HT 1071 SLA

Florida A&M University, Tallahassee
Florida Atlantic University, Boca Raton
Florida Gulf Coast University, Ft. Myers
Florida International University, Miami
Florida State University, Tallahassee
University of Central Florida, Orlando
University of Florida, Gainesville
University of North Florida, Jacksonville
University of South Florida, Tampa
University of West Florida, Pensacola

Slavery Without Sugar

Diversity in Caribbean Economy
and Society Since the 17th Century

Edited by Verene A. Shepherd

University Press of Florida
Gainesville · Tallahassee · Tampa · Boca Raton
Pensacola · Orlando · Miami · Jacksonville · Ft. Myers

Copyright 2002 by Verene A. Shepherd
Printed in the United States of America on acid-free,
TCF (totally-chlorine free) paper
All rights reserved

07 06 05 04 03 02   6 5 4 3 2 1

Library of Congress Cataloging-in-Publication Data
Slavery without sugar : diversity in Caribbean economy and society
since the 17th century / edited by Verene A. Shepherd
p. cm.
Includes bibliographical references and index.
ISBN 0-8130-2552-4 (cloth : alk. paper)
1. Slavery—Economic aspects—Caribbean Area—History. 2. Slave labor—
Caribbean Area—History. 3. Slavery—Caribbean Area—History. 4. Plantation
life—Caribbean Area—History. 5. Caribbean Area—Economic conditions.
I. Title: Diversity in Caribbean ecnonomy and society since the 17th century.
II. Shepherd, Verene.
HT1071 .S54 2002
306.3'62'09729—dc21   2002028937

The University Press of Florida is the scholarly publishing agency for the
State University System of Florida, comprising Florida A&M University,
Florida Atlantic University, Florida Gulf Coast University, Florida International
University, Florida State University, University of Central Florida, University
of Florida, University of North Florida, University of South Florida, and
University of West Florida.

University Press of Florida
15 Northwest 15th Street
Gainesville, FL 32611–2079
http://www.upf.com

Dedicated to the memory of Douglas Hall

Contents

Tables

Introduction

Verene A. Shepherd

The "plantation economy model," one that stresses the role of the sugar-plantation complex in structuring Caribbean society along the lines of a rigid enslaver-enslaved dichotomy, has been the dominant paradigm used to explain the functioning of Caribbean societies during the period of African enslavement. This model has been so pervasive, even in recent publications on Caribbean historiography, that it often masks the fact that diversification was a significant feature of Caribbean society and economy even in the age of sugar.[1] Equally masked are the gender, class, and ethnic heterogeneity of the enslaving class and the variation in the occupations of the enslaved.

In reality, diversity in Caribbean socioeconomic life has a long history: in the pre-Columbian and presugar era, indigenous peoples and early European colonizers cultivated a variety of fruits, vegetables, and agricultural staples, first for subsistence and later for export, and engaged in a variety of maritime activities. As Carlyle Batie has shown, staples like tobacco, indigo, cotton, and ginger, far from being marginal, brought in profits for settlers during the seventeenth century, only giving way to sugar in the British-colonized Caribbean because of market conditions after 1640.[2] The cattle industry in Jamaica, and the Hispanic Caribbean particularly after the mining phase had passed, also generated incomes for early settlers, many of whom later invested in the sugar industry.[3] The early labor force was ethnically diverse, composed as it was of indigenous peoples, white indentured servants, and enslaved Africans. Thus an early phase of diversified production characterized the economic history of most of the areas developed later as plantation economies.

The high price of sugar compared with that of other staples, however, led to an intensive monoculture and a dependence on imports in many Caribbean territories, beginning with the English-colonized island of Barbados, which benefited from the Brazilian economic experience, and spreading to other territories thereafter. By 1750, societies in most of the French- and British-colonized Caribbean were being described as "sugar-plantation societies," with the Hispanic Caribbean enjoying its "sugar revolution" later in the eighteenth and nineteenth centuries.

Similarly, the genocidal impact of European colonization on the indigenous peoples, racism, and comparative labor prices all combined to cause the large-scale exploitation of Africans through a system of slavery that would become dominant by the late seventeenth century. Of course, there continues to be disagreement over the relative role of racism and economic factors in European colonizers' decision to base their labor force on forcefully imported Africans. Eric Williams's early conclusion that "the reason was economic, not racial" (at least in the quantitative dimension of the trade) still does not have complete support in the academy.[4] There is, however, general agreement that the sugar estates gave rise to a dominant sugar-planter class, employed a large proportion of the imported Africans, and, in many cases, occupied most of the arable land in the various territories that experienced a sugar revolution. By the end of the seventeenth century, these features of Caribbean economy and society gave rise to the large-scale application of the plantation economy model to the region. Generally, theorists of this model have conceptualized plantations as monocultural enclaves, lacking economic links with other sectors of the economy.[5] In his summary of the major arguments of the proponents of this model, Alex Dupuy reminds us that they suggest that "economic activities in the colonies are primarily between each plantation and the metropolitan centre, an internal home market fails to develop, and there are no significant 'spread effects' from production within the colony." As a result, all plantation inputs are said to have been imported and all outputs exported. Consequently, it has been stated that limited possibilities for internal capital accumulation existed because of the monopolistic control of trade. In classic sugar-plantation economies, in addition, the life of enslaved people was dictated directly by the regimen of the plantation as an economic unit (be it sugar or another staple).[6]

Yet sugar did not control the whole structure of life in the Caribbean in any deterministic way, and European colonialism did not succeed completely in introducing structural discontinuities by appropriating the land resources of the region for its monopolistic sugar-plantation designs. Jamaica is a good example of this conclusion. The cattle industry, which predated the large-scale cultivation of sugarcane in that island, continued after the shift to sugar. Livestock farms, styled "pens," supplied crucial plantation inputs in the form of grass and working animals and services such as wainage (transportation by animal drawn carts or wagons) and pasturage; these farms also supplied meat to a mostly white consumer market. They helped in the establishment and maintenance of inter-property links through the internal commodity trade and generally supported the sugar industry. Jamaica's economic history during slavery demonstrates clearly, and in contrast to the plantation economy model, that the domestic sector was not incompatible with an export-dominated economy and that the sugar estate market, indeed, facilitated the existence of the cattle industry. There was a complementary interaction between the domestic and export sectors that, if anything, strengthened both. In Jamaica by 1782, close to 50 years after the development of the large-scale sugar-plantation industry, there were 300 livestock farms on the island. By 1832, the island had 176 coffee plantations employing 22,562 enslaved people and 15 pimento plantations employing 1,287 enslaved workers. By that date, sugar employed directly 49.5 percent of the enslaved population; coffee, 14.4 percent; and livestock farms, 12.8 percent.[7] The non-sugar producers were fairly influential in the presugar era and even in the first two decades after the "sugar revolution." In 1755, for example, the pen-keepers of Saint Catherine, Saint John, Saint Dorothy, and Saint Thomas-in-the-Vale successfully petitioned the House of Assembly against the removal of the Courts of Justice from Saint Jago-de-la-Vega, their political stronghold, to Kingston. At that time there were 472 cattle farms and provision farms in the entire area.[8] The extent of Jamaica's departure from the plantation economy model was thus quite significant and cannot be dismissed lightly.

Jamaica was not unique. Other Caribbean economies continued to produce nonsugar crops, with some colonies producing no exportable quantities of sugar at all. Belize, the Cayman Islands, the Turks and Caicos Islands, the Bahamas, Barbuda, Anguilla, the Dutch "ABC" islands (Aruba, Bonaire, and Curaçao), Saint Eustatius, and most of the Virgin Islands never became dominated by the sugar industry, exploiting instead a variety of forest, maritime, and nonsugar agricultural resources. For Belize, the extraction of timber remained the economic raison d'être up to and after 1789, when it became a British colony, and labor organization and work processes for the extraction of timber differed greatly from those of the sugar plantation.[9] Similarly, the Bahamas never developed as a sugar-plantation society. The inhabitants were occupied principally in cotton cultivation (until the 1880s), maritime activities, woodcutting, and subsistence agriculture.

Even the so-called classic plantation colonies of the Eastern Caribbean produced other commodities on land unsuitable for cane. Saint Kitts, Antigua, and Barbados, prototypical plantation economies, exported small quantities of cotton;[10] even at the height of the sugar economy, Cuba, Puerto Rico, Saint Domingue, Martinique, Guadeloupe, and Jamaica grew varying quantities of coffee, tobacco and indigo and produced animals and timber. Before the Haitian Revolution of 1791, Saint Domingue produced most of the coffee exported from the Caribbean. In the late 1830s, Cuba's coffee plantations numbered just over 2,000 and employed some 50,000 enslaved Africans, roughly the same number as on the sugar estates; another 100,000 enslaved peoples were engaged in other rural agricultural pursuits and in urban/nonagricultural tasks.[11] It is also well known that tobacco cultivation played an important role in Cuban agricultural history even in the age of sugar. Similarly, if farther afield, while sugar was very important to Brazil's economy, other economic activities were significant. Stephen Bell, in *Campanha Gaúcha,* and B. J. Barickman, in *A Bahian Counterpoint,* illustrate the ways in which tobacco and cassava cultivation, as well as ranching, interrupted the traditional monocultural interpretation of Brazilian economic history.[12]

The relative dominance of the sugar plantation as a system of production, of course, must be recognized. Only differences in the price and quality of land created variations in the extent to which intensive monoculture came to dominate the economies of particular territories. In the case of Jamaica, for example, physical environmental factors dictated that sugar could not dominate the landscape totally, and that island sustained a degree of diversification during the age of sugar that was unparalleled in most other English-colonized territories. Barry Higman's quantitative analysis of 960 properties returned in the Accounts Produce for Jamaica in 1832 showed that sugar and its by-products accounted for 76 percent of total receipts; these properties had 53.6 percent of the enslaved population.[13] The dominance of the sugar economy was greater in Barbados, where sugar and its by-products accounted for 97 percent of the island's exports and over 75 percent of the enslaved population labored on sugar estates, compared to less than 50 percent in Jamaica.[14] The point, though, is that, for whatever reason, diversification was the real Caribbean experience.

The enslaver class also demonstrated its own diversity, being neither all male nor all elite white; as Evelyn Powell Jennings's essay shows, the state itself participated as enslavers in the early period of Cuba's economic development. The cattle industry in Jamaica and the Spanish Caribbean provided an alternative route for property ownership and capital accumulation for some nonelite whites and free colored men and women. There were also quite wealthy white and free colored coffee farmers in the region during slavery. Diversity in property ownership and in occupations dictated that many of the enslaved lived their lives off the sugarcane fields as domestics in rural and urban households, as hired artisans, as laborers on nonsugar agricultural units, and as workers on roads, wharfs, and construction sites. The importance of the urban context of the life of enslaved peoples in the Caribbean has already been demonstrated in several works, including Higman's quantitative studies based on Jamaica and the wider British-colonized Caribbean, and is picked up in this volume in the essays by Hilary McD. Beckles, Félix V. Matos Rodríguez, Evelyn Powell Jennings, and Pedro Welch.[15] The importance of urban enslavement in the Spanish-colonized Caribbean is particularly evident in Matos Rodríguez's contribution. He has used examples from Puerto Rico to show the centrality of domestic work and urban enslavement in capital formation in the city of San Juan. Enslaved domestics even figured, however tangentially, in the rhetorical strategies of the warring sides of the antislavery debate.

Despite this evidence of diversification, for years Caribbean socioeconomic history displayed a rather totalizing tendency, with historians focusing on the sugar sector and virtually ignoring other agricultural sectors. In this tradition of scholarship, nonsugar-producing units represented a divergent pattern of socioeconomic development and were largely underresearched. Similarly, though enslaved peoples were located outside of the physical context of the sugar plantation, within the context of Caribbean history, slavery became synonymous with sugar-plantation society; among students of rural history, inquiry into class and race dynamics outside of the sugar plantation per se has been confined to a position of secondary importance. In addition, as Matos Rodríguez and Welch show in their essays, the historiography of colonial life in Caribbean societies conceptualized developments in terms of a hegemonic (and male), rural enterprise, with insufficient scholarly investigation of urban regimes.

Recent research, however, indicates that Caribbean socioeconomic history needs to be reproblematized and its history of diversity explored in greater detail. The call for attention to diversity has been strongest among those who study Caribbean slavery, for there is growing awareness of the need to acknowledge the internal diversities and contrasting conditions of slavery within the Caribbean, since one can no longer assume spatial and other homogeneity in the region's enslaver systems. The efforts to identify and classify variation, certainly for the British-colonized Caribbean, took

on new dimension with the publication of Barry Higman's *Slave Population and Economy in Jamaica, 1807–1834* and *Slave Populations of the
British Caribbean, 1807–1834.* Higman essentially provided a demographic framework for a comparative analysis of British Caribbean enslaved populations, taking on board the issue of diversity in commodity
production and the occupations of the enslaved—which in large measure
determined enslaved people's demographic experiences. His 1989 analysis
of the internal economic features of Jamaica's pens does much to illuminate the complex nature of Caribbean economy in the eighteenth and
nineteenth centuries and the ways in which these units contributed to the
variation in the lives of the enslaved.

Demographic work has also been undertaken by other historians, including Michael Craton and Gail Saunders for the Bahamas, Humphrey
Lamur for the Dutch colonies, Meredith John for Trinidad, and Jack Eblen
for Cuba.[16] But there is still need to go beyond the quantitative demographic studies to examine in greater detail the daily and annual cycles of
enslaved life in rural nonplantation and urban settings and explore issues
such as the differences in the gender division of labor, method of labor
organization, degree of autonomy achieved by the enslaved, control, and
patterns of resistance in sugar and nonsugar settings. There is also the
need to expand the study of slavery outside of the context of sugar to take
in places in the Circum-Caribbean region and the so-called marginal colonies, as well as the experiences of male and female enslavers not engaged
directly in the sugar culture. Indeed, the study of the experiences of property owners who were not members of the sugar-planting elite is among
the most underresearched areas of Caribbean history.

This collection of essays is inserted into the discourse of diversification
within Caribbean societies during the operation of enslavement. It is intended as a contribution to the ongoing interpretive debate on the relationship between, on the one hand, commodity production and, on the
other, the occupation of the enslaved, diversity in their lives, and diversity
in the occupation of freed blacks and former enslavers. The volume is pan-
Caribbean in its coverage and testifies to the fact that the socioeconomic
experiences of the region demonstrated remarkable similarities. The volume focuses on the variety of rural and urban contexts in Caribbean society, outside of the context of the sugar estates, within which the enslaved
lived and worked, and the authors explore different dimensions of nonsugar production in the Caribbean.

The essays (some of which appeared in the special issue of *Plantation
Society in the Americas* [fall 1998][17] and are reprinted here with kind

permission) are arranged in a rough chronological order both to reflect the timing of European colonization of the Caribbean and the time frame being explored by the authors. Some attempt has also been made to place the essays that deal with the urban context together. David Geggus begins the discussion with his essay on indigo and slavery in Saint Domingue (Haiti), one of the earliest locations of Spanish and French settlement and a colony until 1804, when Haitian independence was proclaimed by African Haitians. He shows that by the 1680s indigo had replaced tobacco and ranching, about the same time as sugar was introduced. Indigo was not only a viable crop in itself, continuing after the large-scale sugar industry became dominant in the 1700s, but, as was the case with minor-staple or minor-crop production elsewhere, its cultivation was often a stepping stone to a more profitable and socially prestigious sugar estate. Only after 1713 did indigo lose ground to sugar; thereafter, indigo fluctuated in importance depending on the economic state of other crops. Finally, Geggus explores the demographics of the enslaved population on indigo plantations, contrasting these features with demographic features on sugar plantations. His conclusions coincide with those of scholars who have studied other nonsugar properties with respect to six areas: the high residency and low absenteeism of the proprietors; the fluctuating fortunes of the crop, tied as they were to the state of the sugar industry; employment of a significant proportion of the enslaved population; the less frenetic work regime of the enslaved; fostering of some element of intra-Caribbean trading links; and the ways in which the demographic characteristics of the enslaved population contrasted sharply with those of the sugar estates in terms of the African/Creole ratio; male/female ratio; and fertility and mortality rates. But the absence of complete demographic data makes Geggus tentative on the differences in mortality rates between the enslaved working sugar and those working indigo.

In "Timber Extraction and the Shaping of Enslaved Peoples' Culture in Belize," O. Nigel Bolland focuses on the ways in which "Baymen," as the British settlers in the Bay of Honduras were called, organized slavery, the dominant form of labor exploitation by the 1750s, for the extraction of timber, mainly logwood and mahogany. The extraction of timber in this area had a long history. In the seventeenth century, British buccaneers used the coastline of Belize in the Bay of Honduras as a base for attacking Spanish ships carrying logwood from which a dye was obtained for use in the woolen industry. By the 1650s, some buccaneers had changed from plundering Spanish ships to cutting logwood trees in various parts of the Yucatán peninsula. The extraction of timber remained the chief economic rationale up to and after 1798, when Belize became a British colony. Labor organization and work process in the extraction of timber differed greatly from those of the sugar plantation. The timber industry dictated a type of regime not noted elsewhere in the Caribbean. Few of the enslaved engaged in agriculture; there was no gang labor; and there was a strict gender division of labor, with the cutting of logwood and mahogany being almost the sole preserve of enslaved men who were isolated in logging camps for long periods. Most women engaged in domestic work. Only the very young children and the very old men and women engaged in similar occupations. The labor process also affected settlement patterns and demographic characteristics, as well as helped to define gender roles and relations between enslavers and enslaved. Because of the nature of the commodity exploited, Belize had a higher proportion of enslaved men than elsewhere in the Caribbean, enslaved people were expensive, and the demand for young men was high. However, while there has usually been an association between nonsugar production and an increase in the enslaved population, Belize's enslaved population, as elsewhere in the Caribbean, failed to be self-reproducing for most of the slavery period. This had to do with the unique composition of the colony's enslaved population. Bolland also discusses the ways in which commodity production shaped blacks' resistance (with little chance of large, organized revolt but with significant *marronage*, that is, running away and living free) and the culture of the enslaved, particularly in Belize Town.

Barry Higman and Verene Shepherd explore different dimensions of the history of the livestock industry in Jamaica. As indicated, the livestock industry predated the large-scale cultivation of sugar in Jamaica but continued on lands not utilized for cane even after the shift to sugar, and it provided an alternative way of life for some whites, free coloreds, and enslaved peoples. The pens supplied crucial plantation inputs in the form of grass and working animals and services such as transportation of goods and the pasturing of animals; these farms also supplied meat to a mostly white consumer market. The pens helped in the establishment and maintenance of interproperty links through the internal commodity trade. Higman's essay (reprinted here by kind permission of *Social and Economic Studies,* the journal in which it appeared in 1989) offers a quantitative analysis of the internal economy of Jamaican pens primarily for the slavery period, though he provides comparative data on the postslavery period, showing that changes in the structure and technology of the export sector resulted in a shift in the output of pens from draft animals to meat between 1760 and 1890. He outlines the evolution of the pens, their significance to the local market, and the broad changes in the numbers, distribution, and function of the pens and, through a detailed study of a large sample of maps and plans, analyzes their size, land use, and field patterns. Together with Shepherd's 1988 study on Jamaican pens, this analysis does much to illuminate the complex nature of Caribbean economy in the eighteenth and nineteenth centuries, specifically the ways in which the pens contrasted with sugar estates and other agricultural units and contributed to the variation in the lives of enslaved and enslavers.

In their joint essay, Verene Shepherd and Kathleen Monteith revisit the socioeconomic roles and statuses of arguably two of the most significant groups of nonsugar producers in eighteenth-century Jamaica: the pen-keepers and the coffee farmers. Shepherd and Monteith show that the history of nonsugar proprietors who were generally socially marginalized by the dominant white elite and who, consequently, aspired to white, sugar-planter elite status, clearly illustrates the problems in claiming a dialectical relationship between "colonial" and "Creole" Jamaica (to which Kamau Brathwaite alluded in his seminal work on Creole society),[18] and so their history merits further study. Most of the independent pen-keepers and coffee farmers were "Creole" in the sense of being born on the island, and the pen-keepers contributed much to the internal commodity trade, reduced the island's dependence on imported work animals, and provided an alternative location for over 10 percent of the island's enslaved population. But while they did much to develop "Creole economy," broadly defined, it is arguable whether, as Higman claims in his essay, they "contributed to the development of . . . Creole society in every sense."[19] They comprised traditionally antagonistic sections—white and free coloreds, Creole born and metropolitan born, small entrepreneurs and larger, more profitable proprietors—among whom there were few common social goals outside of the context of their similar aspirations to the socioeconomic status of the sugar barons. Those who could afford it invested in the sugar economy as soon as they had built up the capital to do so, and they showed little cultural affinity with "Creole society." Indeed, they helped to reinforce the dichotomy of separate cultures that was a pervasive characteristic of Caribbean societies during slavery. The two authors contrast the socioeconomic marginality of the pen-keepers, who lacked political power and an effective lobby in the House of Assembly, with the position of the coffee farmers. The latter were also primarily resident and, except for the few who were rich and a part of the white elite, were lower down on the social ladder than the sugar planters. But fewer of them were black or colored, guaranteeing their group a higher position on the social ladder than the pen-keepers—a middle-class position within the white social hierarchy. Furthermore, they participated in the export sector, and there was a definite relationship between type of commodity production and social status in colonial Jamaica. Politically, however, they had more power. A few wealthy ones were in the House of Assembly, and, unlike the pen-keepers who were often in an antagonistic relationship with the sugar barons over issues like the tax on animals, they mostly formed an alliance with the sugar planters.[20]

S. D. Smith continues the analysis of the coffee farmers in Jamaica, presenting another perspective on Caribbean economic and social development. He compares the organization of large and small coffee plantations in Jamaica with the experience of slavery as practised on sugar estates, drawing on material from elsewhere in the Caribbean to illustrate further the relationship. He outlines the difficulties inherent in any comparative study of coffee and sugar plantations, not least of which are the lack of comparable data on the history of coffee and the paucity of documentation on resident planters. He also cautions against comparing all coffee properties, regardless of size, with the sugar estates. His view is that large coffee plantations shared some similarities with sugar estates with respect to monocultural tendencies, gang labor, and the form cultivation took (for example, the way in which both integrated backward to regulate raw material inputs and coordinate labor supplies, thereby ensuring that throughput was maximized through the processing plant). In other respects, differences were glaring and similar to other nonsugar units: smaller physical size and enslaved populations; less rigid control; absence of the gang system; the occupation of different geographical zones; the absence of night work; the lower capitalization; less technological equipment; and so forth. And the smaller coffee farms not only demonstrated even fewer similarities with the sugar estates but exhibited marked differences when compared to the larger coffee farms. His essay sheds light on the demographic characteristics of the coffee parishes, which presented a paradoxical combination of a sex ratio skewed toward males and a high fertility rate. He poses new questions about the coffee farmers and adopts some perspectives on their social roles that contrast with Shepherd and Monteith's.

Gail Saunders focuses on the Bahamas, which never developed as a sugar-plantation society. The inhabitants were principally occupied in maritime activities, woodcutting, and subsistence agriculture. Between 1783 and 1810, cotton culture increasingly defined the experiences of the enslaved, American Loyalists having relocated in these islands with their enslaved laborers and capital after the U.S. War of Independence and having established viable cotton plantations. She provides a good summary of the daily and annual regimen of the enslaved laborers in a nonsugar-plantation economy and explores the relationship between commodity production, work regime, and the demographic experiences of the enslaved. She concludes, much as Geggus and Higman have done for other nonsugar settings,[21] that cotton production helped to create favorable demographic characteristics in the Bahamian enslaved population. The decline of cotton around the first part of the nineteenth century had important implications for the enslaved population in the Bahamas. Saunders shows that many of the enslaved engaged in the "self-hire" system, earning wages and acquiring a number of the characteristics of an "assertive proletariat."[22]

In "State Enslavement in Colonial Havana, 1763–1790," Evelyn Powell Jennings, using manuscript sources from Spanish archives, analyzes the crucial role that the Spanish state played in the growth and character of African enslavement in Cuba, especially before 1790. More specifically, she studies an important group of workers enslaved by the Spanish colonial state in late-eighteenth-century Cuba—the king's enslaved laborers—who worked on Havana's fortifications after the British occupation of the city in 1762 and 1763. Indeed, up to 1790, the state was the largest single enslaver in Cuba, divesting itself of its *dotación* (impressment into labor gangs) of enslaved workers only after that date. These enslaved workers were significant not only as an example of the diversity of enslavement in Cuba but also because they represented a sizeable portion of Havana's population of enslaved workers; their recruitment and deployment played an important role in the reorientation of the Cuban economy toward sugar production based on enslaved labor. Her analysis illuminates two important aspects of Cuban history. First, many of the conditions attributed to sugar-plantation enslavement—large importations of enslaved workers, skewed gender ratios in favor of men, gang labor, high mortality, and diminished access to manumission—obtained in the urban context of state defense projects before the advent of the sugar boom. Second, state enslavement in the fort works of Havana between 1763 and 1790 was an integral part of the transformation of Cuba into a plantation economy; in the process of marshaling enslaved laborers and funding defense projects that utilized their labor, the state helped to create the conditions for the sugar boom of the nineteenth century. This latter fact is of great significance for the conversation in which all contributors are engaged, for clearly Cuba's transition to a large producer of sugar departed from the evolutionary model advanced by the Plantation Economy School.

Pedro Welch continues the conversation on urban slavery, pointing out that a majority of the white population and a significant portion of the enslaved and free colored population in the Leeward Islands lived and operated in nonplantation settings. In "The Urban Context of the Life of the Enslaved," he stresses that enslaved people within the Barbadian urban perimeter faced conditions of life different from those faced on rural plantations and that if the complexities of Caribbean slave systems are to be understood, then the peculiar characteristics of urban enslavement need to be identified and analyzed. To illuminate aspects of urban slavery in Barbados, he selects one of the areas of importance in the socialization of the enslaved in the urban, nonplantation environment: occupational culture. His account of the main characteristics of the life of the enslaved and occupations in the urban sector (absence of strict supervisory roles by whites; large proportion of females; lack of gang labor; high incidence of the "self-hire" system; degree of independent activity) facilitates a comparative engagement with already explored aspects of rural slavery. He concludes that the rhythm of urban occupational life, though far from idyllic, was removed in some respects from the regimentation characteristic of life among the rural enslaved. Indeed, as others have shown elsewhere, urban slavery facilitated its own form of opposition to slavery.[23]

Hilary McD. Beckles shifts somewhat from a strict discussion of enslaved peoples to focus on the ethnic and gender diversity among enslavers. He explores the contentious issue of the life options available to blacks in the Atlantic slave system who were freed before 1834, particularly in the period during and immediately after the Haitian Revolution when whites perceived freed black people as potential allies with those engaged in the antislavery struggle. Yet freed blacks in Barbados adapted to the surrounding value hierarchy and purchased enslaved people when they could. This is explained by the fact that the colonial system ensured that there was a close relationship between wealth, status, and enslaving. Did this indicate a total retreat from antislavery politics on the part of free blacks in the interest of self-serving strategic economic relations and political postures? Did their seeming collaboration with the slave-owning mechanism lull whites into a false sense of security? What was their political strategy in the urban sector? These are questions with which the author grapples. The essay also explores the routes to freedom and slave-owning and the ways in which free blacks, the majority of whom were female, functioned in the urban socioeconomic sector as domestics and skilled artisans, although they were denied access to rural sugar-plantation production.

Like Powell Jennings, Franklin Knight focuses on Cuba, but he examines the color diversity among enslaved and enslavers in colonial Cuba. Like Beckles, then, he points us to yet another area of diversity among those who became enslavers in the Americas. Caribbean slave systems were all characterized by the tyranny of color—the "pigmentocracy"—which favored those whose skin color was closest to white and accorded them a higher position on the racially constructed social ladder. The Spanish Caribbean is a fitting location for this analysis of the growth and impact of the free coloreds, for during the operation of the slave system in the Americas, this part of the region had the largest racially mixed population. The rapid growth of this racially mixed group even led some twentieth-century scholars to speak in terms of Catholic benevolence and a "humane" and "superior" Spanish Caribbean slave regime. If slavery in the Spanish Caribbean had displayed racial characteristics not usually associated with a classic plantation/slave system in the sixteenth and seventeenth centuries, however, enslavers corrected this by the nineteenth century when sugar and slavery were firmly entrenched. As Knight shows, the free coloreds were not unaffected by the socioeconomic changes that reinforced social cleavages in nineteenth-century Cuba. They suffered from heightened racism, discrimination, shifting internal demographic characteristics, changed physical location, and occupational possibilities and differential access to educational opportunities. Much like other parts of the Caribbean, free colored property-owners showed a propensity to concentrate in the nonsugar zones and those without land in nonsugar occupations. Indeed, a unifying feature of all Caribbean slave systems was that there were racially motivated laws that affected occupational specialization. These features of Caribbean society fit uncomfortably within the plantation economy model, especially as that model suggests a level of economic (even social) homogeneity that never existed in Cuban society.

In the final essay, Félix Matos Rodríguez, like Beckles, Jennings, and Welch, addresses the issue of urban slavery, reinforcing the fact that the rural dimension represented only one aspect of social reality in Caribbean plantation societies, although the historiography tends to conceptualize development in terms of a hegemonic rural enterprise. His examples come from Puerto Rico and are located within the context of domestic work and urban slavery, particularly with respect to capital formation in the city of San Juan and eventual abolition. His essay, like Beckles's, Powell Jennings's, and Welch's, provides important details on the occupational pattern of urban slavery and the work of domestics, the majority female. More crucially, he intervenes into the debates over the abolition of slavery in Puerto Rico and the role of enslaved urban domestics/urban slavery in that process; while not being a central theme in the abolitionist debates, enslaved domestics did figure in the rhetorical strategies of the warring sides of the debate. Proabolition forces, for example, used the large numbers of blacks engaged in domestic service to show that abolition would not affect the agricultural enterprises. They also pushed the stereotype of the docile domestic to decrease white fears of violence after abolition. Interestingly enough, the behavior of San Juan's elites in their attempts to control the labor time and wages of urban domestics contradicts the docility thesis.[24]

These essays make it clear that the concept of a single type of plantation complex modeled on sugar can no longer be applied sweepingly to the colonial Caribbean. As Smith says of coffee plantations in his present essay, "[t]he study of coffee plantations, therefore, provides further confirmation that the institution of plantation enslavement possessed complex and diverse aspects and that plantation economy based on involuntary servitude was capable of subtle adaptations." The authors all concur that conditions of enslaved labor in the Caribbean varied according to whether the enslaved were located in rural or urban contexts and according to the nature of the agricultural/economic enterprise. Coffee and cotton plantations, pens, indigo farms, and the urban milieu were said to have offered those enslaved a less-arduous regime, unlike the sugar estates where life for the enslaved was described as nasty, brutish, and short. In sum, the main characteristics of life outside of the sugar estates were a more individualized labor regime; an absence or lower incidence of gang labor; less close supervision by whites; lower mortality; higher fertility; a higher incidence of natural increase; an absence of the 24-hour work schedule during crop time; little night work; and a tendency to task over day labor, with the enslaved getting more time to work on their grounds. Of course, similarities also existed, particularly in the layout of large coffee and sugar estates; the use of gang labor on large properties; the allocation of provision grounds to the enslaved; internal marketing by the enslaved; the gender division of labor; the (s)exploitation of enslaved women by owners; and slave resistance. It has been demonstrated that there were significant implications in the co-existence of sugar and nonsugar units within the same territory, for this facilitated interproperty trade, variation in the occupation of the enslaved, internal capital accumulation, and the local provision of some plantation inputs. Clearly, the sugar-plantation economy model that conceptualized plantations as enclaves importing all inputs and exporting all outputs is, along with slavery being defined by the sugar industry, now outdated. The authors have not only demonstrated the importance of nonsugar economic activities quantitatively—that is, in terms of the numbers and percentages of the enslaved workers who were occupied outside of the sugar plantations—but they show the qualitative differences in their lives, their contribution to a domestic economy, the ways in which they had greater success in negotiating the terms and conditions of their enslavement, and their pursuit of freedom with their enslavers. The essays thus focus on diversity as an academic exercise but are also crucial for illustrating and understanding the development of Caribbean societies.

Of importance also is that those authors, like Beckles, Bolland, and Knight, who take on the issue of agency agree that despite the differences in regimes on sugar estates and in nonsugar-plantation settings and despite the ethnic, color, and gender diversity among the working class, the self-liberation ethos was no less developed among enslaved and free working people who lived outside of the physical context of the large sugar plantation. Indeed, as has been shown elsewhere, nonsugar units like pens were considered by planters to be oases of social instability, and those enslaved on pens were engaged in a variety of nonviolent and violent resistance strategies.[25] The revelations in the detailed journals of Thomas Thistlewood, which have now propelled the study of livestock farms and enslaved women's experiences to a prominent position, provide testimony enough of the violence (among which rape can be counted) perpetrated against enslaved peoples whether on sugar or nonsugar properties; the exploitation of their sexuality faced by enslaved urban domestics was cause enough for the enslaved to try and win their freedom.[26] Logically, every form of subjugation and domination generates an opposing struggle for liberation. Despite the importance of the economic explanation of abolition as advanced by Eric Williams, the struggles of the enslaved in the quest for self-liberation must be accorded a position of importance (as he also acknowledged).[27] Above all, the present volume demonstrates that the battle for terrain, economic and ideological, was not unique to modern Caribbean society. It should contribute to the trend, which intensified in the late 1980s, of pluralising the discourse on Caribbean and Latin American economic and social history, which, as Allen Wells has remarked, has for too long focused on export monoculture and *latifundia* (in the case of Latin America).[28]

Notes

1. Those contributors to B. W. Higman, ed., *UNESCO General History of the Caribbean,* vol. 6, *Methodology and Historiography of the Caribbean* (London & Oxford: UNESCO Publishing, 1999), who mentioned nonsugar/nonsugar-planter aspects of Caribbean economy and society did so simply as an indication of the research trend. They did not indicate the potential impact that such a trend has in effecting a radical transformation of the interpretation of Caribbean history.

2. Carlyle Batie, "Why Sugar?: Economic Cycles and the Changing of Staples on the English and French Antilles, 1624–1654," *Journal of Caribbean History* 8–9 (1976): 1–41.

3. See Verene Shepherd, "Pens and Pen-keepers in a Plantation Society: Aspects of Jamaican Social and Economic History, 1740–1845" (Ph.D. diss., University of Cambridge, 1988), chap. 1; and Franklin Knight, *Slave Society in Cuba in the Nineteenth Century* (Madison: University of Wisconsin Press, 1970), 3–24.

4. Eric Williams, *Capitalism and Slavery* (1944; reprint, Chapel Hill: University of North Carolina Press, 1994), 19. For a recent summary of the reasons Africans rather than other ethnicities were used as the primary group of enslaved laborers in the Americas, see David Eltis, *The Rise of African Slavery in the Americas* (Cambridge: Cambridge University Press, 2000), 1–28.

5. See, for example, Lloyd Best, "Outlines of the Model of a Pure Plantation Economy," *Social and Economic Studies* 17 (1968): 283–326; George Beckford, *Persistent Poverty: Underdevelopment in Plantation Economies of the Third World* (New York: Oxford University Press, 1972); J. R. Mandle, *The Plantation Economy* (Philadelphia: Temple University Press, 1973); Frederic L. Pryor, "The Plantation Economy as an Economic System," *Journal of Comparative Economics* 6 (1982): 288–317; and Michael Craton, "The Historical Roots of the Plantation Model," *Slavery and Abolition* 5 (1984): 189–221.

6. Alex Dupuy, "Slavery and Underdevelopment in the Caribbean: A Critique of the 'Plantation Economy Perspective,'" *Dialectical Anthropology* 7 (1983): 139.

7. B. W. Higman, *Slave Population and Economy in Jamaica, 1807–1834* (Cambridge: Cambridge University Press, 1976), 16.

8. Verene A. Shepherd, *Cattle, Cane, and Chattel: Contesting Sugar and Slavery in Colonial Jamaica* (forthcoming).

9. See O. Nigel Bolland, *Struggles for Freedom: Essays on Slavery, Colonialism and Culture in the Caribbean and Central America* (Belize City: Angelus Press, 1997). Bolland's essay in this volume has been reprinted by permission from this collection.

10. Hilary McD. Beckles, *A History of Barbados: From Amerindian Settlement to Nation-State* (Cambridge: Cambridge University Press, 1990), 74; B. W. Higman, *Slave Populations of the British Caribbean, 1807–1834* (Baltimore: Johns Hopkins University Press, 1984), 50–52.

11. See Herbert Klein, *African Slavery in Latin America and the Caribbean* (Oxford and New York: Oxford University Press, 1986), 93–96; and David Watts, *The West Indies: Patterns of Development, Culture and Environmental Change since 1492* (Cambridge: Cambridge University Press, 1987), chaps. 5, 7, 10.

12. Stephen Bell, *Campanha Gaúcha: A Brazilian Ranching System, 1850–1920* (Stanford, Calif.: Stanford University Press, 1998); B. J. Barickman, *A Bahian Counterpoint* (Stanford, Calif.: Stanford University Press, 1998).

13. Higman, *Slave Population and Economy in Jamaica*, 12.

14. Higman, *Slave Populations of the British Caribbean*, 50, 52; W. Dickson, *Letters on Slavery* (London, 1789), 6.

15. Higman, *Slave Population and Economy in Jamaica*; Higman, *Slave Populations of the British Caribbean*.

16. See Gail Saunders's essay in this collection; Michael Craton, "Changing Patterns of Slave Families in the British West Indies," in *Caribbean Slave Society and Economy*, ed. H. Beckles and V. A. Shepherd (Kingston: Ian Randle, 1991), 228–49; Humphrey Lamur, "Demographic Performance of Two Slave Populations of the Dutch-Speaking Caribbean," in Beckles and Shepherd, *Caribbean Slave Society*, 209–20; A. Meredith John, *The Plantation Slaves of Trinidad, 1783–1816* (Cambridge: Cambridge University Press, 1988); and Jack Eblen, "On the Natural Increase of Slave Populations: The Example of the Cuban Black Population," in *Race and Slavery in the Western Hemisphere*, ed. S. Engerman and E. Genovese (Princeton, N.J.: Princeton University Press, 1975), 211–47.

17. The additional authors in this collection are Higman, Jennings, Saunders, Matos Rodríguez, and Knight.

18. [Edward] Kamau Brathwaite, *The Development of Creole Society in Jamaica, 1770–1820* (Oxford: Clarendon Press, 1971).

19. Higman in Brathwaite, chap. 7.

20. This issue is explored more fully in Verene A. Shepherd, "Questioning Creole: Domestic Producers and Jamaica's Plantation Society," *Caribbean Quarterly* 44, no. 1 and 2 (March 1998): 93–107.

21. See Higman, *Slave Populations of the British Caribbean*; and Higman, *Slave Population and Economy in Jamaica*.

22. This essay has been reprinted here with the permission of the author. It first appeared in *Slavery and Abolition* 11 (1990): 332–50.

23. This is one aspect of the focus of Lorna Simmonds's Ph.D. thesis, "Jamaican Urban Slavery, 1780–1834" (University of the West Indies, Mona, Jamaica, 1997) on urban slavery in Jamaica.

24. Taken from Félix Matos Rodríguez and Linda Delgado, eds., *Puerto Rican Women's History: New Perspectives* (Armonk, N.Y.: M. E. Sharpe, 1998), 62–82, and reprinted here with kind permission.

25. See Verene Shepherd, "Pens and Pen-Keepers," and "Liberation Struggles on Livestock Farms in Jamaica," in *Caribbean Slavery in the Atlantic World*, ed. V. A. Shepherd and H. Beckles (Kingston: Ian Randle, 2000), 260–76, 896–904.

26. Thomas Thistlewood, from Tupholme, Lincolnshire, lived in Jamaica from 1750 to 1786. He worked initially as overseer on several properties in western Jamaica before establishing his own pen. The edited journals can be read in Douglas Hall, In *Miserable Slavery: Thomas Thistlewood in Jamaica, 1750–1786* (London: McMillan, 1989). Some historians are still reluctant to use the word "rape" to refer to Thistlewood's sexual activities with enslaved women, preferring to argue that enslaved women "worked" as prostitutes. The fact that Thistlewood gave some enslaved women a few "bitts" after his sexual encounters with them is being used as the "proof of prostitution." Others ignore these sexual activities altogether. I was somewhat surprised to see Thistlewood's enslaved laborers referred to as his "teachers and companions" in Philip Sherlock's and Hazel Bennett's book, *The Story of the Jamaican People* (Kingston: Ian Randle, 1997), 168.

27. Williams, *Capitalism and Slavery.* See in particular chapter 7.

28. Allen Wells, "A Welcome Shift in Emphasis," review of *Campanha Gaúcha: A Brazilian Ranching System, 1850–1920,* by Stephen Bell, and *A Bahian Counterpoint,* by B. J. Barickman, *Plantation Society in the Americas* 6, no.1 (spring 1999): 95.

Indigo and Slavery in Saint Domingue

David Geggus

Well known as the world's major producer of sugar and coffee in the later eighteenth century, the French colony of Saint Domingue also outproduced its competitors for a long period in the indigo market as well. As befits its reputation as an "intermediate" or "transitional" crop requiring moderate capital investment, indigo's history in Saint Domingue has been more studied than that of cacao, tobacco, or cotton, but it is less well known than that of sugar or coffee, which came to dominate the colonial economy. Several articles and one monograph concerning individual plantations have appeared over the years.[1] John Garrigus has investigated indigo cultivation on the south coast and its relation to the local free colored community, and as early as 1736 a Saint Domingue planter published a manual on the crop.[2] Even so, little attention has been paid to its development. This essay is intended as a first step toward an overview of indigo's role in the history of slavery in the eighteenth-century Caribbean's most important colony.

Indigo Cultivation and Processing

Common to tropical regions of the Old and New Worlds, various shrubs of the genus Indigofera have been used since antiquity for the long-lasting dye they contain. Prized by textile producers of five continents, indigo's deep blue tincture had no real rival until the development of synthetic dyestuffs in the nineteenth century. Natural blue dyes were extracted from several local plants in Europe, but it was recognized that the addition of even a small quantity of indigo greatly enhanced their effectiveness.[3] The fraudulent use of such substitutes for indigo became the subject of commercial legislation.[4] Sold wholesale by the pound, not the hundredweight, indigo had a much higher unit value than the other, much bulkier, plantation crops of colonial America. For this reason, and because it grew at high elevations as well as in the plains, it appealed to planters in remote regions, where transportation was difficult. It was also sought after by merchants in wartime, when the risk of running blockades placed a premium on high-value cargoes.

Europe's main supplier of indigo from ancient times until the mid-seventeenth century was India, which either was named for the plant or gave its name to it. The expansion of colonial production in the American tropics caused the sudden demise of Asian imports around 1650. They revived, however, in the 1780s under British stimulus and resumed domination of the world market after 1800. It was during the century or so of American prominence that Saint Domingue rose to be the major indigo producer. Through the third quarter of the eighteenth century, and perhaps a little longer, the French colony exported close to and often more than 2 million pounds per annum. Guatemala, its closest rival, rarely exported more than 1 million pounds at its peak in the late eighteenth century. Production in South Carolina, where indigo took off in the 1740s, peaked at 1.1 million pounds on the eve of the American Revolution. Introduced into Venezuela and Brazil in the 1760s, indigo production attained no more than 0.75 million pounds in the former and 0.26 million pounds in the latter, before declining around the century's end. Jamaican exports peaked at 0.13 million pounds in the 1680s and 1780s.[5] The principal purchasers of indigo were the textile manufacturers of Britain and (in Saint Domingue's case) the Low Countries and Germany. More than half of French indigo imports were reexported, albeit a smaller proportion than of French-grown coffee or sugar.[6] Like Saint Domingue's sugar and coffee, its indigo was in general a mass market rather than premium product.

On Saint Domingue, as in Jamaica, four varieties of the indigo shrub were grown. Whereas in Guatemala they were left three years in the ground, in Saint Domingue they were usually uprooted annually and new ones were planted at the start of the rainy season by slaves working in gangs.[7] Élie Monnereau, writing in the 1730s, when enslaved males substantially outnumbered females, described a sexual division of field labor. Men with hoes moving backward dug holes into which some women placed seeds and other women quickly covered over. Much less hardy than sugarcane, the delicate plants needed weeding every two weeks. Indigo bushes were usually harvested at the height of two or three feet and took from 6 to 12 weeks to grow. Cut off one inch above the ground with a curved knife, they took six weeks to grow back and could be harvested two to five times per season. The cut plants were bundled in large cloths and carried to the *indigoterie*, which consisted of three rectangular basins made of masonry, arranged one below the other.

The first and largest basin measured about 100 square feet and some 3 feet deep. It required 30 or 40 bundles to fill it. The bundles of plants were covered with water and left to ferment between 12 and 30 hours. As the leaves and stems rotted, the water turned into a sticky violet liquid with a consistency thicker than egg white. Sometimes bubbling violently, it sent up pyramids of scum and gave off noxious gases that some claimed could be fatal. When fermentation was judged complete, the liquid was released via connecting pipes into the second and deepest basin. There it was kept churning for two or three hours by enslaved males using paddles set into the stonework. Extremely tiring work, this was the only job truly monopolized by males.[8] It was made more unpleasant by flies attracted by the rotting plants in the first basin. By the 1770s, most substantial planters had installed a paddle wheel that was turned by a horse or mule or by a waterwheel. The purpose of this "beating" was to cause the dyestuff suspended in the liquid to coagulate. Drained into the third basin, it settled as sludge on the bottom, as the water was progressively run off through taps at different levels. The sludge was drained into long cloth bags that were hung up to dry. Having achieved the consistency of soft cheese, it was laid out in the sun inside wooden cases. Finally, it was cut into inch cubes that eventually dried hard inside a shed.

On lowland plantations, a single basin-load yielded 20 to 30 pounds of dyestuff; on mountain plantations, the cooler temperatures lowered yields but improved quality. Inexperienced beginners, like the hapless Regnaud de Beaumont family in the hills of Léogane, might make less than 7 pounds per basin-load. An acre of indigo was expected to fill about 3.5 basins and an annual yield of 1,000 pounds to require 15 to 18 enslaved workers.[9] In the Artibonite plain, an acre supposedly yielded more than 35 pounds; 50 pounds would be a good crop, and some claimed 75 pounds per acre a feasible target.[10] But even the smallest figure seems exaggerated. Indigo dye was classified into five grades: from *bleu flottant* through *violet/cuivré fin* and *gros cuivré* to *ardoise* and *inférieur*. The best quality sold for more than three times the price of the worst. Ships' captains were known to empty out sack-loads before purchasing to examine each cake.[11]

The work regimen of indigo plantations was less harsh than that of sugar estates. Planting, weeding, and harvesting were all stoop labor, as with sugar, but there was no night work and much less heavy lifting. Planting did not require the digging of large holes, and the harvest doubtless lacked the frenetic pace dictated by the needs of sugarcane. Even so, Monnereau tells us, the indigo harvest was a race against the dual threat of rot and caterpillars, such that "every moment is so full that one can hardly distinguish holidays and Sundays from workdays."[12] Moreover, the frequent weeding through four to six months of the year, the working in full sunlight, the tendency to replant annually, and working with the paddles of the second basin probably made indigo a more demanding crop than coffee, cacao, or cotton.[13] This was certainly true of plantations where the workers had to fill the main basin with water.

In Guatemala, indigo planters were forbidden to employ Indian laborers because the work was considered so harmful.[14] Contemporaries disagreed whether the gases given off in fermentation really could poison workers, but the belief was found in both Brazil and the French colonies.[15] As most indigo plantations were located in the humid plains, they additionally shared the deadly disease environment of sugar estates rather than the healthier climate of the highland coffee plantations. Indigo was no doubt also a harder crop to work than tobacco, although seventeenth-century tobacco farms in the French Caribbean sometimes did demand a degree of night work. It is unclear to what extent, as tobacco was declining in the late seventeenth century, the demands of indigo plantations reinforced those of sugar in causing the replacement of white indentured labor with enslaved Africans. It is suggestive, however, that the few surviving inventories from this period show a similar, low ratio of servants to enslaved workers on sugar and indigo plantations, distinct from that found on ranches and tobacco farms.[16] Writing in the 1780s, the lawyer Moreau de Saint-Méry thought the harsher work regime of indigo and, especially, of sugar dictated the switch to slaves, which those crops' greater profitability also facilitated.[17]

In the eyes of the colonists, indigo was a difficult and fickle crop. It was particularly vulnerable to weeds, insect pests, and heavy rains, and the *franc* variety to drought as well. "There are few plants that have more enemies."[18] Some said indigo exhausted the soil more than any other crop.[19] Not only soil quality but water quality affected the finished product. Successful manufacture of the dyestuff required expert judgment in timing the various processes involved. Bad coffee might be sold locally; poor quality cane juice was used for rum or molasses; but low-grade indigo could be almost unsalable. After the Seven Years War (1756–63), depressed prices, exhausted soil, and declining output caused many planters to switch to cotton and sugar. It cost as much to produce 1,000 pounds of indigo as 5,000 pounds of cotton, which was then yielding 40 percent more revenue.[20] Though indigo prices greatly improved thereafter, indigo planters in the 1770s and 1780s were still diversifying into cotton or coffee.[21]

Spatial Distribution and Chronology

Spanish settlers cultivated indigo for export in late-sixteenth-century Hispaniola, but the island was already in commercial decline and faced strong competition from Guatemala and Mexico.[22] The crop was introduced into Saint Domingue by migrants from Samaná in 1676.[23] Indigo began to replace tobacco and ranching in the French colony in the 1680s, about the same time sugar cultivation was introduced.[24] The French presence, contested by Spain until 1697, was at this time still limited to a few enclaves on the north and west coasts. In 1692, a partial census recorded 164 plantations in the western part of the colony, and by 1703 there were another 32 along the south coast.[25] In the Caribbean, indigo plantations frequently served as stepping stones to the creation of sugar estates. This trend was already evident in Saint Domingue's northern plain by 1700. Nevertheless, the two crops developed almost in parallel until the 1740s— indigo cultivation expanding more rapidly before 1720, sugar accelerating thereafter. High prices during the War of the Spanish Succession stimulated both crops. By war's end in 1713, Saint Domingue had 138 sugar estates and 1,182 (much smaller) indigo plantations, of which half were in the west province.

After 1713, indigo rapidly lost ground to sugar cultivation in the northern plain and the Cul de Sac and Léogane plains of the west, but it expanded into areas of pioneer cultivation. New plantations now were more often cut out of the forest and underbrush than assembled from existing tobacco farms. Growth was strongest in the west's Artibonite plain and along the south coast, dominated by the plain of Les Cayes. Growth in the north was confined to the dry northeast region around Fort Dauphin and the northwest parishes of Jean Rabel, Port de Paix, Gros Morne, and Saint Louis. When the recorded number of indigo plantations peaked at 3,445 in 1739, 27 percent were located in the Artibonite and 22 percent on the south coast.

Though Pierre Pluchon depicts the number of plantations remaining stable in the second half of the century, Saint Domingue's indigo sector seems to have in fact experienced extraordinary instability.[26] Despite expansion in the central parishes of Mirebalais on the Santo Domingo frontier and Arcahaye on the western seaboard, the number of plantations fell in the 1740s, only to recover when prices rapidly peaked in the mid-1750s.[27] Prices then fell and stagnated through the 1760s. Artibonite planters turned to cotton; those with sufficient capital, to sugar; and those with land in the mountains to the new boom crop, coffee.[28] The 1771 census recorded only 1,027 plantations; the biggest decline occurred in the north. That year, however, saw the bursting of the coffee bubble, which, along with rising textile production, seems to have contributed to indigo's reviving fortunes in the early 1770s. Prices rose and stabilized after the mid-1770s. The number of plantations more than doubled in three years. Some marginal coffee planters abandoned their trees and planted indigo.[29] The number of plantations was back to 3,000 by 1780, but it dipped again to around 2,400 in 1785–86, perhaps because of the Artibonite flood of 1784.[30] Yet it soon regained and exceeded the 3,000 level in the final years before the slave revolution that began in 1791. In these last decades of the colony, the number of *indigoteries* grew to more than 1,000 in the Artibonite plain, from where more than a third of the colony's production was exported.[31] Growth was also marked in the plain of Les Cayes and at the tip of the southern peninsula, whereas in the north numbers fell again through the 1780s.

According to the colonial censuses, the area planted in indigo expanded from some 134,000 acres in 1780 to around 176,000 acres in 1787–88 and then fell to 83,000 acres in 1789.[32] But the reliability of these figures is highly suspect. Overall, indigo retained the image of a marginal and declining crop in Saint Domingue. In 1785, an Artibonite planter, the marquis d'Aussigné, wrote a memoir deploring the decline in quality and quantity of Saint Domingue's indigo production and urged government action. The crop was vital for French industry, he argued, but he had himself abandoned its cultivation because of a mystery disease affecting the plant.[33] The same year, it was estimated that fewer than 5 percent of indigo plantations were owned by absentees, whereas half of the sugar estates and nearly 10 percent of coffee and cotton plantations supported owners in France.[34]

Although broadly correlated with price movements, the violent fluctuations in the total number of plantations are hard to explain.[35] Colonial statistics do not merit much confidence, but it is unlikely that the tallying of indigo plantations should have been radically less reliable than that of all other plantation types. Coffee, cotton, and sugar also experienced falls of 50 percent in market prices without undergoing such instability. Sugar's growth was indeed inexorable, its heavy investment in fixed capital doubtless precluding rapid adjustment to market forces. The fact that indigo was quite often grown along with other cash crops (cotton, coffee, or sugar) on the same estate probably facilitated the reclassification of individual plantations, when the emphasis of their crop mix changed. Perhaps much of the variation occurred among the small indigo farms in the mountains that produced only plant seeds for sale, not dye. Finally, some of the decline in plantation numbers must have reflected the consolidation of larger indigo estates.

Indigo Production

Due to its high unit value, indigo can never have occupied more than a tiny proportion of the shipping tonnage servicing Saint Domingue. In the early eighteenth century, indigo cultivation employed more of Saint Domingue's enslaved laborers than any other sector, and it is generally thought to have been the main source of colonial income until about 1730.[36] According to Clarence Munford, however, in 1714 sugar exports were valued at 850,000 livres; those of indigo, at 612,000 livres.[37] Trade figures are sparse and frustratingly contradictory and, because of the extent of smuggling, almost invariably understatements. Colonial export statistics do not match imports into France and are often lower. One may assume indigo exports peaked at something over two million pounds in the third quarter of the century, or possibly earlier, when plantations were more numerous though smaller.

Indigo exports from Saint Domingue were recorded at 1.69 million pounds in 1753 and were estimated at 1.88 million pounds in 1764 by the colony's Superior Councils, which commented the first figure was "much below" the reality. In the late 1760s, when production was said to be declining, Hilliard d'Auberteuil put total exports at 2 million pounds including contraband, reckoned at 25 percent.[38] Annual imports into France fell from 2.0 million pounds in 1765 to 1.6 million pounds in 1767–68.[39] In 1771, the single port of Bordeaux, which normally imported about 0.6 million pounds, supposedly received 3.59 million pounds solely from Saint Domingue, but this can be ignored as a clerical error.[40] Official exports were recorded at 1.7 million pounds in 1772–73, and for the period 1774–77 they averaged between 2.0 and 2.2 million pounds according to different sets of statistics.[41] During the 1780s, they averaged 1.3 million pounds, declining steadily from 1.8 million pounds to less than 1.0 million pounds in 1788 and 1789.[42] Indigo still accounted for about a quarter of the value of Saint Domingue's exports to France in the 1730s and 1740s, 12 percent in the late 1760s, but little more than 5 percent 20 years later.[43]

The paradox here, as John Garrigus points out, is that official exports from Saint Domingue declined while the price of indigo in France and the rest of Europe remained strong.[44] Except for the slump of the late 1760s, the price of indigo improved relative to most other colonial products for most of the period 1750–90.[45] The decline in exports in the 1780s is all the more surprising; according to the censuses, the number of indigo plantations and the area planted in indigo tended to expand. Production techniques also improved.[46] The failure of trade figures to match up with statistics on plantation numbers, crop area, and even modest estimates of output per acre was doubtless due to a combination of smuggling, faulty record-keeping, and increasing soil exhaustion.

The relative importance of these factors is impossible to gauge. Many complained of soil exhaustion. Moreau de Saint-Méry reckoned in the late 1780s that soil exhaustion, parasites, and declining rainfall in the Artibonite plain had cut output per acre on older estates by more than half.[47] Smuggling was extensive, especially on the south coast and from the Artibonite. Nonetheless, it is difficult to believe it was much more extensive in the late 1780s than before. Given the opening of freeports in 1784 and the unusually vigorous efforts of the unpopular intendant Barbé-Marbois (1786–89), one would expect smuggling to have declined in that period.[48] However, it is possible the intendant's efforts were counteracted by the burgeoning demands of the British textile industry, exerted through Jamaica. Some contemporary commentators writing about contraband trade did not include indigo at all in their estimates.[49] Yet Venault de Charmilly claimed that two-thirds of the colony's indigo was smuggled to Jamaica. Antoine Dalmas thought the contraband trade took 15 percent of the colony's sugar and coffee but 20 percent of its indigo and cotton. Everyone knew, he claimed, interlope traders carried to Jamaica almost all of the indigo and cotton of the Artibonite and the south, especially in the year 1789.[50] This assertion seems highly unlikely; the customs duties paid in Saint Marc, the main outlet of the Artibonite plain, made it the colony's third most important port, and Dalmas was perhaps misled by a misprint in the intendant's *Etat de finances* for 1789.[51] On the other hand, if just the lowest estimates of output per acre and the lowest statements of total acreage in indigo were accurate, then de Charmilly would seem to have been correct. Whatever smuggling's precise extent, it clearly bolsters Saint Domingue's claim to be considered the premier source of indigo of the mid-eighteenth century.

Plantation Size and Value

By the end of the colonial period, the average Saint Domingue sugar estate had a workforce of close to 200 enslaved people, an area of 750 acres with 230 acres planted in cane, and a capital value of around 1.5 million livres coloniales (42,000 pounds sterling).[52] Coffee plantations averaged between 250 and 350 acres, with 65 acres of coffee trees, about 50 enslaved laborers, and a capital value in the region of 225,000 livres coloniales (6,250 pounds sterling).[53]

Much less is known about indigo plantations. The only census that permits calculation of average workforce size is a census of 1720 limited to the southern parishes of Les Cayes, Cavaillon, Saint Louis, and Aquin. There we find an average of only 14 enslaved workers on 209 plantations, whose ateliers ranged from 2 to about 30 workers. The region's 21 sugar estates at that time had workforces in the range 21 to 119 enslaved workers, with a mean average of 60. Three decades later, indigo plantations in the same area averaged 156 acres and sugar estates, 562 acres.[54]

A sample of 84 indigo (and indigo/cotton) plantations from all parts of Saint Domingue, assembled from secondary works and manuscript records, shows the average workforce increasing from less than 30 enslaved people before the Seven Years War to about 80 (with a range of 10 to 214) during the colony's final decade (table 1.1).[55] Of these cases, 39 reveal an average area of 582 acres and 16 an average value of 245,000 livres coloniales (6,800 pounds sterling), with a range between 22,000 and 758,000 livres coloniales. The area planted in indigo also varied enor-

Table 1.1. Workforce structure, 1730–93

	Slaves per plantation		Number of cases	Sex ratio	Creole (%)	Adults (%) Creole
	Median	Mean				
North	42	50	23	109	55	45
West	76	83	32	145	45	25
South	55	63	29	192	39	31
1730–59	25	30	12	275	27	23
1760–79	63	68	29	134	44	33
1780–93	80	77	49	128	47	34
1730–93	56	67	84	148	44	33

Source: See notes 55 and 56.

mously, from a few acres producing just indigo grain up to nearly 300 acres.[56] Regrettably, such surviving sources undoubtedly overrepresent the largest property holdings, and it remains unclear whether indigo plantations were generally bigger or smaller than coffee plantations. Although Monnereau claimed there were indigo plantations in the Artibonite plain with 500 or 600 enslaved laborers, another writer estimated in 1771 that the average was worth only 25,000 livres coloniales (700 pounds sterling), less than coffee plantations (30,000 livres coloniales) or sugar estates (300,000 livres).[57] Twenty years later, however, the average value of land, buildings, and crops was reckoned at 30,000 livres coloniales for indigo plantations and only 20,000 livres coloniales for coffee plantations. By this reckoning, the indigo sector accounted for 27 percent of the capital invested in the Saint Domingue countryside excluding the enslaved and livestock.[58]

According to the 1780s censuses, the average area planted in indigo per plantation fluctuated through the decade from 40 to 60 to 25 acres, and in the north the acreage was nearly ten times as great as elsewhere.[59] Some 70 percent of the colony's indigo grew in the north, if we are to believe the 1780 census. As less than 30 percent of official indigo exports came from the region, as it included some of the most productive land planted in indigo, and as its workforces appear to have been relatively small, this is puzzling.

The Workforce

Table 1.1 illustrates the gradual and incomplete movement during the eighteenth century toward workforces that were balanced between the sexes and between Africans and locally born Creoles. Creolization proved slowest in the West Province, where new plantations continued to appear, although even there they were in the aggregate less dominated by Africans than the much newer coffee sector. In the north, however, where Creolization was most advanced, indigo plantations still had markedly fewer Creoles than the oldest sugar estates. This was because the earliest indigo plantations had long since converted to sugar. The proportion of children (under age 15) generally increased through the century and was higher on indigo than on sugar estates. In the 1720 south coast census, children constituted 21 percent of indigo workforces and 14 percent of those of sugar plantations. In the north, they made up 30 percent of indigo enslaved laborers (22 percent of sugar and coffee slaves) in the colony's last

25 years. While this difference may reflect different purchasing patterns, it also reflects somewhat higher fertility levels among indigo workers. A sample of 20 plantations revealed a mean fertility index of .346 (children aged 0–4/women aged 15–44) and a median index of .300. These figures from the prerevolutionary decades place indigo exactly midway between sugar and coffee plantations as regards slave fertility.[60]

The evidence concerning health is less clear. People enslaved to the Mauger family, which had both a sugar and an indigo plantation in the Artibonite plain, suffered higher mortality as well as lower fertility on the sugar estate.[61] The 1720 south coast census recorded 3 percent of the enslaved sick on 209 indigo plantations and 6 percent sick on 21 sugar estates. However, a later sample of 19 indigo plantation inventories shows 15 percent of enslaved adults suffering permanent ailments, substantially more than usually found on sugar or coffee plantations. The large number of hernias and other disabilities is suggestive of a punishing work regime. However, it may be that indigo farmers, like coffee planters, were willing to purchase partially incapacitated laborers because their work routines were less demanding than that of sugar.[62] Slave ships with Africans considered unsalable in premium markets were sometimes sent to the Artibonite.[63]

These different degrees of selectivity are also apparent in the ethnic composition of the enslaved Africans on the three types of plantations. Sugar planters made greater efforts than coffee planters to purchase those Africans exported from the Bight of Benin (or Slave Coast), who were considered the best workers, and to avoid those from Central and Southeast Africa and the Bight of Biafra, regarded as less robust. The ethnic composition of workforces also varied considerably between each of Saint Domingue's three provinces, but within each the coffee sector tended to absorb about 50 percent more Central Africans than did the sugar sector.[64]

With indigo workers, too, we find the same regional variation in ethnic makeup (table 1.2). Central Africans dominated in the north, where the coffee planters' prominence shaped the regional market; Africans transported from the Bight of Benin were at their most numerous on western plantations; and the south imported substantial numbers of Biafrans, partly from British contraband traders. Despite echoing regional trends, the indigo workforces had within each province an "ethnic profile" quite distinct from that of the sugar estates. In the north and south, it resembled that of the coffee plantations; in the west, it was perfectly intermediate between those of coffee and sugar. The resultant structure was the expres-

Table 1.2. Origins of enslaved Africans on 33 indigo plantations, 1742–92 (selected regions)

	Slave coast	Central Africa	Biafra	No. of Africans
North	14%	63%	1%	174
West	30%	38%	5%	659
South	16%	37%	22%	318

Source: See notes 55 and 56.

sion of attitudes of planters like the Maugers, who tried to insist on Slave Coast purchases for their sugar estate but found Central Africans acceptable for their indigo plantation.[65]

Conclusion

As Jean Tarrade wrote 25 years ago, the history of indigo is yet to be written.[66] Surveying the growth of indigo cultivation in the colony that for a time was its leading producer, this essay points out certain difficulties in interpreting the primary sources and sheds further light on the crop's economic, developmental, and demographic "intermediate" character. Given the inconsistencies uncovered in the documentary record and with only 80 or so of Saint Domingue's 3,000 indigo plantations studied in any detail, the indigo sector continues to constitute a weak link in our knowledge of the colony.

Notes

1. Gabriel Debien, "Une Indigoterie à Saint-Domingue à la fin du XVIIIe siècle" *Revue d'Histoire des Colonies* 33 (1940–46): 1–49; Henri Teychenié, "Les Esclaves de l'indigoterie Belin à Saint-Domingue (1762–1793)," *Revista de Ciencias Sociales* 4 (1960): 237–66; Roseline Siguret, "Esclaves d'indigoteries et de caféières au quartier de Jacmel (1757–1791)," *Revue Française d'Histoire d'Outre-Mer* 55 (1968): 190–230; Jacques de Cauna, "Indigoteries à Saint-Domingue: Les habitations Gandérats et Pascal," *Cahiers du Centre de Généalogie et d'Histoire des Isles d'Amérique* 47 (1994): 25–31; François Girod, *Une Fortune coloniale sous l'Ancien régime* (Paris: Les Belles-Lettres, 1970).

2. John Garrigus, "Blue and Brown: Contraband Indigo and the Rise of a Free Colored Planter Class in French Saint Domingue," *The Americas* 50 (1993): 233–63; Élie Monnereau, *Le Parfait indigotier ou description de l'indigo*, nouvelle ed. (Marseille, 1765). For reference to the work's first edition, see 112–13.

3. Denis Diderot and Jean d'Alembert, eds., "Teinture," in *Encyclopédie; ou dictionnaire raisonné des sciences, des arts, et des métiers* (Paris, 1751–76), 16: 8–32. One pound of indigo was the equivalent of 16 pounds of woad.

4. Archives départementales des Pyrénées-Orientales, Perpignan, C 1045, Arrêt du Conseil d'État, January 29, 1735, Règlement sur le commerce du grabeau d'indigo.

5. Statistics taken from R. S. Smith, "Indigo Production and Trade in Colonial Guatemala," *Hispanic American Historical Review* 39 (1959): 181–211; José Fernández Molina, "Colouring the World in Blue: The Indigo Boom and the Central American Market, 1750–1810" (Ph.D. diss., University of Texas at Austin, 1992); and the invaluable Dauril Alden, "Growth and Decline of Indigo Production in Colonial Brazil," *Journal of Economic History* 25 (1965): 35–60, which slightly underestimates production in Saint Domingue.

6. Jean Tarrade, *Le Commerce colonial de la France à la fin de l'Ancien régime*, 2 vols. (Paris: P.U.F., 1972), 2: 753; François-Georges Pariset, *Bordeaux au XVIIIe siècle* (Bordeaux: Fédération Historique de Sud-Ouest, 1968), 233; John G. Clark, *La Rochelle and the Atlantic Economy during the Eighteenth Century* (Baltimore: Johns Hopkins University Press, 1981), 163.

7. On Jamaica, see Thomas Coke, *A History of the West Indies*, 3 vols. (1808; reprint, London: Frank Cass, 1971), 1: 377; for Guatemala, see Smith, "Indigo Production," 186–89. The following description derives mainly from Monnereau, *Parfait indigotier*, 17–21, 34–59; Diderot and d'Alembert, *Encyclopédie*, 8: 679–83, Suppl. 3: 586–92.

8. Archives Départementales de la Charente-Maritime, La Rochelle (hereafter ADCM), E514, letter of May 17, 1776.

9. Ibid., and letter of July 15, 1776.

10. Debien, "Une indigoterie," 47–48; Gabriel Debien, *Etudes antillaises* (Paris: Armand Colin, 1956), 57.

11. New York Public Library, West Indies Collection, box 2, folder L, De La Rue to Mme. de Ramera, August 28, 1785.

12. Monnereau, *Parfait indigotier*, 105.

13. Cotton was also replanted annually and similarly did not benefit from the shade trees found on cacao and sometimes coffee plantations, but it is described as the least demanding of Caribbean crops in Félix Carteau, *Soirées bermudiennes* (Paris, 1802), 297.

14. Smith, "Indigo Production," 186–89.

15. Diderot and d'Alembert, *Encyclopédie*, 8: 681, Suppl. 3: 590; Alden, "Growth and Decline," 57.

16. See the data in Gabriel Debien, "Les Engagés des Antilles au Travail," *Notes d'Histoire Coloniale* 223, (n.p., n.d.).

17. M.L.E. Moreau de Saint-Méry, *Description topographique . . . de la partie française de l'isle Saint-Domingue*, 3 vols. (1797; reprint, Paris: Société de l'Histoire des Colonies Françaises, 1958), 1: 45.

18. Diderot and d'Alembert, *Encyclopédie*, Suppl. 3: 586.

19. AN, 505 Mi 85, Foäche & Cie. to La Lorie, April 1, 1789; AN, C9B/40, "Mémoire sur les terres"; Diderot and d'Alembert, *Encyclopédie*, Suppl. 3: 589–92. The necessity of frequent weeding and cutting and the lack of shade and of leaf trash exposed the topsoil to intense sunlight, which turned it to dust.

20. See the 1768 report printed in Pierre Léon, *Marchands et spéculateurs dauphinois dans le monde antillais du XVIIIe siècle* (Paris: Les Belles Lettres, 1963), 202–3; Monnereau, *Parfait indigotier*, 28; Gabriel Debien, *Lettres de colons* (Laval: Madiot, 1965), 11.

21. Debien, *Études antillaises*, 44–46, 64; Maurice Begouen Demeaux, *Mémorial d'une famille du Havre: Les fondateurs* (Le Havre: Etaix, 1948), 171; Debien, "Une indigoterie," 38; Lucile Bourrachot and Gabriel Debien, *Une famille de l'Agenais à Saint-Domingue d'après sa correspondance: Les Redon de Monplaisir (1740–1778)* ([Agen]: Société acadé mique d'Agen, 1975).

22. Antonio Sánchez Valverde, *Idea del valor de la isla Española* (Santo Domingo: Editora nacional, 1971), 63; Smith, "Indigo Production," 197; Alden, "Growth and Decline," 38.

23. Michel Hector and Claude Moïse, *Colonisation et esclavage en Haïti* (Port au Prince: Henri Deschamps, 1990), 60. However, Alden, "Growth and Decline," 42, states the crop was introduced from Martinique.

24. On the colony's first sugar estate, see Moreau de Saint-Méry, *Description*, 2: 1091.

25. Saint Domingue's surviving census data contain widely varying amounts of information. Most of the census data cited here come from Archives Nationales Section d'Outre-mer, Aix-en-Provence (hereafter ANOM), G1/509 (years 1692–1786); Archives Nationales, Paris (hereafter AN), C9A/160, ff. 335–36 (years 1787–88); and (for 1788 and 1789) the two reports written, respectively, by François Barbé Marbois and chevalier de Proisy entitled *État des finances de Saint-Domingue* (Paris, 1790). The boundaries of the colony's three provinces were changed several times. Here I define the west as all districts bordering the Gulf of Gonave and the Grande Anse region, including the parish of Tiburon.

26. Pierre Pluchon, *Histoire de la colonisation française* (Paris: Fayard, 1991), 461–62.

27. On prices, see Tarrade, *Commerce colonial*, 2: 771–73.

28. Léon, *Marchands*, 202–3.

29. ADCM, E514, correspondence 1769–74; Michel-René Hilliard d'Auberteuil, *Considérations sur l'état présent de la colonie française de Saint Domingue*, 2 vols. (Paris, 1776–77), 1: 71.

30. AN, C9A/158, ff. 177–78, and C9A/157, letter of April 28, 1787.

31. Official exports from Saint Marc, the Artibonite plain's port town, accounted for 37 percent of Saint Domingue's legal indigo exports in 1788–89. In addition, some Artibonite produce was shipped to Le Cap, and a large quantity was sent illegally to Jamaica.

32. AN, C9A/160, ff. 335–36; AN, Dxxv/72/719, report by Legrand.

33. Thésée, *Négociants bordelais*, 48.

34. C9A/158, ff. 177–78.

35. I ignore patently aberrant estimates of plantation numbers, such as the "700" in the 1786 census summary and the "600" found in Hilliard d'Auberteuil, *Considérations*, 1: 71.

36. As in Alden, "Growth and Decline," 42.

37. Clarence Munford, *The Black Ordeal of Slavery in the French West Indies in the Seventeenth Century* (New York: Mellen, 1991), 521.

38. Léon, *Marchands*, 203; Hilliard d'Auberteuil, *Considérations*, 1: 71.

39. Tarrade, *Commerce colonial*, 2: 747.

40. Pariset, *Bordeaux*, 230. The recorded coffee imports of the same year were similarly aberrant.

41. AN, C9B/37, dossier "Commerce"; Tarrade, *Commerce colonial*, 2: 747. The statement in James McClellan, *Colonialism and Science: Saint Domingue in the Old Regime* (Baltimore: Johns Hopkins University Press, 1992), 67, that production peaked in the 1740s, "declining steadily thereafter," overlooks the revivals in the 1750s and 1770s.

42. AN, C9B/37, dossier "Commerce"; Tarrade, *Commerce colonial*, 2: 747; Emilio Cordero Michel, *La Revolución haitiana y Santo Domingo* (Santo Domingo: Editora Nacional, 1968), 21. The figure for total indigo exports in de Proisy, *État des finances*, (Paris, 1790), tableau X, is evidently a misprint. It is repeated in Drouin de Bercy, *De Saint Domingue* (Paris, 1814), appendix.

43. Pariset, *Bordeaux*, 230; Léon, *Marchands*, 204; Drouin de Bercy, *De Saint Domingue*, appendix; Maurice Begouen Demeaux, *Jacques-François Begouen* (Le Havre: Geuthner, 1957), 195; AN, Dxxv/72/719, report by Legrand; AN, C9B/38, report entitled "Commerce direct." These sources present different figures for the 1780s but differ little as to proportions. I ignore the figures in T. C. Mozard's tables also in C9B/38, and Avalle, *Tableau comparatif des productions des colonies* (Paris, 1799), as they are greatly at variance with most other sources. They show France importing from Saint Domingue 1.9 million pounds of indigo worth 17 million livres tournois in 1788.

44. Garrigus, "Blue and Brown," 240–43.

45. Robert Stein, "The State of French Colonial Commerce on the Eve of the French Revolution," *Journal of European Economic History* 12 (1983): 112. However, unlike in France, indigo prices on the Amsterdam market declined in the 1780s. Nicolaas Posthumus, *Inquiry into the History of Prices in Holland*, 2 vols. (Leiden: Brill, 1946–64), 1: 417, 419.

46. Improved techniques that greatly reduced waste apparently became generalized between the 1740s and 1770s: Diderot and d'Alembert, *Encyclopédie*, Suppl. 3: 590. However, see also Thomas Southey, *Chronological History of the West Indies*, 3 vols. (London, 1827), 3: 178.

47. Moreau de Saint-Méry, *Description*, 2: 816–17. However, on the Detroit

plantation, output increased from 5,000 pounds to 8,000 pounds between 1762–78 and 1779–87, although the estate was then half a century old: Bermondet de Cromières Papers, Château de Cussac.

48. See David Geggus, "The Major Port Towns of Saint Domingue in the Late Eighteenth Century," in *Atlantic Port Cities: Economy, Culture, and Society in the Atlantic World, 1650–1850*, ed. Franklin Knight and Peggy Liss (Knoxville: University of Tennessee Press, 1991), 96–98.

49. AN, Dxxv/72/719, report by Legrand; Charles Malenfant, *Des colonies et surtout celle de Saint-Domingue* (Paris, 1814); *Philadelphia General Advertiser*, May 21, 1792; Archivo General de Indias, Seville, Audiencia de Santo Domingo 1031, memoir by Urizar, September 25, 1793.

50. Pierre-François Venault de Charmilly, *Lettre à M. Bryan Edwards* (London, 1797), 78; Antoine Dalmas, *Histoire de la Révolution de Saint-Domingue* (Paris, 1814), 294.

51. See note 42.

52. David Geggus, "The Sugar Plantation Zones of Saint Domingue and the Revolution of 1791–1793," *Slavery and Abolition* 20 (1999): 31–46.

53. David Geggus, "Sugar and Coffee Cultivation in Saint Domingue," in *Cultivation and Culture: Labor and the Shaping of Slave Life in the Americas*, ed. Ira Berlin and Philip Morgan (Charlottesville: University Press of Virginia, 1993), 73–98.

54. ANOM, G1/509, censuses of 1720 and 1753. Details of individual properties in multiple holdings are not provided; the largest (Boisrond family) consisted of three indigo plantations with 89 slaves. In the 1753 census and the 1733 survey of the Grande Anse, one in six proprietors were non-whites.

55. The number of cases in table 1 refers to columns 1 and 2; the last three columns were derived from smaller samples. The number of cases in the subperiod samples is greater than the overall total, as some plantations provided data from more than one subperiod. For the regional and overall samples, I chose the most complete or the latest data for each estate. The table shows the mean average sex ratio (males per 100 females) at the plantation level. Since sexual imbalance was greatest on the smallest plantations, aggregate sex ratios were lower, 99, 127, and 143, respectively, for the north, west, and south.

56. The sources include the works cited above in notes 1, 2, and 21; ADCM, E295, E513–514; Archives Départementales de l'Aveyron, Rodez, E 2832; Archives Départementales de la Vendée, Roche-sur-Yon, 87 J 55; Archives Départementales de la Vienne, Poitiers, F3; Archives Départementales des Yvelines, Versailles, J 39; ANOM, Notsdom 258, 292, 405, 435, 1154, 1210, 1627, 1712, and Notariat (old-style) 418; ANOM, Greffe 51; Bibliothèque Nationale, Paris, Manuscrits, NAF 22,367, f. 151; Château de Cussac, Bermondet de Cromières Papers; Louisiana State Museum, Mossmeier Collection, New Orleans; New York Public Library, West Indies Collection, box 1, folder C; South Caroliniana Library, Dugas-Kerblay Papers, Columbia; Marcel Châtillon Collection, Paris; University

of Florida Library, Special Collections, Slaves and Plantations in Saint Domingo collection; *Affiches Américaines* (1781, 1788, 1790, 1791); Thésée, *Négociants bordelais*; Françoise Thésée, "Sur deux sucreries de Jacquezy," *Actes du 92e congrès national des sociétés savantes Strasbourg et Colmar, 1967; Section d'histoire moderne et contemporaine, vol. 2, Le Commerce et l'industrie* (Paris: Bibliothèque nationale, 1967), 217–95; H. Branche, *Plantations d'Amérique et papiers de famille, II* (n.p., 1960); Bernard Foubert, *Les Plantations Laborde*, 2 vols. (Lille: Atelier National de Reproduction des Thèses, 1990); Debien, *Lettres de colons*; Gabriel Debien, *Plantations et esclaves* (Dakar: Université de Dakar, 1962); Gabriel Debien, "Les Esclaves de la plantation Mauger," *Bulletin de la Société de la Guadeloupe* 43–44 (1980): 1–136; Eileen Glotin, *Vers la fortune* (n.p., 1959); Gabriel Debien et al., "Les Origines des esclaves antillais," *Bulletin de l'Institut Français de l'Afrique Noire*, ser. B, 27 (1965).

57. Monnereau, *Parfait indigotier*, 28; Tarrade, *Commerce colonial*, 1: 33.

58. Report to Legislative Assembly, in James Barskett, *History of St. Domingo* (London, 1818), appendix 3. Legrand's report in AN, Dxxv/72/719, attributed to indigo 25 percent of the capital in rural buildings and 8 percent by value of rural land excluding crops.

59. See note 25; Legrand's report in AN, Dxxv/72/719 (for 1789).

60. See Geggus, "Sugar and Coffee," 91.

61. Debien, "Plantation Mauger," 25–29.

62. Geggus, "Sugar and Coffee," 89.

63. AN, 505 Mi 85–86, Foäche & Cie. correspondence.

64. Geggus, "Sugar and Coffee," 79–84; Geggus, "Sugar Plantation Zones," table 5.

65. Debien, "Plantation Mauger," 14–18.

66. Tarrade, *Commerce colonial*, 1: 34.

2

Timber Extraction and the Shaping
of Enslaved People's Culture in Belize

O. Nigel Bolland

In the seventeenth century, British buccaneers used the coastline of Belize in the Bay of Honduras as a base to attack Spanish ships, many of which carried logwood from which a dye valuable in the European woolen industry was obtained. By the 1650s, some buccaneers changed from plundering Spanish logwood ships to cutting the trees in various parts of the Yucatán peninsula. The shift from buccaneering to logging and more permanent settlement was encouraged by the 1670 Treaty of Madrid, in which the European powers agreed to suppress piracy. Despite continuing conflicts with Spain, the British expanded their logwood trade and settlement in the Bay of Honduras.

In the 1760s, the logwood trade declined because of a glut in the market, and mahogany became Belize's chief export. By the Convention of London, signed in 1786, Britain acknowledged Spanish sovereignty over the area and agreed not to build forts, establish any form of government, or develop plantation agriculture. In return, the Baymen, as the British settlers in the Bay of Honduras were called, were allowed to cut and export logwood and mahogany. They elected magistrates from among the wealthiest settlers, and the British government appointed a superintendent to act as the chief executive. In 1798, with the defeat of a Spanish attack, Belize became a British colony in all but name and in 1862 was formally declared a colony with the name of British Honduras.[1] The extraction of timber remained the chief economic raison d'être of the colony until the mid- twentieth century.

In Belize, the Baymen organized slavery for the extraction of timber. The earliest reference to enslaved Africans in the British settlement at Belize was in 1724, when a Spanish missionary observed that enslaved people had been imported a short time before from Jamaica and Bermuda.[2] By the 1750s, enslaved Africans constituted a majority, and by the turn of the century they were about 75 percent of the population. The cutting of logwood and mahogany, which was almost the sole occupation of enslaved men in Belize, had a pervasive influence upon the organization and conditions of work. The organization of work for the extraction of timber, in turn, created a unique slave system in Belize.

Few enslaved people in Belize engaged in agriculture, and, unlike most places in the Americas, there was a sharp gender division of labor.[3] The vast majority of enslaved men were woodcutters, and most enslaved women engaged in domestic tasks. The labor process affected settlement patterns and demographic characteristics and helped define gender roles and relations between enslavers and enslaved. These aspects of the slave system shaped the patterns of resistance and Afro-Belizean or Creole culture. The decline in the logwood trade and shift to mahogany cutting in the 1770s resulted in an increase in the amounts of capital, land, and labor required for timber extraction. Logwood, a small tree that grows in clumps near the coast, could be cut by Baymen with just one or two enslaved persons, but mahogany is huge, and it grows sparsely in the interior. Various tasks involved in mahogany extraction created several distinct occupations, including axe-men, huntsmen, and cattlemen. The work units, though necessarily larger in extracting mahogany than logwood, were generally small and lacked drivers. The extraction of timber, particularly mahogany, entailed the frequent shifting of workers from one location to another in the extensive and virtually uninhabited bush. Mahogany camps were isolated and more or less temporary, and logging was seasonal. At the end of the logging season, enslaved men were reunited with each other and with their families in Belize Town, where the holiday season between Christmas and Epiphany became the occasion of a community festival. In this urban context, social interaction between the enslaved of different African cultures gave rise to Belizean Creole culture.

The Enslaved Population: Numbers and Demographic Composition

During the eighteenth and early nineteenth centuries, enslaved Africans were brought to Belize via the British Caribbean, chiefly Jamaica. From about the middle of the eighteenth century, people of African origin comprised the majority of the population of Belize. With the development of the demand for mahogany in the 1770s, the settlement expanded, and hundreds more enslaved people were imported. When Spaniards captured the settlement in 1779, there were an estimated 3,000 enslaved people in

Belize, who comprised about 86 percent of the population. After the resettlement following the peace of 1783, about 75 percent of the population comprised enslaved Africans, 14 percent free people of color, and about 10 percent white.[4] While the proportion of enslaved Africans as distinct from those of Caribbean birth is unknown, an 1823 estimate indicates that in an enslaved population of about 2,300 there were "near 1500 Africans," and the rest were "Creoles and descendants of Indians," the latter from the Mosquito Shore.[5] If about three-fifths of those enslaved were African-born in 1823, Creoles almost certainly had always been a minority of the enslaved population. Following the abolition of the transatlantic trade in enslaved African captives in 1807, the number of enslaved people in Belize decreased from about 3,000 to under 2,000 at the time of emancipation in 1838. During this period, the enslaved population declined from about 75 percent to less than 50 percent of the population, while free people of color increased from about 25 percent to almost 50 percent, and whites remained about 10 percent of the population.

Apparently, the majority of enslaved people born in Africa who were located in Belize were from the Niger and Cross deltas in the Bight of Benin, from where most of the captives exported were probably Ibo. In Belize, as in Jamaica, the Ibo seem to have been numerous. Many other enslaved Africans came from the Congo and Angola and were predominantly Bantu peoples. The African contingent in the free population was reinforced when discharged members of the West India regiments, many of whom had been recruited in West Africa, were settled in Belize in 1817 and 1818. An attempt to augment the labor force in the 1830s with liberated Africans from Spanish and Portuguese slavers was only partly successful. Some of those who landed died of cholera, drowned, or killed themselves, but at the end of 1837 some 357 of these Africans remained in Belize.

As long as enslaved Africans could be imported to Belize their numbers increased, but with the abolition of the trade in African captives the number of enslaved persons and their proportion to the rest of the population declined rapidly. A relatively high incidence of manumission, combined with the large number of successful runaways, speeded this decline. About 600 enslaved people were manumitted between 1807 and 1834, and more than 200 escaped. Had all these people remained in slavery, there still would have been fewer enslaved persons in 1834 than there were in 1807. The enslaved population was unable to reproduce itself, the decrease resulting, in particular, from high mortality rates. The sex ratio of 162.5

males per 100 females, which was "by far the highest sex ratio" in the British Caribbean, and the top-heavy age structure suggest that the growth of the enslaved population was dependent on the transatlantic trade in enslaved Africans.[6] While the enslaved population appears to have been unable to increase by natural means, the proportion of the enslaved who were nine years old or less increased from 16 percent in 1823 to 19 percent in 1834. As Barry Higman suggests, the population may have been "emerging into a position of positive natural increase shortly before emancipation."[7]

The enslaved population in Belize, especially vigorous, seasoned men, were more highly valued than those in other British colonies, in part because they had to be imported through the Jamaican market for African captives. In 1834, 25 percent of the enslaved were men aged 40 years or more, reflecting the great importation of young men in the years immediately preceding the abolition of the trade. In 1809, a recently imported African was worth between 120 pounds and 160 pounds Jamaican currency, and a seasoned one between 200 pounds and 300 pounds.[8] The average price for an enslaved person in the 1820s was over 120 pounds. Some enslaved persons who purchased their own freedom paid 200 pounds or more, one paying as much as 450 pounds in 1829.[9] The high value placed upon enslaved people in Belize was confirmed by the rate of compensation per enslaved person after emancipation which, at more than 53 pounds, was the highest rate in any British colony. The high value of the enslaved and the preference for young men reflected the nature of the labor demands in an economy devoted almost exclusively to the arduous tasks of mahogany extraction.

Labor Organization and Work Regime

The organizational requirements of timber extraction in Belize were unlike those of plantation crops such as sugar and cotton, producing some marked differences in the experiences of the enslaved, including the patterns of residence associated with work, the nature of the work itself, and the gender division of labor.

First, the extraction of timber entailed the continual shifting of production units from one location to another as timber resources became exhausted in one area and settlers laid claims to new areas of exploitation.[10] The nature of timber extraction also led to the existence of many timber works, large in area but small in personnel, that dotted the rivers of Belize, while the vast intervening spaces remained untouched bush. The enslaved worked in small, more or less temporary and isolated camps in the middle of an uncultivated and essentially uninhabited forest.

The second difference between the experience of enslaved men cutting timber in the forests of Belize and those working on agricultural plantations resulted from the work process. The extraction of logwood was a small-scale operation. Initially, it was possible for Baymen to undertake it themselves "with a single Negro, some without one."[11] With the shift to mahogany extraction in the second half of the eighteenth century, however, the settlers required more labor. The mahogany tree was larger and grew further inland and in a more scattered manner than logwood. Also, while logwood was exported in chunks, the giant mahogany trees were squared whole for shipment. Though logwood continued to be exported for many decades, the chief occupations for enslaved men after about 1770 were connected with mahogany extraction.

The extraction of mahogany was a seasonal occupation, each season requiring laborers to spend long periods of time in isolated camps. The first season began after Christmas, at the end of the rainy season, when the men cut and trucked out the trees. Mahogany cutters went to their locations by a little fleet of pitpans or dories and made a depot for storing provisions on the riverbank. At the various works where the trees were to be cut, the men built temporary shelters using palm leaf or grass thatch. These makeshift dwellings were described as "nothing more than huts composed of a few sticks and leaves."[12] Work sites were determined not for the men's comfort but for their accessibility to mahogany trees, to the means of feeding the draft animals with which to truck the trees, and to the rivers down which the logs would float in the rainy season.[13] The mahogany trees—once located, cut, and trimmed—were trucked during the dry season by teams of cattle through temporary paths in the bush to the nearest riverside, at the place called the *barquadier,* and the trees were marked with the owner's initials. At the end of May, the rains made the roads impassable and the rivers swell. In the second season, beginning in about August, the logs were floated downriver, followed by men in pitpans who kept them free from obstacles, to a boom. The logs were then re-sorted and formed into rafts according to their owners' marks for the trip to the proprietors' wharves at the river's mouth. There the gigantic logs were lifted from the water and finally squared ready for shipment. The isolation of the gangs from each other and from their families during the logging seasons was similar to "a long confinement on shipboard."[14]

Labor organization and work process in the extraction of timber differed greatly from those of the sugar plantation. While most enslaved people on sugar plantations worked in large gangs, those engaged in mahogany extraction worked in small groups. Gangs employed in cutting mahogany were said to "consist of from ten to 50 each; few exceed the latter number. The large bodies are commonly divided into several small ones, a plan which it is supposed greatly facilitates labor."[15] Other than the teams that trucked the huge logs to the riverbanks, most gangs consisted of only 10 to 12 men. The small size of the gangs involved in timber extraction and the isolation in which they worked may have created a uniquely intense kind of solidarity within the logging gang, whose members would soon come to know and depend on each other, but their isolation inhibited the extension of such solidarity beyond the gang. The smaller gangs also reduced the owners' need for supervising the enslaved. The foreman or captain of a logging gang assigned the daily tasks and was responsible for integrating their productive activities. Though he had some authority and probably some coercive power, the whip-wielding drivers—ubiquitous on the plantations—were "not known to any Gang" in Belize.[16]

A number of distinct tasks required by mahogany extraction became the basis of identifiable occupations. First, there were huntsmen who searched and surveyed the forest to locate mahogany trees. This task, generally carried out in the fall when the tinge of the leaves distinguished the mahogany from other trees, was solitary and highly skilled and, like that of boilermen on sugar plantations, was the basis of the success of the entire enterprise. Captain G. Henderson records that huntsmen were the "most intelligent" and "often valued at more than five hundred pounds."[17] A master depended not only on the huntsman's skills in discovering the mahogany but also on his sense of duty in reporting it. Given the irregular and unsystematic nature of land tenure, a successful huntsman was known to trick his owner by bargaining with other masters when he found a considerable stand of timber. The nature of the huntsman's work and the master's reliance upon him gave the huntsman considerable independence.

Second, there were the men who cut the trees, a dangerous and highly skilled job, swinging heavy axes on a springy platform about 12 feet above the ground. This platform permitted axe-men to sever the tree above the great buttresses and also provided a flexible base that enabled them to achieve more momentum with each stroke. Axe-men worked singly or in pairs rather than in a gang. Since their work required great physical strength and skill, axe-men, like huntsmen, may have derived some satisfaction, pride, and status from it.

Following the axe-men were less skilled enslaved men whose task was to trim the tree after it had been felled, to clear the rough track upon which the tree was to be drawn to the riverside, and to square the trunks at the river's mouth. The more accessible trees were rolled or slid down to the riverbanks or, if the path declined suitably, hauled over skids. When trees were widely dispersed, however, an extensive network of roads was needed, with smaller tracks leading from individual trees converging onto a main road leading to the riverbank, perhaps eight or ten miles in all. Large trees and undergrowth alike had to be removed, by cutting and burning, in order that trucking could begin in the dry season. The larger trees were sawed into various lengths and squared roughly in order to reduce their weight and to prevent them from rolling dangerously on the carriages.

Another important occupation was that of the cattleman, who fed and drove the animals used in trucking the huge trunks. A gang of as many as 40 men worked with six trucks—which were specially constructed on broad wooden wheels—drawn by seven pairs of oxen and led by two drivers, the whole occupying a quarter mile of road. At least 12 men were needed to raise a mahogany log by means of inclined platforms up which the log was gradually pushed, each end alternately, onto the trucks. Because of the intense daytime heat, trucks usually started from the *barquadier* at 6 o'clock in the evening, were loaded in about three hours, and returned to the river by 11 o'clock the next morning. While strong and healthy enslaved men were extracting timber, enslaved women and children prepared their food. Rationed allowances—including salt pork, flour, rum, and sugar—accounted for most but not all of the slaves' diet.[18]

Beginning in the eighteenth century, the enslaved were occupied in "making plantations," an expression used to this day in Belize to refer to the cultivation of small plots of ground-foods, vegetables, corn, plantains, and other subsistence crops. That owners encouraged enslaved people to grow provisions in order to cut the costs of maintaining the labor force is supported by an observation made in 1806 that "the slaves have pieces of ground allotted them for cultivation, which enables the most industrious, to make an agreement with their Masters in lieu of Provision."[19] These arrangements were more necessary in times of war, when the price of imported food tended to rise. In order not to lose the labor of those enslaved workers who were unfit for the demanding job of timber extraction, owners sometimes put them to work growing provisions.[20] Of the 48 listed as plantation laborers in the Slave Register, a census of the enslaved population taken in 1834, 11 were enslaved women. Thirty of the men were 50 years old or more, and the remainder were under 16 years.[21]

Although most of the enslaved men and women who grew provisions were required to do so by their owners, some did so on their own initiative. In 1788, a settler described how the enslaved were "ever accustomed to make Plantation as they term it, by which means they support their wives and children, raise a little Stock and so furnish themselves with necessaries etc."[22] Most of the produce grown by the enslaved on their own account was for their families' consumption. Enslaved people in Belize also participated in a rudimentary marketing system, whereby they sold some of their produce in Belize Town. Though the extent of the provision grounds is unknown, Henderson wrote that "every Settlement at Honduras has its plantain walk . . . the pine-apple and melon, being very commonly interspersed between the rows of plantains." The banks of the Sibun River, today one of the chief sources of small farm produce for the Belize City market, were "thickly studded with plantations."[23] Such cultivation had to be compatible with timber extraction and was therefore shifting or seasonal rather than settled agriculture. Forest workers, whether enslaved or free, had little time or opportunity for cultivation. Even though the provision grounds were usually on the riverbanks, the time needed to transport produce to the market in Belize Town and, even more, to return upriver was generally prohibitive. The exigencies of the woodcutting economy and its associated patterns of settlement and migration inhibited the growth of the provision-ground system and made the enslaved and their descendants dependent chiefly on allowances of imported food.

The enslaved population in Belize had other customary allowances—including food, tobacco and pipes, and clothing—and other ways of gaining subsistence. They sometimes received payments in cash from their owners for labor that was considered to be extra or on their own time. Henderson reported that "Saturday's labor, invariably the privilege of the slave, [was] generally engaged by his owner [at the] established rate of 3s 4d per day." He pointed out, however, that this allowance, "though it be paid at the nominal rate of 3 shillings 4 pence per day, seldom actually amounts to any thing like so much; it being in most instances accounted for in slops, trinkets, or liquors, of the most inferior kind; and which no doubt are given out in this way at a profit of more than 200 percent."[24]

If Henderson's statement of allowances was the ideal, it is not known to what extent or how often it was attained. Nor is it known how such customary allowances and usages were negotiated between the enslaved and their owners. Presumably, the enslaved people had some input in the exchange of their labor for provisions and payments. This experience was important in the transition to wage labor after 1838.[25]

Gender Division of Labor

The gender division of labor among the enslaved in Belize was so marked that only young children and, to a lesser extent, old men and women shared similar employment: the children waited at table and some of the old people cultivated provisions. Young boys and girls experienced their first work as domestics, where they were taught to be obedient. The majority of boys would then become "attached to the Mahogany works," and a few became assistants to blacksmiths or carpenters.[26] In 1834, the 795 woodcutters, all men, amounted to 41 percent of the enslaved population and 67 percent of the enslaved men. Of the enslaved males between the ages of 10 and 59 years, 82 percent were woodcutters, and many of the others were in occupations, like cattlemen, associated with timber extraction. As the men became older or infirm, they were shifted to agricultural or some other less strenuous labor, and only about half of the men aged 60 years or more were still woodcutters.

The Belizean economy was so devoted to timber extraction and this work was so exclusively the business of men that women were largely confined to varieties of domestic work. Of the 729 enslaved women in 1834, 73 percent were identified as washerwomen, housemaids, servants, chambermaids, cooks, seamstresses, drudges, or other domestics. Among the enslaved females, the occupational transition was from one kind of domestic work to another: from waiting girl to housemaid, chambermaid, or seamstress, and then, as they reached their 20s, to the more skilled or heavy work of cook, washerwoman, or drudge. The handful of other occupations held by women included nurses (five), bakers (three), and a single vendor. There was more variety among the men, who included 13 sailors or boatmen, 13 footmen or other domestics, five blacksmiths, two draymen, two pen-keepers, one cooper, one bank keeper, one stove boy, and one butcher.

Although it is difficult to evaluate the impact of the division of labor upon women's status, particularly in terms of their authority and control over their households, the peculiar organization of work in Belize had implications for the definition of gender and the position and treatment of women in the colony, both during slavery and after. On the one hand, as

Marietta Morrissey suggests, a division of labor that favored men would tend to result in women having less authority and control in the households, but, on the other hand, the absence of most men for long periods must have left the women, if only by default, in positions of authority and control.[27] Perhaps there were conflicts between women and men when the latter, returning from work in the forests, tried to reassert their authority in the home.

Women were sometimes subjected to vicious and sadistic punishments by their masters and mistresses in Belize Town. Enslaved women, by virtue of their occupations and the absence of their men, were particularly vulnerable to such abuse. Some of the free colored mistresses, feeling jealous or insecure in their status, were especially harsh. One such case was recorded in 1820, when an enslaved woman, Kitty, was chained and whipped so badly by her free colored mistress that she was said by a physician to be scarcely recognizable.[28]

The patterns of employment experienced by both enslaved men and women in Belize must have appeared as binding and unalterable, not simply because they were enslaved but also because there were so few observable alternatives, particularly for women. Some men could hope to become captains of gangs or huntsmen in mahogany extraction or to acquire a skilled trade. For most of the enslaved, woodcutting for men and domestic work for women constituted almost their whole work experience. The lack of development of what Sidney Mintz has called a protopeasantry among the enslaved, and of the associated development of trade and marketing of foodstuffs, affected all those enslaved in Belize, but it especially affected the women vis-à-vis the men.[29] After the abolition of slavery, women could not begin to match the wages earned by men, and women's status in the household probably suffered as a consequence. The limited pattern of work experience during slavery contributed to the continued dependence of the majority of the formerly enslaved men on employment as mahogany cutters, to the continued and perhaps increased dependence of women upon men, and to the relatively retarded development of a peasantry in Belize in the century after abolition.[30]

Settlement Pattern and Timber Extraction

The pattern of settlement in colonial Belize, as shaped by the economy of timber extraction, differed from that prevailing in the sugar colonies. Much of the northern half of the territory, in which most of the logging took place during the slavery period, was inhospitable lowland penetrated by rivers and lagoons or inundated by swamps covered with mangrove and infested by insects. Until 1779, the chief British settlement was on Saint George's Cay, but after the peace of 1783 the principal establishment, located at the Belize River mouth, became Belize Town. During the period of slavery, most enslaved persons and free people of color resided in Belize Town when they were not in the seasonal logging camps. When the mahogany cutters returned from the forest to join their families at Christmas, the population of the town almost doubled, to between 2,000 and 3,000 people. This largely urban context was the crucible of Belizean Creole culture.[31]

The presence of a culturally varied population gave rise to complex cultural exchanges. The seasonal rhythm of work and the pattern of settlement that was affected by it had a great effect on the process of cultural change in Belize. Little is known of the enslaved's social and cultural life in the logging camps. Their greatest opportunity for communal recreation and cultural creativity occurred when they returned to the town between logging seasons. In the early nineteenth century, a large proportion of the population of Belize Town, both enslaved and free, was of diverse African origins; most others were Creole, born either in the West Indies or Belize. While elements of several African cultures persisted in the nineteenth century, the process of cultural interchange produced a new, Belizean Creole culture. Thus paradoxically, the social context of Belize Town may have encouraged the retention of elements of African cultures and also promoted the rapid emergence of Creole culture. The way in which the free and enslaved and the European and African sectors of Belize intersected offered opportunities for African continuities while at the same time providing a context within which Creole institutions and culture were created among blacks and whites, enslaved and free.

Despite its small size, Belize Town was socially and culturally heterogeneous. It was bounded by the sea on the north, east, and south and divided through the middle by the Belize River. On this low, swampy, and humid site, dry ground was created in the eighteenth and nineteenth centuries by filling in the swamp with sand and wood chips. On these inauspicious foundations, the British erected several sizeable public buildings, including Government House, the courthouse, the public hospital, and the Anglican cathedral. Between these edifices there were about 200 houses. "Many of these, particularly such as [were] owned by the opulent merchants, [were] spacious, commodious, and well finished," built entirely of wood and raised eight or ten feet from the ground.[32] The dwellings of the wealthier inhabitants were mostly along the shore on North and South

Front Streets, where they could catch a breeze. The population was sharply differentiated by legal status (until 1838), race, ethnicity, and class, as well as age and gender. Most poor people lived behind Back Street in crowded situations, away from sea breezes and close to the swamp. One of these areas—between South Street, Back Street, and the Burial Ground—was referred to as Eboe Town in an 1829 plan of Belize Town.[33] A later account described Eboe Town as "consisting of numerous yards, flanked with long rows of what are called Negro houses, being simply separate rooms under one long roof, which used to be appropriated to slaves, and now accommodate the poorer laborers."[34]

The Culture of the Enslaved

Evidence of African cultural elements occurs in many aspects of culture in Belize, including religion, music, folklore, and the festivals that took place at the end of the year. While direct continuities between particular cultural phenomena reported in Belize and social or cultural forms from specific African societies are hard to demonstrate, there nonetheless was a broad pattern of African cultural influence. As in the Old World, Africans did not maintain boundaries between religion, music, and dance in Belize. Musical instruments, styles, and events that were derived from African sources persisted. The use of gombay drums, for example, was frequently reported, often in complaints by white settlers. In 1806, several white settlers bemoaned "a very large assemblage of Negroes either free or Slaves . . . who have resorted to certain appointed Huts situated in different parts of the Swamps on the South side of this Town, whose apparent motive for which is Dancing."[35] The next year, the superintendent of Belize complained about the enslaved being accustomed "to beat Gumbays or other Instruments sounding like drums, and to be strolling about the Streets at all hours of the Nights."[36] These events persisted, despite attempts by the magistrates to limit them. In 1830, they were recognized as "importations from the coast of Africa; large parties meet at night, at some appointed negro yard, where they commence dancing to the beat of the drum, and the music of their voices. . . . There can be nothing more calculated to impress a stranger with surprise, than the different formations of their drums and the variety of their dances."[37] Such large parties of African and Creole Belizeans were made possible by the dense settlement pattern in Belize Town.

The period between Christmas and Epiphany was called the Christmas holiday, though little about it suggests that Afro-Belizeans were celebrat-

ing any event in the Christian calendar. Several nineteenth-century accounts describe festivals in this period—involving music, songs, street
parades and dances, feasts, and boat races—that were similar in many
respects to African and other Afro-American festivals. "At Christmas,"
according to a local almanac,

> the slaves enjoy a saturnalia which continues without interruption
> for the space of a fortnight. During this time there is an entire relax-
> ation from all toils; Negroes of all conditions join in sets, and peram-
> bulate the streets from morn till night, with colours flying and music
> playing, to which they keep time in graceful movements, waving
> their flags and umbrellas to the measured beats of the drum.[38]

Licentious behavior began on Christmas morning with "the discharging
of small-arms in every direction."[39] For a period of one or two weeks,
enslaved people enjoyed

> the pleasures of town in Belize, according to the respective ideas of
> what was enjoyment peculiar to the several tribes. These congre-
> gated in several bodies, and followed the African rites they had
> brought with them, but all displaying the same wonderful endurance
> in undergoing the fatigues of dissipation that they undoubtedly did
> in sustaining those of toil—"keeping it up" day and night.[40]

People of African origin, both enslaved and free, organized themselves
in sets or nations, a common feature of Afro-American festivals and mas-
querades from Jamaica to Brazil.

> The members of the several African tribes, again met together after
> a long separation, now form themselves into different groups, and
> nothing can more forcibly denote their respective casts of national
> character than their music, songs, and dances. The convulsed rapid
> movements of some, . . . [and] the occasional bursts of loud chorus,
> with which all are animated, contribute greatly to heighten the sin-
> gularity of the entertainment.[41]

During the festivals, these ethnically distinct sets were generally involved
in a degree of rivalry in costume and dance that sometimes led to fights.
Thus it was sometimes "necessary to institute a guard to control the slaves
during the annual Christmas holidays, the different African tribes, no
doubt, occasionally indulging in faction-fights."[42] The drums, the "bursts
of loud chorus," and the flagmen in the street dancing were all of African
derivation.

The dory or pitpan races on the river were a feature of the Christmas holidays that was established during the period of slavery and survived until the twentieth century. Sets may have first organized these races as another form of rivalry, but mahogany firms came to sponsor them because such competition between gangs of enslaved people developed skills and feelings of teamwork that were valuable to the business of timber extraction. "At this season," reported Henderson,

> water-sports are also common, and Dory-racing affords a very general amusement; and on these occasions large sums of money are frequently betted both by owners and slaves. This species of diversion has no small share of utility attached to it, as it contributes to render the latter highly expert in a kind of exercise that is inseparably connected with the labor in which they are principally engaged.[43]

The largest pitpans were "manned by crews of from 20 to 40 paddlers, appropriately dressed and representing rival mahogany firms."[44]

Although the accounts stress the variety of African peoples and cultural activities, the Christmas holiday, which was "the single season of relaxation granted to their condition," was the major occasion on which they came together with Creoles and other Belizeans.[45] Even while each group was emphasizing its distinctiveness and trying to re-create its own particular heritage, there was an intensified flow of cultural interchange during this period of heightened contact. In this period when the usual discipline was relaxed, as is evident by the discharge of guns and the absence of sobriety, there was a special opportunity for creativity, during which some new Belizean customs developed, such as the boat races.

During slavery, the majority of the population of Belize, both those enslaved and free people of color, had strong cultural links with Africa. In the 1830s, an observer remarked that free blacks, who previous to emancipation constituted almost half the population of the settlement, were organized in "tribes" or "nations." They tried to maintain their ethnic identity and customs and even to re-create some sort of rudimentary political organization. "The blacks," according to a local almanac,

> present almost as many varieties as there are countries whence they come; and seem to uphold their original systems, prejudices, superstitions, and amusements, to as great a degree, as they can be allowed consistently with the regulations of civilized society. . . . [T]hey maintain, as far as in them lies, the customs of the countries whence they came; and hence their habits in a great measure con-

tinue. In order to preserve themselves distinct and to uphold their customs, each nation selects one from their body to whom they give the title of king. This is observed by almost every tribe or nation.

These kings exercised "a certain species of lordship over their respective subjects" and, in return, received "the most marked attention and respect."[46]

In 1850, there were in Belize "Congoes, Nangoes, Mongolas, Ashantees, Eboes, and other African tribes," an indication that ethnic identities persisted after emancipation.[47] The area known as "Eboe Town, a section of the town of Belize reserved for that African tribe," reportedly burned in 1819 but was still referred to by that name in 1850.[48]

Language and folklore were further examples of the persistence of African influences in Afro-Belizean culture. The peculiar concentration of people, especially of women and children, in Belize Town must have facilitated the rapid development of Creole, which was probably established as the most widespread lingua franca of Belize by the end of the eighteenth century. Folktales and proverbs, told in Belizean Creole, had and still have African roots. Belizean Anansi stories and proverbs were adapted to the new environment and social context, while continuing to express, and thus to preserve, traditional values and views of the world.[49] Skill with words and the ability to perform publicly have a premium in Afro-American cultures, and Belize was no exception. The tradition of storytelling, including Anansi stories, is less common in Belize City today than in the past, though there are still some well-known raconteurs.[50] Such storytelling occurred in the logging camps but was probably more important in Belize Town, where the women and children lived. Both African and Creole folklore must have been especially prominent during the Christmas season, when men returned from the camps and families were reunited. African men would have adapted traditional tales to fit their experience in the Belizean bush. Henderson reported that the men made "a variety of small articles, from the less valuable mahogany, for domestic use . . . either as presents to their wives, or as matters for sale . . . on their return from the woods."[51] The folktales of enslaved peoples, like the woodcarvings they brought back from the bush, were crafted in African-derived styles.

The Baymen suppressed some specific aspects of African culture. For example, a 1791 regulation based on Jamaican law banned under threat of death

the wicked art of Negroes going under the appellation of Obeah Men and Women, pretending to have communication with the Devil

and other evil spirits, whereby the weak and superstitious are de-
luded into a belief of their having full power to exempt them whilst
under protection from any Evils that might otherwise happen.[52]

Despite the threat of capital punishment, obeah persisted, though doubtless chiefly in secret. Indeed, in the middle of the nineteenth century, the
practice of obeah, though long suppressed, had even spread to whites.[53]

The influence of the established Anglican church and the dissenting
missionaries seems to have been less potent in Belize than elsewhere in the
British Caribbean, probably because of the missionaries' reluctance to
visit the remote logging camps. The unusual settlement pattern resulting
from the timber economy gave clergymen less access to enslaved men but
easier access to women and children. In 1794, an Anglican cleric was
appointed to the settlement. Although the cleric baptized his own enslaved
people and a few others, Anglican clergy did not have much to do with the
enslaved. Instead, the Anglican church worked more closely with the military establishment as a "Garrison church."[54] The first Baptist missionary
arrived in 1822, but four years later he had only 21 communicants.[55] He
was soon followed by the first Wesleyan. Baptists and Wesleyans, like
Anglicans, centered their congregations in Belize Town and rarely took the
gospel into the mahogany camps. These missionaries, unlike their counterparts in Barbados and Jamaica, were generally permitted to preach without hindrance, though Anglican marriages alone were considered legal.
Hundreds of enslaved people, free blacks, and free coloreds were baptized
in the 1820s, and some were given Christian marriages and burials.[56]
Many of these baptisms may have been simply nominal and may not reflect much involvement with the Church or with Christianity, but some of
those who remained unbaptized may have been influenced considerably
by Christian beliefs and practices. There does not seem to have been any
equivalent of the Jamaican native churches in Belize, though doubtless
some reinterpretations and syntheses of African and European religious
elements occurred. Over many years, the missionaries' goal of suppressing
African religious beliefs and practices and replacing them with Christianity was largely realized, though styles of worship and views of the cosmos
continued to reflect African influences.

A description of the wake of an enslaver, presumably of British origin,
illustrates the juxtaposition, mingling, and synthesis of different cultures
that took place in Belize. "Different African nations and Creoles, each in
parties," participated in the wake with their own songs and dances, while
people played cards, dice, and backgammon and drank rum, coffee, and
ginger-tea. Music was provided by the sheck'ka and drums.

After a night thus spent, the corpse was carried in the morning to the churchyard, the coffin being borne by labourers, who in their progress used to run up and down the streets and lanes with their burden, knocking at some door or doors, perhaps visiting some of the friends of the deceased, professing to be impelled by him, or to be contending with the spirit who opposed the interment of the body. At length some well known friend came forward, speaking soothingly to the dead, and calling him Brother, urging him to go home, and promised him rest and blessing. They then moved all together towards the grave, and the sheck'ka's jingle, the voice of song, and latterly, the funeral service of the Established Church were mingled together in the closing scene.[57]

The custom of carrying the corpse from house to house and visiting friends of the deceased was widespread in West Africa as well as Afro-America. Bearers of the corpse were believed to be controlled by the deceased's spirit, who could reveal the cause or source of his or her demise. This part of the funeral rite was a kind of divination, a way of giving the spirit of the deceased an opportunity to disclose whether he or she had enemies, that would have been familiar to most Africans. This account shows that it was being learned by Creoles in Belize, perhaps by white as well as black ones. The music, too, suggests a juxtaposition, if not yet a synthesis, of African and European elements, the drums and sheck'ka mingling with the Anglican funeral service.

Africans of Belize, both enslaved and free, could not communicate with their homelands as easily as British settlers could maintain ties with England, but Africans tried to keep a sense of identity by keeping some of their original customs. However, in addition to the acts of repression directed against particular cultural forms, such as obeah and drumming parties, the entire structure of slavery and colonialism militated against the persistence of African cultures. The flow of Africans into the settlement was reduced to a trickle after the abolition of the trade in enslaved Africans in 1807, so the maintenance of African traditions during the nineteenth century depended heavily upon the sense of ethnic solidarity among the enslaved and free blacks, often reinforced at the Christmas festivals, and upon the continuance of traditions in black families.

Family Life

The family life of enslaved people in Belize was affected by the seasonal nature of employment in timber extraction and by the resulting settlement pattern. There was no law to protect the families of the enslaved, but it was considered contrary to custom to sell enslaved people in such a way that families would be divided. The expense of importing and maintaining enslaved Africans in Belize was greater than in the sugar colonies, so some enslavers may have encouraged the development of stable families among the enslaved. Familial stability not only would have encouraged enslaved women to have and care for children, but it would also be a way of tying the men to Belize Town and discouraging flight.

Some among the enslaved enjoyed a stable family life, despite the seasonal pattern of employment, and some had the opportunity to maintain quite large kinship networks, which may have included free people.[58] Such family groups and kin networks affected the processes of cultural persistence and change in two ways. On the one hand, the existence of large networks of people who maintained contact over generations provided an opportunity for the transmission of African cultural traditions. On the other hand, such networks also constituted one of the important social contexts within which Creole Belizeans created their own, new culture. Through miscegenation, such networks were expanded to include whites, thereby linking the various groups in the society that were "implicated in the development of a single Creole culture."[59] By the early 1830s, almost half the settlement's population were free people of color, consisting of about 20 percent free black and 26 percent free colored.

As a colonial society based upon the enslavement of Africans, Belize was organized around a core of European-derived institutions—economic, political, military, legal, religious, and educational—all of which were concentrated after 1783 to an extraordinary degree in Belize Town. Many of the institutions established by the British settlers excluded not only the enslaved but also free people of color. Nevertheless, these institutions mixed with African ones, resulting in the development of Belizean Creole culture. The 1830 *Honduras Almanack* stated that the free blacks could organize their "nations" and "uphold their original systems, prejudices, superstitions, and amusements" only as far "as they can be allowed consistently with the regulations of civilized society," that is, within the limits imposed by the colonial administration.[60] This was also true with regard to the enslaved.

Sidney Mintz and Richard Price argue that "continuities between the Old World and the New must be established upon an understanding of the basic conditions under which the migrations of enslaved Africans occurred."[61] Among the particular conditions in Belize that were a consequence of the timber economy (and which differed from those prevailing in the sugar colonies) was a largely urban African Belizean population in Belize Town beginning in the late eighteenth century. Bounded by sea and swamp, this town was not large, but it was densely populated and culturally heterogeneous. While British settlers determined the spatial organization of Belize Town, including its street plan and the locations of the principal buildings and residences, the concentration of some groups of Africans into particular areas, such as Eboe Town, was done by the Africans themselves. This phenomenon, in which "urban slaves and 'free blacks' were formed into 'nations' with their own 'kings' and 'governors'" has been observed in other parts of urban Afro-America in Argentina, Brazil, and Peru.[62] To the extent that the "comparative prevalence of African survivals . . . will to a large extent depend on the density of the black population in certain areas," this feature of the social organization of Belize probably facilitated continuities in African cultures.[63] The activities of large parties of Africans, both free and enslaved, who met regularly in "certain appointed Huts" or in "some appointed negro yard" and, in particular, during the period between Christmas and Epiphany, reinforced these groups' sense of ethnic identity, often in rivalry with other nations.

At the same time, members of these African nations rubbed shoulders with each other in close proximity on a regular basis, along with the British, British Caribbean, and Belizean Creole inhabitants of the town, in a context that encouraged cultural interchange. As no evidence suggests that the "nations" were ever endogamous, it may be assumed that kin networks quickly linked together people who, in other contexts, viewed themselves as culturally distinct. Thus ethnic mixing as well as miscegenation occurred, and it became increasingly difficult for successive generations to see themselves as anything but Creole. As the number of Africans declined from 894 in 1861 to 110 in 1901, the Africanness of distinct groups became impossible to sustain in the midst of the prevailing Creole culture.[64] At the risk of considerable oversimplification, it may be said that an aggregate of ethnic groups, among which the various Africans were numerically predominant during slavery, was transformed to a largely Creole community in Belize Town by the end of the nineteenth century.

Resistance

The patterns of resistance of enslaved Africans and Creoles in Belize, like those of residence, were influenced by the economy of timber extraction. The dispersal of enslaved men in small groups throughout the forest, separated from their families for most of the year, affected opportunities and motivation for escape and revolt. Four revolts and countless and continual desertions from the settlement gave evidence of discontent among the enslaved. The British settlers, who were a minority of the population from the middle of the eighteenth century, were constantly haunted by the spectre of revolts by enslaved people. These fears were compounded by the treaties Britain signed with Spain in 1763, 1783, and 1786, which prevented British settlers from maintaining a permanent police or military force in the settlement. Consequently, the settlers had little power, other than their own resources and an occasional warship from Jamaica, to suppress rebelliousness among the enslaved in the eighteenth century.

During the economic crisis of the 1760s and 1770s, when the logwood trade was severely depressed but not yet superseded by mahogany, the enslaved—who were undoubtedly forced to bear a great deal of the hardship engendered by the crisis—rebelled three times. In the absence of police power, even the small-scale revolts of 1765 and 1768 exposed the helplessness of the Baymen and threatened the existence of the settlement.[65] The biggest revolt, lasting five months, occurred in 1773 on the Belize River. A warship was sent from Jamaica, but the marines failed to prevent 11 of the rebels from escaping over the Rio Hondo to the Spanish post of Bacalar.[66]

Although there were no reported revolts in the late eighteenth century, white settlers were continually apprehensive about the possibility and tried to exclude what they defined as "dangerous slaves" from the settlement, especially after the revolution in Saint Domingue. They were also afraid that the enslaved people would join Mayas in the interior, though they apparently never did. In 1817, the magistrates feared that "a very small Gang of desperate runaway slaves, who would join and lead these Indians, must instantly overpower us and the destruction of every British subject would be inevitable."[67] By this time, the British had soldiers from the West India regiments stationed in Belize.

The last revolt of enslaved people in Belize occurred in 1820 on the Belize and Sibun Rivers. The superintendent reported that the settlers were "earnestly praying for immediate protection" because "a considerable number of slaves had formed themselves into a Body in the Belize River, and being well armed, and having already committed various depredations the most serious consequences were to be apprehended."[68] Martial law was declared, and troops were sent up the rivers. It was found that "the Negroes who had first deserted and had excited others to join them, had been treated with very unnecessary harshness by their owner, and had certainly good grounds for complaint."[69] On May 3, about ten days after the revolt began, the superintendent offered rewards for the apprehension of two enslaved blacks, Will and Sharper, "reported to be the Captains and Leaders of these Rebels," and offered "a Free Pardon to any of the other Runaways, who will at this time voluntarily come in and deliver themselves."[70] This inducement to divide the rebels may have succeeded. On May 22, martial law was ended as "there no longer exists any Combination amongst the slaves."[71]

The other major evidence of discontent among enslaved people can be found in the continual complaints from settlers that the neighboring Spaniards gave asylum to runaways. The organization of timber extraction made such escape relatively easy. In the eighteenth century, most of the enslaved who escaped went north into Yucatán. This was partly because the south and west of Belize was unexplored but also because the Spaniards had outposts just across the Rio Hondo and the commandant at Bacalar offered freedom and protection to runaways. When the settlement expanded to the west and south early in the nineteenth century, some of the enslaved went still farther, through the bush into the Peten, Guatemala, or by boat down the coast to Honduras. In 1823, the superintendent stated that in a little over two months 39 enslaved persons had "absconded" and fled to the Peten, which "is believed to be well known to many of the Negroes, it has also been long known that Negroes who have absconded some years ago during the War are residing there."[72]

In 1824, shortly after they became independent, the territories bordering on Belize abolished slavery, and complaints that enslaved people were escaping to these republics increased. A complaint from the superintendent to the Peten authorities drew the response that there was "a Town of black People" that was joined by those who "emigrated from your Establishment" and who "already enjoy the privileges of Citizens."[73] In 1825, settlers were desperate, "having just learnt that 19 slaves have left their employments up the river in a body, and taken the road to the Town of Peten at the head of the River, and 12 to Omoa . . . instant ruin stares us in the face."[74] A Colonial Office official commented in 1830 that "[British] Honduras is now in the center of countries which have declared Slavery illegal, and if we persist in maintaining it we must look for a rapid depopulation of the settlement by the slaves passing the border line, and returning no more."[75]

The geography of Belize, unlike that of some small islands of the Caribbean, certainly favored the enslaved. Some fugitives created independent Maroon communities on the fringes of the settlement. In 1816, one such community existed "near Sheboon River, very difficult to discover, and guarded by poisonous Stakes."[76] The following year, it was reported that "a considerable body of runaway Slaves [were] formed in the interior" and, in 1820 "two Slave Towns" were said to have been formed north of the Sibun.[77] In addition to the settlements of escapees in the neighboring countries, then, there were also Maroon communities in Belize, particularly near the Sibun River, a tributary of which is still called Runaway Creek. While these Maroon communities sometimes communicated with the enslaved and, as in 1820, provided a refuge for black rebels on the run, they were never the basis for any organized or protracted guerrilla action against the Baymen. As a response to enslavement, revolt was not such a pressing alternative in Belize when freedom could be obtained by slipping away into the bush of the interior or over the borders of the settlement. However, many of the men must have been inhibited from escaping because their wives, mothers, sisters, and children remained in Belize Town. It was much harder for the women and children to escape, and the enslavers could threaten to punish them if their male relatives took flight. Though owners deplored the frequent desertion of their human property, they also recognized that the facility with which enslaved men could escape reduced the likelihood of insurrections. Indeed, the revolt of 1768 may be more accurately described as an armed thrust by the enslaved to force their way out of Belize, and the 1773 revolt ended with the survivors escaping across the Rio Hondo. In 1825, enslaved people—having "almost a total absence of all respect" for their owners—were said to be discussing whether to continue escaping or to seize the settlement.[78] Given the favorable geographical conditions and the great numerical superiority of the enslaved, the fact that they never actually took over the settlement may best be explained by the availability of freedom beyond the boundaries of British jurisdiction.

The small, isolated units in which enslaved people in Belize worked also reduced the likelihood of a successful large-scale revolt. This pattern of settlement, which encouraged solidarity within each group but inhibited communication between groups, favored small-scale revolts and escapes but hindered the organization and coordination of a large-scale insurrection, such as occurred in many plantation societies. Another factor that detracted from the development of large revolts was the limited identification enslaved people had with Belize as a permanent home. Only a minority of those enslaved were Creole, most being Africans of diverse ethnic origin or natives of the Caribbean or the Mosquito Shore. In Belize, where the enslaved were continually shifted from one temporary logging camp to another, the only place of continued residence was Belize Town. The limited time that most enslaved males had spent in Belize and the seasonal, migratory nature of their residence patterns inhibited their identification with the area, which otherwise might have motivated them to take control of the settlement. The enslaved, however, were less concerned with achieving political control of Belize than with avoiding enslavement. The latter could be more easily and safely accomplished through withdrawal than confrontation, thereby reducing the impulse to rebel.

The extent to which the treatment and conditions of enslaved people were different in Belize than elsewhere was partly the product of the different economic functions of slavery and its consequent mode of organization, but it was also a product of the enslaved's own understanding of his or her situation. Their propensity to revolt and escape was among the chief factors that inhibited their owners from ill-treating them. That enslavers themselves recognized this was frequently indicated. For example, George Hyde, a leading free colored merchant and enslaver, stated in 1825 that "as for punishments or ill-usage, you are aware (if ever so deserved) we dare not inflict it, so easy is their retreat to the Spaniards."[79]

The situation in the timber camps, in which one or two white men lived in remote isolation for long periods of time with between 10 and 50 enslaved males, all of whom possessed machetes, axes, and sometimes muskets, must have made the owners cautious about rousing the enslaved. Enslaved males' possession of arms, including firearms that were used for hunting, was the object of frequent comment. In 1788, a Bayman said that "it has always been a Custom with us to allow our Negroes Firearms," and Henderson noted 20 years later that "the whole of the slaves of [British] Honduras are permitted to use arms, and possibly a more expert body of marksmen could no where be found."[80] Soon after he arrived in 1814, a new superintendent reported with amazement that some enslaved men

> leaving their Works in the interior of the Country came down in a body to the Town of Belize to dictate who should be their masters. . . . [T]he several Thousand Slaves in this Settlement . . . by some unfortunate mismanagement, have been allowed to be provided with Arms, and therefore it requires additional attention to keep them quiet and peaceable, and certainly to give them no just grounds for discontent.[81]

The enslaved men, among whom were huntsmen who knew the territory better than their owners, possessed such means and capacities for affecting their enslavers' behavior that they were able to modify the institution of slavery itself.

Conclusion

The extraction of timber was the basic economic activity in the British settlement in Belize in the eighteenth and nineteenth centuries. This had far-reaching implications for shaping the lives of enslaved Africans and Creoles and for the shaping of the lives of all people in that society. In particular, the organization and experience of work, the gender division of labor, the patterns of residence and resistance, and the cultural processes that gave rise to Belizean Creole culture were all affected by the central activity of timber extraction.

Notes

This chapter is reprinted from my article "Slave Labor and the Shaping of Slave Culture" in *Historia y Sociedad* 6 (1993): 7–32, by permission of the University of Puerto Rico, Department of History, San Juan. An earlier version of this essay was written for and presented at the conference "Cultivation and Culture: Labor and the Shaping of Slave Life in the Americas" at the University of Maryland, College Park, in 1989. I wish to thank Ira Berlin and Philip Morgan for inviting me to participate in that conference and for their advice when I revised the article. Another version of this article was published in my book *Struggles for Freedom: Essays on Slavery, Colonialism and Culture in the Caribbean and Central America* (Belize City: Angelus Press, 1997), 55–80.

1. Belize, originally called the Belize Settlement or the Settlement in the Bay of Honduras, was known as British Honduras until 1973. Belize Town, renamed Belize City in 1943, is the chief town and, until 1970, was the capital. To avoid confusion, Belize is used throughout this article to refer to the territory, which has been independent since 1981, and Belize Town is used for the town. For a historical analysis of the settlement up to the creation of a Crown colony in 1871, see O. Nigel Bolland, *The Formation of a Colonial Society: Belize, from Conquest to Crown Colony* (Baltimore: Johns Hopkins University Press, 1977).

2. H. H. Bancroft, *History of Central America*, 3 vols. (San Francisco: A. L. Bancroft, 1883–87), 2: 626.

3. Herbert Klein, in summarizing the organization of enslaved labor on plantations in the Americas, draws attention to "the absence of sexual differences in all major labor tasks associated with the planting, cultivation, and harvesting of crops. . . . Women did almost all the same physical labor as men." Between 50 and 60 percent of all those enslaved on plantations "were engaged in field labor related to production of agricultural crops," and women often predominated in the work gangs. See Klein, *African Slavery in Latin America and the Caribbean* (New York:

Oxford University Press, 1886), 60–62. Marietta Morrissey states that "there is virtually no task in Caribbean commodity production not at some time carried out by female slaves." See Morrissey, *Slave Women in the New World: Gender Stratification in the Caribbean* (Lawrence: University Press of Kansas, 1989), 33. The situation in Belize was almost entirely different.

4. "General Return of the Inhabitants," October 22, 1790, Colonial Office Records, Public Records Office, Kew, CO 123/9.

5. Supt. Codd to R. Wilmot, February 23, 1823, CO 123/34.

6. B. W. Higman, *Slave Populations of the British Caribbean, 1807–1834* (Baltimore: Johns Hopkins University Press, 1984), 117.

7. Ibid., 307.

8. Capt. G. Henderson, *An Account of the British Settlement of Honduras* (London: C. & R. Baldwin, 1809), 60. Captain George Henderson, whose account of the British settlement is a major source, was stationed in Belize with a West India regiment in the early nineteenth century.

9. Supt. Cockburn to Lord Goderich, April 25, 1831, CO 123/42.

10. O. Nigel Bolland and Assad Shoman, *Land in Belize, 1765–1871: The Origins of Land Tenure, Use, and Distribution in a Dependent Economy* (Mona, Jamaica: Institute of Social and Economic Research, 1977).

11. Supt. Despard to Lord Sydney, August 17, 1787, CO 123/5.

12. Capt. G. Henderson, *An Account of the British Settlement of Honduras* (London: C. & R. Baldwin, 1809), 51.

13. E. G. Squier, *Notes on Central America* (New York: Harper & Brothers), 173–74.

14. Henderson, *An Account*, 75.

15. Ibid., 47.

16. Br. Gen. Montresor to Gov. Coote, October 22, 1806, CO 123/17; see also Maj. Gen. Pye to Earl Bathurst: "The Name of Driver is here unknown," July 26, 1822, Belize Archives (hereafter BA), Belmopan, BA, R2. The watchman, well known on sugar estates, was also unknown in Belize because there were no export crops that could be threatened from theft, arson, or the depredations of livestock (Higman, *Slave Populations*, 175).

17. Henderson, *An Account*, 47–48.

18. Ibid., 57–59.

19. Montresor to Coote, October 22, 1806, CO 123/17.

20. Supt. T. Barrow, "Remarks upon the Situation Trade etc.," May 1, 1809, CO 123/18.

21. Slave Register, 1834, BA.

22. Richard Hoare to Robert White, August 25, 1788, CO 123/7.

23. Henderson, *An Account*, 42.

24. Ibid., 59.

25. O. Nigel Bolland, "Proto-Proletarians? Slave Wages in the Americas: Between Slave Labour and Free Labour," in *From Chattel Slaves to Wage Slaves: The*

Dynamics of Labour Bargaining in the Americas, ed. Mary Turner (Kingston: Ian Randle, 1995), 123–47.

26. Slave Register, 1834, BA.

27. Morrissey, *Slave Women in the New World,* 64.

28. Supt. George Arthur to Bathurst, October 7, 1820, CO 123/29.

29. Sidney W. Mintz, *Caribbean Transformations* (Chicago: Aldine, 1974), 151.

30. O. Nigel Bolland, "Labor Control and Resistance in Belize in the Century after 1838," *Slavery and Abolition* 7 (1986): 175–87.

31. O. Nigel Bolland, "African Continuities and Creole Culture in Belize Town in the Nineteenth Century," in *Afro-Caribbean Villages in Historical Perspective,* ed. Charles V. Carnegie (Kingston: African-Caribbean Institute of Jamaica, 1987), 63–82.

32. Henderson, *An Account,* 12–13.

33. *Honduras Almanack,* 1829.

34. Frederick Crowe, *The Gospel in Central America, containing . . . a History of the Baptist Mission in British Honduras* (London: Charles Gilpin, 1850), 33.

35. Thomas Potts et al. to Supt. Hamilton, May 3, 1806, CO 123/17.

36. Hamilton to Gov. Coote, November 26, 1807, CO 123/17.

37. *Honduras Almanack,* 1830, 18.

38. Ibid., 17.

39. Henderson, *An Account,* 76.

40. Archibald Robertson Gibbs, *British Honduras: An Historical and Descriptive Account of the Colony from its Settlement, 1670* (London: Sampson Low, 1883), 75–76.

41. Henderson, *An Account,* 76.

42. Gibbs, *British Honduras,* 52.

43. Henderson, *An Account,* 76–77.

44. Gibbs, *British Honduras,* 76.

45. Henderson, *An Account,* 77.

46. *Honduras Almanack,* 1830, 6–7.

47. Crowe, *The Gospel,* 50.

48. Gibbs, *British Honduras,* 79.

49. Marlis Hellinger, "The Study of Creole Proverbs," *National Studies* 3 (1975): 28–38.

50. Richard Hadel, "Anansi Stories and Their Uses," *National Studies* 1 (1973): 4–10.

51. Henderson, *An Account,* 52.

52. Sir John Alder Burdon, *Archives of British Honduras,* 3 vols. (London: S. Praed, 1935), 1: 195–96.

53. Crowe, *The Gospel,* 324.

54. D. Gareth Lewis, "The 1794 Register of St. John's Cathedral," *Belizean Studies* 5 (1977): 19–26.

55. Crowe, *The Gospel,* 329.

56. "Return of Baptisms . . ." by Rev. John Armstrong, December 16, 1823, CO 123/34; "Return from the Church Register . . ." by Mathew Newport, October 19, 1829, BA R2.

57. Crowe, *The Gospel,* 324–25.

58. Bolland, *Formation of a Colonial Society,* 201–5.

59. Arnold Sio, "Commentary" on Harry Hoetnik's "Slavery and Race," *Roots and Branches: Current Directions in Slave Studies,* ed. Michael Craton, *Historical Reflections* 6 (1979), 272.

60. *Honduras Almanack,* 1830, 6.

61. Sidney W. Mintz and Richard Price, *An Anthropological Approach to the Afro-American Past: A Caribbean Perspective* (Philadelphia: Institute for the Study of Human Issues 1976), 43.

62. Roger Bastide, *African Civilizations in the New World,* trans. Peter Green (New York: Harper & Row, 1971), 9.

63. Ibid., 12–13.

64. *Census of British Honduras, 9th April 1946* (Belize: n.p., 1948), xxix.

65. Joseph Maud to Gov. Lyttleton, October 7, 1765, CO 137/62, and Allan Auld to Lord Hillsborough, July 1768, CO 137/63.

66. O. Nigel Bolland, "The Social Structure and Social Relations of the Settlement in the Bay of Honduras (Belize) in the 18th Century," *Journal of Caribbean History* 6 (1973): 15–16.

67. Magistrates to Bathurst, February 26, 1817, CO 123/26.

68. Arthur to Bathurst, May 16, 1820, CO 123/33.

69. Ibid.

70. Proclamation, May 3, 1820, CO 123/33.

71. Proclamation, May 22, 1820, CO 123/33.

72. Codd to Bathurst, March 8, 1823, CO 123/34.

73. Leon Baldison to Codd, November 15, 1823, CO 123/34.

74. Magistrates to Codd, January 28, 1823, CO 123/36.

75. James Stephen to Horace Twiss, October 13, 1830, CO 123/41.

76. Burdon, *Archives,* 1: 184.

77. Arthur to Major Fraser, June 12, 1817, CO 123/26; Arthur to Bathurst, May 16, 1820, CO 123/29.

78. Codd to Bathurst, February 18, 1825, CO 123/36. Codd expressed anxiety about the reliability of the black soldiers and militia in the event of a revolt and requested white troops.

79. Crowe, *The Gospel,* 321.

80. Hoare to White, August 25, 1788, CO 123/7; Henderson, *An Account,* 73.

81. Arthur to Bathurst, December 2, 1814, CO 123/23.

3

The Internal Economy of Jamaican Pens, 1760–1890

B. W. Higman

Of the many factors that inhibited long-term growth in the plantation economies of the Caribbean, the limited development of linkages was among the most crucial. Industries created through backward and forward linkages did emerge, and final demand linkage produced a significant market for consumer goods, but the metropolitan orientation of the economies meant that such industries and consumption were commonly located outside the region. Thus these linkages contributed to metropolitan rather than Caribbean development.

Most of the plantation economies passed through an initial phase of diversified production, but the high prices commanded by sugar and other export staples during the seventeenth and eighteenth centuries led quickly to intensive monoculture and a dependence on imported inputs in the British Caribbean.[1] Differences in the price and quality of land, however, created variations in the profitability of production for the domestic market.

Jamaica's colonial economy sustained significant elements of diversification, in contrast to the pure plantation economies of the Eastern Caribbean. This diversification was of course constrained by external, metropolitan influences and by the island's physical environment, but it extended beyond a simple broadening of the range of export staples to generation of an important internal commodity trade. A general recognition of these features of the Jamaican economy exists in the literature, but relatively little research effort has been applied to their study. Thus the economic history of the minor staples (such as coffee, pimento, ginger, cotton, indigo, and logwood) is known only in outline, and domestic trade other than the "internal marketing system" of enslaved people and peasants has been largely ignored.[2]

The role of livestock in the development of the plantation economies has received little attention from economic historians.[3] Before mechanization and chemical fertilizers industrialized agricultural systems, animals played a major role in supplying traction, manure, milk, meat, and leather. In the case of Jamaica, the market for livestock was central to the internal (plantation) trade of the island. Smallholders increased their share of this market after emancipation, but it was dominated by large-scale producers both before and after 1838. The production of draft animals by specialized "pens" constituted the most important example of backward linkage within the Jamaican plantation economy, while the production of meat by the same units was a type of final demand linkage. Trade in these commodities was largely confined to the plantation sector until the end of the nineteenth century. At the time of emancipation, pens contributed as much as 10.4 percent of the total value of slave-produced output in Jamaica, almost as much as coffee and significantly more than the remaining minor staples.[4]

The economic history of the pen, its changing function and internal organization, as well as the changing social status and role of the pen-keeper, are subjects deserving thorough investigation. The symbiotic relationship of pen and plantation and the impact of pens on the efficiency of resource allocation, distribution of landownership, and levels of profitability are poorly understood. Similarly, the causes and implications of observed differences between pens and plantations in demographic structure and work regimes require fuller study. The present essay makes no claim to providing a complete discussion of these issues. Rather, it seeks first to sketch in some broad areas that merit further historical research and then to present the results of a detailed cartographic study of land-use patterns on pens between 1760 and 1890, a critical period of change.

Definitions

The use of the word "pen" to denote a cattle farm or ranch is apparently a Jamaicanism dating from the late seventeenth century.[5] In 1774, Edward Long referred interchangeably to "breeding pens," "grass pens," "farms," and "breeding farms or penns," and J. B. Moreton in 1790 talked of "grass pens" or "farms."[6] In 1835, Bernard Senior wrote that the Jamaican "penn" was equivalent to an English breeding-farm, and "on it are bred horses, mules, steers (i.e. oxen), and all kinds of stock, and from which the butcher is supplied with cattle for the market."[7]

Difficulties of definition or classification arise, however, because by the later eighteenth century the term "pen" was used also to designate relatively small properties producing a variety of minor crops. Further, the term was commonly applied to residential units on the fringes of towns. The *Jamaica Almanack* for 1838, for example, referred to "pens for breeding and feeding stock," "grazing farms," "breeding pens of note," and "large breeding pens," distinguishing all of these from small "settlements" producing coffee, ginger, provisions, grass, and wood. But, it said, "A great part of the plain adjoining Kingston, is taken up with small settlements as places of residence for merchants, and others generally called pens."[8] Some of these pens supplied Kingston with "firewood, grass, milk, fruit, and vegetables."[9]

The census of 1844 identified 378 "breeding pens"; 822 "pens, with residences and woodland and pasture"; and 22,703 "farms and other settlements."[10] All three of these types of enterprises produced some livestock for sale, but there is clear evidence that the "breeding pens" dominated the market throughout the eighteenth and nineteenth centuries. In 1844, the pens in which the residential function was uppermost were located principally in the peri-urban areas of Saint Andrew (221 units) and Saint Catherine (82 units), though a substantial proportion occurred in Saint Ann (174 units) and Saint Elizabeth (85 units), and these latter two parishes also contained nearly half of the island's breeding pens. These partially overlapping categories do create problems of classification, but the analysis that follows is centered strictly on those pens that had the production of livestock as their major activity and belonged to persons calling themselves pen-keepers.

Numbers and Distribution

Whereas the increasing dominance of sugar in Jamaica during the eighteenth century stifled the production of competing staple crops other than coffee, the growing demand for livestock on sugar estates was met by an increasing number of pens. The demand was so great that cattle and cane competed for land space in some lowland regions, but the pens were generally confined to marginal backlands and relatively infertile hilly areas. Where land of this type was limited, as in Trelawny and Portland, pens were few and livestock was purchased from other parishes. Specialized livestock-producing regions emerged in response to this market, particularly in Saint Ann, Saint Elizabeth, and Westmoreland.[11] The abandonment of sugar estates, which began as early as 1790 and increased rapidly after 1820, provided an expanded stock of land for grass and livestock raising, so that pen-keeping approached its maximum extent around 1900.

According to Edward Long, there were 500 "breeding pens" in Jamaica in 1768, but this figure probably included at least some peri-urban, residential units.[12] At the time of emancipation there were 400 pens, with an average population of 100 enslaved persons and accounting for 12.8 percent of the total enslaved population.[13] The census of 1844 listed 378 "breeding pens" (including 91 in Saint Elizabeth, 81 in Saint Ann, and 57 in Westmoreland). By 1852, however, the number of "cattle pens" was put at 636, and in 1881 there were 604 "cattle pens of over 200 acres," so that pen-keeping was said to be "only second, if that" to sugar.[14] The census of 1891 identified 691 "pen-keepers" (105 of them in Saint Ann) employing 31,594 laborers, compared to only 445 sugar planters and their 38,423 laborers.[15] In 1913–14, the *Handbook of Jamaica* particularized 350 "grazing pens having 100 heads of cattle and over" (62 in Saint Ann, 49 in Saint Elizabeth, and 44 in Westmoreland), but almost all of these properties covered more than 1,000 acres, so these data are not easily compared with those for 1881.[16] Some land was, however, returned to sugarcane after 1900, and the process accelerated after 1920. In 1884, guinea grass and common pasture accounted for 79 percent of the total acreage "under cultivation and care," but this share dropped to 71 percent by 1914.[17]

All of these data must be interpreted with caution, bearing in mind the problems of definition, but it is at least certain that pens controlled a substantial proportion of Jamaica's agricultural land and labor force and extended this control to reach a maximum toward the end of the nineteenth century when sugar was deeply depressed. Even before the abolition of African enslavement it could be said that the pens ranked with the sugar estates in "respectability and responsibility."[18] The decline of sugar and the expansion of pen-keeping after 1838 further enhanced the pens' economic and social roles, particularly because of their contribution to domestic trade and the Creole character of the pen-keepers. In 1832, for example, only 25 percent of pens belonged to absentee proprietors, compared to 79 percent of sugar estates.[19] By 1852, the proportion of absentee pen-keepers had fallen to only 18 percent, while 55 percent of planters were absentee, and the proportion for sugar increased rapidly after 1880.[20] Thus pens and pen-keepers contributed to the development of Creole economy and Creole society in every sense.[21]

Changing Functions

In the eighteenth and nineteenth centuries, Jamaican pens performed two major functions: they raised livestock to supply motive power and manure on estates and plantations, and they fattened cattle for the meat market. In the long term, there was a shift from the first to the second function as a consequence of changes in technology and the structure of the island's economy, but the transition was not completed until the middle of the twentieth century.

The livestock raised and fattened by pens consisted largely of cattle. Mules were bred, as were a smaller number of horses and asses, but horsekind were imported to a much larger extent than cattle. In 1831–32, for example, the island imported 1,323 horses, 618 asses, and 608 mules but only 591 cattle.[22] Mules and asses played an important role as draft animals on estates in the early eighteenth century but came to be largely replaced by cattle after 1750, and horses were required only as riding animals for supervisory whites during slavery. In 1768, there were, according to Long, 67,000 cattle and mules on the island's pens; 40,000 road and mill cattle and 25,000 mules and horses on sugar estates; and another 4,000 cattle and mules on minor staples plantations.[23] By the early nineteenth century, cattle predominated on both estates and pens. In 1822, for example, the Irwin estate in Saint James had 301 head of stock, distributed as follows: 134 working steers, 33 working spayed heifers, 11 young spayed heifers, 1 bull, 10 young heifers, 21 young steers, 28 cows, 14 calves, 26 fattening cattle, and 23 mules.[24] Irwin then had an enslaved population of 260. On pens, the ratio of livestock to enslaved people was much higher, but cattle remained much more important than horsekind. Retirement Pen in Saint Ann, for example, had a typical enslaved population of 117 in 1830 but ran 213 head of livestock: 2 bulls, 80 cows, 40 calves, 33 open heifers, 23 spayed heifers, 34 young steers, and 1 ass.[25] These examples are sufficient to show the dominance of cattle by the early nineteenth century.

Edward Long reported a population of 135,753 livestock in 1768.[26] By 1815, taxable stock (excluding working animals on estates and plantations) numbered 218,306 and peaked at 240,990 in 1822. A rapid decline then set in, stock numbers falling to 138,527 by 1832.[27] Trends during the remainder of the nineteenth century are less certain. Cattle numbers declined from the 1880s, at least, but totaled 116,000 in 1900 and then increased rapidly to 160,000 in 1911 and 248,500 in 1950.[28] Between 1890 and 1900, the number of cattle on estates decreased from 25,870 to

17,840, while the same period showed an increase on pens from 78,950 to 83,870. In 1900, smallholders accounted for 14,630 head of cattle, almost as many as on estates, but planters and peasants together owned less than half as many cattle as the pen-keepers. On the other hand, smallholders owned the majority of the island's 55,800 horses and mules by 1900, only 16,200 being on pens. Thus there was a steady increase in the ratio of people to livestock (cattle, horses, mules, and asses) from 1.4 persons per head in the 1760s to 1.6 in 1822, 2.5 in 1832, and 4.0 in 1900, reflecting the declining role of animals in Jamaica's agricultural economy.

The long-term decline in the ratio of livestock to people during the eighteenth and nineteenth centuries occurred alongside an increase in the number of pens. Two major factors explain this apparent paradox. First, a large proportion of the livestock population was always found on estates and plantations rather than on pens. Thus in 1822 the livestock numbers of Saint Ann (30,380), Saint Elizabeth (29,048), and Westmoreland (21,960) were rivaled by the plantation parishes of Trelawny (20,605), Hanover (18,638), Saint Mary (18,488), and Saint James (17,696). During the eighteenth century, animal power was gradually replaced in the sugar and coffee mills by water and wind. As late as 1804, however, James Robertson's map of Jamaica showed 422 sugar estates dependent on cattle mills, compared to 318 using water and 86 wind.[29] By 1854, water power was employed on 125 estates, steam on 108, and wind or cattle on only 97.[30] At the end of the nineteenth century, a mere 2 estates used cattle mills, while 79 depended on steam, 31 on water, and another 10 on a combination of steam and water.[31]

This transition from animate to inanimate power in the sugar mills went together with a decline in the absolute number of functioning estates, the total falling from 827 in 1804 to 330 in 1854, 200 in 1800, and 125 in 1900. Animals were also replaced in the fields to some extent—by tramlines and imported fertilizers, for example—but the changing mill technology and the absolute contraction in the sugar sector were most important in reducing demand. Gisela Eisner has argued that emancipation "increased demand for draft cattle by sugar estates following the replacement of animal for human motive power" and that this led to the establishment of new pens.[32] There seems little evidence to support this contention, but Eisner is surely correct in arguing that the abandonment of estates led to a reduced demand for livestock and impelled pen-keepers to turn to the exploitation of logwood, pimento, and other commodities found on their properties. This is the second factor explaining the paradoxical association between growth in the number of pens and decline in livestock numbers after 1822.

In the period of slavery, the demand for beef was limited largely to the white population and was readily supplied by the pens. Some cattle were killed for meat, while young, old, lame, and scrawny working cattle were returned to the pens for fattening and sale to urban and rural butchers. By the 1880s, it was said that an annual surplus of 6,000 cattle remained after supplying the estates and draft animals and meeting butchers' demands, and that "unless these can be utilized either by consumption in the island or by export the future prospects of cattle owners are gloomy."[33] In the late 1870s and again in the decade before 1914, there was a significant export of cattle to Cuba, but this trade was hindered by quarantine difficulties. Although prices for beef fell significantly after 1870, consumption failed to increase because the purchasing power of the working people was limited and strong preferences for salted fish persisted until the shortages of World War I.[34] Attempts to salt beef had no great success, while pens produced butter only for the owners' households. Townspeople were supplied with fresh milk, but no real dairy existed before 1900.

By 1950, however, a mere 5 percent of Jamaica's cattle were draft animals. Beef cattle accounted for 38 percent of the herd and dairy for 22 percent, while the remaining 35 percent were dual purpose beef-dairy animals.[35] Supplementary sources of income, such as pimento and logwood, ceased to be the necessity they had been at the end of the nineteenth century.

Cartographic Evidence of Land-Use Patterns

The economic history of Jamaican pens may be traced through a wide range of sources. The remainder of this essay is concerned with only one of these—the rich but little studied collection of manuscript plans at the National Library of Jamaica. This collection contains some 20,000 plans dating from the eighteenth and nineteenth centuries. It has its origins in the gradual accumulation of papers by nineteenth-century land surveyors and therefore includes a large proportion of unfinished plans, the most polished works having naturally found their way on to the walls of the commissioning planters and pen-keepers. Although the survival of these working papers is helpful for the study of surveying and plan-making techniques, it means also that many of the plans are in too unfinished a state to be fully interpretable. Of the total collection, 856 plans portray the internal layout of agricultural holdings, almost all of them large-scale estates, plantations, or pens. This is a far larger sample than that known for any other Caribbean territory. For the period of slavery, roughly 30 percent of the island's pens are represented by at least one plan. This is a smaller proportion than the 40 percent for sugar estates but larger than the 20 percent for coffee plantations. These differential rates of representation reflect the relative wealth, absenteeism, and social status of planters and pen-keepers, lending support to the notion that the pens were second only to sugar. The spatial distribution of the surviving plans matches closely the known distribution of breeding pens, while the weighting of the sample around 1838 reflects the great surveying activity associated with emancipation.[36]

The sample of plans of Jamaican pens analyzed here consists only of those that show internal layout in its entirety, possess full reference tables, and can be dated precisely. Of the total 856 plans, only 88 relating to pens satisfy these stringent conditions. This remains a substantial number, however, and the sample reflects closely the structure of the total collection, providing a reasonably representative cross section of Jamaican experience between 1760 and 1890.

Information regarding the number of field units devoted to each type of land use and their area can be obtained directly from the reference tables of the plans. In addition, a range of measurements has been taken from the plans relating to the distances between fields, pasture, provision grounds, works, great house, and laborers' housing. An index of the shape of holdings is provided by a measure of circularity.[37] Field shape has not been measured precisely, but a subjective classification is used, distinguishing square, rectangular, elongated, straight-sided irregular figures, and sinuous irregular types. A number of physical environmental indexes have also been calculated. Distance to the coast, rainfall, maximum altitude, relative relief (the difference between the highest and lowest point), and average slope are established for each of the three-kilometer-square quadrats of the Jamaica 1:50,000 topographic map and taken to be typical of the pens located within them.[38] A total of 63 variables enter the analysis, though not all are relevant to every one of the plans in the sample.

Any assessment of the accuracy and quality of the plans must be framed in terms of the aims and limitations of the surveyors and plan-makers. Almost all of the plans were commissioned for primarily utilitarian purposes, such as the conveyance of land ownership, establishment of boundaries, or measurement of area for contract labor. Thus a premium was placed on accuracy of representation and measurement and a low value on decorative qualities. Cartometric analysis shows a distortion error of less than 2 percent for the gross dimensions of boundaries, but not all internal elements were treated with equal care. Fields planted in export staples were measured more carefully than woodland and ruinate, for example, since the areas calculated for the former affected estimates of yield, productivity, and labor cost. Land planted by the enslaved in "Negro grounds," on the other hand, was of less concern to planters or pen-keepers and so required less exact plotting. The same principle applied to buildings. Works buildings were the first to be measured carefully and plotted in plan, while precise measurement of the location and dimensions of slaves' houses and even great houses was of less concern. These distinctions are important, but for present purposes it is fair to conclude that the plans are highly reliable in their representation of the location and area of major land-use elements.

Size, Shape, and Land Use

In the sample of 88 plans showing the internal layout of pens for the period 1760–1890, the mean size of the properties was 693 acres, compared to 699 acres for coffee plantations and 1,036 acres for sugar estates (table 3.1). The long-term trend was toward an increase in size, but growth was not considerable until the period following 1860, when large numbers of estates and plantations were converted to pens.

Pens increased in size with distance from the coast (r = .28; p = .00) and increasing rainfall (r = .18; p = .05), but there were no significant correlations between size and the slope, altitude, or relative relief of the land. Pen-keepers sought locations in ecological zones very similar to those preferred for sugar cultivation, but pens were unable to compete with sugar and so tended to be pushed inland, away from shipping points and the most fertile lowlands. Thus 51 percent of the pens in the sample were located below 1,000 feet compared to 64 percent of the sugar estates, and 16 percent of the pens were above 2,000 feet compared to only 6 percent of the sugar estates. On the other hand, pen-keepers avoided the constricted river valley sites with scattered pockets of rich soil, which beckoned sugar planters during the later eighteenth century, and preferred open, rolling country of a greater elevation. Only 35 percent of the pens were located in quadrats with mean slopes exceeding ten degrees, compared to 47 percent of the sugar estates.

The shape of pens was similar to that of sugar estates and coffee plantations, but pens scored slightly lower on the measure of circularity (0.40

Table 3.1. Land use on livestock pens, 1760–1889 (acres)

Date of plan	Total Area[a]		Coffee		Pimento		Guinea grass		Common pasture		Corn		Plantains		Woodland		Ruinate		Provision grounds		No. of plans
1760–69	2,700	—	—	—	—	—	20	—	998	—	—	—	—	—	—	—	—	404	55	—	1
1770–79	348	—	—	—	—	—	—	—	274	—	—	—	—	—	65	—	—	—	—	—	1
1780–89	741	795	—	—	—	—	163	218	233	315	11	22	5	11	223	328	72	24	1	3	9
1790–99	314	87	—	—	—	—	13	17	274	73	—	—	—	—	—	—	—	—	10	12	3
1800–1809	788	609	—	—	—	—	182	259	171	237	46	80	1	2	251	309	192	104	34	56	7
1810–19	473	249	2	5	—	—	173	161	170	95	2	6	—	—	10	24	92	41	94	113	6
1820–29	541	435	2	7	65	199	165	166	87	72	6	14	2	5	108	176	130	64	37	39	12
1830–39	702	685	1	4	31	111	269	282	177	167	10	20	—	—	168	326	107	35	36	57	21
1840–49	536	464	1	2	4	14	110	137	117	168	—	—	—	—	174	298	86	41	48	142	14
1850–59	658	568	—	—	22	53	262	390	140	109	—	—	—	—	88	103	112	81	2	3	6
1860–69	1,083	775	—	—	—	—	226	108	284	191	—	—	—	—	—	—	489	266	—	—	4
1870–79	967	380	—	—	—	—	496	427	277	160	—	—	—	—	—	—	116	125	—	—	3
1880–89	2,034	—	—	—	—	—	479	—	146	—	—	—	—	—	997	—	—	—	—	—	1
Total	693	623	1	4	18	91	198	240	181	199	8	27	1	4	142	267	155	66	32	75	88

Source: Sample of plantation maps (National Library of Jamaica).
a. The left column under each heading is the mean; the right column is the standard deviation.

compared to 0.45 for estates and plantations) and tended more often to be elongated or star-shaped. This may be explained by the process of accretion, which added blocks in a somewhat arbitrary fashion. There were no significant correlations between shape and any of the ecological variables, however. Nor did shape have any impact on the overall structure of land uses within pens.

Grass covered 55 percent of the total area of the pens represented in the sample of plans (table 3.1). Although there was little change in this proportion between 1760 and 1890, the relative balance between common pasture and guinea grass did alter significantly. Common pasture was dominant throughout the eighteenth century. Guinea grass, introduced accidentally in 1744 and regarded as superior feed for stabled and working cattle, forged ahead after 1800. Crab or pimento grass was also found on pens, particularly in Saint Ann and Manchester, but did not appear on any of the sample plans. Para grass, introduced in the late nineteenth century, did not appear either.[39] Scots, or Scotch, grass, a type of rough pasture on sugar estates, was indicated on the brackish land of some pens. Guinea grass achieved the greatest supremacy on the pens, however, and common pasture always covered a greater area on sugar estates (64 percent of all pasture) and coffee plantations (57 percent) than on pens (48 percent).

Woodland, ruinate, and provision grounds accounted for 34 percent of the total land area on pens, significantly less than the proportion on sugar estates (44 percent) and coffee plantations (58 percent). This difference can be explained by the relative lack of rugged land on pens, most of the rolling hills being suited to pasture. Thus there was a positive correlation between the proportion of woodland on pens and mean slope ($r = .30$; $p = .00$). The area in ruinate, generally land formerly in pimento, coffee, or cane, increased in an erratic fashion and was not associated with variations in topography. Provision grounds appear to have reached their maximum extent on pens around 1815 and disappeared from the plans after 1850.

Pimento was the most important of the export crops produced by pens but appeared on plans only between 1820 and 1859, with a peak mean of 65 acres during the 1820s. Most often the pimento was spread through pastures of guinea and common grass rather than being treated as a separate crop. A small number of monocultural pimento properties did exist in Saint Ann around 1830, but these were all called plantations rather than pens.[40] Only one plan of such a specialized holding is found in the National Library's collection: the adjacent Mount Edgecombe and Hilton

Hill Plantations, surveyed in 1816.[41] On this 772-acre unit, 237 acres were devoted exclusively to pimento, 11 acres to pimento and provisions, and 78 acres to guinea grass. A plan of Prospect Pen, Trelawny, in 1826, on the other hand, distinguished 30 acres in "guinea grass and pimento" and another 31 acres in "common and pimento" from a total area of 76 acres.[42] A more complex mix of land uses occurred at Devon Pen and Plantation in Manchester, a property of 1,682 acres when surveyed in 1858.[43] Even the unusual title "Pen and Plantation" suggests uncertainty about the property's proper categorization. The seven specialized "pimento walks" covered 125 acres, but another nine fields accounting for 163 acres were in "common and pimento." In addition, there were 37 acres in coffee, 32 acres in Guinea grass, and 26 acres in common. All of these land uses were intermixed spatially. The remainder of the property was in ruinate, coffee, and woodland.

Guinea corn was also a common crop on pens in the period from the American Revolution to emancipation (table 3.1). Some of it was consumed on the pens, but much was sold to estates and plantations. Other food crops, such as plantains, yams, cocos, and arrowroot, also entered this internal trade, operated by pen-keepers rather than slaves from their provision grounds.

Coffee and cotton appeared as supplementary crops on a few pens, but the mean area in coffee was only one acre and cotton even less. These crops generally appeared in combination with food crops, outside the specialized zones of pen-keeping, being most common in Manchester.

Logwood, used in the production of dye, rarely appeared on plantation maps, though other historical data show it to have been a significant source of income in some periods. The reason for this omission was chiefly that logwood was not planted systematically and was often used only to form hedges or fences. Introduced from Honduras in 1715, logwood was self-sown and came to overrun extensive areas by the 1780s, particularly in Saint Elizabeth and Westmoreland. It was exploited most intensively in times of hardship, notably the later nineteenth century, when other products were relatively unprofitable. The only plans in the sample for 1760–1890 to show significant areas of logwood relate to the 1860s. Often it was listed under the land-use classification "ruinate and logwood." Thus the exploitation of logwood was opportunistic, and this is one of the few respects in which the cartographic evidence fails to provide a true picture of land-use patterns.

Works, Great House, and Village Locations

The works complex played a much less significant role on pens than on sugar estates or coffee plantations, and many of the plans fail to indicate such a site. Where pens concentrated strictly on the production of livestock for sale as working animals, the development of processing centers was always limited. Stone-walled stockyards or "pens" were built to contain cattle when they were being drafted, branded, spayed, or treated for disease. Complexes of this sort were simple and could be split into smaller units or relocated at no great cost. Pens that produced cattle and sheep for the meat market occasionally had their own butcheries, but most sold fat stock to butchers in towns, where demand for fresh meat was concentrated. Only about 30 pens operated butcheries at the time of emancipation.[44] Similarly, pens close to towns supplied milk, although butter and cheese were generally imported. No plan has been found clearly indicating the site of a butchery or dairy on a pen before 1890. Pens that produced pimento or coffee as well as livestock had the small-scale works necessary to process these crops, but the mills and barbecues were sometimes separated from the cattle pens.

Most pens had a set of cattle pens located near to the great house larger than any sprinkled about the pastures, however, and this complex may reasonably be regarded as equivalent to the works of sugar or coffee plantations, though bearing a much lighter significance in terms of labor time and contribution to output. In the following analysis of works–village–great house relationships, the principle employed in cases of confusion has been to regard the cattle pens nearest the great house as the works. Obviously, this procedure weights the analysis, but it has been necessary to employ it for only a small proportion of the sample. In any case, the results of the analysis are of less significance than for estates or plantations simply because the works were less important in the economic life of the pens.

An index of centrality of works on pens and plantations can be obtained directly from the sample plans by measuring the distances from the works to the nearest and farthest boundary lines and calculating their ratio. The results are remarkably consistent. The index of centrality was 0.18 on pens, only marginally less than the 0.20 found on sugar estates and 0.19 on coffee plantations. For the period 1770–1860, the works on cattle pens were a mean 372 yards from the nearest boundary (S.D. = 225) and 2,078 yards from the farthest (S.D. = 1,129). There was no significant correlation between this index of centrality and the size or shape of pens. There was, however, an unexpected but weak association between increased centrality and steeper slopes ($r = 0.24$; $p = 0.10$). In general, it would appear that placing works near the center of properties was as important for pen-keepers as it was for sugar and coffee planters. The same principles of movement minimization applied, even though works on pens were less important centers of activity and might be supplemented by satellites scattered through the pastures.

Measurements of the distances between works, village, and great house have been obtained from 50 plans of pens, the remaining 38 plans in the sample lacking at least one element of the complex (table 3.2). The shortest axis was the works–great house distance, with a mean of 179 yards over the period 1770–1860, slightly less than that found for coffee plantations and less than half that for sugar estates. This result may be weighted by the definition of works used here, but it is important to notice that the works on a pen were not tied to sources of water or wind power and so could be located relatively freely. Equally important is the fact that the works on pens had a mean area of only 0.8 acres, compared to 7.1 acres for sugar estates and 1.7 acres for coffee plantations. There were no significant correlations between the works–great house distance and any of the ecological or land-use variables included in the analysis. Thus the requirements for a works site were easily satisfied in the rolling country occupied by most pens.

The longest axis of the complex was the village–great house distance, as on sugar estates, with a mean of 313 yards (418 on estates). Variations in this distance were significantly correlated only with the area in pimento ($r = 0.39$; $p = 0.00$) and the area occupied by the village ($r = 0.31$; $p = 0.02$). Thus the larger the workers' village, the farther it was pushed from the great house. This relationship suggests an association with absenteeism, though the argument that resident-proprietorship drew the village closer to the great house seems not to apply to pens. The distance in fact shortened somewhat after the abolition of slavery, but at the same time a number of pen-keepers pushed the villages off their properties entirely. Villages on pens increased to a maximum area of 13 acres during the 1820s, when their enslaved populations were growing and averaged about 100, but contracted to a mean of only 4 acres by the 1850s. None of the eight post-1860 plans included in the sample indicated a village site. Great house sites fluctuated very little in size, however, and approximated the mean of 4 acres from 1760 to 1890.

The third axis of the complex, the works-village distance, had a mean of 285 yards over the whole period. This placed the village nearer the works than to the great house, as on sugar estates. The works-village

Table 3.2. Mean distances between works, great house, and village on livestock pens, 1770–1859 (yards)

Date of plans	Works–village[a]		Works–great house		Village–great house		Number of plans
1770–79	145	—	185	—	92	—	1
1780–89	n.c.[b]	n.c.	66	—	224	169	6
1790–99	517	358	88	31	403	336	3
1800–1809	n.c.	n.c.	450	451	193	39	2
1810–19	146	77	143	133	157	78	4
1820–29	403	71	176	187	343	256	10
1830–39	271	139	213	398	399	362	15
1840–49	294	194	148	157	266	161	7
1850–59	275	47	179	198	363	109	2
Total	285	168	254	179	313	262	50

Source: Sample of plantation maps (National Library of Jamaica).
a. The left column under each heading is the mean; the right column is the standard deviation.
b. n.c. = no cases.

distance increased with the total size of pens ($r = 0.32$; $p = 0.04$) and with the area in common pasture ($r = 0.49$; $p = 0.04$). It also lengthened with the size of the village site ($r = 0.30$; $p = 0.02$). There was no significant correlation between the works-village and works–great house distances, but there were strong correlations between the other two pairs of axes ($r = 0.69$; $p = 0.00$). Thus it appears that the works element was the most free to move on pens, as on coffee plantations. But the elements of the works–village–great house complex on pens fell within a larger circle than circumscribed them on coffee plantations. This suggests a looser relationship, resulting from the lesser role of the topographic constraints and the more limited importance of the works as a focus of activity.

Field Patterns

The distribution of land uses within pens was relatively simple, since pasture was always dominant. The mean distance from the works to the farthest pasture was 1,571 yards, which means that grass very often spread throughout the pens rather than forming a zone enclosed by woodland and provision grounds as on sugar and coffee plantations. Where present, coffee and pimento were often pushed to the fringes of pens, since they were strictly marginal crops. In contrast to the pattern on estates and plantations, the mean distance from works and village to the farthest provision ground was actually less than that to the farthest pasture. On some pens the "Negro grounds" were located adjacent to both the village and great house, while pastures spread beyond. Most often, however, grounds were near the boundaries of pens at a mean 1,480 yards from the village site.

For the period 1760–1890, the typical pen was divided into 22 fields (S.D. = 14.5), with a mean area of 31.5 acres (S.D. = 33.7). Thus the field units of pens were larger than those of coffee plantations. The fields devoted to guinea grass and common pasture were much more uniform on pens, however, since grass was not forced into available spaces between cane and coffee pieces. After about 1820, of course, the field patterns of some pens were artifacts, reflecting previous cultivation in sugar and other staples, and so contributed to a greater uniformity.

Mean field size increased along with total area ($r = 0.64$; $p = 0.00$), as on estates and plantations. The size of fields in common pasture, guinea grass, and wood also increased together with total size. The only ecological variable to have an effect on field size was relative relief, which reduced the size of pastures where the land was particularly rugged ($r = 0.22$; $p = 0.03$). Field shape was affected in a similar way. Pens with rectangular fields were all located in quadrats with mean slopes of less than 10 degrees, while the proportion with irregular, natural field shapes increased steadily from 21 percent below 5 degrees to 67 percent above 20 degrees. Some 10 percent of the pens in the sample had field patterns composed of geometric figures, while 53 percent had irregular but straight-sided fields and only 33 percent had fields of irregular shape with boundaries following natural features. The last were most common beyond 2,000 feet above sea level.

The fabric of the fences that divided the fields of pens were rarely recorded by surveyors in a systematic manner. Hedges of the plant *Bromelia penguin,* its extremely prickly leaves forming an effective barrier, were popular throughout the eighteenth and nineteenth centuries. In some cases, these "penguin" fences were combined with ditches or banks and, after 1860, post-and-wire on external boundaries. Stone walls had always been popular where materials were ready to hand, and by the 1870s fences of stone, rails, wire, penguin, banks, and ditches frequently occurred together on a single pen.[45] As noted, logwood fences were often put to economic use in hard times.

Conclusion

The analysis of the internal economy of Jamaican pens presented in this essay has depended on a systematic study of the collection of plans in the National Library of Jamaica. Map evidence has clear advantages and disadvantages for this purpose. It provides unique information about spatial organization, permitting precise answers to questions discussed only loosely in impressionistic literary sources. On the other hand, plans are less useful indicators of land use and output for pens than they are for sugar or coffee plantations. Pasture types and field size provide only a rough guide to the size and composition of the livestock population. Similarly, the opportunistic exploitation of pimento and logwood meant that these items appeared in the account books of pens but were not always indicated on plans, since they were often seen only as shade trees or fences. A more precise and complete analysis of the changing pattern of resource use and productivity on pens must necessarily rest on a much wider range of sources, such as the public Accounts Produce and the private accounts of individual pens. It is also important to emphasize that even the information regarding spatial organization that may be derived from the plans has its limitations. For example, the plans provide precise dimensions for the works–village–great house triangle but less reliable data on the internal layout of these elements, such as the spatial organization and fabric of workers' houses.

Although the plans are a valuable source, then, it is obvious that any comprehensive study of pens and pen-keepers will have to be based on the creative use of a wider range of materials and placed in comparative perspective.[46] Such work is needed to establish the social and economic implications of the peculiar role of Jamaica's pens within the agrarian structure. It is needed also to address the larger question of why the linkage and spread effects commonly associated with livestock production were so limited in the plantation economies before 1900, even in Jamaica.

Notes

The research reported here was supported in part by a grant from the Joint Committee on Latin American Studies of the Social Science Research Council and the American Council on Learned Societies.

1. Richard B. Sheridan, *Sugar and Slavery: An Economic History of the British West Indies, 1623–1775* (Barbados: Caribbean University Press, 1974), 121.

2. S. W. Mintz and Douglas Hall, "The Origins of the Jamaican Internal Marketing System," *Yale University Publications in Anthropology* 57 (1960): 3–26.

3. Sheridan, *Sugar and Slavery,* 105.

4. B. W. Higman, *Slave Population and Economy in Jamaica, 1807–1834* (Cambridge: Cambridge University Press, 1976), 17.

5. F. G. Cassidy and R. B. Le Page, *Dictionary of Jamaican English* (London: Cambridge University Press, 1980).

6. Edward Long, *The History of Jamaica* (London, 1774), 1: 283, 380, 496; J. B. Moreton, *Manners and Customs in the West India Islands* (London, 1793), 58.

7. Bernard Martin Senior, *Jamaica, As It Was, As It Is, and As It May Be* (London, 1835), 39.

8. *Jamaica Almanack* (Kingston: Government Printing Office, 1838), 110.

9. Ibid., 11.

10. B. W. Higman, ed., *The Jamaican Censuses of 1844 and 1861* (Kingston: The Social History Project, University of West Indies, Mona, Jamaica, 1980), 1.

11. Higman, *Slave Population*, 25; and Long, *History of Jamaica*, 1: 380.

12. Long, *History of Jamaica*, 1: 495–96.

13. Higman, *Slave Population*, 16.

14. Philip D. Curtin, *Two Jamaicas: The Role of Ideas in a Tropical Colony, 1830–1865* (New York: Atheneum, 1970), 262; A Pen-keeper, "Pen-keeping or Cattle farming," *Handbook of Jamaica* (hereafter *HBJ*) (1882): 491–93.

15. The other censuses are not helpful. That for 1871 listed 1,004 "pen-keepers and their employees" and 1,948 "sugar planters and their employees," as well as 105,474 agricultural laborers (26). In 1881, the census identified only 275 pen-keepers, completely omitting Saint Ann but finding 20,660 laborers on pens and 49,441 on sugar estates (366). The 1911 census listed 582 "pen-keepers and proprietors" and 393 sugar planters (38).

16. *HBJ* (1913–14): 442–50.

17. *HBJ* (1885–86): 433; (1915): 423.

18. Senior, *Jamaica, As It Was*, 58.

19. Higman, *Slave Population*, 13.

20. Curtin, *Two Jamaicas*, 262.

21. [Edward] Kamau Brathwaite, *The Development of Creole Society in Jamaica, 1770–1820* (Oxford: Clarendon Press, 1971), 83.

22. *Votes of the House of Assembly of Jamaica* (1832), 481.

23. Long, *History of Jamaica*, 1: 495–96.

24. List of Slaves and Stock on Irwin Estate, 1820–27, Manuscript A/10, National Library of Jamaica, Kingston.

25. John Taylor Papers 1771–1813, Powell Collection, Box 29–F, Historical Society of Pennsylvania, Philadelphia.

26. Long, *History of Jamaica*, 2: 46–223.

27. *Jamaica Almanack*, 1838

28. *HBJ* (1883): 31; (1893): 289; (1902): 275; *Report of the Cattle Industry Enquiry Board, Jamaica, B.W.I.* (Kingston: Government Printing Office, 1952), 9.

29. James Robertson, *Map of the Island of Jamaica, Constructed from Actual Surveys* (London, 1804).

30. Douglas Hall, *Free Jamaica, 1838–1865* (New Haven, Conn.: Yale University Press, 1959), 71.

31. *HBJ* (1900): 406–10.

32. Gisela Eisner, *Jamaica, 1830–1930,* (Manchester: Manchester University Press, 1961), 199.

33. A Pen-keeper, "Pen-keeping," 493.

34. *Report of the Cattle Industry Enquiry Board, 9.*

35. Ibid., 3

36. B. W. Higman, *Jamaica Surveyed: Plantation Maps and Plans of the Eighteenth and Nineteenth Centuries* (Kingston: Institute of Jamaica Publications, 1988).

37. The measure of circularity is given by $100.A / (3.1416) (B/2)^2$ where A is the area of the pen and B is the distance between the farthest points of the pen. See Jack P. Gibbs, ed., *Urban Research Methods* (Princeton, N.J.: Van Nanstrond, 1961); Peter Haggett, *Locational Analysis in Human Geography* (London: Edward Arnold, 1965); and H. Kishimoto, *Cartometric Measurements* (Zurich: Geographisches Insitut der Universitat Zurich, 1968).

38. The method is explained in Higman, *Slave Population,* 51–52, 246. Average slope is derived from the number of grid/contour crossings by Wentworth's formula: G. H. Dury, *Map Interpretation* (London: Pitman, 1960), 176.

39. A Pen-keeper, "Pen-keeping," 491–93.

40. Higman, *Slave Population,* 24.

41. Richard Weightman, Plan of Mt. Edgecombe and Hilton Hill Plantations, St. Ann, 1816, St. Ann 13, plans, National Library of Jamaica, Kingston.

42. Nicholas Smith, Plan of Prospect Pen, Trelawny, 1826, Trelawny 4, plans, National Library of Jamaica, Kingston.

43. James L. Windett, Plan of Devon Pen and Plantation, Manchester, 1858, Manchester 17, plans, National Library of Jamaica, Kingston.

44. Higman, *Slave Population,* 26.

45. For example, Thomas Harrison, Plan of Thetford Pen, St. Catherine, 1889, St. Catherine 857, plans, National Library of Jamaica, Kingston; Archibald Edgar, Plan of Cow Bay Pen, St. Thomas (St. David), 1789, St. Thomas 15, plans, National Library of Jamaica, Kingston; Thomas Harrison, Plan of Spring Plain Pen, Clarendon (Vere), 1860, Clarendon 26, plans, National Library of Jamaica, Kingston.

46. For companion studies of sugar estates and coffee plantations, see B. W. Higman "Jamaican Coffee Plantations, 1780–1860: A Cartographic Analysis," *Caribbean Geography* 2 (1986): 73–91; and B. W. Higman, "The Spatial Economy of Jamaican Sugar Plantations: Cartographic Evidence from the Eighteenth and Nineteenth Centuries," *Journal of Historical Geography* 13 (1987): 17–39. Verene A. Shepherd has now done a full-length study of Jamaican pens and pen-keepers. See her Ph.D. dissertation, "Pens and Pen-keepers in a Plantation Society: Aspects of Jamaican Social and Economic History, 1740–1845" (University of Cambridge, 1988). See also her coauthored essay in this volume.

4

Pen-Keepers and Coffee Farmers in a Sugar-Plantation Society

Verene A. Shepherd and Kathleen E. A. Monteith

Jamaica's political economy has been deeply influenced by the sugar plantations that dominated the island's history from the beginning of the eighteenth century. Contemporary and modern writers stress the superordinate position occupied within the sugar-plantation structure by the sugar-planting elite—the class that owned and controlled most of the means and markets of production and dominated the social and political life of the island.[1] The resultant socioeconomic order, defined by George Beckford as the "plantation system," constituted the empirical basis for the formulation of the classic "plantation economy model."[2] Among the stated characteristics of plantation societies are the limited possibilities for internal capital accumulation; the absence of a significant home market; monoculture; the importation of inputs, usually from the "mother country"; and the exportation of all outputs.[3] But some colonial economies conformed more rigidly than others to this model. Studies have shown that, in contrast to Eastern Caribbean islands like Barbados and Saint Kitts, Jamaica's more varied physical environment resulted in significant entrepreneurial and economic diversification and the evolution of an important group of nonsugar proprietors.[4] While some of these, notably the "minor staple" cultivators such as the coffee planters, catered primarily to the export market, others geared their activities essentially to the domestic market. Among those concerned with producing primarily for the local market were those who engaged in the rearing of animals (called "pen-keepers" in Jamaica), who participated only minimally in the direct export trade, accumulating their capital locally. Although coffee and sugar planters sold some animals locally, the pen-keepers dominated the internal trade in animals and, by catering primarily to the sugar estate market, determined that the plantations did not conform to the traditional "enclave theory."[5]

However, despite the importance of coffee and livestock production in the export and local markets, the coffee planters and pen-keepers were never successful in bringing about any fundamental changes to the institutional arrangement of Jamaican society during slavery. They, like other nonsugar or nonstaple producers, were relegated to secondary roles and remained ancillary to the sugar sector. The dominant sugar sector, indeed, exploited those dependent on it, thereby reinforcing its superordinate position. This essay demonstrates that in spite of the growth in importance of coffee and the rearing of animals in Jamaica in the eighteenth and nineteenth centuries, which resulted in significant economic diversification, the island remained very much a "sugar-plantation society," with nonsugar producers being accorded an inferior social position.

The Pen-keepers

Many people reared animals in Jamaica in the eighteenth and nineteenth centuries—enslaved people, free people of color, free blacks, large sugar planters, coffee planters, and other small-scale white entrepreneurs. The essay is, however, primarily concerned with those specialized graziers commonly styled "pen-keepers" in the contemporary literature. They are to be distinguished from the enslaved male "pen-keepers" in charge of animals on sugar estates and other properties and from the overseers of livestock farms, who were also frequently referred to as "pen-keepers." Large sugar planters, resident or absentee, who established satellite pens as adjuncts to their estates and owners of urban residential pens must also be excluded from this analysis.

The livestock industry predated the establishment of sugar as the dominant crop and the rise of the plantation system. The earliest specialized graziers were, in fact, the Spaniards whose *hatos* dotted the southern savanna lands of early-seventeenth-century Jamaica. At that time, the industry was more export oriented, supplying dried, cured meat to passing ships and to Cuba and lard, hides, and tallow to the metropolitan Spanish market. With the English invasion, subsequent settlement, and the rise of the sugar economy, pen-keepers increasingly catered to the estates' demand for animals for draft purposes and millwork. Edward Long, an active apologist for slavery, for example, stressed the positive correlation between the expansion of the pen-keeping industry and the extension of the sugar culture, pointing out that far from declining in the face of the expansion of the sugar estates, pens increased to meet the estates' demand for working animals.[6] By 1782, there were an estimated 300 pens on the island.[7]

The earliest pen-keepers in English-colonized Jamaica were among the soldier-settlers of the Cromwellian expeditionary force. At first they established pens on the south coast, but with the competition for land resulting from the development and expansion of the more lucrative sugar industry, some were pushed onto marginal interior lands. In this regard, they were among the pioneers of the frontier society and were numbered among the early settlers in the Pedro's Cockpit area of the northern parish of Saint Ann.

Jamaica's varied topography and physical environment clearly provided possibilities for small-scale entrepreneurs, and the ready market for animals on the sugar estates contributed to the growth of the small-settler population. By 1820, pen-keepers also included attorneys and overseers in charge of estates. Attorneys and overseers, according to Benjamin M'Mahon's somewhat exaggerated description, made their "fortunes" while in charge of properties belonging to their absentee proprietors. They invested these "fortunes" in pens, which provided not only a ready source of animals for the estates they managed but also markets for the estates' old animals, which were fattened and sold to the butchers.[8]

In addition to whites, the pen-keepers also comprised free coloreds. Before the enactment of a law in 1761 curtailing the value of inheritance, free coloreds had managed to acquire substantial property.[9] Some inherited pens. Benjamin Scott-Moncrieffe, for example, inherited Soho Pen from his father and later also acquired Thatch Hill Pen in Saint Ann.[10] Pen-keepers also included women, though Kamau Brathwaite is essentially correct in his impression that it was a male-dominated occupation.[11] Female pen-keepers were comprised of whites, free coloreds, and free blacks. White female pen-keepers seemed to have been essentially widows and were less numerous among the pen-keepers than freedwomen.[12] Catherine Buckeridge from Sonning, County Berks, in England, for example, was a widow and owner of a rather substantial pen, Salt Pond Hut, in Saint Catherine.[13] Free colored and freed black women were more numerous among the female pen-keepers. Anna Woodart was, arguably, the wealthiest free colored woman in 1762, owning Dirty Pit and Hoghole Pens in Saint Catherine. Freedwomen were also noted among the pen-keepers in Westmoreland, Saint Elizabeth, Saint Thomas-in-the-East, and Saint David. The pens owned by freedwomen were among the smallest and were also confined to marginal lands.[14] Other distinguishing characteristics of the pen-keepers were that they were primarily Creole-born and resident.

The Coffee Planters

Coffee was grown in Jamaica from as early as 1728. However, a distinct coffee-planter class did not emerge until the late eighteenth century, when coffee became an important export crop within the Jamaican economy.[15] The catalyst for this expansion was provided largely by the revolt of enslaved people in Saint Domingue. The dislocation in production and supply caused by events after 1791 on that French colony, which at the time was the world's leading supplier of the product, led to a rapid escalation in the price on the international market.[16] In response to this hike in price, and with the added impetus of a further reduction in import duty on coffee entering Britain, Jamaican coffee planters extended their fields, while new settlers were attracted to the industry, thereby contributing to its expansion.[17]

Unlike the pen-keepers, there was never any competition for land between the coffee farmers and the sugar planters. Coffee lands were at higher elevations totally unsuitable for sugarcane, and this factor helped in the spatial differentiation of agrarian economic activities on the island. This also assisted in the unimpeded expansion of coffee plantations.[18]

The rapid development that followed this expansion led to coffee becoming the second most important export crop in Jamaica by the beginning of the nineteenth century. By 1800, the crop accounted for the second largest percentage of the total value of exports after sugar and its derivatives. In 1805, the sector contributed more than 25 percent of the total value of exports, reaching a maximum of 28 percent in 1814.[19] It remained the second most important export crop within the Jamaican economy up to the time of emancipation in 1834.[20] Like the pen-keepers, the majority of the coffee planters were resident proprietors. In 1799, of a total of 519 coffee plantations, at least 467, representing 90 percent, were owned by resident farmers, and 46 were owned by absentees.[21] While the level of absenteeism within the industry had risen by 1808, the number of properties owned by resident proprietors was still high. In that year, out of a total of 607 properties, 478, or nearly 80 percent, were owned by residents. This pattern of ownership only underwent change in the 1830s and 1840s when the industry was in decline and creditors foreclosed on properties, resulting in a higher level of absentee ownership within the sector.[22]

Most of the coffee planters were white. However, like the pen-keeping sector, some free coloreds were among this group.[23] Their entry into plantation agriculture was also primarily through the avenue of the legacies provided by their white fathers. For example, free coloreds William Peart and John Morgan were both owners of considerable properties in Manchester. There were also William Alcock, owner of Seamones Garden in Saint David, and Thomas William Powell, who owned Cassava River Mountain in Saint Thomas in the Vale. Free coloreds were also involved in the industry as superintendents and overseers. For instance, Halberstadt coffee plantation in Port Royal was overseen by Johann Casper Weisse, while Charly McNally of Manchester was reported to be "doing duty on a coffee plantation," as was William Mortimer Taylor of Saint Elizabeth who worked as an overseer.[24]

However, the number of free coloreds owning coffee plantations was probably lower than the number owning pen properties, and it must be stressed that the above-mentioned individuals were atypical of their class, as the majority of free coloreds in Jamaica were kept out of the plantation sector. This was mainly because the expansion of the industry occurred after the enactment of the Inheritance Law of 1762.[25]

A small number of French émigrés from Saint Domingue were also among the coffee planters in Jamaica in the early nineteenth century, though the number of émigrés who eventually settled in Jamaica numbered approximately 200. The vast majority of them arrived penniless and were not in a position to invest in the plantation economy.[26] Those who established themselves were mostly men of privileged position who had occupied the upper echelons of Saint Domingue society and were able to escape with most of their resources. Notable among them was Pierre Joseph Laborie, whose contribution to the island's industry included his manual, *The Coffee Planter of Santo Domingo*.[27] There was also Raymond Chevolleau, who owned Friendship in Saint George, and Louis Rene Malabre of Mahoe in the same parish. Louis Carre Desquottes owned Silver Hill in Saint George, which was leased to another French émigré, Paul La Mothe DeCarrer. Desquottes also owned Mocho in Saint George and Florence Hill in Saint Andrew.[28]

Economic Dependence and Independence

Pen-keepers were heavily dependent on the sugar industry, as the sugar estates provided the largest outlet for the products of the pens. A small sample of 11 percent of the pens returned in the Accounts Produce for 1820 revealed that these units earned more from the sale of working animals to the estates than from other income-generating activities such as jobbing, wainage, pasturage, and the sale of food and miscellaneous items. While livestock sales amounted to just over 20,014 pounds Jamaican currency representing 69 percent of total earnings of around 28,939 pounds, other resources combined accounted for 31 percent. Taken as single categories, jobbing represented 9 percent, pasturage 4 percent, wainage 4 percent, provisions 9 percent, and miscellaneous items 5 percent. For individual pens, however, livestock sales often accounted for as much as 98 percent.[29]

The size of the sugar estate market for animals was considerable. Large estates like Golden Grove in Saint Thomas-in-the-East needed an estimated 100 "steers" (oxen) annually in addition to mules and spayed heifers.[30] Indeed, between the late eighteenth century and the early nineteenth century, the estimated annual total island demand for working animals was put at somewhere between 56,000 and 71,000.[31] At 18 pounds (currency) each in the late eighteenth century and between 20 and 30 pounds (currency) in the early nineteenth century, estates would need to spend a considerable sum on oxen alone.[32]

Theoretically, Jamaica's sugar economy afforded a relatively substantial market capable of acting as a dynamic factor in the development of the pen sector. In reality, this dynamism was not directed completely toward the local pen-keeping industry. In the first place, Jamaican sugar planters continued to import working animals, primarily from Spanish-colonized America, even after the local pen-keeping industry had been well established. Some sugar planters also established their own pens or rented existing ones in attempts to exclude the intermediary suppliers. The "ingivings" of 1815 reveal that 84 sugar planters owned 96 satellite pens serving 122 estates.[33] As their sugar estates could not always use all the animals reared on such related units, sugar farmers who also raised cattle competed on the local market with the specialized pen-keepers. Therefore, even that section of the sugar market to which pen-keepers had access was not always stable.

During and after the period of African enslavement, fluctuations in the demand for work animals on the sugar estates created by the depression in the sugar market often resulted in bankruptcy for some pen-keepers. For example, between 1810 and 1817—good years for sugar—George Forbes of Thatchfield Pen in Saint Elizabeth was confident of making profits of between 2,000 and 2,500 pounds from his property.[34] The decline in profitability of some estates in the mid-nineteenth century caused a decrease in their demand for estate work animals and wiped out his savings.[35] Likewise, in the immediate postslavery period, the depressed state of the sugar sector caused by labor and capital shortages created an oversupply of animals on the market and a fall in their prices. Pen-keepers then complained of the "death of pen-keeping."[36] Competition from foreign suppliers and the precariousness of depending almost completely on the sugar estates caused pen-keepers to diversify their activities and restrict their output of animals—reducing their dependence upon sugar estates but making them vulnerable to downturns in the new markets they entered.

On the other hand, the coffee planters, because they were involved in production for export, were largely independent of the sugar plantation economic complex. Like the sugar planters, their fortunes were determined mainly by international forces, as was evident in the timing of the expansion of the industry. The industry clearly exhibited a genuine increase in the late eighteenth and early nineteenth centuries as a result of the escalation in prices on the international market caused by the revolutionary upheaval in Saint Domingue after 1791. This was indicated by the rapid extension of settlements and increased production and export levels. Correspondingly, with the prevalence of high prices in this early period, significant profits were realized by the coffee planters. Indeed, while the average return on capital invested in coffee production for export averaged 5 percent in 1790, between 1800 and 1810 this had increased to an average of 14 percent.[37]

Another favorable market condition for coffee in the early period was the preferential rates of duty accorded to British Caribbean coffee over those imposed on East Indian and foreign-grown coffee entering Britain. In 1792, the duty on coffee from the British-colonized Caribbean was 10⅝ pence per pound, while imports from the East attracted 2 shillings and ⅛ pence. This preference was increased in 1799, when an additional ad valorem tax of 2 pounds was imposed on East Indian coffee. Thus, as Lowell Ragatz notes, "the more than doubling of prices between 1793 and 1799 and the favored position in the British market brought undreamed of wealth to British coffee growers beyond the Atlantic."[38] However, the following century brought far less favorable conditions.

Perhaps the most serious crisis affecting the fortunes of coffee planters prior to emancipation was the Anglo-French war, which resulted in the Napoleonic blockade of the European continent against British exports. Coffee from the British-colonized Caribbean was primarily produced for reexportation to the Continent.[39] As a result, the effective blockade of this market between 1807 and 1813 had a devastating impact on the Jamaican coffee industry, as imports reaching Britain remained unsold in warehouses.[40] The pile up of stocks was also evident on the plantations, and in 1811, 1812, and 1813 the level of unshipped coffee stood at 16.6 percent, 26.4 percent, and 16.9 percent, respectively.[41] The large quantities of unsold coffee meant that there was a drastic reduction in price on the international market. This in turn meant that coffee planters were unable to sell enough coffee to cover their expenses. As a result, many of them became heavily indebted during the period of the blockade. For example, Halberstadt plantation in 1809 had expenses totaling 4,864 pounds 12 shillings and 10 pence, while receipts amounted to 2,756 pounds 18 shillings and 1 pence. In 1810, the situation had worsened in spite of some saving on expenses—which totaled just over 3,081 pounds 1 shilling and 11 pence—as receipts were only 1,550 pounds 4 shillings and 8 pence. Barracks plantation's expenses for 1809 amounted to 2,760 pounds 13 shillings and 7 ½ pence, and as coffee sales were not forthcoming, a mortgage of 2,364 pounds 5 shillings and 8 pence had to be taken out against 65 tierces of coffee in order to offset the expenses incurred for that year.[42]

The industry never really recovered from the impact of the Napoleonic blockade because many of the coffee planters continued to be saddled with huge debts as prices remained generally lower than in the early 1800s. Prices remained lower in the post-1814 period as a result of substantial increases in the amount of coffee produced within and outside of the British empire. This increased competition was also influenced by changes in British fiscal policy begun in the 1820s and extended in the 1830s and 1840s. In the 1820s, Britain began to reduce the preferential margins on British Caribbean coffee over coffee produced in the East, and by 1835 the duty on coffee produced in Ceylon was equal to that imposed on the British Caribbean product. In 1842, this liberalization policy was extended to foreign-grown coffee, and a further reduction was made in 1844. As the cost of producing Jamaican coffee was higher than that of its competitors, many coffee planters were forced to abandon their properties altogether, and at least 300 properties were abandoned in the 1830s. Emancipation in 1838 only exacerbated an already worsening situation, and between 1842 and 1848 an additional 159 properties were thrown out of production.[43]

Social and Political Status

In her analysis of white society in the British Leeward Islands in the eighteenth century, Elsa Goveia suggests that, despite class stratification among whites, an unconscious sense of solidarity existed and that, further, they were all, because of their "race," members of the elite. Of course, as both Goveia and Brathwaite acknowledge, this did not mean an absence of class divisions, for phenotype affinity did not seem to have been sufficient to guarantee elite status.[44] This analysis is supported by aspects of the history of the livestock and coffee industries, as white coffee planters and livestock farmers, particularly overseers and managers, were clearly differentiated socially from the top echelons of white, sugar-planter society and typically occupied ambiguous positions within the class configuration during the eighteenth and nineteenth centuries. Neither Brathwaite's nor M. G. Smith's account of white society lists such whites among the elite or "principal" whites. According to Smith, "principal whites" formed a closed social class from which "secondary whites," coloreds, and blacks were vigorously excluded—with the possible exception of mistresses.[45] The basis of such "social marginality" for the poorer class of whites was linked to economic factors and social class differences.

From the early eighteenth century, pens were considered to be less prestigious properties than sugar plantations, and their differential rate of remuneration made them unable to attract white workers. J. B. Moreton emphasized that "grass pens were considered as despicable objects for enterprising individuals to hunt after, nor would any man accept the management of one who had hopes of preferment on sugar plantations."[46] He stressed that managers and overseers of sugar estates would not even associate with people in similar occupations on the pens. Furthermore, because pens were considered to be simply "moderate sized farms," their owners were more likely to be residents and less likely to join the elite group of absentees. Therefore, resident proprietors, particularly Creoles, were regarded as socially inferior.[47]

Relationships of superordination and subordination were also clearly discernible between "principal" and "secondary whites" according to Smith's categorization.[48] This was because a significant number of Jamaican pen-keepers and coffee planters worked as attorneys and overseers of sugar estates. Dominant-subordinate relations were thus partly the result of the delegation of authority in the administration of estates.

In his seminal work on the development of Creole society in Jamaica, Kamau Brathwaite outlined the main social divisions within the society and differentiated between the several categories of settlers.[49] White pen-keepers, along with "minor staple" producers, who included the coffee planters, were grouped among those categorized as "other whites." More specifically, he referred to them as "country whites" and "small settlers" not numbered among the "upper class whites."[50] The free colored pen-keepers and coffee planters were already regarded as socially inferior by white society. Even pen-keepers such as Robert Anguin and Benjamin Scott-Moncrieffe, whose economic position ranked them at the top of the free colored social ladder, were marginal vis-à-vis white elites, as were other groups of "unappropriated people."[51]

Despite their involvement in an important export crop, coffee planters, like pen-keepers, were accorded a social position inferior to that of the sugar planters. Most of them occupied a middle-class position within the white social hierarchy.[52] Evidence of this is provided by a description of them in a petition to the British Crown in 1811 as being resident proprietors of "easy circumstances [and] independent."[53] These planters owned relatively modest properties, ranging between 200 and 500 acres, with the majority of them being worked by 100 or fewer enslaved people.[54] This meant that a significant number of these proprietors were engaged in the daily management of their properties. Many of them had arrived on the island between 1780 and the early 1800s and had availed themselves of credit from merchants, investing modestly at first in 10 or 20 enslaved Africans and 200 to 300 acres of land.[55] The personal inventories of these planters also attest to their overall middle-class background. The furnishings recorded included double loop dining tables, tea and card tables, other mahogany fittings, and an array of crockery and utensils, which suggests a modest, though comfortable, lifestyle.[56]

Despite the fact that social differences separated sugar planters from pen-keepers and coffee planters, the necessity to forge economic links between economic sectors on the island determined that a certain level of interaction occurred.[57] Sugar planters or their representatives at times visited pens to select the stock for their estates. Pen-keepers similarly visited the sugar plantations to seek business and to see about the welfare of their jobbers. The crucial question is: did such interaction extend beyond that dictated by economic necessity? There is no definitive answer. Caribbean social history highlights the social divisions between broad social groups but sheds very little light on the more complex subject of intra- and inter-class interaction within ethnic and color groupings. Nevertheless, it can be safely assumed that interaction dictated by economic necessity did not result in complete egalitarianism.

Yet it seems reasonable to assume that some amount of egalitarianism must have prevailed between some sections of the coffee- and sugar-planting community, given the significant number of coffee planters who were members of the Jamaica House of Assembly during the first half of the nineteenth century.[58] Many of these coffee planters were linked with the sugar economy as trustees and/or as attorneys for absentee sugar proprietors.[59] A few also owned sugar-producing properties. For example, Samuel Vaughan (1762–1827), a member of the House of Assembly, owned Flamstead sugar estate as well as Vaughansfield, a combined pen and coffee unit.[60] Hugh Fraser Leslie, who represented the parish of Saint David between 1830 and 1847, managed several sugar and coffee properties located in the eastern section of the island.[61] Henry Lord Garrigues of Vere was also engaged in both sugar and coffee cultivation for some 30 years. At least eight sugar estates and three coffee plantations in the parishes of Saint Mary, Clarendon, Manchester, Vere, Saint David, and Saint Thomas-in-the-East fell under his management.[62] Therefore, one would assume that given this membership and the commonality of interests that existed between the two economic sectors, a great deal of social interaction would have occurred.

While most possessed the franchise, in general, specialized pen-keepers never occupied high political positions.[63] Up to 1845, none was noted in the Assembly or Legislative Council. Even in prominent pen parishes where pen-keepers managed to occupy public positions, these were usually low-status parochial positions (such as waywardens and jurors).[64] To gain access to positions of political power meant that rural pen-keepers had to diversify into export-oriented economic activities, such as sugar or coffee production. Only those pen-keepers who joined the sugar-planter class eventually gained seats in the Assembly. A notable example was the landowner Hamilton Brown.

The Response of Pen-keepers and Coffee Planters

The majority of the Jamaican pen-keepers could do very little about their dependent economic position. Until the late nineteenth century, they lacked a viable alternative market for their outputs, were restricted in the scale of their operations as sugar planters monopolized most of the suitable pasturelands, and could not compete effectively with foreign suppliers of animals. For the majority of pen-keepers, therefore, economic constraints affected the extent to which they could improve their sociopolitical position. This situation, in fact, caused some to sell out and emigrate. Others were frustrated in their attempts to achieve an economic position that would enable them to join the ranks of the absentee class; as J. Bigelow points out, very often residency was forced by low economic status. He notes that "nothing less than the profits of a very large estate could compensate . . . for the trouble and expenses of keeping up a force of attornies [sic] agents and book-keepers, and for the absence of that personal devotion to its management which none but a proprietor ever feels."[65] Thus the Saint Elizabeth pen-keeper George Forbes informed his brother that he would return to live in the United Kingdom as soon as his financial circumstances allowed him to do so.[66] Others invested in alternative economic activities such as sugar, coffee, pimento, and logwood, often in combination with livestock farming, or sought jobs as overseers on sugar estates.[67]

Free colored pen-keepers, notably Anguin and Scott-Moncrieffe, were among those who successfully petitioned the Assembly for privileges in order to improve their social position. But these strategies were largely individualistic. Internal diversities and disorganization—notably the absence of group cohesion and consciousness and the acceptance of the dominant social ideology by the poorer white and free colored pen-keepers—meant that responses to their ascribed position were not all designed to achieve the upliftment of the pen-keepers as a "group."

Collective group action was not totally absent, however. Despite the existence of internal divisions, when their economic welfare was threatened, pen-keepers collectively agitated for legislation favorable to their economic interests. The primary form of political action was petitioning the Assembly. This action was taken by white and free colored male and female pen-keepers. It would seem that free colored women were directly affected by sexist attitudes prevalent during this period. Sheena Boa records that as it was considered unseemly for women to be involved in political activities, free colored women were excluded by their male counterparts from the civil rights movement.[68] By contrast, petitions at times originated with female pen-owners. For example, in 1843 Catherine Buckeridge spearheaded the protest over the planned diversion of the Rio Cobre to facilitate the laying of railway lines. The construction of the railway from Spanish Town to Kingston would have encroached on the lands of some of the Saint Catherine pen-owners, including Buckeridge. She petitioned the Assembly to reconsider its plans, as the diversion of the river would create hardships for pen-owners who relied on it: "in its present course [the river] had afforded a constant supply of water to the grass pieces of petitioner's pen and had thereby fertilized them, and given the occupier the means of conveying grass to market."[69] Her petition was unsuccessful. Most of the other petitions related to the import trade in animals from Spanish America, the low level of import duties imposed, and general matters of taxation.

The planters' continued support for imported animals caused the pen-keepers to restrict production to a low level to avoid having a surplus and a consequent drop in prices. As early as 1790, the pen-keepers in the Saint Ann Vestry petitioned the governor about the "distressing Prospect arising [in] the Community in general . . . and this Parish in particular of the trade carried on between the Spaniards of Cuba and a few of the trading or commercial Persons of this country."[70] They stressed that the trade posed an obstacle to the further expansion of the industry "which [is] being partly discontinued by the introduction of Spanish horses, mules, mares and neat cattle, subject to no Impost or Duty whatsoever, and at a time when we [are] paying taxes towards the support of Government from the time of sale."[71] The pen-keepers of Manchester and Saint Elizabeth echoed these sentiments in the early nineteenth century. In 1816, they implored the House of Assembly to impose a tax on imported "stock." The Saint Elizabeth graziers complained that "from the late large importation of horned or neat cattle, mules and horses, the stock of the native breeder and grazier has become unsaleable."[72] The petitioners of Manchester complained similarly that "the petitioners are sorely aggrieved by the constant importations into this island of horses, mules, asses and neat cattle from the Spanish Main and other ports, to the great loss and injury of the petitioners; and that such importations enable the importers very considerably to undersell the breeders of the island."[73]

In their defence, the sugar planters maintained that the trade with Spanish America was vital, as animals from that source sold at cheaper rates and this served to regulate better the price of beef and planters' stock. Edward Long, however, accused them of being, in general, prejudiced in favor of foreign articles "despising their own though far superior in value."[74] In addition to differences in cost, planters maintained that the form of payment demanded by the local producers was at variance with the customary method employed by the importers of foreign cattle. That is, while local producers wanted immediate cash payment, importers supplied stock on a one-year credit at 6 percent interest. Although by the mid-nineteenth century some pen-keepers had adopted the credit system, this did not reduce significantly the level of importations; though the few livestock farmers in the Assembly were able to press for the imposition of a tax on animals imported, this was too low to stem importation. Hamilton Brown, for example, had proposed a tax of 80 shillings, but instead the low level of one pound per head of cattle was implemented in 1817.[75] Though changes occurred afterward, the duty never exceeded two pounds per head of livestock in the period of slavery.

In the postslavery period, pen-keepers collectively protested the Assembly's attempt to tax them unfairly. Where the parish vestry was dominated by sugar planters, the fight for fair taxation was even more protracted. In 1840, for example, Saint Mary pen-keepers consistently petitioned the Assembly to get the vestry to remove the five shillings Jamaican currency tax imposed on all breeding stock. The vestry had levied this charge with the explanation that it was to offset the cost of road repair incurred in the parish in the previous year. The pen-keepers objected on the grounds that, in the past, little of the money raised for this purpose was actually correctly applied. Rather, it was "appropriated towards the disbursement of the general accumulated debts of the parish."[76] They accused the vestry of using this devious means of achieving its real purpose, which was "to evade a recent law prohibiting Vestries from assessing any tax on stock for parochial purposes, to an amount exceeding treble the amount per head, levied as a public tax on stock."[77] The livestock farmers claimed that "the nominal road tax . . . is most unequal and oppressive in its operation and amount, falling on a description of property which makes no use of the roads for the repairs of which it is alleged to be imposed."[78] They claimed that estates had been assessed only a third of the sum levied on pens.

In 1843, other pen-keepers from various parishes added their voices to those of the Saint Mary protestors. They claimed that the "petitioners are heavier taxed than any other proprietors in the island."[79] Without adequate representation in the Assembly, however, the island's pen-keepers could not hope to win favorable legislation to protect their industry.

The coffee planters, despite their comparatively inferior social status, fared better in the House of Assembly with respect to having their interests looked after on account of their dual interests in sugar and coffee and because they were a significant part of the exporting sector. Legislation was not passed that militated against them, unlike the pen-keepers. Indeed, one could go as far as to say that the interests of the coffee farmers were well represented. This is reflected in the petitions and inquiries made on their behalf to the British Parliament. For example, an inquiry was made into the possible effects on the coffee industry resulting from the abolition of the transatlantic trade in enslaved African captives by the Assembly in 1792.[80] In 1811, the Assembly sent a petition to the Crown highlighting the debilitating effects of the Napoleonic Wars (1803–15) not only on the sugar industry but also on the coffee industry.[81] In 1848, extensive investigations were made into the industry to report on the impact of the abolition of slavery.[82]

On the other hand, the equalization of the coffee duties in 1844 did not raise a furor as did the Sugar Duties Equalization Act of 1846. One may argue that this reflected the importance of sugar vis-à-vis coffee to the total economy.[83] This is true; but it should also be remembered that by that time the coffee industry was already in decline, with a significant number of properties having been abandoned, and to have raised a protest would have been pointless. However, the fundamental issue is that the plight of the producers of cattle and other animals never attracted the same level of internal attention as the plight of the sugar planters in the postslavery period.

Sugar continued to be the main export crop, and the wealthiest resident planters were to be found in this industry as attorneys.[84] Naturally, many of them continued to occupy seats of high political power. Jamaican society of the eighteenth and nineteenth centuries, in contrast to the seventeenth century when nonsugar producers had more influence, was politically dominated by the sugar planters. In this society, many groups were politically marginalised. Race, color, or gender factors had already marginalised women and free coloreds of all categories (except for those free coloreds who had successfully applied for privileges). But even among the whites—usually the ruling class in plantation societies of the American hemisphere—there was differential access to political power. "Secondary whites," among whom rural pen-keepers were numerous, were clearly politically subordinate to the "principal whites."

Conclusion

Owners of units other than sugar estates, then—except where they formed an alliance with the sugar-planter class—seemed to have been relegated to secondary roles and social positions in a plantation society dominated by the sugar sector. But it would also seem safe to argue that though all nonsugar proprietors were marginalised to some degree in the sugar-dominated economy, those not directly linked to the export sector were even more marginalised. This helps to explain the differences evident in the political experiences of coffee planters and pen-keepers. It is undeniable that for some of the latter, their ascribed inferior position was derived from race, color, gender, and class considerations; but the nature of their primary economic activity and the lesser extent to which they invested directly in the sugar industry were crucial contributory factors.

A few other concluding observations are necessary. The Jamaican plantation society, though characterized in a generalized sense by a dichotomy of class—the white exploiting class and an exploited non-European class—showed significant intraclass diversities. In the case of whites, internal socioeconomic and political differentiation and antagonistic relationships derived from competitive economic activity lend support to the notion that Caribbean plantation societies were not characterized by a homogenous white race that formed the ruling class. Political power was not exclusively held by the sugar planters, as a few nonsugar producers managed to gain access to the Assembly—the traditional bastion of "sugar power." Admittedly, the success of a few individuals did not significantly change the position of the marginal groups. The effectiveness of the pen-keepers' attempts to change this position of marginality was diminished by external factors relating to the state of the sugar market; economic dependence on the sugar sector; their own internal disorganization and the absence of a true coalition that cut across color, race, class, and gender lines; and their acceptance of the dominant ideology. In the case of the free colored pen-keepers, responses to their subordinate position represented individualistic and pragmatic strategies for upward social mobility in a society where one's position was determined not only by class considerations but also by color and race. They used their education and wealth accumulated from the pen-keeping industry to seek acceptance within white elite society, not to challenge the dominant ideology.

The coffee farmers were also internally differentiated, though fewer of them were non-European. Their resident status and modest economic activity marked them off from the sugar planters; but the fact that they were a part of the export sector and that many were linked to the sugar economy seems to have caused them to fare better than the pen-keepers.

Notes

1. See Edward Long, *The History of Jamaica* Ad Ms 12, 404–6, British Library, 3 vols. (London, 1774); J. B. Moreton, *Manners and Customs in the West India Islands* (London, 1790); M. G. Smith, "Social Structure in the British Caribbean about 1820," *Social and Economic Studies,* 1, no. 4 (1955): 55–78; [Edward] Kamau Brathwaite, *The Development of Creole Society in Jamaica 1770–1820* (Oxford: Clarendon Press, 1971); R. B. Sheridan, *Sugar and Slavery: An Economic History of the British West Indies, 1623–1775* (Barbados: Caribbean University Press, 1974); and B. W. Higman, *Slave Population and Economy in Jamaica 1807–1834* (Cambridge: Cambridge University Press, 1976).

2. G. Beckford, *Persistent Poverty: Underdevelopment in Plantation Economies of the Third World* (New York: Oxford University Press, 1972).

3. L. Best, "Outlines of the Model of a Pure Plantation Economy," *Social and Economic Studies* 17 (1968): 283–332; F. L. Pryor, "The Plantation Economy as an Economic System," *Journal of Comparative Economics* 6 (1982): 288–317;

and A. Dupuy "Slavery and Underdevelopment in the Caribbean: A Critique of the Plantation Economy Perspective," *Dialectical Anthropology* 7 (1983): 239.

4. Higman, *Slave Population and Economy in Jamaica,* 16; V. A. Shepherd, "Pens and Pen-keepers in a Plantation Society: Aspects of Jamaican Social and Economic History, 1740–1845" (Ph.D. diss., University of Cambridge, 1988); Kathleen E. A. Monteith, "The Coffee Industry in Jamaica, 1790–1850" (M.Phil. thesis, University of the West Indies, Mona, Jamaica, 1991).

5. Dupuy, "Slavery and Underdevelopment," 169–226.

6. Long, *History of Jamaica* 1: fol. 308.

7. W. J. Gardner, *History of Jamaica* (London, 1874), 161.

8. B. M'Mahon, *Jamaica Plantership* (London, 1835), 171–73.

9. G. Heuman, *Between Black and White: Race, Politics and Free Coloreds in Jamaica, 1792–1865* (Westport, Conn.: Greenwood Press, 1981).

10. Shepherd, "Pens and Pen-keepers," 182.

11. Brathwaite, *Development of Creole Society,* 146–47.

12. S. Boa, "Free Black and Colored Women in a White Man's Slave Society" (M.Phil. thesis, University of the West Indies, Mona, Jamaica, 1985), 64–69

13. Shepherd, "Pens and Pen-keepers," 183.

14. Boa, "Free Black and Colored Women," 66.

15. Brathwaite, *Development of Creole Society,* 147. L. J. Ragatz, *The Fall of the Planter Class in the British Caribbean 1763–1833: A Study in Social and Economic History* (New York: Octagon, 1928), 205.

16. Ragatz, *Fall of the Planter Class,* 205; M. R. Trouillot, "Motion in the System: Coffee, Color and Slavery in 18th century Saint Domingue," *Review* 3 (winter 1982): 337.

17. Ragatz, *Fall of the Planter Class,* 205.

18. Monteith, "Coffee Industry," 24–40.

19. B. W. Higman, "Jamaican Coffee Plantations 1780–1860: A Cartographic Analysis," *Caribbean Geography* 2 (1986): 73.

20. D. G. Hall, *Free Jamaica 1838–1865: An Economic History* (New Haven, Conn.: Yale University Press, 1959), 39.

21. Monteith, "Coffee Industry," 82.

22. Jamaica Archives, Spanish Town, Accounts Produce, 1B/11/4/39–41; 1B/11/4/44, fol. 154; 1B/11/4/45, fols. 230–39; 1B/11/4/48, fols. 176–77. Accounts Produce, 1B/11/4/93–94.

23. Brathwaite, *Development of Creole Society,* 105, 172. See also Monteith, "Coffee Industry," 72–77.

24. Monteith, "Coffee Industry," 74.

25. Ibid., 74–75.

26. Patrick Bryan, "Conflict and Reconciliation: The French Émigrés in 19th century Jamaica," *Jamaica Journal* (September 1973): 14.

27. David Geggus, *Slavery, War and Revolution: The British Occupation of St. Domingue, 1793–1798,* (Oxford: Oxford University Press, 1982), 169, 274.

28. Ms. 37a National Library of Jamaica, "Louis Malabre Baptismal, Marriage and Burial Records of the French Families of St. Domingue and Jamaica."

29. Jamaica Archives, Accounts Produce, 1B/11/4/54–56.

30. Simon Taylor to Chaloner Arcedeckne, October 29, 1792, Vanneck MSS, Jamaican Estate Papers, box 2, bundle 10.

31. Calculated on the basis of the number of estates each year and their estimated demand for working animals.

32. Accounts Produce, 1B/11/4/3, 4, 9, 54.

33. *Jamaica Almanack* (Kingston, 1815), 221–83. Satellite pens represented about a third of the total number of pens.

34. Jamaica Archives, Gunnis Papers, Private Deposits 4/110/30, George Forbes to Peter Forbes, June 11, 1817.

35. Ibid.

36. For further information on the experiences of livestock farmers during the Apprenticeship and post-Apprenticeship periods, see V. A. Shepherd, "The Apprenticeship Experience of Jamaican Livestock Pens," *Jamaica Journal* 22, no. 1 (1989): 48–55; and V. A. Shepherd, "The Effects of the Abolition of Slavery on Jamaican Livestock Farms (Pens)," *Slavery and Abolition* 10, no. 2 (1989): 187–211.

37. Monteith, "Coffee Industry," 211–13.

38. Ragatz, *Fall of the Planter Class,* 215–16.

39. Ibid., 328; Seymour Drescher, *British Slavery in the Era of Abolition, 1760–1810* (Pittsburgh: University of Pittsburgh Press, 1977) 90; Eli Heckscher, *The Continental System: An Economic Interpretation,* trans. C. S. Fearenside, ed. Harold Westgaard (Oxford: Clarendon Press, 1922), 95–96.

40. Ragatz, *Fall of the Planter Class,* 329.

41. Monteith, "Coffee Industry," 219–22.

42. Ibid., 225–26.

43. Ibid., 230–46.

44. Elsa Goveia, *Slave Society in the British Leeward Islands at the End of the Eighteenth Century* (New Haven, Conn.: Yale University Press, 1965), 314–15.

45. Brathwaite, *Development of Creole Society,* 105–50; Smith, "Social Structure," 55–59.

46. Moreton, *Manners and Customs,* 58.

47. J. Bigelow, *Jamaica in 1850* (London, 1851), 104; Shepherd, "Pens and Pen-keepers," 100, 180.

48. Smith, "Social Structure," 55–59.

49. Brathwaite, *Development of Creole Society,* 105–50.

50. Ibid., 135–48.

51. See Heuman, *Between Black and White;* and Boa, "Free Black and Colored." See also D. Cohen and J. Green, eds., *Neither Slave nor Free* (Baltimore:

Johns Hopkins University Press, 1972); and J. Handler, *The Unappropriated People* (Baltimore: Johns Hopkins University Press, 1973).

52. Brathwaite, *Development of Creole Society*, 105.

53. *Representation and Petition* (1811), 1.

54. Monteith, "Coffee Industry," 41–43, 45–47.

55. Edgar Corrie, "Letters on the Subject of the Duties on Coffee," *Slavery Pamphlets* 6 (1808): 8.

56. Monteith, "Coffee Industry," 81, 84.

57. See Higman, *Slave Population and Economy in Jamaica;* B. W. Higman, *Slave Populations of the British Caribbean, 1807–1834* (Baltimore: Johns Hopkins University Press, 1984); B. W. Higman, "Slave Population and Economy in Jamaica at the Time of Emancipation," (Ph.D. diss., University of the West Indies, Mona, Jamaica, 1970); and Shepherd, "Pens and Pen-keepers," 135–50.

58. Monteith, "Coffee Industry," 83.

59. *Further Proceedings of the House Assembly of Jamaica, Relative to a Bill introduced into the House of Commons for effectually preventing the Unlawful importation of Slaves and holding—taken upon oath before a Committee of that House for the Disproving the allegations of the said Bill* (London, 1816), 65, 68; *First to Eighth Reports from the Select Committee on Sugar and Coffee Planting, together with the Minutes of Evidence and Appendices* (London, 1848), 7th Report, Appendix 1, 162, 165, 173.

60. Philip Wright, ed., *Lady Nugent's Journal of Her Residence in Jamaica from 1801–1805* (Kingston: Institute of Jamaica Publications, 1966), 320.

61. *Select Committee on Sugar and Coffee Planting*, 7th Report, Appendix 1, 166.

62. Ibid., 184.

63. Shepherd, "Pens and Pen-keepers," 216.

64. Ibid., 218–20.

65. Bigelow, *Jamaica in 1850*, 104.

66. George Forbes to Peter Forbes, January 12, 1811.

67. The Crop Accounts and the Returns of the Registration of Slaves were usually made up by the overseers. Many of these overseers were pen-owners.

68. Boa, "Free Black and Colored Women," 202.

69. *Jamaica House of Assembly Votes* (hereafter *JHAV*) 1843, 113–14.

70. St. Ann Vestry Minutes, 2/9/1, Jamaica Archives.

71. Ibid.

72. *JHAV*, 1816, 114.

73. Ibid., 115.

74. Add. Ms 12,404, fol. 329.

75. *Blue Books of Jamaica (BBJ)*, 1832, C.O. 142/45.

76. "Petition of Certain Proprietors of St. Mary," *JHAV*, 1840.

77. Ibid.

78. Ibid.

79. *JHAV,* November 16, 1843.
80. *Journal of the House of Assembly of Jamaica 1792,* November 23, 1792.
81. *Representation and Petition* (1811), 1–6.
82. *Select Committee on Sugar and Coffee Planting,* 7th Report, Appendix 1.
83. Hall, *Free Jamaica,* 185.
84. John Stewart, *An Account of Jamaica and its Inhabitants* (London, 1808), 128.

5

Coffee and the "Poorer Sort of People" in Jamaica during the Period of African Enslavement

S. D. Smith

Interpretations of the economic development and social evolution of the British Caribbean during the two centuries after 1640 have been dominated by one crop—sugar.[1] Of particular influence has been Eric Williams's "plantation economy model," which stresses, using a rigid enslaver-enslaved dichotomy, the role of the sugar plantation complex in structuring Caribbean society.[2] Important though sugar was, however, cane cultivation was not the only economic activity undertaken in the Caribbean, and it is misleading to equate enslavement solely with the sugar estate. The investigation of the world of slavery outside of sugar has recently been a prominent feature in studies of Jamaica, a colony that experienced a degree of diversification greater than other sugar-producing islands in the English-colonized Caribbean. There has been a revival of interest in the creation of Jamaica's internal market for commodities grown on the enslaved's provision grounds as an example of an area in which the enslaved, rather than the enslavers, were able to make independent decisions over how to allocate a significant part of their labor time. The relationship between sugar and other economic sectors has also been subject to more careful scrutiny, particularly the livestock-rearing or pen-keeping sector, which expanded alongside cane during the eighteenth century in order to supply animate energy to power mill equipment.[3] This essay compares the organization of Jamaican coffee plantations with the island's sugar estates. Additional material from elsewhere within the Caribbean is drawn on to illustrate further the practice of enslavement without sugar.

Characteristics of the Larger Coffee Plantations

Coffee plantations are difficult agricultural units to study by comparison with sugar estates. Surviving source material documenting both sectors is heavily biased toward the representation of large-scale properties owned by absentee proprietors. But whereas absenteeism was commonplace in the sugar sector, coffee growing was carried out largely by resident planters, and the scale of operation was typically smaller. Where financial resources allowed, plantations were able to expand to upward of 500 acres, and a few even attained 1,000 acres. Minimum efficient scale, however, lay under 100 acres, permitting entry to occur at a threshold level of investment that was small in comparison with sugar, though still large relative to that of other staples and even coffee plantations elsewhere in the Caribbean.[4] These aspects of cultivation are illustrated in table 5.1, which is compiled from surveys of Grenada in 1772 and Jamaica in 1832. The coffee sectors of both islands featured large concentrations of small producers cultivating less than 100 acres: Grenada had a majority of growers operating at this scale (52.1 percent), Jamaica a sizeable minority (23.8 percent). As well as featuring a host of small-scale units, 46.3 percent of plantations on Grenada and 29.2 percent on Jamaica fell into the midrange of 101–500 acres. It is striking, however, that Jamaica in 1832 also possessed a sizeable minority (27 percent) of large-scale plantations greater than 500 acres, and these units were probably the largest of their kind in the Caribbean. In Jamaica, the number of larger units may have been a comparatively recent development in the industry, brought on by the effects of depression created by the closure of European markets during the Napoleonic Wars (1803–15).[5]

Jamaica is much the best-documented coffee-producing colony in the British Caribbean, and its early-nineteenth-century coffee boom has been subject to detailed study by Barry Higman and Kathleen Monteith.[6] Even in the case of Jamaica, however, sources detailing medium to large plantations predominate by virtue of the fact that the administration of the properties of absentee owners generated written records. Such evidence reveals that coffee cultivation resembled that of sugar in a number of important respects, even though the industry was located away from the coastal plain where most of the sugar estates were located. Higman's study of estate surveys, maps, and plans reveals that the layout of the larger coffee plantations, like that of the sugar estates, was devised to conform to the ideals of centralization and symmetry. This view receives support from accounts detailing best practice on other islands. Treatises by P. J. Laborie

Table 5.1. Percentage distribution of coffee plantations: Grenada, 1772, and Jamaica, 1832

Acreage	Grenada (%)	Jamaica (%)
<50	28.7	11.8
51–100	23.4	12.0
101–150	14.4	6.3
151–200	12.8	7.6
201–250	5.3	5.9
251–300	3.2	10.2
301–350	4.8	5.5
351–400	1.6	6.1
401–450	2.1	3.5
451–500	2.1	4.1
501–1000	1.6	19.2
>1000	0.0	7.8

Sources: Select Committee on Sugar and Coffee Planting, 7th Report (1848), Appendix 1; P.R.O., C.O. 101/19, "State of the Parishes in Grenada."

and William Lowndes describing cultivation on Saint Domingue and Dominica feature illustrations designed to reinforce how, in Lowndes's words, "neatness in Plantership is, as in everything else, a very desirable object" and how "symmetry and regularity contribute to increase of revenue."[7] Similar descriptions of coffee works appear in Captain Stedman's account of Surinam (now Suriname) and Henry Bolingbroke's description of Demerara. Stedman's account contains a fine illustration intended to demonstrate how a well-designed coffee plantation united elegance, convenience, and safety. The print is accompanied by the following commentary: "It is elegant, as being perfectly regular; convenient, as having everything at hand and under the planter's own inspection; and safe, being surrounded by a broad canal, which by floodgates lets in the water fresh from the river, besides a draw-bridge, which during the night cuts off all communication from without."[8] Bolingbroke likewise noted how on the coffee plantation he visited, everything appeared in perfect order: "the dwelling house—an elegant brick mansion—stood in the midst of a garden, which the occupier took the greatest delight in; even the Negro cottages were built on brick foundations, neatly boarded, and covered in with shingles."[9] Not every setting in which coffee was planted can have proved as conducive to harmonious design as these examples of large-scale planting, and in practice plantations were frequently obliged to deviate from ideal layouts. Symmetry was far easier to achieve in lower-lying cultivating areas than in more mountainous regions, and it was also rare for a complete set of works to be constructed from scratch. As Lowndes himself noted on Dominica, "they have commonly gradually sprung up as the Estate has been advanced in extent of cultivation and revenue."[10] Nevertheless, the language used to describe model examples of coffee planting strongly suggests the extent to which owners of substantial properties aspired to imitate the layout of the sugar estate.

Most large coffee-producing properties in Jamaica further resembled sugar estates by engaging in monoculture. Higman reports that 176 units solely given over to coffee were listed in the 1832 crop accounts. Though it was possible to practice other crop combinations with coffee, multiple units were much less common. Coffee cultivation was combined with jobbing or livestock on just 28 properties and with the production of other staples (primarily pimento) on only a further 15.[11] The data, however, also reveal certain important differences. Higman's sample of maps and plans suggests that the average size of coffee holdings was 699 acres compared with 1,036 acres for sugar estates—a significant differential, even though the sources indicate an increase in the mean size of coffee holding from 400 to 800 acres between 1780 and 1850. According to Higman's analysis of the crop accounts and slave registration returns, in 1832 an average of 128 enslaved people lived on coffee plantations compared with 223 on sugar estates. The slave registrations spanning the years 1829 to 1832 highlight a further difference by suggesting that the sex ratio on coffee plantations, at 101 males per 100 females, was somewhat higher than the figure of 93.9 males per 100 females for the enslaved population as a whole. Also striking is the fact that the major coffee parishes of Port Royal, Manchester, and Saint Elizabeth enjoyed generally higher rates of fertility and lower rates of mortality than other Jamaican parishes.

On the larger coffee holdings, the size of the labor force permitted owners to organize enslaved field workers along the same lines as on sugar estates. The enslaved were organized into first, second, and children's gangs headed by drivers. By working the gang members in unison, planters attempted to economize on supervision costs. Much of the work was allocated by the use of the task system; for example, a gang might be ordered to weed a field in a day.[12] The practical operation of the institutions for regulating labor on large coffee properties may be illustrated with references to two surviving plantation journals: Radnor plantation, which possessed a labor force of 213 enslaved people in 1825, and Oldbury plantation, which in 1832 had a corps of 147 enslaved people rising to 186 by 1834. Radnor in 1807 produced more than 150,000 pounds of coffee, but by 1832 production had fallen to 42,554 pounds while the workforce remained roughly the same. Output on Oldbury varied from 15,000 to 65,000 pounds between 1830 and 1834.[13]

Radnor's and Oldbury's journals both feature the regular combination and division of field workers among the first and second gangs in order to coordinate work effort in picking the coffee crop, weeding the coffee pieces, and clearing, lining, or planting fresh seedlings on new grounds. The regime of task work and the gang system was, however, modified in several important respects. On both plantations every Sunday and every other Saturday was designated "a Negro day" set aside for the growing of provisions and the sale of goods in local markets. A small number of the enslaved were required to attend the works or mind coffee drying on platforms on these days, and on Radnor and Oldbury they were compensated by "taking days" during the week, suggesting an ability on the part of the enslaved to bargain with their enslavers over the loss of customary privileges.[14] The system of "Negro days" not only gave the enslaved the opportunity to cultivate their provision grounds, but during the first year of apprenticeship it also granted the workforce at Oldbury experience of paid labor rates during crop time for hours worked in excess of 40.5 hours per week. During the 1833–34 season, a total of 2,938 barrels of cherry berry were picked on the plantation, but of this total only 1,640 barrels (55.8 percent) were picked by the first or second gangs in normal working time. The remainder was either gathered by hired jobbing gangs or by the plantation's own labor force on a free day. Oldbury's journal records one page of cash expenditure relating to picking during the period November to December 1833 that illustrates the wage payments received for such excess work. Typical entries read: "November 30th [Saturday]: Oldbury Negroes paid 2/6 per barrel for picking 41 barrels; driver and cook paid 2/6 each: total 7 pounds 8 shillings and nine pence. James Green and Lewes paid 2/6 for 2 day's [sic] each: total 10 shillings." In the case of the hire of jobbing gangs, in addition to the owners receiving payment, the enslaved themselves received "allowances to Negroes in lieu of days" if during their hiring they were put to work on a free day.

The plantation journals contain additional details shedding light on the organization of labor on larger units. Variation in the quantity of bushels picked per enslaved worker plus marginal comments in the journal stating on occasion the time that specific gangs finished weeding or picking a coffee piece suggest that the daily task was conditioned by the season and could be light outside peak crop time. The separation of laborers tending the works from field workers also implies that night work, the double or long shifts of the sugar estates, was not normal practice on coffee plantations, though this statement should be qualified by the fact that Lowndes does refer to the running of mill equipment at night on Dominica.[15] The journals also provide limited insights into the working practices of the white plantation employees. Radnor's accounts show that, in addition to the manager, three workers were employed on the plantation: an overseer hired at the rate of 160 pounds per annum (raised to 180 pounds in May 1824), a head bookkeeper at 70 pounds, and a junior bookkeeper at 60 pounds. Turnover in these posts was strikingly high. Between March 1822 and March 1825 the plantation was obliged to make 16 staff changes (13 resulting from personnel leaving voluntarily), in the course of which three separate overseers and 11 bookkeepers were hired. In contrast, at Oldbury the vestry accounts reveal that the manager, John Harrison, lived on the plantation with his wife and five children throughout the period covered by the journal.

The Radnor and Oldbury journals are very similar in layout, and the descriptions of the tasks to which the enslaved were assigned on specific dates closely match each other. On Radnor, a monthly average of 10 enslaved laborers (maximum 23, minimum 4) were employed "about the works" processing cherry berry, while on Oldbury the figures were similar, with an average of 10.6 (maximum 20, minimum 6). In comparison, on Saint Domingue in the later eighteenth century, where the scale of plantations was generally smaller, Gabriel Debien reports that 10 laborers (2 operating the pulping mill, 1 a smaller grating mill, plus 6 and a superintendent to feed the mills and carry out other daily processing tasks) was the norm on the works, suggesting that this was a fixed cost of production.[16]

Surviving plantation survey maps and plans indicate that coffee was processed on larger Jamaican plantations in the same manner as on Radnor and Oldbury. Laborie's treatise describes how a plantation's coffee works processed coffee using the "parchment method," whereby the coffee bean's outer covering was removed early in the processing cycle by a mill.[17] The parchment method required a mill house in which planters installed a grating or pulping mill and a winnowing or peeling machine. Adjacent to the mills were large stone cisterns for soaking the berries and level drying platforms called "barbecues." Processed beans or semiprocessed beans in the husk were placed in a nearby coffee store to await transportation to market. The layout of the works and the design of mill equipment remained remarkably consistent during the eighteenth and nineteenth centuries, but this is not to say that coffee plantations were technologically stagnant. During the first half of the nineteenth century, iron replaced wood as the main construction material employed in mill equipment, and steam power was applied successfully to processing techniques. Multiple pulpers were also developed that combined several processing functions, including the separation of skin and berry. On some plantations, kiln drying replaced sunlight and the labor-intensive barbecues. In essence, however, coffee cultivation was characterized by simple technologies that were adaptable to both large- and smaller-scale production. It is notable that even though the form of energy input and the material of construction had both altered radically, the pulpers advertised for sale in 1914 closely resembled those pictured by Lowndes and Laborie more than a century previously.

Throughout the period of African enslavement, nearly all of the capital equipment used in coffee production was imported, as in the case of sugar, though in both sectors machinery was maintained by local millwrights. During Jamaica's coffee boom, a number of British firms were established to supply plantations with machinery, including the Aberdeen concern of William McKinnon and Company, which was founded in 1798 during the Jamaican coffee boom. By the later nineteenth century, McKinnon and Company were exporting coffee-, cacao-, rubber-, and sugar-processing machinery throughout the British empire.[18]

Jamaican inventories drawn up during the 1820s suggest that the capital outlay in processing facilities ran between 1,000 pounds and 1,200 pounds for a medium-sized concern.[19] This sum was less than the investment in boiling houses and crushing mills required on sugar estates and reflected the reduced energy input into milling equipment. Nevertheless, though relatively cheap and simple to install and operate, the technology of coffee production generated an organizational structure similar to that of sugar production. In comparison with staple cultivation elsewhere in the Americas, particularly tobacco, coffee plantations were sizeable, even if their extent could not match that of sugar plantations. The scale of coffee plantations reflected the fact that cultivation and processing were combined on a centralized site. Despite a smaller absolute scale of operation, the level of investment involved encouraged mill owners in both the coffee and sugar sectors to integrate backward in order to regulate raw material inputs and to coordinate labor supplies, thereby ensuring that throughput was maximized through the processing plant.

A major difference existed, however, between coffee berries and sugarcane. While both staples had to be processed quickly after harvest to prevent fermentation setting in, in the case of coffee it was possible to interrupt curing after the pulping stage was complete. Evidence that planters took advantage of the possibility of delay is provided by Jamaican estate inventories, which frequently refer to coffee appraised by valuers "in the husk" awaiting the removal of its parchment covering by winnowing. Storing coffee in this state reduced labor requirements since it permitted the reallocation of enslaved laborers from the field to the works as the harvest neared its end.[20]

Characteristics of the Smaller Coffee Plantations

The larger plantations provide most of the material that informs historical understanding of how coffee plantations operated in Jamaica by dominating the crop accounts and contemporary surveys of industry. But these units were not representative of the coffee sector as a whole. In 1799, for example, a contemporary report stated that only 8.9 percent of Jamaica's 519 monoculture coffee plantations were owned by absentees.[21] Another measure of comprehensiveness is provided by export data. In 1814, the crop accounts record that only 3.5 million pounds of coffee were consigned to Great Britain or sent to Kingston for sale, compared with total exports of 34 million pounds. Even if the additional 0.9 million pounds of coffee that were picked and processed but not yet marketed are added to the total, the 98 agricultural units listed in this source account for only 13 percent of exports.[22] During the 1820s, the ratio of production recorded in the crop accounts to total exports climbed until, by the period 1830 to 1835, it consistently exceeded 25 percent. Moreover, surveys of plantations carried out in 1808 and 1832 report that the proportion of plantations owned by absentees had risen to 21.3 percent and 25 percent, respectively.[23] The information presented in the previous section, therefore, is most applicable to the coffee sector as a whole during the last years of enslavement and even then only to about a quarter of the properties. The later period was a difficult one for coffee. Napoleon's Continental System (1806–12) cut Jamaican planters off from European markets, and in the aftermath of the Napoleonic Wars the industry faced fierce competition from rival Caribbean producers. From the 1830s, dwindling tariff protection caused further problems. An important reason for the improved coverage of the crop accounts stems simply from the number of plantations going into liquidation. Bankruptcy led both to the generation of accounts by estate administrators and to the consolidation of holdings into larger units held by absentee owners. The most detailed and accurate information about coffee growing, therefore, becomes available only after Jamaican coffee growing had reached its zenith and entered a period of decline.

In view of the preceding discussion, there are grounds for questioning whether the organization of coffee plantations during the decades of prosperity after 1790 was the same as that observed at a later stage of the sector's history. In consequence, it is dangerous to assume that the details of the technology of coffee cultivation and processing outlined in the previous section set inflexible parameters within which all plantations large and small were obliged to operate. To obtain more insights into coffee cultivation on smaller properties run by resident owners before decline set in, it is necessary to turn to the inventories of deceased planters. A sample of 49 inventories drawn up between 1811 and 1814 has been compiled for this purpose. Estates left by persons engaged in coffee planting may be easily identified during these years because of the effects of Napoleon's continental blockade, which shut off valuable European markets from Jamaican producers and caused the amount of coffee remaining "on hand" at the end of the crop year to mount up from season to season. Such surplus stocks were valued as assets by the executors and overseers charged with appraising a decedent's moveable property and, therefore, feature prominently in the inventories. These records may be used to build up a picture of coffee cultivators who had been in business during the years leading up to the Napoleonic Wars but who died during the blockade.

In table 5.2, the distribution of the enslaved population listed in the inventories has been compared with listings in the *Jamaica Almanack* for 1818, the 1832 Select Committee report, and the earlier 1772 survey of Grenada. Though the number of Jamaican holdings that possessed 100 enslaved people was greater than on other Caribbean islands, these sources emphasize the small-scale nature of coffee cultivation even more clearly than the acreage accounts considered above.[24] The distribution of slaveholding preserved in the inventories is virtually the same as that of the other Jamaican accounts, indicating that the sample is an unbiased one. It is striking, however, that the average number of enslaved laborers in the sample is higher than that suggested by the 1832 survey, reflecting the fact that the sample is based on all inventories listing significant amounts of coffee on hand or coffee-processing equipment, including mixed coffee and livestock properties. Since the numbers of enslaved laborers employed on livestock pens was normally greater than on coffee monoculture, the average is boosted.[25] The sample confirms several of the features of coffee growing suggested by the records of larger plantations, but it also points to some notable differences.

Table 5.2. Plantation size by slaveholding: Jamaica, 1811–32, and Grenada, 1772

Number of slaves	Jamaica 1811–14		Jamaica 1818		Jamaica 1832		Grenada 1772	
0–50	25	(51.0%)	145	(47.9%)	267	(58.7%)	136	(76.8%)
51–100	11	(22.5%)	97	(32.0%)	112	(24.6%)	32	(18.1%)
101–200	8	(16.3%)	47	(15.5%)	66	(14.5%)	8	(4.5%)
201–300	3	(6.1%)	12	(4.0%)	7	(1.5%)	1	(0.6%)
>300	2	(4.1%)	2	(0.7%)	3	(0.7%)	0	
mean	81		—		59		41	

Sources: Jamaica Archives, Inventories, 1B/11/3 libers 118, 119, 121, 122, 123, 124, 126, 127; Kathleen E. A. Monteith, "The Coffee Industry in Jamaica, 1790–1850," unpub. (M. Phil. thesis University of the West Indies, Mona Campus, Jamaica, 1991), 48; P.R.O., C.O. 101/19, "State of the Parishes of Grenada."

The majority of plantations in the sample were small and held less than 50 enslaved workers, with a quarter of the properties possessing fewer than 25 hands. Only a minority of the enslaved labor force, however, lived on the smallest units: 10 percent of the enslaved were located on plantations with under 50 workers and 4.5 percent on properties numbering less than 25 workers. Most of the enslaved were situated on medium-sized plantations, as only 44 percent of laborers lived on units with a workforce larger than 149 and only 35.9 percent on estates with more than 199 hands. These findings have implications for the prevalence of the gang system. The division of the workforce into three large teams each headed by an overseer, as practiced on the sugar estates, is unlikely to have been the experience of many of the enslaved living on coffee plantations. In the previous section, it was suggested that even on the largest plantations the system of close supervision of laborers organized into gangs was modified in important respects by assigning to the enslaved a specific task such as weeding or planting, after which they were free to dispose of their remaining time. On the smaller plantations, these tendencies were probably more marked and the opportunities for individual work specified on a task basis correspondingly greater.

Irrespective of the size of the unit, however, the methods employed at crop time to harvest cherry berry contained a strong element of individual task work. Coffee berries were typically picked by enslaved workers equipped with canvas bags hung around their necks and emptied into a larger basket. A daily target was set, which was normally around three bushels or a barrel, but this task, as Laborie points out, was abated if the weather was poor or ripe berries scarce.

There is evidence that planters experimented with incentive schemes as well as relying on the threat of coercion in order to secure a steady flow of ripe berries of requisite quality to the processing works. Bryan Edwards, for example, cautioned against reliance on the threat of punishment, noting that "it is not provident to urge him on too fast, as probably a great deal of unripe fruit will in that case be mixed in with the ripe."[26] Picking coffee, therefore, appears to have been suited to individual task work where performance could be monitored at the central coffee works by weighing the berries and inspecting them for quality. Two possible departures from this practice, however, should be noted. First, Laborie records how a local planter "being short of Negroes, offered a gratuity for each second barrel; two Negroes generally completed it, and shared the gratuity." In this account the initiative for teaming field workers in this way appears to have come from the enslaved themselves. Second, Laborie also warns how "the Negroes, with a view to get more quickly over the work, are apt to take the branch in their hands, and to strip the fruit at once into their baskets; but that must be carefully prevented, because it tears the bark and strips off the leaves." Effective protection of coffee trees from damage caused by careless picking may have required the provision of supervisors and encouraged planters, where possible, to use a form of gang system. The need was probably greater on larger properties, where it was harder to hold a specific worker to account for the state of a given cluster of trees.[27] Notwithstanding these qualifications, it is apparent that the rigors of working in line under close supervision were considerably less on coffee plantations than was the case on the sugar estates during crop time, which was the busiest period in the case of both staples.

Another important difference between large and small plantations appears in their respective sex ratios. The sample reveals that there were on average 108 males per 100 females on small coffee plantations, a figure that differs from that of 101 males to 100 females on the larger coffee properties recorded in the slave registration documents between 1829 and 1832. Inclusion of smaller properties in the analysis in consequence accentuates the differences between the demographic profile of coffee labor forces and the African Caribbean population as a whole suggested by examination of the larger units. Moreover, it is difficult to attribute this difference to the influence of the inclusion of livestock properties since Higman's data for the years 1829 to 1832 suggest that the sex ratios on properties combining coffee and livestock or that engaged in livestock only were 94.1:100 (males to females) and 96.7:100, respectively.[28] The reduced sex ratio reported in the 1830s by Higman may, however, be the result of the consolidation of units after 1815, which resulted in an increase in the mean size of plantations and a skew in the distribution toward larger units.

Can the reasons for the preponderance of males on smaller units be located in the sexual division of labor practiced on coffee plantations? It is difficult to explore such an hypothesis because the evidence detailing the allocation of labor by gender for all crops is scanty, and data for coffee are currently only available in the form of five occupational listings, each of which describes larger Jamaican properties (table 5.3). Despite considerable variation across these accounts, the documents share several common features. On each property, women formed in excess of 50 percent of the field laborers, irrespective of the overall sex ratio. Moreover, the percentage of females of working age employed in the field consistently exceeded that of males, and in no case did it fall below 60 percent. Whereas field work was carried out by both sexes but featured a disproportionate amount of female participation, the work of carpenters, sawyers, masons, and stockkeepers was exclusively carried out by male enslaved workers. Enslaved females, in contrast, dominated domestic and hospital work. All these features are consistent with the limited number of studies on the gender division of labor practiced on Jamaican sugar estates and also the mainland tobacco and rice plantations in the Chesapeake and in South Carolina. Planters in general appear to have utilized female labor disproportionately for field work but confined female skilled labor to lowly regarded domestic service or hospital work.[29] The principal difference between the occupational listings of coffee and sugar lies in the comparatively narrow range of skilled employments practiced on the plantation, resulting in a less hierarchical and more standardized occupational structure.[30] This very flexibility is paradoxical since the relative absence of skill differentials should have raised demand for female labor. Indeed, across the five properties surveyed in table 5.3, the sex ratio was approximately 100 males to 100 females, albeit with a high degree of variance about the mean.

Did the male bias featured on the smaller properties reflect a markedly divergent occupational structure to that of the larger plantations? In the absence of firm evidence it is impossible to answer this question definitively, but it is worth noting that several of the male employments were required early in a plantation's working life, particularly woodcutters who cleared the site, and it was usual for planters starting up a coffee unit to

Table 5.3a. Occupational structure on five large Jamaican plantations, 1812–25

Occupation		Lawrie Estate 1812	Israel Estate 1812	Maryland 1822	Radnor 1825	Oldbury 1832
Field	males	42	22[a]	79	59	36
	females	53	38[b]	78	70	50
Watchmen/pens	males	3	9	22	11	11[f]
	females	0	1	8	0	0
Artisan	males	10	17[c]	22	10	9[g]
	females	0	0	0	0	0
Hospital	males	0	0	0	1	0
	females	2	2	6	4	4
House	males	1	2	4	1	4
	females	7	7	11	6	7
Invalids/yaws	males	0	6[d]	11	10	0
	females	2	4	28	16	4
Children		32	30	62	25	18
Runaways	males	1	2	0	0	2
	females	1	0	0	0	0
Not specified and other		15	4[e]	0	0	1[h]
Total		169	142	269	213	147

a. includes 3 members of the small gang
b. includes 12 members of the small gang
c. includes 6 field and sawyers combined
d. includes 2 children also enumerated below
e. includes 3 tenders of barbecues, 1 male and 2 female
f. includes 1 tender of barbecue
g. includes 7 combined field
h. includes 1 male tender of barbecue.

Table 5.3b. Summary

	Lawrie	Israel	Maryland	Radnor	Oldbury
Sex Ratio (M/F)	0.88	1.09	1.05	0.96	0.97
% field female	56	63	50	54	58
% female field	82	70	60	73	77
% male field	74	37	57	64	57

Sources: Jamaica Archives, Inventories, 1B/11/3 libers 119, 121; B. W. Higman, *Slave Population and Economy in Jamaica, 1807–1834* (Cambridge: Cambridge University Press, 1976), 197; National Library of Jamaica MS 180, Radnor Plantation journal, fol. 104; Devon Record Office, John Harrison Account Book, 49/14, Oldbury Plantation journal.

begin with a mostly male workforce.[31] It is possible that some of the inventories in the sample of small properties are embryonic plantations that reflect this early bias. Moreover, fully fledged crop units would also tend to have more men than women working on the plantation because the work of the craftsmen (such as masons preparing the drying barbecues and the stones required for foundations and roads) was necessary whatever the size of the unit. Smaller properties, however, usually lacked great houses and thus generated less employment for exclusively female labor.

The inventories do not provide any direct indication of the age of the enslaved workers enumerated in them, but they do normally assign a separate valuation to each. Enslaved infants, young children, people with disabilities, runaways, and aged men and aged women were capable of making only a minimal contribution to plantation output, yet, with the exception of runaways, their owners were obliged to maintain them and, therefore, the values assigned to this collective group were low and often zero. Higman has shown how age was a prime determinant of the value attached to the enslaved and how the age-value profile of the enslaved follows an almost universal bell-shaped curve, as value rose steadily from about age 15 to peak at the age of 20, where it remained steady before falling off sharply after 40 to 45 years.[32] In table 5.4, the distribution of valuations of enslaved people by the overseers drawing up the inventories is compared with the distribution of the enslaved laborers by age within three coffee parishes and on the two best-documented large Jamaican plantations. It is striking that between 35 percent and 46 percent of enslaved people living in the coffee parishes or the selected plantations were either under 10 years or over 40 years of age. This suggestion of a high dependency burden is reinforced by the sample's finding that 30 percent of enslaved people were valued at under 50 pounds, while only 43.6 percent were valued at more than 100 pounds as prime field hands.

The data suggest that Britain's ending of the legal transatlantic trade in African captives in 1807 made it increasingly difficult for owners to augment the size of their workforces by purchase. Reports of labor scarcity became prevalent during the 1820s. John Wemyss, the manager of Hermitage plantation in Saint Elizabeth's parish, for example, wrote in 1822 how "there is great difficulty now in purchasing any Negroes since the abolition of the slave trade and if there are any Negroes for sale many applications are prior made to obtain a preference of purchase and cash or a good Bill of Exchange given for the payment."[33] The phenomenon described here has been studied in depth by Higman, who details how plantation owners responded by starting enslaved workers in the field at younger ages and by keeping them there for more of their lives.

A number of contemporary observers drew connections between the scale of coffee cultivation and the low social status of coffee planters. Indeed, coffee planting on Jamaica was originally advocated in order to stem the exodus of white settlers from the island in the wake of the sugar revolution. A petition to the British Parliament submitted in 1731 argued that coffee was well suited to "the poorer sort of people, whose stocks and plantations are small." The committee established to look into the matter also heard evidence the following year that coffee might prove "a means to bring in the poorer sort of people there, which is very much wanted."[34] The sample of inventories is sufficiently large to examine the status of planters. Whereas contemporaries stressed the comparative poverty of the coffee planters, the data suggest that the social profile of the proprietors was so diverse that it is not possible to define a typical plantation owner.

Coffee cultivation was not necessarily the sole activity and may not even have been the primary source of income of the deceased owner. The sample lists three plantations held by carpenters comprising 52, 53, and 25 enslaved laborers respectively, plus one coppersmith who owned a plantation with 20 enslaved laborers. There were also two overseers in the sample, one with 5 and one with 13 enslaved laborers who were employed on coffee properties situated close to their own. Three owners drawn from the ranks of the professions practiced coffee growing as a supplementary activity. Jacob Stamp, a Kingston merchant, owned a large property numbering 236 enslaved people, while John Powell Reynalls, "Practitioner in Physic and Surgery" at Spanish Town, owned Glengoff coffee plantation

Table 5.4. Distribution of enslaved people by value and by age: Jamaica, 1811–23

Range (£)	Sample 1811–14 (%)	Range (years)	Port Royal 1817 (%)	Manchester 1817 (%)	Saint Elizabeth 1817 (%)	Maryland 1822 (%)	Hermitage 1823 (%)
<50	30.3	<19	37.7	37.0	39.1	41.0	38.3
51–100	26.1	20–44	51.9	50.6	43.6	31.0	55.0
>101	43.6	>45	10.4	12.4	17.3	28.0	6.7
		<10	22.9	23.4	22.3	18.6	15.0
mean	£92.60	>40	17.1	19.4	24.0	21.8	20.0

Sources: Jamaica Archives, Inventories, 1B/11/3 libers 118, 119, 121, 122, 123, 124, 126, 127; B. W. Higman, *Slave Population and Economy in Jamaica, 1807–34* (Cambridge: Cambridge University Press, 1976), 260–261, 263; National Library of Jamaica, MS 250, Hermitage Plantation inventory.

and 100 enslaved people. Robert Barker Wray of Saint George's parish was also a doctor and at the time of his death owned a property with 34 enslaved people. In addition to these specified occupations, other plantation owners were engaged in raising livestock.[35] It was usual for most properties to possess some stock, since mules were the principal means of transporting coffee down from the hills to the wharves for shipment or to power the mill equipment where water or wind power was impractical. Wealthier planters often owned horses for use with a chaise, while a few kept fillies for racing.

In the sample as a whole, the average value of inventoried stock held at the time of death was 608 pounds, and the ratio of stock to slaves was 7.6 pounds worth of stock per enslaved worker. A total of 30 of the 49 inventories possessed a stock–to–enslaved worker ratio of less than or equal to 5 pounds, while 14 inventories fell into the range of greater than 5 pounds but less than or equal to 10 pounds, and 5 inventories featured higher ratios, indicating that raising livestock formed a major source of the decedent's income. One of the largest stock owners was the physician John Reynalls.

Summing up, though coffee cultivation appears to have been the dominant activity of the greater part of owners in this sample, at least 13 of the owners (26.5 percent) enjoyed other substantial sources of income. A further 10 coffee growers (20.4 percent) derived significant income supplements from other activities. Seven planters enjoyed high enough ratios of stock to enslaved worker to suggest that they sold amounts of livestock sufficient to boost their incomes from growing coffee, while on five properties (including one pen-keeper and one carpenter) the inventories enumerate significant quantities of ginger, pimento, and logwood in addition to coffee stocks lying on hand.

The sample reveals that coffee plantation owners were neither all male nor all white, though the great majority of planters fell into these categories. Two female owners are listed: Martha Cole, a widow with a plantation of 27 enslaved laborers in the parish of Saint Ann, and Eleanor Smith, whose inventory describes her as a "gentlewoman" owning a plantation with 39 enslaved people in the parish of Vere.[36] Two "free men of color" also appear in the sample: James McLean of Clarendon, who owned 25 enslaved people, and Thomas Bonner of Saint Catherine's, who owned 10 enslaved people. Bonner's estate was valued at 828 pounds, which was the smallest in the sample. McLean's estate was more substantial and was valued at 3,740 pounds, a rating that exceeded the old limit of 2,000 pounds placed on the transfer of property between free people of color imposed by the Jamaican Inheritance Law of 1762 but which had been rescinded in 1813.[37]

Ownership details and total wealth holding complete the impression of the social composition of planters available in the inventories. Joint ownership of coffee properties was very unusual. The sample records only two examples, and in one of these cases, that of Andrew Anderson of Saint Ann's parish, the joint owner was a son with a sixth share. Ownership of multiple properties was also rare, and only three examples are recorded. John Longlands of Saint Elizabeth's parish owned Hermitage Pen (209 enslaved people), Roseberry Coffee Plantation (47 enslaved people), and (jointly with James Miller) Malpern Hill Coffee Plantation (116 enslaved people). Robert Hamilton of Saint Andrew's parish owned four properties, but two were very small: Clifton Mount (185 enslaved people), Hamilton Estate (97 enslaved people), Vineyard Pen (26 enslaved people), and Enfield Hall (7 enslaved people). The other joint owner was Alexander Ector, also of Saint Andrew's, who owned the medium-sized properties of Prospect Hill (62 enslaved people) and Charlton Pen (39 enslaved people). Over 90 percent of the plantations in the sample, therefore, were held by single owners owning one property.

Inventories were compiled primarily as a record of the possessions of persons at the time of death, yet ironically they are deficient as indicators of wealth. The appraisers swore to a declaration that the accounts submitted amounted to an exact "inventory and appraisement of all and singular the goods and chattels and credits which were of [name] late of [parish] deceased." In nearly all of the inventories collected, the appraisers discharged their obligation to the letter and, therefore, failed to record either the value of real estate held by the testator or the value of the debts owed by the decedent.[38] The level of detail also varied considerably as some inventories itemized all possessions of value while others grouped articles together, rendering it difficult to analyze trends in the possession of specific household goods or tools. It is also likely that the level of inventoried wealth is understated owing to the fact that the sample spans a period of depression in the industry, though the distribution in the pattern of wealth holding should not be distorted by the circumstance.[39]

In spite of these deficiencies, some meaningful inferences may still be drawn from the data. Table 5.5 illustrates the breakdown of wealth holding among coffee planters. The mean value of inventoried wealth in the sample was 10,678 pounds, but the dispersion around the mean was considerable. The standard deviation was 11,760 pounds, and the sample rates from an estate rated at 828 pounds to a maximum value of 60,864 pounds. Nevertheless, despite the high level of variance, only 4 inventories were appraised at less than 2,000 pounds and only 4 at more than 25,000 pounds, whereas 35 of the estates fell into the range of 2,001 to 15,000 pounds, with 15 worth between 2,001 and 5,000 pounds and 12 worth between 5,001 and 10,000 pounds. The distribution of wealth was influenced strongly by the pattern of enslaving, since enslaved people accounted for 68.3 percent of property recorded in the inventories. During peacetime conditions (when European markets were open to trade), it is probable that the importance of the enslaved as a component of wealth was even greater due to a reduction in the amount of coffee lying unsold. In general, the smallest planters held the greatest proportion of their wealth in the form of slaves. Decedents worth less than 10,000 pounds held only 24.5 to 27 percent of their wealth in nonhuman form, compared to the 35.4 to 38.4 percent characteristic of the larger inventories.

The importance of enslaving as a component of inventoried wealth among coffee planters was not as great as that of the owners of Jamaica's sugar estates, who held 81.6 percent of their wealth in this form during the years 1771 to 1775. Nevertheless, even the smaller coffee planters held a greater proportion of their wealth in chattel than other regions of British colonial America. In comparison, the value of enslaved workers (and servants' contracts) in the southern continental colonies amounted to 62.1 percent of physical wealth excluding real estate, and the proportion across the 13 continental colonies as a whole was 43.5 percent.[40]

While only four inventories mentioned cash, credits were owing to 29 of the estates; after enslaved workers, these formed the next most valuable component in the inventories. Financial assets most commonly consisted of loans, book debts, and judgments for the recovery of debts, though balances in the hands of merchants for crop sales and annuities are also mentioned. The larger planters held between 13.8 percent and 21.6 percent of their enumerated wealth in this form, whereas the smaller planters held only around 11 percent. Larger estates also tended to have proportionately more livestock, but they held a smaller share of their wealth in the form of household goods. This latter tendency reflects the fact that the category includes essential tools and equipment, which all producers were obliged to own as well, as consumer durables and furniture. Of the 49 inventories, 11 explicitly mentioned coffee-processing equipment: fanning mills ranging in value from 10 to 40 pounds appeared eight times; sieves from 10 to 40 shillings are listed four times, pulping mills appraised at between 5 and 18 pounds appeared three times. These items were all employed in the parchment method of processing coffee, and their presence

Table 5.5. Major components of inventoried wealth of Jamaican coffee planters, 1811–15 (currency: £140 Jamaica equivalent to £100 sterling)

Range (£)	N	Mean (£)	Slaves (%)	Stock (%)	Goods (%)[a]	Credits (%)	Coffee (%)
Sample	49	10,678	68.3	5.7	2.4	15.7	7.3
<5000	19	2,812	75.5	3.1	2.9	11.0	6.1
5001–10,000	12	6,839	73.0	3.9	3.9	11.3	6.6
10,001–20,000	12	14,613	64.6	7.3	1.9	21.6	5.8
>20,001	6	35,396	67.8	5.7	2.1	13.8	9.1
>20,001[b]	5	33,210	61.6	5.1	2.0	17.6	11.7

Source: Jamaica Archives, Inventories, 1B/11/3 libers 118, 119, 121, 122, 123, 124, 126, 127.
a. Includes furniture, consumer durables, tools and equipment.

b. Excludes one large estate where slaves account for 90 percent of inventoried wealth.

in some of the smallest as well as largest estates suggests that the alternative method of processing coffee "in the pulp" was not in widespread use. Jamaican planters large and small preferred to invest in mill equipment in order to process coffee more quickly and to reduce the drying times on barbecues.[41]

At the top end of the distribution, the dozen inventories listing estates valued at over 15,000 pounds sterling exclusive of real estate indicate that the top quartile of coffee planters included individuals who could count themselves among Jamaica's white social elite. The nature of some of the household possessions of this group points to a degree of gentility, since the larger estates were more likely to have silver plate, chinaware, and chaises listed separately. Books also appear in some of the estates, and holdings could be considerable. William Lawrie's estate was valued at 11,161 pounds and included a library of 100 individually named volumes. Nonetheless, a love of reading was not confined to the elite, as the inventories of Robert Farquarson and Thomas Daly reveal. Farquarson left an estate worth 3,332 pounds and owned 30 pounds worth of books, while Daly left 3,914 pounds of moveable goods at the time of his death and possessed 2 pounds worth of books and a spyglass worth 2 pounds 10 shillings. The existence of an upper echelon of cultivators is reinforced by Monteith's identification of 24 coffee planters who served as members of the Jamaica House of Assembly between 1772 and 1852.[42] Such conspicuous individuals, however, were not typical of the coffee growers as a whole. The majority of coffee planters consisted of a diverse array of whites of middling to lower status, supplemented by a few free men of color.

A final piece of information that can be readily extracted from the inventories is the parish of residence of the decedent, which is stated in 43 of the 49 cases. The parish distribution of the sample can be compared with the location of plantations listed in two contemporary reports drawn up in 1799 and 1836 and also with the list of plantations appearing in the crop accounts.[43] No less than 14 parishes appear in the sample, which testifies to its broad geographical coverage. Both it and the surveys of 1799 and 1836 confirm that coffee growing was concentrated in two regional clusters. The first concentration embraced the eastern and relatively more mountainous parishes of Port Royal, Saint Andrew, Saint David, Saint Thomas-in-the-East, and Saint George. The second cluster covered the western and relatively lower-lying parishes of Vere, Saint Elizabeth, and Clarendon (out of parts of which the parish of Manchester was created in 1815) and extended northward into the parishes of Trelawny and Saint Ann. According to the 1799 survey, 40.9 percent of Jamaica's coffee plantations were located in the mountainous cluster and 25.5 percent in the lower-lying parishes, whereas by 1836 the shares had altered to 35.1 percent and 42.5 percent, respectively. The sample falls between these benchmarks, with 46.5 percent of inventories falling into the mountainous region and 44.2 percent falling into the low-lying cluster.

In contrast, the crop accounts overstate the share of the mountainous parishes where premium coffee was grown. The accounts for 1800 and 1815 have 56 percent and 61.6 percent of plantations in the mountainous group, but only 24 percent and 10.8 percent in the low-lying cluster. In the crop accounts for 1835, the Blue Mountains' share at 51 percent is still too high, but the Manchester parishes' share of 43.5 percent is in line with the other sources. Since coffee produced from the Blue Mountain region fetched a premium in the market, estimates of the value of output per enslaved worker could be biased upward if properties listed in the crop accounts are not weighted in line with the relative importance of each region. A further interesting feature of the sample is the location of four properties (9.3 percent of inventories) in the westerly parishes of Westmoreland and Hanover, a region that featured a concentration of sugar estates. These four plantations ranged in size from 46 to 123 enslaved laborers and included one pen-keeper. While their close proximity to cane cultivation does not question the overall conclusion that coffee and sugar were geographically separated crops, it does indicate that the location of just one property in this area in the 1832 crop accounts forms another source of bias contained within this set of records.

Conclusion

Coffee became a significant export crop in Jamaica during the 1790s, relatively late in the history of enslavement, and its cultivation was for the main part concentrated in areas remote from sugarcane. Despite physical separation, the organization of coffee plantations paralleled that of the sugar estate in a number of important aspects. The lower setup costs and smaller scale of the majority of coffee plantations relative to sugar should not be permitted to disguise the fact that both staples combined growing and processing in a centralized location even on the smallest identifiable units surveyed. In consequence, the typical coffee plantation in Jamaica was very far removed from the family holding that the original promoters of coffee cultivation envisaged in their submissions to the British Parliament in 1731 and 1732. The example of Jamaica's coffee planters, therefore, provides a measure of support for Williams's sugar-orientated model of Caribbean development during the two centuries after 1640.

Sugar's influence on coffee is most apparent in the case of the largest crop units. Literature describing best practices on the coffee-producing islands of Saint Domingue and Dominica illustrates how planters drew on concepts familiar to the sugar estate in an attempt to obtain maximum returns from coffee cultivation. The journals and occupational listings for surviving plantations reinforce this impression by providing details of labor management on coffee plantations that feature extensive use of the gang system and task work. In the case of the smaller holdings, the profile of cultivators provides further evidence for the existence of links between the two crops since a significant proportion of coffee planters consisted of carpenters, coppersmiths, doctors, merchants, and stock rearers. The followers of these occupations were likely to derive income from servicing the dominant staple, and these earnings probably funded their initial investment in coffee. Moreover, as Monteith points out, the owners of coffee plantations were not precluded from supplying managerial services to the absentee proprietors of sugar estates, and a number of coffee cultivators who sat in the Jamaica Assembly performed this function.[44]

Notwithstanding the fact that the culture of coffee shared common features with that of sugar, it is clear that the concept of a single type of plantation complex modeled on sugar cannot be applied crudely to coffee. On smaller crop units the conventional pattern of labor organization derived from sugar was inappropriate in view of the small labor forces. Even on the larger plantations, the dichotomy of white enslaver and black enslaved was modified in important respects through the granting of "Negro days," the negotiation of payment for additional work during leisure time, and modifications in the intensity of the work regime in line with the season. It is also striking that the four coffee planters in closest proximity to the sugar estates (in Westmoreland and Hanover) did not rank among the largest coffee units and therefore would have stood out from their neighbors.

Demographically, the parishes into which the bulk of the coffee plantations were concentrated presented the combination of a sex ratio skewed toward males and a high fertility rate. The socially accepted image of coffee farming being carried on by poor white families is not supported by the sample data. The patterns of ownership featured great diversity, and a small number of plantations were owned by free coloreds and women. The study of coffee plantations, therefore, provides further confirmation that the institution of plantation enslavement possessed complex and diverse aspects and that plantation economy based on involuntary servitude was capable of subtle adaptations.

Notes

1. Since this essay was written and first published in *Plantation Society in the Americas* 5 (1998): 227–53, a new study of Jamaica's colonial coffee plantations has been published: James A. Delle, *An Archaeology of Social Space: Analyzing Coffee Plantations in Jamaica's Blue Mountains* (New York and London: Plenum Press, 1998). In his study, Delle develops Barry Higman's pioneering geographical and archaeological analysis of Jamaica's plantations. Delle's analysis of coffee plantations prior to abolition, however, is primarily concerned with the larger properties that generated written evidence in the form of journals and cartographic records. I believe, therefore, that the reprinting of the material in this essay (with only minor changes) is justified because, in the case of coffee plantations, archaeology has not yet overcome the bias inherent in the creation and survival of written records. Earlier versions of this essay were presented at the LSE Business History Unit seminar and at the 24th Conference of the Association of Caribbean Historians in Martinique. I am grateful for the comments of participants on both occasions. The essay draws on research carried out with the aid of a British Academy Small Personal Research Grant (BA-AN 1392/APN 2170). To Verene Shepherd is due a special debt of thanks for her gracious assistance and warm hospitality during a research trip to Jamaica. Monetary values are given in Jamaican currency unless otherwise stated (£1.4 Jamaican equaled £1 sterling).

2. Eric Williams, *Capitalism and Slavery* (London: Andre Deutsch, 1964), 65–97; Hilary McD. Beckles, "The Williams Effect: Eric Williams' *Capitalism and*

Slavery and the Growth of West Indian Political Economy," in *British Capitalism and Caribbean Slavery: The Legacy of Eric Williams,* ed. Barbara L. Solow and Stanley L. Engerman (Cambridge: Cambridge University Press, 1987), 303–12; George L. Beckford, *Persistent Poverty: Undevelopment in Plantation Economies of the Third World* (New York: Oxford University Press, 1972).

3. See, for example, S. W. Mintz and Douglas Hall, "The Origins of the Jamaican Internal Marketing System," *Yale University Publications in Anthropology* 57 (1960); Richard B. Sheridan "From Chattel to Wage Slavery in Jamaica, 1740–1860," *Slavery and Abolition* 14 (1993); Verene A. Shepherd, "Livestock and Sugar: Aspects of Jamaica's Agricultural Development from the Late Seventeenth to the Early Nineteenth Century," *Historical Journal* 34 (1991); Verene A. Shepherd, "Alternative Husbandry: Slaves and Free Laborers on Livestock Farms in Jamaica in the Eighteenth and Nineteenth Centuries," *Slavery and Abolition* 14 (1993).

4. It is important to bear in mind, however, that only a proportion of the acreage of a plantation was kept in coffee at one time. For estimates of the acreage under coffee, see B. W. Higman, "Jamaican Coffee Plantations, 1780–1860: A Cartographic Analysis," *Caribbean Geography* 2 (1986): 82–83; S. D. Smith, "Sugar's Poor Relation: Coffee Planting in the British West Indies, 1721–1833," *Slavery and Abolition* 19 (1998): 76–77.

5. Higman, "Jamaican Coffee Plantations," 75–78. For comparison, in 1775, when coffee and cocoa were the main crops being raised on the island, 34 percent of the concessions granted on Saint Lucia were less than 62 acres and 69 percent under 190 acres, with only 14 percent greater than 316 acres. See J. Megemont, "Sainte Lucie de 1763 à 1789"(Ph.D. dissertation, no university accreditation, n.d.), University of York copy, 40, 46. The only regions to rival the largest Jamaican coffee plantations were the mainland Dutch colonies of Surinam and Essequibo-Demerara, where geographical conditions were different.

6. Higman, "Jamaican Coffee Plantations"; B. W. Higman, *Slave Population and Economy in Jamaica, 1807–1834* (Cambridge: Cambridge University Press, 1976), 9–29, 73–83, 103–23, 197–226; B. W. Higman, *Jamaica Surveyed: Plantation Maps and Plans of the Eighteenth and Nineteenth Centuries* (Kingston: Institute of Jamaica Publications, 1988), 159–91; Kathleen E. A. Monteith, "The Coffee Industry in Jamaica, 1790–1850," (M.Phil. thesis, University of the West Indies, Mona, Jamaica, 1991).

7. William Lowndes, *The Coffee Planter* (London, 1807), front and end plates; P. J. Laborie, *The Coffee Planter of Saint Domingo* (London, 1797). Laborie's diagrams are reproduced in Higman, *Jamaica Surveyed,* 160–63.

8. Capt. J. G. Stedman, *Narrative of a Five Years' Expedition Against the Revolted Negroes of Surinam,* 2 vols. (London, 1796), 2: 355.

9. Henry Bolingbroke, *A Voyage to Demerary, 1799–1806,* ed. Vincent Roth (London: n.p., 1947), 115. This account was originally published in London in 1807.

10. Lowndes, *Coffee Planter,* 41.

11. Joint coffee and sugar cultivation was hardly ever undertaken, reflecting the geographical separation of the two sectors.

12. Higman, *Slave Population,* 23–24; Philip D. Morgan, "Task and Gang Systems: The Organization of Labor on New World Plantations," in *Work and Labor in Early America,* ed. Stephen Innes (Chapel Hill: University of North Carolina Press, 1988), 192–93, 204. Drying coffee berries on the stone barbecues was the most important job not organized on a task basis.

13. Higman, *Jamaica Surveyed,* 168–72; National Library of Jamaica MS 180, Radnor Plantation Journal; Devon Record Office, 49/14, John Harrison's Account Book. The discussion in the text is based on these sources.

14. On slave bargaining elsewhere in British colonial America, see Betty Wood, "Never on a Sunday: Slavery and the Sabbath in Lowcountry Georgia, 1750–1830," in *From Chattel Slaves to Wage Slaves: The Dynamics of Labor Bargaining in the Americas,* ed. Mary Turner (Bloomington: Indiana University Press, 1995), 79–96.

15. Lowndes, *Coffee Planter,* 35; Morgan, "Task and Gang Systems," 192–93.

16. Gabriel Debien, *Les Esclaves aux Antilles Françaises, XVIIe–XVIIIe Siècles* (Basse-Terre, Guadeloupe: Société d'Histoie de la Guadeloupe; Fort-le-France, Martinique: Société d'Histoire de la Martinique, 1974), 143–44.

17. A detailed account of coffee processing practiced in the Caribbean area is given in the Abbé Raynal, *A Philosophical and Political History of the Settlements of the Europeans in the East and West Indies,* 4 vols. (originally published in French [Paris, 1774]; Dublin, 1776), 3: 253–54.

18. William McKinnen & Co. Ltd., *Coffee: Its Treatment* (Aberdeen, 1914). Lowndes's and Laborie's diagrams should be compared with the plates on pages 6–7, 14–15, 20–21, 26–27, 28–29.

19. Monteith, "Coffee Industry," 294–96. For estimates of the cost structure of coffee plantations in Jamaica, Dominica, and Surinam, see Smith, "Sugar's Poor Relation," 76; and A. Blom, *Verhandeling van den landbouw in de colonie Suriname* (Amsterdam, 1787), 82–106, 178–87.

20. Richard Sheridan, *The Development of the Plantations to 1750* (Barbados: Caribbean Universities Press, 1970; London: Ginn and Company, 1970), 17–18; Monteith, "Coffee Industry," 116–17. Evidence of variation in work allocation between the works and the field during crop time, combined with lags between picking and delivery of coffee to the wharf, is provided by the Radnor and Oldbury plantation journals.

21. Monteith, "Coffee Industry," 86. By comparison, 30 percent of Jamaica's sugar estates were owned by absentees in 1775, rising to 80 percent in 1790 (Sheridan, "Chattel to Wage Slavery," 13–24).

22. Jamaica Archives, Accounts Produce, 1B/11/4, liber 48.

23. Monteith, "Coffee Industry," 64; Higman, *Jamaica Surveyed,* 17.

24. On Saint Domingue, the average number of slaves living on coffee planta-
tions lay between 34 and 45, 1767–89, rising to 82, 1790–92; David P. Geggus,
"Sugar and Coffee Cultivation in Saint Domingue and the Shaping of the Slave
Labor Force," in *Cultivation and Culture: Labor and the Shaping of Slave Life in
the Americas,* ed. Ira Berlin and Philip D. Morgan (Charlottesville: University
Press of Virginia, 1993), 76–77; Michel-Rolph Trouillot, "Motion in the System:
Coffee, Color, and Slavery in Eighteenth-Century Saint-Domingue," *Review* 5
(1982): 346–47.

25. Higman's 1832 data record that the average number of slaves employed on
mixed coffee and livestock holdings was 171, considerably higher than the average
of 128 for coffee monoculture (Higman, *Slave Population,* 15).

26. Bryan Edwards, *The History, Civil and Commercial, of the British Colonies
in the West Indies,* 2 vols. (Dublin, 1793), 2: 279–80; Laborie, *Coffee Planter,* 151.

27. Laborie, *Coffee Planter,* 1510. Laborie's general enthusiasm for supervisors
is revealed 14 pages later where he declares that "it is commonly and justly said,
that Drivers and Commanders are the soul of a plantation."

28. Higman, *Slave Population,* 23.

29. Marietta Morrissey, *Slave Women in the New World: Gender Stratification
in the Caribbean* (Lawrence: University Press of Kansas, 1989), 7, 9, 37, 65–75;
Shepherd, "Alternative Husbandry," 45–47.

30. Higman, *Slave Population,* 24.

31. Laborie advised that 12 men plus one or two women were a sufficient initial
labor force to bring a new settlement into cultivation (Laborie, *Coffee Planter,* 15).

32. Higman, *Slave Population,* 190–205.

33. National Library of Jamaica, MS 250, Hermitage Plantation Letterbook,
fol. 60.

34. "Petition of Several Planters . . . of Jamaica," March 2, 1731, reprinted in
F. R. Augier and Shirley C. Gordon, eds., *Sources of West Indian History* (London:
Longmans, 1962), 62; Leo Francis Stock, ed., *Proceedings and Debates of the
British Parliament Respecting North America,* 5 vols. (Washington, D.C.: Car-
negie Institute of Washington, 1927–37), 4: 149–52.

35. Shepherd has detailed how pens listed in the crop accounts turned to grow-
ing coffee after 1800, exports exceeding 50 percent of earnings on some properties
(Verene A. Shepherd, "Trade and Exchange in Jamaica in the Period of Slavery," in
Caribbean Slave Society and Economy, ed. Hilary Beckles and Verene A. Shepherd
[Kingston: Ian Randle, 1991], 112).

36. On small-scale female planters, see also [Edward] Kamau Brathwaite, *The
Development of Creole Society in Jamaica, 1770–1820* (Oxford: Clarendon Press,
1971; reprint, New York: Oxford University Press, 1978), 146–47.

37. Gad J. Heuman, *Between Black and White: Race, Politics, and the Free
Coloreds in Jamaica, 1792–1865* (Westport, Conn.: Greenwood Press, 1981), 24–
29.

38. Three inventories did include real estate, and a further inventory enumerated a large irrecoverable debt. These atypical items have been excluded from the wealth totals in the sample data set.

39. John Mackerson recorded that, while his property had been worth £20,000, in 1812, it could not be sold for half this amount (Alan Furness, "The Jamaican Coffee Boom and John Mackerson," *Jamaican Historical Review* 3 [1962]: 16–17).

40. B. W. Higman, "Economic and Social Development of the British West Indies from Settlement to ca. 1850," in *The Cambridge Economic History of the United States,* ed. S. L. Engerman and R. E. Gallman, 3 vols. (Cambridge: Cambridge University Press, 1996), 1: 323; Alice Hanson Jones, *Wealth of a Nation to Be: The American Colonies on the Eve of the Revolution* (New York: Columbia University Press, 1980), 90.

41. Description of coffee at the time the inventories were drawn up "in the husk" or "in the shell" also suggests the prevalence of the parchment method. For more information regarding the different techniques, see Laborie, *Coffee Planter,* 46–48; Monteith, "Coffee Industry," 166–92; S. D. Smith, "Accounting for Taste: British Coffee Consumption in Historical Perspective," *Journal of Interdisciplinary History* 27 (1996): 211.

42. Monteith, "Coffee Industry," 87.

43. Ibid., 31, 34–35; Verene Shepherd, "Pens and Pen-Keepers in a Plantation Society: Aspects of Jamaican Social and Economic History, 1740–1845" (Ph.D. diss., University of Cambridge, 1988), 67.

44. Monteith, "Coffee Industry," 88. See also Trouillot, "Motion in the System," 350.

6

Slavery and Cotton Culture in the Bahamas

Gail Saunders

As a number of historians have demonstrated, work was central in the experience of enslaved peoples. Slavery was "first and foremost an institution of coerced labour."[1] Until the conference "Cultivation and Culture: Labor and the Shaping of Slave Life in the Americas" and publications emanating from it, scholars writing on slavery in North America traditionally emphasized links between the staple and the white society, the economy and the mentality, but gave little attention to work and the society built on slavery and how that institution shaped the lives of the enslaved.[2] This was not the case for the British Caribbean, as evidenced by the work of Sydney Mintz and Douglas Hall, B. W. Higman, W. K. Marshall, and Michael Craton, among others.[3]

However, historians traditionally concentrated on analyzing the domestic economy of the enslaved and labor on sugar plantations or in sugar production. Since the late 1970s, however, Caribbean historians and Caribbeanists have made a concerted effort to examine nonsugar activities and nonplantation or "marginal colonies."[4]

As Higman has argued in his thorough and comprehensive study *Slave Populations of the British Caribbean,* slavery in the British Caribbean and the Americas in general "took a variety of characteristic forms, dependent on the type of economic activity in which the enslaved were employed." He found that the material conditions of enslaved populations living on sugar estates were similar and were characterized by high mortality and a failure to show natural increase. On the other hand, "material conditions" of the lives of the enslaved "associated with coffee, cotton, cocoa, pimento, and provisions plantations, as well as wood-cutting and salt-raking, each took on a characteristic form associated with typical patterns of demographic structure and natural increase."[5]

This essay will examine the lives of enslaved peoples in the Bahamas who were involved in the growing of cotton between 1783 and 1834. It will describe how cotton was grown in the Bahamas and how labor was organized. An attempt will be made to analyze how cotton production and its failure as a staple shaped the life of the enslaved and labor in the Bahamas.

The Bahamas, like Belize, was not a true plantation colony. It never grew sugar commercially. Before the coming of the American Loyalists and their enslaved males and females between 1783 and 1785, the inhabitants were principally occupied in seafaring activities such as fishing, wrecking, and turtling. They also engaged in woodcutting, mainly dye woods and other varieties such as mahogany, madeira, and boxwood. There was no staple crop and very little agriculture. Subsistence crops such as guinea corn, peas, beans, potatoes, yams, plantains, and bananas were grown. Salt was also raked but mainly for local consumption.[6]

Planter Loyalists who settled mainly in the south and southeastern islands introduced the growing of cotton on a commercial scale. The crop had been planted, but in small quantities, by the old inhabitants. Between 1784 and 1785, many cotton plantations were established, and by November 1785, 2,476 acres of cotton were under cultivation.[7]

Initially, it seemed as though the hopes of Loyalists would be realized. In 1785, the Bahamas produced 124 tons of cotton from 2,476 acres. During the following two years, 150 and 219 tons were produced from 3,050 and 4,500 acres, respectively. Hopes were high for 1788 when 394 tons were expected from 8,000 acres. However, only 122 tons were actually produced, the remaining 282 tons having been almost completely destroyed by the chenille and red bugs.[8] Despite these losses, cotton production continued. In 1790, for example, 4,160 bales weighing 442 tons were exported from the ports of Nassau and Exuma. Further, there was an increase in 1791, when 5,163 bales weighing 492 tons were exported.[9]

However, in 1794, the chenille attacked the cotton crops of the Bahamas again, and two-thirds of the cotton crop was destroyed. Four years later in 1798, cotton bugs almost demolished the crop, and between 1794 and 1805 cotton exports seriously diminished (table 6.1).[10] Daniel McKinnen, a British traveler, noted that although the Caicos Islands, then a part of the Bahamas, had the best soil and that cotton was still a staple in 1803, on most of the southern islands cotton production had declined. Of Crooked Island, where the Loyalists had settled and established about 40 plantations and planted over 2,000 acres of cotton, McKinnen states: "I beheld some extensive fields originally planted with cotton, but which from the failure of crops were now abandoned, and had become covered

Table 6.1. A return of sundry articles: Bahamas, 1794–1805

	Lignum vitae (tons)	Mahogany (feet)	Braziletto (tons)	Cotton (pounds)	Hides	Eleuthera bark
1794	52½	25,700	½	3,000	224	0
1795	458	4,220	½	600	666	0
1796	756	7,724	¼	1,200	540	0
1797	277	5,380	¾	1,800	424	0
1798	1,188	700	0	0	0	0
1799	120	8,306	0	0	56	0
1800	898	1,040	0	0	200	0
1801	673	2,000	1½	600	358	0
1802	301	0	0	1,500	0	0
1803	147¼	500	0	0	0	17,309
1804	427	0	½	600	0	2,650
1805	267	12,000	0	0	0	5,900

Source: Nassau Naval Office, February 5, 1807, CO/23/51 Folio 47.

with a luxuriant growth of indigenous shrubs and plants. . . . I found the plantations of Crooked Island for the most part deserted."[11]

It was evident that cotton as a staple crop was a failure, although statistics show that more cotton was produced in 1809 and 1810 than in any average year between 1789 and 1799.[12] It is therefore difficult to say exactly when the decline of cotton finally set in. By 1800, however, most of the cotton planters were facing ruin. This is evident by the searching questionnaire sent out to 25 of the leading cotton growers in that year by the government of the Bahamas in order to determine the causes of the failure. Most attributed the decline of cotton to the exhausted state of the soil, the inexperience of the planters and injudicious planting, the attack of the chenille and red bug, bad management, and the climate.[13]

There is a dearth of literature on cotton production and, until recently, on the work routine of the enslaved in the Bahamas. According to a House of Assembly report in 1826, few planters were capable of keeping records. Additionally, a large number of plantations were supervised by free people of color and also enslaved people who were mostly illiterate.[14] In the absence of testimonies of the enslaved, it is necessary to depend solely on the enslavers' point of view. Only one journal of a Bahamian plantation has survived, as far as can be ascertained, and this only records happenings for 1831 and 1832, years immediately before emancipation when cotton cultivation had drastically declined and was then "little more than a nominal article of export."[15]

Work Routine on Cotton Plantations

Cotton cultivation in the late eighteenth and early nineteenth centuries was dependent on enslaved labor. Its production dictated the work routine of the enslaved, at least for a short period. One of the first tasks of the enslaved was to clear the land and prepare it for cultivation. The Loyalists and their enslaved laborers established extensive cotton plantations, most on islands that had not been settled or very sparsely so. Establishing new plantations was rigorous work. After the trees were felled and bushes cleared, the stumps and undergrowth were burned until the field was cleared for planting. This "slash-and-burn" method is still used in the Bahamas. It destroyed much vegetable substance that might have been converted into excellent topsoil. In addition, manure was hardly employed as a fertilizer, being a scarce commodity owing to the shortage of cattle.[16] William Wylly, attorney general and an enslaver, complained that many of the fields laid out were too large and often not sheltered, which left the cotton plants exposed to winds.[17] Margins were made around the field and were often used by the enslaved as a place for shelters from the sun and for cooking.

The soil in the fields was then hoed, a tedious job using simple hand tools. Shallow holes were dug probably with a dibble stick, and seven or eight seeds were planted in each hole. Planting was done in rows, leaving a space between each row varying from six or eight feet. Seeds were typically planted about four feet apart. Indian corn was usually cultivated between the rows of cotton. Planting took place in March and between May and September, and cotton crops were harvested seven to ten months after planting. There was usually a winter and a spring crop. Two major types of cotton were planted in the Bahamas, the seeds from Anguilla and from the Georgia Sea Islands. Anguilla cotton could not withstand the "wet season" or the "cold winds." Georgia cotton, which was introduced later, was found to be hardier and more easily managed.[18]

In the early stages of growth, the cotton plants required close attention. Usually there were at least two weedings when all available workers would be employed. When about eight inches high, the plants were thinned out, leaving two of the best plants. At a height of about two feet, the cotton plants were pruned. Three or four inches were lopped from the top, "the extremities must be pinched off, which will force the fruit."[19]

Cotton plants blossomed at the end of five months and formed a pod two months later. From then until the tenth month, the pods ripened and burst open in three partitions displaying the cotton wool, which was then gathered by hand.[20] Harvesting of cotton usually took place in January or February or March, but as all cotton did not mature at one time, gathering continued with occasional intervals to July. Charles Farquharson records in his journal that on June 29, 1831, his workers had "finished gathering this year's crop." However, they were also employed in picking the lighter crop known as "spring" cotton, referred to in the journal as "one-one cotton."[21]

Picking cotton was "hard and distasteful work."[22] On the American plantations, quotas had to be met. In the Bahamas, planters were anxious to gather the cotton before the rainy season. All enslaved field hands were employed in the picking of cotton on large plantations, while on smaller estates "all hands" were used at harvest time.[23] Shoulder baskets made of straw or cloth were probably used in the picking of cotton. Cotton was taken from the fields either by the enslaved or by horse or mule to the barns where it was stored.

The cotton was then ginned, whereby the seeds were removed from the wool either by hand or by machine. Ginning cotton required few skilled workers and, unlike sugar processing, was a relatively simple operation. Before the invention of Joseph Eve's gin in about 1790, a simple foot gin was used.[24] Comprised of two small rollers placed close and parallel to one another in a frame, it was turned in opposite directions by different wheels, which were moved by foot. The cotton was placed by hand on the rollers spiked with nails. As they moved round, the cotton readily passing between them, leaving the seeds that were too large to pass through. After this process, the wool was handpicked to rid it of decayed leaves, broken seeds, or damaged wool. The cotton was then packed into bales of about 200 pounds and shipped to Nassau, from where it was exported.

Eve's gin was a modified version of the foot gin, but it was turned by wind, horse, cattle, or water power if there was an inlet. While it was estimated that the common gin could clean between 25 to 40 pounds of cotton in one day, Eve's gin cleaned between 90 and 100 pounds of cotton in the same time. Some plantations could gin as much as 360 pounds of cotton in one day. Besides increasing production and saving valuable time and money, Eve's gin made it unnecessary to handpick cotton. It also meant that the cotton was stored for brief periods, making it less exposed to dangers of rodents and other pests. Additionally, Eve's gin was less taxing on the enslaved. It was said that the common gin was "apt to rupture negroes."[25]

A planter, Alexander Drysdale, who used Eve's wind gin on both of his estates congratulated Eve: "Preparing our cotton for Market was formerly considered as the most tedious, troublesome and laborious part of the agricultural process in this country. To you we are indebted for its having been pleasant, easy and expeditious."[26] William Wylly informed the House of Assembly in 1795 that the "[u]se of this indigenous invention is equivalent to the labor of at least eight Negroes . . . it is certain that this machine attended only by two men will clean more cotton and do it in a more effectual manner than what was usually accomplished by ten negroes with the common foot Gin."[27]

Cotton Culture versus Sugar Culture

As Michael Craton demonstrated, cotton production even before the introduction of Eve's gin "was far less labor intensive than sugar."[28] Sugar cultivation was a highly capitalized industry, being both an agricultural and manufacturing enterprise. A factory was necessary, and it needed raw materials, that is, the sugarcane. Large areas of land had to be planted, requiring a large labor force, some of which needed to be highly skilled in order to grow and process sugar. Sugar required one enslaved person for every two acres as compared to one slave for five or six acres of cotton.[29]

The essential difference between cotton and sugar production, however, was the nature of the economic system in which the enslaved were employed. In the production of sugar on British Caribbean plantations, the enslaved usually worked in gangs, while those who labored on cotton plantations in the Bahamas were employed mostly by the task system. As Phillip Morgan has argued, there were parallels in the experience of the Caribbean plantation and the Low Country rice economy. In the British Caribbean, as Higman has shown, coffee and pimento, crops that required little supervision or regimentation, were, like rice, grown by an enslaved labor force organized by tasks rather than in gangs.[30]

It may be conjectured from Morgan's findings that the enslaved people who were brought by the Loyalists from the Carolinas and Georgia were already accustomed to the task system. As Morgan explained, the task system by the late eighteenth century had taken deep root in the Low Countries. The task system employed in rice cultivation was extended to the cultivation of sea island cotton.[31] Tasking became a way of life in the antebellum Low Country.

Task Labor, Gang Labor, and Slave Drivers

Owners of enslaved peoples in the Bahamas claimed that task work as a system of labor was all they remembered. It was used to employ all the enslaved except those employed as domestics, as sailors, as tradespeople, or in salt production. Howard Johnson contends that salt production continued to be profitable in the closing years of slavery; it was only in the salt-producing areas that gang labor was employed on a regular basis.[32] Wylly, answering to a committee of the House of Assembly in 1815, stated: "And whenever the nature of the work will admit of it, our Negroes are regularly tasked. The tasks are one fourth of an acre in extent, they are usually marked out by permanent stations in every field, and two, three, sometimes four slaves (but in general more than one) are put into each Task, at the discretion of the Driver according to the actual state of the fields."[33]

From the available evidence and frequent references to the "taskable negroes," it seems that the task system predominated, although gang labor was also employed. McKinnen graphically described the system:

> Their labor is allotted to them daily and individually, according to their strength; and if they are so diligent as to have finished it at an early hour, the rest of the day is allowed to them for amusement or their private concerns. The master also frequently superintends them himself; and therefore it rarely happens that they are so much subject to the discipline of the whip as where gangs are large, and directed by agents or overseers.[34]

Gang labor was usually employed at planting, using the hoe, during thinning phases, and at harvesting times, and the enslaved were rewarded with extra time. Wylly informed members of the House of Assembly that "in seed time and Harvest when it would hardly be possible to assign set Tasks, they are allowed one Hour at Breakfast and two Hours at Dinner."[35]

Farquharson seemed to have employed the gang system on his plantation. However, he also rewarded enslaved people on his property for extra labor. On Saturday, July 9, 1831, he "employed in the same way as above (weeding)—One part of the gang and the other part has today to themselves having gained a day this week by extra work."[36]

While positive incentives were offered, some coercion by owners or drivers must have been practiced. But according to Wylly, the whip was rarely used in the field. Whippings, however, were inflicted at the whipping post as punishment for disobedience and misdemeanors. Whipping was, in fact, the most common form of punishment for minor offences. The cowskin and cat-o'-nine tails were used in the Workhouse in Nassau and were probably employed on some Out Island plantations, but by 1815 the use of the cowskin had been prohibited. The cartwhip employed in the sugar colonies apparently was not used in the Bahamas.[37] Enslaved peoples also suffered confinement in the stocks for theft and disobedience.[38]

Drivers, who were chosen for reliability and loyalty and who held the highest post of enslaved field workers, administered punishments but were not as significant in the Bahamas as in the sugar colonies. At emancipation, there were 80 drivers out of a total enslaved population of 10,000, representing only about 0.8 percent of the total. In contrast, Jamaica had 14,043 head people (praedial attached, that is, those employed on lands belonging to owners and attached to the soil) listed in 1834, comprising 4.51 percent of the total slave population.[39]

The importance of the driver varied from plantation to plantation. In the Bahamas, slaveholdings were generally small. Nearly 75 percent of the enslaved lived in holding units of 50 or less.[40] Very often plantation owners oversaw the slaves themselves. Charles Farquharson, for example, who in 1834 had 52 enslaved persons along with his son, James, seemed to have supervised the work himself. No driver is listed for his estate.[41] On the other hand, at the Wylly plantation at Clifton in New Providence in 1818, there was a driver called Boatswain and an underdriver, Jack, both Africans, who supervised the enslaved. Boatswain was literate, which was very rare for an enslaved male, and was instructed to read prayers to the enslaved population on the plantation every Sunday.[42] He was also paid a fee for teaching them to read but was "not to be paid for more than ten pupils in any one year." Moreover, Boatswain and Jack were paid an allowance of 12 guineas a year for being drivers, and additionally they were given a "brood mare each, for the purpose of enabling them the more frequently and expeditiously to ride over the pasture grounds and other lands."[43]

Just how many hours owners or drivers got the enslaved to work a year is difficult to determine. As Higman has demonstrated, it depended on a variety of factors, including type of plantation, the length of the crop season, the size of the slaveholding, the use of the task system, the existence of provision ground system, and "the sex, age and strength of the slaves themselves."[44] Enslavers in the Bahamas, in defending conditions of their human property there and protesting ameliorative measures in 1823, stated that enslaved people were not overworked, rarely working over seven or eight hours.[45] In view of the system of task work and the serious decline of cotton, this might have been the case, especially out of the planting and harvesting season. In 1815, Wylly informed the House of Assembly that "it rarely happens that the setting sun ever leaves a Negro in our Fields."[46]

Daily routines for the enslaved varied according to the season, and occupations changed to suit the job at hand. At the Farquharson estate on Watlings Island, for example, when cotton was harvested, "all hands" in gangs were usually employed. In February 1831, Farquharson devoted 11 days solely to the gathering of cotton. On some days cotton was gathered half of the day and corn picked during the other half. Other days were employed in weeding, planting, heaping and burning bush, and handpicking cotton.[47]

As Higman has demonstrated, field laborers on all types of plantations were involved in a variety of tasks in the out-of-crop season.[48] This was evident at the Farquharson estate and at Wylly's Clifton plantation and, in view of the decline of cotton, was probably generally practiced throughout the Bahamas. As Wylly informed the members of the House of Assembly in January 1823:

> A crop of cotton, or provisions being raised, or a few small cargoes of cedar or dye woods cut from the woods, the slaves are frequently sent, for the season, to rake and manufacture salt at the ponds; from thence they are, in due time, called back to the fields, the provision grounds, or the orchards or gardens, where fruits are raised for exportation. The produce has next to be taken to the market; and a portion of the same gang become sailors for the occasion; and at other times, through the year, fishermen, wreckers . . . and even domestic servants, to attend to the business of their master's house, his cattle and other stock, for use, or for consumption or sale. Thus, with all the varieties of season and casualty, the nature of the Bahama negro's occupation changes.[49]

Similar to enslaved pen-workers on Jamaican plantations involved in driving cattle and horsekind to and from estates, enslaved people in the Bahamas were generally allowed a great deal of mobility.[50] Their occupations changed not only according to the season but also according to their age.[51] For example, among black males, approximately 40 percent after the age of 10 worked in the field all their life until they became sick, disabled, or simply too old. However, between the ages of 11 and 15, 55

Table 6.2. Occupational distribution by sex and color: Bahamas, 1834

Occupation	Males			Females			Total
	Black	Mulatto	Total	Black	Mulatto	Total	
Nil	1,049	180	1,229	1,113	192	1,305	2,534
Domestic	370	58	428	1,394	181	1,575	2,003
Field	1,682	96	1,778	1,622	100	1,722	3,500
Mariner	528	57	585	—	—	—	585
Salt	496	42	538	354	26	380	918
Driver/overseer	74	5	79	1	—	—	80
Nurse/midwife	12	2	14	71	9	80	94
Trade/craft	228	18	246	15	2	17	263
Sundry	8	—	8	3	—	3	11
Unknown	9	—	9	5	—	5	14
Total	4,456	458	4,914	4,578	510	5,083	10,002

Source: Calculated from Returns of the Registration of Slaves (RRS), 1834.

percent were in the field, but between 16 and 24 years of age, only 43 percent were in the field. At 16 to 24, about 12 percent left the field for another occupation, probably salt production, seafaring activities, or the trades.[52]

Color, Gender, Use, and Task Allocation

Enslavers did not discriminate by sex but by color as far as female field labor was concerned. In 1834, there were nearly as many female field laborers as males (see table 6.2).[53] Among enslaved black females, about 45 percent after the age of 10 worked in the field all their life. Among colored females, 50 percent worked as domestics all their lives. Enslaved black women between the ages of 16 and 39 usually worked in the field. Enslaved females, as in Jamaica and the plantations in the American South, were considered as valuable or more so than enslaved men as far as cotton production was concerned.[54] Farquharson employed women in every phase of the growing of cotton. McKinnen in his travels throughout the Bahamas witnessed a scene in Acklins: "I amused myself in passing over the shrubberies at the time of gathering in the crop, which was performed with much more dexterity by the women than the men, although their utmost exertions were stimulated and put forth by the hope of a reward. One lusty female slave, with a child upon her back, gathered in between forty and fifty pounds for each day's work."[55]

The Decline of Cotton and Diversification

The decline of cotton and the failure to replace it with a staple caused Bahamian enslavers to diversify. Many turned to developing salt production. Some turned to stock raising and the growing of ground provisions. Many estates became little more than subsistence farming by the end of slavery. These developments obviously affected the intensity of labor and the occupational distribution in the Bahamas. The enslaved were usually underemployed. At emancipation, just over half (55 percent) of enslaved people in the Bahamas were employed in field work as compared to several sugar colonies, including Jamaica and Barbados, which registered 73.3 and 70.8 percent, respectively.[56] The Bahamas' low percentage of praedial tradesmen and head people and its high percentage of the enslaved involved in domestic work, in shipping, and in working around the wharves reflected a decayed plantation system and the absence of sugar (see table 6.3)

Independent Production

These economic conditions and the employment of the task system (used earlier in cotton production), as Morgan has established, allowed "the slaves a certain latitude to apportion his [sic]own day, to work intensively at this task and then have the balance of his time." If the enslaved completed their work by midafternoon, they had "leisure time to cultivate for themselves tend their stock or amuse themselves."[57] Although tasking could be onerous and fast-paced, it had the advantage of allowing the enslaved some flexibility in determining the length of the workday. As Michel Ralph Trouillot stated, "slaves employed in the cotton era production . . . routinely used the task system to shorten the length of time spent in their masters' fields."[58]

Enslaved peoples who worked by tasks in the Low Country region of South Carolina and Georgia in the Bahamas had much time to work for themselves. Some who lived in New Providence also had time to attend the Saturday market in Nassau and to accumulate cash. Similar to that in the Low Country and British Caribbean colonies, a significant internal economy developed. The enslavers in the Bahamas and in the Caribbean generally were either by custom or law pledged to provide for the enslaved population. Certain provisions and clothing and other necessities had to be given. To supplement the provisions, they often gave enslaved people extra rations. For example, Farquharson at Christmas 1832 gave each of

Table 6.3. Comparative occupations in seven British Caribbean colonies, 1834

Occupations (August 1, 1834)	Jamaica	Barbados	Trinidad	Antigua	Grenada	Tobago	Bahamas
Praedial attached							
1. Head people	14,043	1,963	1,100	593	1,164	209	68
2. Tradesmen	11,244	1,821	345	990	741	350	0
3. Inferior tradesmen	2,635	784	333	306	278	248	0
4. Field labor	107,053	27,693	8,018	11,250	8,649	3,734	2,688
5. Inferior field laborers	63,923	15,615	2,448	6,502	5,728	3,567	1,280
Praedial unattached							
1. Head people	1,329	32	86	9	10	6	3
2. Tradesmen	1,133	224	51	39	21	5	0
3. Inferior tradesmen	322	163	34	10	10	5	0
4. Field laborers	11,670	2,330	1,101	472	214	74	184
5. Inferior field laborers	5,104	1,568	357	197	125	68	73
Nonpraedial							
1. Head tradesmen	1,759	391	92	252	95	40	162
2. Inferior tradesmen	780	408	220	215	125	19	48
3. Head people on wharves, shipping, etc.	1,428	64	59	80	28	66	459
4. Inferior people on wharves, shipping, etc.	901	1,071	133	203	498	55	321
5. Head domestic servants	12,883	3,816	1,678	303	350	316	1,264
6. Inferior domestic servants	19,083	8,695	1,584	1,929	975	316	1,186
Children under 6 years at March 1, 1834	39,013	14,732	2,246	4,327	3,320	1,479	1,986
Aged, diseased, or otherwise noneffective	15,692	1,780	872	1,444	1,309	1,032	293
Runaway	1,075						
Total	311,070	83,150	20,757	29,121	23,640	11,589	9,995

Source: T/71/851; R.M. Martin, Colonies of the British Empire (London, 1843).

the "grown hands" four pounds of pork, four pounds of beef, a bottle of rum, and "a large cup full of sugar." Children received half-rations of meat and sugar. Additionally, Farquharson gave enslaved people on his property "half a sheep and 2 flasks of rum to make them a super [*sic*]" at the end of the corn crop. In the same year, they received the meat of two cows, one in February and the other in August.[59] Owners also allowed the enslaved customary use plots of land on which to grow their own provisions.[60]

The provision ground system, which by the early nineteenth century was such an integral part of the Jamaican and indeed the Caribbean domestic economic system of the enslaved, probably developed in the Bahamas in the latter part of the eighteenth century. No clauses relating to provision grounds appear in the early-eighteenth-century slave regulations. In fact, the early beginnings of the provision ground system remain obscure.[61] However, an act in 1767 forbade the enslaved to plant except on the land of their owners. This indicated that enslaved people in the Bahamas were accustomed to organizing and planting their provision grounds.[62] By 1796, in addition to being given "sufficient provisions" and "proper clothing," enslaved people in the Bahamas were also given a "sufficient quantity of land" in order to grow their own provisions. A later act in 1824 reiterated this demand.[63]

As Johnson has argued, after the collapse of cotton the enslaved "were left with more time for productive labor of their own grounds." The enslavers, faced with the problem of maintaining an increasing "underemployed labor force," were "willing to shift the burden of slave maintenance to the provision grounds since there was no crop of comparable commercial importance to replace cotton."[64]

There is evidence that some enslavers in the Bahamas allowed provision grounds on their plantations. Wylly, for example, directed that on his plantations at Clifton and Tusculum "sufficient land is set apart from the use of the people, and half an Acre is annexed to each house as the property of the occupant for the time being; separate pastures are allotted for their hogs; and each head of a family is permitted to keep one sow." This regulation seems to have been carried out. Enslaved people on Wylly's property at Clifton were given two days to work on their own grounds. Each man and his "wife" were expected to plant two acres of provisions. Wylly claimed the right to purchase "all hogs, pigs, poultry, and eggs which the people might have for sale, and for which he is to pay Nassau prices; to be fixed by the drivers and two other men chosen by the seller." The enslaved were allowed Saturdays to take their produce, pigs, and poultry, sometimes using Wylly's boat, to the Nassau market, where they exchanged their produce for rum and cash. For work such as wall building done on his plantations in their own time, enslaved people could accumulate cash.[65]

As Mintz and Hall, and Marshall, have shown, the provision ground and internal marketing systems gave the enslaved latitude to participate in independent activities. Enslaved people 'pushed hard' to 'establish and expand' the right to produce and market independently. They also attempted to exploit their own positions creating "intense 'competition' between themselves and plantation owners and managers for labor services and land rsources."[66]

Nassau was the main market for the produce of the provision grounds of the enslaved in New Providence and the nearby islands. In competition with white farmers, the enslaved also sold foodstuffs to local residents and "crews of incoming ships." On the more isolated Out Islands, they had intermittent opportunities to participate in the market economy. However, on some islands, it seems that local markets existed to sell products of the provision grounds of the enslaved.[67]

The provision ground system was particularly important in Exuma. Lord John Rolle, an absentee enslaver, owned five plantations at Exuma.[68] Because of the rapid increase in the enslaved population and falling profits brought by the collapse of cotton, he allowed those he enslaved access to their own provision grounds in order that they could provide for their families. They grew peas, beans, and corn and owned poultry and some pigs. When they were given notice that they would be moved to Cat Island, they objected and subsequently staged a revolt led by Pompey, a 38-year-old black Creole. Despite the fact that they were given three days to pick their crops and dispose of their animals, they resisted, not wishing to leave their provision grounds. Notice was too short; their fields were under cultivation, and they wished to pick, thrash, and pack their peas and beans. The enslaved also feared that their poultry would die "if they were put on board a crowded vessel tied together."[69]

This act of resistance was significant, as it underscored the prevailing opinion in the Bahamas that the "labor of those enslaved by Rolle applied chiefly to their private benefit while the expense of their maintenance etc. was supplied by Lord Rolle."[70] With no agricultural staple and a surplus labor force, the practice of enslaved people maintaining themselves became common throughout the Bahamas in the closing years of slavery.[71] Despite the fact that earlier the enslaved had been offered money for their crops and would have been allowed either to sell their hogs and fowls or to carry them with them if they agreed to be moved, they refused. The participation of the enslaved in the market economy supports Craton's argument that "the transition from 'protopeasant' to true peasant was probably more advanced in Exuma and similar Bahamian islands than anywhere in the British colonies."[72]

The Rolle and Wylly examples do not prove conclusively that the provision ground and internal marketing systems were generally employed throughout the Bahamas. However, the decayed plantation system and dire economic conditions may have encouraged the use of the system operated primarily to the enslavers' advantage. At the Farquharson estate, "Negro Ground" is referred to, and there was usually a garden around each house.[73] But according to the journal, the enslaved worked six days a week with only Sundays off. There is no indication that they used their day off to farm for themselves. Farquharson's estate, an owner-controlled plantation, therefore differed from the Rolle holdings, where the enslaved were under the charge of a single overseer and left increasingly to their own devices.

As Johnson has suggested, the decline of cotton as an export staple had implications for labor routines and the labor systems employed. The collapsed plantation system made for changes and the "restructuring of the relationships between slaves and their owners."[74] By the time of full emancipation, labor tenancy and sharecropping had been adopted in the transition from slavery to free labor in the Bahamas.[75] Labor tenancy, adopted by 1828, allowed African apprentices and enslaved peoples to cultivate a plot of land for their "own support and maintenance" for two and a half days a week. For the remainder of the week, they were expected to work for their owners. Sharecropping, introduced during the apprenticeship period, involved the apprentices making voluntary agreements to remain on the former proprietor's estate to work on "liberal and beneficial terms." The usual agreement between the proprietors and their tenants was on the share system.

Without a profitable staple crop to replace cotton and with a surplus of labor, the operation of labor tenancy and sharecropping was found to be a more satisfactory and profitable arrangement for the proprietors in directing the operation of their estates. It was an amicable solution for both the landlords and the tenants. The latter gained access to the land, while the proprietors retained the services of the freed people.[76]

The self-hire system, as Johnson argues, also emerged in the Bahamas in the late eighteenth century.[77] The collapse of cotton, the absence of an export staple to replace it, and agricultural "stagnation" led to the underutilization of the enslaved population. The short-lived cotton boom witnessed some redistribution of the enslaved labor force to cotton-producing islands. However, with the decline of cotton and the plantation system, many owners, especially those in the Out Islands, had difficulty finding work for their enslaved workers, who not only had time to tend their provision grounds but also to hire out their own time. Governor Smyth wrote in 1831, "Many of the slaves pay a monthly sum to their owners to look out for work and employment as they please."[78] While some of the enslavers on the Out Islands employed enslaved people in cultivating foodstuffs and raising livestock for the Nassau market, others transferred their underutilized workers to Nassau, which offered greater opportunities for skilled and unskilled labor to be sold, to be hired out, or to work on the self-hire system.[79] This practice had evolved before the arrival of the American Loyalists.

Many of the enslaved who were transferred preferred to work on the self-hire system. Those in the urban areas worked at a variety of tasks. Enslaved males on self-hire found employment as stevedores, in woodcutting, or in road building. They also engaged in seafaring activities. Enslaved female on self-hire were employed primarily as domestics and itinerant vendors. By the closing years of slavery, "slaves on the self-hire system dominated the urban scene."[80] Johnson contends that the self-hire system was advantageous to both enslavers and enslaved. Owners could look forward to cash payments and not have to supervise or supply food, clothing, or shelter. The enslaved recognized the system as giving them an opportunity to "exercise extensive control over their lives."[81] In fact, "slave owners steadily lost their authority over slaves who were wholly dependent on waged work," and by the end of the eighteenth century, "slaves on self-hire were successfully dictating wage levels in their negotiations with prospective employers."[82]

Some of the enslaved, after paying "wages" to their owners and maintaining themselves, probably saved some cash. A number of them indulged in leisure-time activities such as drinking and gambling, to which the ruling elite reacted by tightening regulations licensing retailers of spirits and prohibiting gambling.[83] Many enslaved people purchased their freedom. Higman notes that the manumission rate in the Bahamas between 1808 and 1834 was the highest in the British Caribbean for that period.[84]

Conclusion

Cotton production and the less arduous labor it required in contrast to the making of sugar helped to create favorable demographic characteristics in the Bahamian enslaved population. With the abrupt ending of cotton production on a commercial scale and the subsequent diversification into salt and stock production and the growing of provisions for the Nassau market, cotton became a marginal product.

Work routines before and after the decline of cotton were organized mainly on the task system. This provided enslaved Bahamians in rural areas with spare time to work for themselves. They organized and farmed their own provision grounds and engaged in an internal marketing system, which was limited on the more remote Out Islands. Labor tenancy and sharecropping emerged on the Out Islands. In the urban areas, especially in Nassau, the enslaved hired out their time, dictated their wages, and were able to acquire material goods and some cash, forming "an incipient (an increasingly assertive) proletariat."[85] The failure to develop a staple to replace cotton made for a "loosening of ties" between the enslaved and the staple crop.[86] Enslavers found alternative methods to employ and extract labor from a steadily increasing enslaved population. In the rural areas, where there was a shift from cotton to the growing of provisions, owners received a "labor rent" and in the urban setting, a cash payment.[87] The enslaved in both settings enjoyed much independence within slavery.

Although the enslavers still had some control, the enslaved "operated effectively as peasants," insisting on working their own grounds on their own terms for a large part of the day.[88] Their labor relationship with their owners by 1834 had, in Howard Johnson's words, "moved decisively from a coercive to a contractual one," foreshadowing postslavery labor systems.[89]

Notes

A version of this essay was given at the conference and published as "Slave Life, Slave Society and Cotton Production in the Bahamas" in *Slavery and Abolition* 2, no. 3 (December 1990): 332–50.

1. Ira Berlin and Philip D. Morgan, eds., *Cultivation and Culture: Labour and the Shaping of Slave Life in the Americas,* (Charlottesville: University Press of Virginia, 1993), 1. See also Douglas Hall, "Slaves and Slavery in the British West Indies," *Social and Economic Studies* 11 (1962): 305–18; Elsa Goveia, *Slave Society in the British Leeward Islands at the End of the Eighteenth Century* (New Haven, Conn.: Yale University Press, 1965); [Edward] Kamau Brathwaite, *The*

Development of Creole Society in Jamaica, 1770–1820 (Oxford: Clarendon Press, 1971); B. W. Higman, *Slave Population and Economy in Jamaica, 1807–1834* (Cambridge: Cambridge University Press, 1976).

2. Berlin and Morgan, *Cultivation and Culture,* 1. See also Philip Morgan and Ira Berlin, eds., *Slavery and Abolition* 12, no. 1 (May 1991).

3. See especially S. W. Mintz and Douglas Hall, "The Origins of the Jamaican Internal Marketing System," *Yale University Publications in Anthropology 57* (1960): 3–26; S. W. Mintz, *Caribbean Transformations* (Chicago: Aldine, 1974); Higman, *Slave Population and Economy in Jamaica;* B. W. Higman, *Slave Populations of the British Caribbean, 1807–1834* (Baltimore: Johns Hopkins University Press, 1984); Michael Craton, "Hobbessian or Panglossian? The Two Extremes of Slave Conditions in the British Caribbean, 1783 to 1834," *William and Mary Quarterly 35* (1978): 324–56; Michael Craton, *Searching for the Invisible Man: Slaves and Plantation Life in Jamaica* (Cambridge: Harvard University Press, 1978); and Woodville K. Marshall, "The Establishment of a Peasantry in Barbados, 1840–1920," in *Social Groups and Institutions in the History of the Caribbean,* ed. Thomas Matthews (Rio Piedras, Puerto Rico: Association of Caribbean Historians, 1975), 84–104. See also Woodville K. Marshall, "Provision Ground and Plantation Labor in Four Windward Islands: Competition for Resources during Slavery," in Berlin and Morgan, *Cultivation and Culture,* 203–20.

4. See Higman, *Slave Population and Economy in Jamaica;* Verene Shepherd, "Pens and Pen-keepers in a Plantation Society: Aspects of Jamaican Social and Economic History, 1740–1845," (Ph.D. diss., University of Cambridge, 1988); Verene Shepherd, "Trade and Exchange in Jamaica in the Period of Slavery," in *Caribbean Slave Society and Economy,* ed. Hilary McD. Beckles and Verene A. Shepherd (Kingston: Ian Randle, 1991), 111–19; K. Monteith, "The Coffee Industry in Jamaica 1790–1850" (staff/postgraduate seminar paper, University of the West Indies, Mona, Jamaica, 1988; Howard Johnson, *The Bahamas in Slavery and Freedom* (Kingston and London: Ian Randle and James Currey, 1991). See also Howard Johnson, *The Bahamas from Slavery to Servitude 1783–1933* (Gainesville: University Press of Florida, 1996).

5. Higman, *Slave Populations of the British Caribbean,* 396.

6. For information on the Loyalist influx, see Thelma P. Peters, "The American Loyalists and the Plantation Period in the Bahama Islands" (Ph.D. thesis, University of Florida, 1960); Gail Saunders, *Slavery in the Bahamas 1648–1838* (Nassau: D. G. Saunders, 1985), 11–47; and Gail Saunders, *Bahamian Loyalists and Their Slaves* (London: Macmillan, 1983).

7. "An Account of all Cotton Plantations in the Bahama Islands," November 1, 1785, CO 23/37/335. See also Robert Millar, "On the Cultivation of Cotton in the Bahamas," *Journal of the Bahamas Historical Society for the Diffusion of Knowledge* (May 1835): 49.

8. *Bahama Gazette,* March 14–21, 1789. See also *Votes of the House of Assem-*

bly *1787–1794*. Report of a Committee of the House, April 28, 1789. *Fausse Chenille* is a worm that looks like a caterpillar. It has a long body and is variegated with beautiful colors and many legs.

9. *Bahama Gazette,* December 16–20, 1791.

10. Castlereagh to Cameron, January–June 1807, CO 23/51/47.

11. Daniel McKinnen, *A Tour through the British West Indies in the years 1802–1803 giving particular account of the Bahama Islands* (London: J. White, 1804), 154–60.

12. Peters, "American Loyalists," 157.

13. Questionnaire and answers sent to planters, May 7, 1800, CO 23/39/167–211.

14. Report on the Committee on the Bill respecting Melioration, November 14, 1826. *Votes of the House of Assembly 1824–1828,* 63.

15. A. D. Peggs, ed., *A Relic of Slavery: Farquharason's Journal, 1831–1832* (Nassau: Dean Peggs Research Fund, 1957).

16. Questionnaires and Answers sent to Planters, May 7, 1800.

17. William Wylly, born in 1757 and called to the English bar, fought as a Loyalist in the American War of Independence. Migrating to the Bahamas in 1787, he became solicitor general in the same year. In 1797, he was promoted to attorney general of the Bahamas. In 1818, William Wylly had 67 slaves on three plantations at the western end of New Providence. The main estate was Clifton, the largest, where provisions were raised for the slaves. Of the other two, one was at Tusculum between the present-day Orange Hill and Gambier Village and the other at Waterloo just west of Lightbourn Creek. The latter two estates were turned over to stock raising. See Saunders, *Bahamian Loyalists,* 32–33; and Michael Craton and Gail Saunders, *Islanders in the Stream: A History of the Bahamian People* (Athens: University of Georgia Press, 1992), 1: 202, 258–59, 279–302.

18. Millar, "On the Cultivation of Cotton," 49–51. See also Bryan Edwards, *The History, Civil and Commercial of the British Colonies in the West Indies* (London: J. Stockdale, 1805), 3: 91.

19. Millar, "On the Cultivation of Cotton," 51. See also *Farquharson's Journal,* 22, 26, 27.

20. Edwards, *History,* 91.

21. *Farquharson's Journal* (February 1831), 5–9.

22. Eugene D. Genovese, *Roll, Jordan Roll: The World the Slaves Made* (New York: Pantheon Books, 1975), 322.

23. See *Farquharson's Journal* (February 1831), 5–9.

24. Joseph Eve was a Loyalist who settled on Cat Island. He was probably born in South Carolina and lived in Pennsylvania at the time of the American Revolution and was thought to be a Quaker. See Saunders, *Bahamian Loyalists,* 39.

25. *Bahama Gazette,* March 18–21, 1794.

26. Ibid., December 24, 1890; March 18–21, May 1, May 17, 1794.

27. Votes of the House of Assembly, 1795–1798 (manuscript) December 12, 1795.

28. Craton, "Hobbessian or Panglossian?" 349.

29. Eric Williams, *From Columbus to Castro: The History of the Caribbean 1492–1969* (London: Andre Deutch, 1971), 122; McKinnen, *A Tour,* 182. McKinnen notes that "it is generally supposed by good planters, that about or six acres of land may be employed in the culture of Anguilla cotton to each working slave or taskable hand: but in the Georgian (or as it is properly called Persian) cotton, not more than four" (182).

30. Philip Morgan, "Work and Culture: The Task System and the World of Low Country Blacks, 1700–1800," *William and Mary Quarterly,* 3rd series, 39, no. 4 (October 1982): 568; Higman, *Slave Population and Economy in Jamaica,* 24–25.

31. Morgan, "Work and Culture," 575–76. See also Berlin and Morgan, *Cultivation and Culture,* 582.

32. *An Official Letter from the Commissioners of Correspondence the Bahama Islands* (Nassau, 1823), 41, cited in Higman, *Slave Populations of the British Caribbean,* 179. See also Johnson, *Bahamas,* 31.

33. Report by Wylly to the House of Assembly, December 26, 1815, CO 23/63/37–41.

34. McKinnen, *A Tour,* 172–73, 45.

35. Report by Wylly to the House of Assembly.

36. *Farquharson's Journal,* 24.

37. Report by Wylly to the House of Assembly, CO 23/63/39. See also the act of 1824 (4 Geo IV c. 6). This act mandated that enslaved people were not to receive more than 20 lashes at one time or for only one offence, unless the owner or employer of the enslaved or the supervisor of the workhouse or keeper of the gaol was present.

38. This was evidenced by the case of "Poor Black Kate." *Poor Black Kate. Cruelties perpetuated by Henry and Helen Moss, on their slave Kate, in The Bahamas* (London, ca. 1828). Kate was an enslaved domestic belonging to Henry and Helen Moss who had a plantation at Crooked Island. In July 1826, she was confined to the stocks for 17 days. During her confinement, she was beaten repeatedly. Tasks were given to her which she was incapable of performing. Red pepper was rubbed on her eyes. When taken out of the stocks, Kate was flogged and sent to the fields to work. There she died of a fever. The Mosses were found guilty of a misdemeanor and were sentenced to the gaol in Nassau for five months and fined £300. A group of 28 citizens, including seven members of the House of Assembly, petitioned the secretary of state asking for a mitigation of their sentence. When they were released they were entertained at a public dinner. Saunders, *Slavery in the Bahamas,* 160–61.

39. D. Gail Saunders, "The Slave Population of the Bahamas, 1783–1834" (M.Phil. thesis, University of the West Indies, Mona, Jamaica, 1978), 259, 386.

40. Ibid., 198; Saunders, *Slavery in the Bahamas*, 94.
See also the act of 1824 (4 Geo IV c. 6). This act mandated that enslaved people were not to receive more than 20 lashes at one time or for only one offense, unless the owner or employer of the enslaved or the supervisor of the workhouse or keeper of the gaol was present.

41. Saunders, "The Slave Population of the Bahamas, 1783–1834" (M.Phil. thesis, University of the West Indies, Mona, Jamaica, 1978), 259, 386.

42. William Wylly to Munnings, August 31, 1818, CO 23/67/147–49.

43. Regulations for the Government of the Slaves at Clifton and Tusculum in New Providence, July 1815, CO 23/67/147.

44. Higman, *Slave Populations of the British Caribbean*, 188.

45. *An Official Letter from the Commissioners of Correspondence of the Bahama Islands,* cited in D. Gail North, "The Amelioration and Abolition of Slavery in the Bahamas 1808–1833" (B.A. thesis, University of Newcastle Upon Tyne, 1966), 32.

46. Report by Wylly to the House of Assembly, CO 23/63/39.

47. *Farquharson's Journal,* 13–24.

48. Higman, *Slave Populations of the British Caribbean*, 168. See also Shepherd, "Trade and Exchange," 113.

49. Votes of the House of Assembly, 1821–1824, 31–32.

50. See Shepherd, "Trade and Exchange," 114.

51. Saunders, "Slave Population," 287.

52. Ibid. About 30 percent of colored enslaved males worked in the field their entire life after the age of 10. Approximately 25 percent worked as mariners their entire life. Between 11 and 15 years of age, about 48 percent, were engaged in the field, but by 16 to 24 years of age this dropped to about 34 percent—about 15 had left the field to engage in mariner activities, in salt production, and in domestic work (ibid., 289).

53. Ibid., 273, 292.

54. Higman, *Slave Populations of the British Caribbean*, 190–91; Genovese, *Roll, Jordan, Roll,* 319.

55. McKinnen, *A Tour,* 183.

56. Higman, *Slave Populations of the British Caribbean*, 48. See also Craton and Saunders, *Islanders in the Stream,* 1: 311–13.

57. Morgan, "Work and Culture," 578, 585.

58. Michel Rolph Truillot, "Coffee Planters and Coffee Slaves in the Antilles: The Impact of a Secondary Crop," in Berlin and Morgan, *Cultivation and Culture,* 137.

59. *Farquharson's Journal,* 4, 5, 28, 82, 83, cited in Higman, *Slave Populations of the British Caribbean,* 213.

60. Saunders, *Slavery in the Bahamas,* 157–58.

61. Barry Gaspar, "Slavery, Amelioration and Sunday Markets in Antigua,

1823–1833," *Slavery and Abolition* 9, no. 1 (May 1988): 5. See also Mintz and Hall, "Origins of the Jamaican Internal Marketing System," 57.

62. An Act for governing of Negroes, Mulattoes and Indians, 1767 (MS).

63. 37 Geo III c.2; 4 Geo. IV, c.6.

64. Johnson, *Bahamas*, 49; see Berlin and Morgan, *Cultivation and Culture*, 23–24.

65. Regulations for the Government of the slaves at Clifton and Tusculum. See Howard Johnson, "A Slow and Extended Abolition: The Case of the Bahamas 1800–1838," in *From Chattel Slaves to Wage Slaves: The Dynamics of Labor Bargaining in the Americas*, ed. Mary Turner (Kingston: Ian Randle, 1995), 167. See also Enclosure in Munnings to Bathurst, September 9, 1818, CO 23/67/150–51; folios 147–49; and Johnson, "Slow and Extended," 52.

66. Marshall, "Provision Ground and Plantation Labor," 203. See also S. W. Mintz, "Slavery and the Rise of Peasantries," *Historical Reflections* 6 (1979): 213–42; and Mintz and Hall, *Origins of the Jamaican Internal Marketing System*, 3–26.

67. Johnson, *Bahamas*, 52

68. John Rolle, an ardent follower of Pitt in the English House of Commons, was raised to the peerage as Baron Rolle in Stevenstone in 1796, taking the title of his uncle who had died without issue. Lord Rolle inherited the five plantations in Exuma situated in Rolleville, Rolletown, Steventon, Ramsey, and Mount Thompson from his father, Denys Rolle of Devonshire, England. Denys Rolle had laid out a town, Charlotia, later called Rollestown, on the eastern bank of the Saint John's River. The settlement comprised about 300 persons from the London slums. The venture failed, as many of the original settlers fled, seeking an easier life. To some extent they were replaced by enslaved Africans. At the time of the evacuation of East Florida, Rolle had about 140 enslaved people whom he transported along with his livestock and other possessions on the *Peace and Plenty* (the name of a present-day hotel in George Town) to Exuma Island in the Bahamas. Rolle's first grant comprised two tracts totaling about 2,000 acres. The original holdings were called Rolleville and Rolletown. Later, Rolle expanded his holdings to 5,000 acres in the center of Exuma. He called the additional settlements Steventon, Ramsey, and Mount Thompson. Saunders, *Bahamian Loyalists*, 21. See also Craton, "Hobbessian or Panglossian?" 327.

69. Police Magistrate Report. Enclosed in Smyth to Murray, May 11, 1830, CO 23/82/346.

70. Cited in Craton and Saunders, *Islanders in the Stream*, 1: 383. See Lewis Grant, December 27, 1828, CO 23/78, 182.

71. Johnson, *Bahamas*, 32, 49.

72. Craton, "Hobbessian or Panglossian?" 355; Johnson, "Slow and Extended," 168.

73. Saunders, "Slave Population," 158.

74. Johnson, *Bahamas*, 158.

75. Ibid., 64.

76. Ibid., 86.

77. Ibid., 33.

78. Smyth to Goderick, May 2, 1831, CO 23/84–134.

79. Johnson, *Bahamas,* 37.

80. Ibid., 37.

81. Ibid. See also Loren Schweninger, "The Underside of Slavery: The Internal Economy, Self-Hire and Quasi-Freedom in Virginia, 1780–1865," *Slavery and Abolition* 12, no. 2 (September 1991): 1–22, for a discussion of the evolution of the self-hire system in Virginia.

82. Johnson, "Slave Life and Leisure in Nassau, Bahamas 1783–1838," *Slavery and Abolition* 16, no. 1 (April 1995): 55; Johnson, *Bahamas,* 46.

83. Johnson, "Slave Life and Leisure," 56–57; see also 1795 Police Act in Duplicate Manuscript Laws of the Bahamas, 1795–1799, and 1824 Slave Act, 4 Geo. IV, c. 6.

84. Higman, *Slave Populations of the British Caribbean,* 380.

85. Johnson, "Slave Life and Leisure," 55.

86. Howard Johnson, personal communication, November 25, 1996.

87. Johnson, "Slow and Extended," 178.

88. Craton and Saunders, *Islanders in the Stream,* 1: 298.

89. Johnson, "A Slow and Extended," 178. See also Johnson, *Bahamas,* 46.

7

State Enslavement in Colonial Havana, 1763–1790

Evelyn Powell Jennings

The nature of African enslavement in Cuba has long been central to wider debates about the nature of African enslavement in the Americas. But much of the historiography on African enslavement in Cuba has focused on the production of sugar on plantations by enslaved workers in the nineteenth century. This focus has obscured the crucial role the Spanish state played in the growth and character of enslavement on the island, especially before 1790. Cuba ultimately developed two distinct but inter-related sectors using enslaved labor, which converged at the end of the eighteenth century. The first of these sectors was urban and was directed in large measure by the needs of the Spanish colonial state, reaching its height in the 1760s. The second sector, which flourished after 1790, was rural and was directed by private enslavers involved in the production of export agricultural commodities, especially sugar.[1] Urban enslavement in Cuba has attracted relatively few scholarly investigations. Although scholars have recognized the importance of the Spanish state to Cuban economic development before 1790, none has treated state enslavement in an urban setting in any detail.[2] Some scholars have highlighted the importance of Spanish law in creating a more open and fluid version of enslavement in the Iberian colonies, using Cuba as their primary example.[3] To a lesser extent, some have argued that the vibrant and diversified economy of Cuba, especially in Havana, also contributed to greater opportunities and mobility for the enslaved and for freed people.[4]

The historiography on Cuba that posits a more open and fluid regime for the enslaved up to 1790 and a progressive "hardening" thereafter in the wake of rapidly expanding sugar production has missed the importance of the crucial moment when the Spanish state became the largest enslaver on the island.[5] The scale and urgency of defense projects after 1763 forced the state to recruit and deploy many of its enslaved workers in ways that were to anticipate the work regimes on sugar plantations in the nineteenth century. That the state soon scaled back its use of the enslaved in favor of other kinds of forced laborers does not negate the importance of that initial moment. Reforms were initiated and precedents set in the structure and funding of colonial administration and in the recruitment and deployment of enslaved labor for public works that later helped to shape the expansion of enslavement in rural Cuba.

This essay examines an important group of workers enslaved by the Spanish colonial state in the late eighteenth century, the king's enslaved laborers who worked on the city's fortifications. This group of the enslaved is significant not only as an example of the diversity of enslavement in Cuba. The enslaved workers purchased by the king in the 1760s for the fort works represented a sizeable portion of Havana's population of enslaved workers.[6] Their recruitment and deployment also played an important role in the reorientation of the Cuban economy toward the better-known axis of sugar and enslavement.

The experience of the workers enslaved by the state in the fortification projects of the 1760s had some features quite different from those usually attributed to the experience of enslavement in cities. The majority of the king's enslaved who worked on the fortification projects in Havana in the second half of the eighteenth century did not enjoy the privileges of living apart from their overseers, hiring themselves out, or controlling some of their conditions of work. Instead, their work regime showed more similarities to the regime attributed to enslaved labor on plantations in the nineteenth century. The 1760s in Havana was an instance in which geopolitical and economic factors such as imperial defense, the Spanish Crown's overextended resources, and the nature of the work to be performed often overshadowed the influence of legal tradition, custom, and urban setting in shaping the experience of the king's enslaved workers.

The Spanish state had a long history of being an enslaver in its own name and of deploying the enslaved in public works.[7] Throughout the Americas, Spanish colonization decimated the Indian population. The precipitous decline of the indigenous population over the first 50 years of conquest was particularly acute in the Caribbean, prompting the Crown in 1518 to authorize the importation of enslaved Africans directly from Africa without the earlier acculturation period in Spain or the Atlantic island colonies. While enslaved Africans were vital to the initial conquest and colonization of Spain's American colonies, they were also employed in the empire's defense. Originally the Crown relied on private initiative and resources to protect colonial shipping and settlements. Various documents

from a number of early defense projects mention the purchase and maintenance of enslaved Africans as part of the costs of construction. In some
cases they were hired out or "donated" (it is not always clear how will-
ingly) by residents or purchased outright by the Crown.[8] All of these
projects used enslaved African labor in some measure. Up through the end
of the seventeenth century, however, those enslaved by the state itself were
a smaller portion of the enslaved employed in defense works.[9]

By the eighteenth century, the Caribbean had become a major theater
for warfare among the competing western European powers. The new
Bourbon monarchy in Spain was acutely aware of the inadequacies of
Cuba's defenses. As open war with England loomed in 1760, the Crown
sent a mission of engineers to report on Havana's defenses. The forts built
at the end of the sixteenth century had made the mouth of the bay of
Havana reasonably secure. The fort of El Morro guarded the point of land
facing the city across the bay, and the smaller La Punta fort guarded the
port area of the city itself. A serious problem was the high ground surrounding the city. The threat of an English invasion made the security of
these hills essential since an enemy with artillery could subdue El Morro
and eventually the city in short order. In addition, the city wall had fallen
into serious disrepair in sections and lacked the height and thickness to
repel a concentrated attack by land.[10] To further complicate Havana's
defenses, the western outer rim of the city also was dominated by three
hills that would give an enemy with artillery command of that approach to
the city.[11]

The new captain-general Prado Portocarrero arrived in 1761 with such
wide-ranging instructions to improve defenses that any administrator
would have found them difficult to implement. Most important, he was to
see to the many repairs necessary on the existing forts and the city wall, as
well as undertaking the construction of a new fort on La Cabaña hill. The
Crown promised to send troops, munitions, and tools to facilitate the
project. Some relief came with a group of *presidiarios* (state convict laborers) sent from Veracruz.

Yet the captain-general still found himself stymied by the fact that the
island was perpetually short of labor for such large projects. An outbreak
of yellow fever in the summer of 1761 felled one of the engineers, many of
the Spanish troops and laborers sent to begin these defense works, and the
small contingent of enslaved workers. By the summer of 1762, little progress had been made on improving Havana's defenses, as Portocarrero frag-
mented his laborers and resources around the many repair projects.[12]
When the British invading force arrived in June, even the ravages of tropi-

cal diseases on the British troops could not save the city.[13] The British took possession of Havana on August 13, 1762, and occupied the island for ten months.

The shock and humiliation of the British occupation spurred the Crown to a major reorganization of the political and military administration of Cuba. In contrast to Spain's usual administrative policies that encouraged overlapping jurisdictions and lengthy consultation, the king appointed the Count of Ricla as captain-general of Cuba with wide-ranging powers to shore up the island's defenses. Once in possession of the island, his first and most urgent task was to repair the city's fortifications and to undertake the reorganization of the military forces on the island. While these instructions were similar to those given his predecessors, Ricla was granted extraordinary authority to marshal resources and make decisions about their deployment. The king had approved a general plan for the building and repair of the fortifications, but Ricla was authorized to make adjustments as he saw fit.[14]

Ricla arrived in Havana in June 1763. After reviewing the state of the plaza, he quickly began organizing the fortification projects. As an initial measure, he solicited donations of laborers from enslavers in Havana, as many as they could spare without detriment to their own properties. The viceroy of New Spain promised some Indians and convicts, along with the subsidy payment granted to Cuba by the Crown. To offset the extreme shortage of skilled workers on the island, Ricla requested that 120 masons and 40 stonecutters be sent from Spain as quickly as possible.[15] But these groups of workers were small compared to the large numbers needed to undertake the building of a new fort and all the many repairs now required after the fighting during the British siege.

Since the shortage of laborers had proven to be a crucial factor in the fall of Havana, Ricla was given the power to determine the number of workers needed and to make contracts and purchase enslaved Africans on royal account. He could import enslaved workers from foreign colonies (something the Crown was usually loath to do) or to transport them directly from Africa, under Spanish or foreign flag, on commission or contract. He was also allowed to include in these contracts the importation of enslaved Africans for the private sector.[16] To make these contracts, Ricla was permitted to grant trade concessions to encourage contractors. Where the Crown had previously employed groups of several hundred enslaved workers on various projects, Ricla signed contracts for thousands of the enslaved to be delivered over the next two years. The contractors agreed to sell enslaved workers to the Crown at a discount in return for permission to import such things as flour or to export molasses.[17] This direct resort by the state to the Atlantic trade in enslaved workers was not new, but the scale of state demand at this moment for enslaved labor was certainly unprecedented and allowed Ricla to negotiate deals at prices very favorable to the Crown.[18] It also encouraged the state to facilitate the provision of enslaved workers to the private sector.

The general defense plan for the city under Ricla's direction concentrated on the repair of the main existing fort of El Morro and on the building of two new forts, one on the hill of La Cabaña and another called Atarés, south of the city's arsenal. The repairs and La Cabaña were given priority. Without the successful completion of these two projects, all others were deemed superfluous. The work of clearing the trees from La Cabaña was begun immediately with the help of hundreds of enslaved laborers donated by neighboring sugar-plantation owners for a period of two months.[19] Once this was completed, the first order of business would be to begin the digging of the fort's foundation and trenches. Virtually all of the work required for the building and repairs of the fort in this early phase was arduous, backbreaking labor that required considerable physical strength. These requirements are reflected in the contracts, as the enslaved workers designated for purchase by the Crown were largely young adult males. The gender ratios were sharply skewed among those destined for state service, with estimates of 3,959 enslaved males and 400 enslaved females purchased by Ricla.[20]

As the work was difficult and exhausting, private enslavers were reluctant to loan or rent their own enslaved workers for these tasks after the initial rush to secure the city in 1763. The most intense phase of the fortification works spanned the years from 1764 through 1769. Unfortunately, available data on the entire period are not continuous or complete, but good data sets of the workers employed there exist for the years 1765 (seven monthly summaries) and late 1767 and 1768 (ten monthly summaries). Ricla was taking proposals of contracts for the importations of enslaved workers in the late summer of 1763. A portion of 1764, then, was probably consumed in bringing together the necessary workers through the forced recruitment of convicts from Cuba and from New Spain and of enslaved Africans through the Atlantic trade. Estimates of state purchases list 795 enslaved people brought to the island through Havana in 1763. But once contractors had organized financing and the logistics of the Atlantic passage, in 1764 an estimated 7,255 enslaved people were disembarked in Havana.[21] With this large influx of enslaved workers to the city, Ricla also was occupied with organizing their maintenance, as he wrote numerous letters seeking supplies for their sustenance, clothing, and medical care.[22]

By the early spring of 1765, there were over 2,000 workers employed in the three main sites of fortification work around Havana. The largest group of workers on these projects was recently arrived enslaved Africans (*bozales*), who accounted for between 54 percent and 67 percent of the total workforce over the year. A much smaller group of Hispanized workers enslaved by the Crown (*ladinos*) made up 0.5 percent of the total workforce. Two other groups of the enslaved were employed on the fortification projects in 1765, a group of the enslaved who had fled the English, most probably during the occupation, and a smaller group of the enslaved hired out from private owners. Together they constituted 2.7 percent of the total workforce. The only other group that came close in numbers to the recently arrived enslaved Africans was that of the convict laborers, who accounted for between 19 and 29 percent of the total workforce over the year of 1765. Free workers of color also constituted a very small group of the total workforce in 1765, an average of 1.9 percent. Native Cubans who were designated by Spanish authorities as white (*paysanos*, as opposed to the free people of color designated as *mulatos* or *negros libres*) were a similar portion of the total workforce for 1765 at 2 percent. Clearly, enslaved Africans recently purchased through the Atlantic trade were crucial to Ricla's plan to reinforce the battered defenses of Havana quickly. Free workers, black and white, were never more than 5 percent of the total workforce. They were usually skilled workers hired to do the careful work of stonecutting and masonry. Because the bulk of the work, especially at the beginning of the projects, involved heavy, unskilled labor, the state resorted to using a mix of coerced laborers. Since convicts from New Spain were not numerous in 1763, the urgency of the projects and the difficulty of the labor necessitated the state buying and maintaining a large contingent of enslaved workers in its own name to advance its defense program.

The monthly summaries list some of the many tasks at which those employed on the fortifications worked. Besides those assigned to the fort sites for digging, hauling, and construction, others quarried and cut stone, and some made fascines to fill trenches and build batteries. Some worked the ovens and hauled lime and charcoal.[23] The summaries also reveal some specialization among the coerced workers assigned to state defense works. The carting of materials around the fort sites with mules and oxcarts was exclusively the province of prisoners, a group of 60 to 67 convicts over 1765. After this date, the figures for carting were subsumed under one of

Table 7.1. Workers on fort projects, March–October 1765

Month	Native Cubans	Prisoners	Free mulatos	Free blacks	Ladinos	Bozales del Rey	Black fugitives	Private slaves	Hospital workers	Total
March	55	513	23	20	13	1,429	41	16	NA	2,110
April	36	446	18	16	12	1,217	46	18	424	2,233
May	44	510	20	21	13	1,352	46	18	331	2,355
June	43	430	22	23	13	1,303	42	18	378	2,272
July	50	616	19	30	11	1,511	49	18	[375]	2,304
August	52	624	20	31	13	1,473	48	20	[375]	2,281
October	50	629	16	30	13	1,399	43	12	[443]	2,192

Source: This table was constructed from figures given in tables found in AGI, SD, 1647, "Estado de la Revista pasada por Don Nicolas Joseph Rapun Cavallero de la orden de Santiago y Comisario de la Guerra de los Extractos a los Negros Esclavos del Rey y demas individuos que se hallan desterrados en los Travaxos de fortificacion en esta Plaza en los dias 9 de marzo 1765," "Estado . . . en los dias 21, 22, 23, 24 del presente mes [abril]," "Estado . . . en los dias 26, 27, 28, de mayo 1765," and "Estado . . . en los dias 29 y 30 de junio 1765."

the fort sites. Carpentry, on the other hand, was carried out by a group of 21 to 25 workers enslaved by the king (*bozales del Rey*) whose numbers remained constant throughout the period from 1765 through 1768. Although it was only listed separately for two months of 1765, the making of fascines was done exclusively by 90 of those enslaved by the king.

Other tasks drew mixed groups of workers. The stone quarries were worked by a handful of *paysanos,* some convicts, and groups of several hundred workers enslaved by the king. The lime and charcoal ovens employed both convicts and some of the king's enslaved laborers, but the proportion of convicts to the enslaved grew over the period from March 1765 to October 1768. Work in the warehouses (holding foodstuffs, salt, water, and so forth for the fort workers) showed a similar progression to greater reliance on convicts over enslaved workers between 1765 and 1768.

Still, the vast majority of those enslaved by the king and the prisoners were employed at the fort sites themselves. In spite of inconsistencies in the data due to some groups of workers being listed under fort sites in several months and separately by task in others, general trends in the patterns of state employment are visible.[24] There was a gradual increase in the numbers of free workers employed, especially at the fort works, over the years from 1765 to 1768. The state also increased its use of convict labor both at the forts and at other tasks. But this growing use of free workers and convicts did not offset an overall decline in the total number of workers in all the state's defense works by October 1768. It was the decline of the use of enslaved workers of all provenances, particularly those enslaved by the king, that accounted for the overall decline in the total workforce.

Besides the heavy work of digging trenches and foundations necessary for fort building, some of the workers enslaved by the state were assigned to work with the free skilled workers to learn their trade. The state preferred to use its own enslaved workers for this for several reasons. On the one hand, convict laborers were rarely sentenced to fort works in perpetuity. Some had sentences as short as several months.[25] With skilled workers enslaved by the Crown, the fortification projects could count on benefiting from their training for as long as the project demanded, and the state would benefit from the higher price that an enslaved worker with skills would bring in the always tight market for skilled labor on the island.

In addition to the large number of the enslaved working on the forts themselves, there were smaller groups of workers enslaved by the king employed in a number of sites in Havana. The reports of the Hospital of San Ambrosio de la Havana (one from 1765 and ten from 1768) listed a total workforce of 30 to 36 employees. The hospital, which was established to care for ailing Spanish troops, employed an average of 19 free civilians (servants, medical personnel, and administrators), 12 prisoners (some of whom were listed as Guachinango Indians), and between seven and nine workers enslaved by the king. These lists include the king's enslaved listed by name, their consistency indicating that a core of seven Crown enslaved persons worked at the hospital over a number of years.[26]

The military reorganization of the island after its return from the British prompted the Spanish to reestablish the two artillery companies that had defended Havana before the occupation, and a group of the Crown's enslaved workers was assigned to this company. The summaries for the year 1765 listed a group of 90 to 99 persons enslaved by the king as the only workers under the Artillery Brigade. This group of king's enslaved workers disappears from the general reviews of the forts' workforce, but the royal commissioner was keeping separate records of the group by the end of 1767. Certain conditions for this particular group of workers enslaved by the king seem to have been better than those of other enslaved laborers working on the fortifications, which suggests that some of the former had acquired skills that made them particularly valuable to the state, perhaps as metalworkers and armorers. During the British siege, enslaved workers skilled in the operation of cannon also had proved very valuable to the defense of El Morro.[27] The number of workers enslaved by the king in the artillery company reached around 200 in 1768, but instead of the overwhelmingly male *dotación* (contingent) assigned to fort works, the king's enslaved workers in artillery were almost perfectly divided between men and women. They seem to have been allowed to marry and live with their wives and children in the quarters of the artillery company. Such accommodations for family life suggest that the state highly valued their skills and planned to keep them as a permanent part of that company.[28]

Workers enslaved by the king also were employed at the other major sites of state enterprises in Havana. They worked in the Royal Shipyard, building and outfitting ships for the royal navy and merchant marine. They labored in the Royal Arsenal constructed just outside the city wall in the 1740s and in the Royal Tobacco Factory. Besides being employed in myriad other tasks around the city, some of the Crown's enslaved people worked in the homes of the colonial officials stationed in the city.

The reasons for the state's declining use of its own enslaved workers in the defense works were varied, but most seem to be related in some measure to the expense of purchasing and maintaining its own force of enslaved laborers. Even though the Crown had been able to purchase thou-

Table 7.2. State purchases of enslaved laborers for fort works, May 1763–65

Year	Slave purchases	Average price/ pesos	Total/pesos	Total/reales
1763	795	150	119,250	954,000
1764	1,967	150	295,050	2,362,420
1765	1,436	140.8	202,235	1,617,884
Total	4,198		616,684	4,934,304

Source: AGI, SD, 2129 "Estado que manifiesta los gastos, y costos . . ." December 31, 1772.

sands of enslaved laborers at less than market price, the expense was still considerable and revenues were short. A summary of expenses in the royal fortification projects compiled in December 1772 listed the state's purchases of enslaved workers at 4,198 individuals. Table 7.2 shows the state's expenditures in these purchases.[29]

The purchase of enslaved workers alone accounted for 50.5 percent of the expenses incurred in the first two and a half years of the fortification projects. Labor costs more generally, which included the purchases of the enslaved, rations and medical care for the enslaved and prisoners, the cost of the desertion guards, and the salaries of other employees (not including the engineers), constituted 65 percent of the total expenses recorded for fort works between May 1763 and the end of 1765.

Unfortunately for colonial officials on the island, Cuba never generated enough revenue to pay for its own defenses. During the 1750s, the Havana treasury recorded an average annual income of some 162,000 pesos, and the Crown also needed to assign to the island a portion of the Mexican *situado,* a subsidy from the Mexican treasury, to cover the costs of the permanent garrison, shipbuilding, fort repair, and other state expenses.[30] Still, before the British occupation of Havana, the *situado* payments were modest compared with their escalation over the second half of the eighteenth century. Between 1750 and 1755, the *situado* amounted to an annual average of 267,000 pesos. During the late 1750s, as expenses for shipbuilding rose, the *situado* climbed to an annual average of 437,000 pesos. But the most intense period of the fortification projects in Havana saw the subsidy payment more than triple to an average of 1,485,000 pesos per year from 1763 to 1769.[31] While the state assigned the cost of the fortifications to the Mexican *situado,* the island was supposed to fund its army and militia.

The purchase and maintenance of a large dotation of workers enslaved by the Crown constituted a significant investment of state resources, but the expense was compounded by losses of enslaved workers through disease, desertion, and death. And the state had to expend some resources on medical attention for its enslaved workers. Two hospitals were built in Havana for their treatment, staffed with a doctor, two surgeons, three bloodletters, an aide, and a chaplain. At times the Crown replaced some of the medical personnel with prisoner attendants as a cost reduction measure. The state also assigned an interpreter to help recently arrived enslaved Africans communicate with their doctors.[32] A significant portion of the total workforce on the fort projects was incapacitated over the first five and a half years. Prisoners were consistently more likely to fall ill than were the king's enslaved workers. One reason for this may have been that the population of prisoners was constantly being supplemented with new arrivals, particularly from New Spain. On the other hand, no new enslaved workers were purchased by the Crown after 1765. In the unfamiliar disease environment of Havana, new forced recruits had a greater chance of becoming ill. For instance, the spike in the percentages of prisoners in the hospital from May to July 1768 may be due to the arrival of 294 Guachinango Indians from Mexico in May and June of that year.

These Indians also seemed to be particularly prone to desertion, as the monthly summaries for the three months list 61 Guanchingos as having deserted out of a total of 110 desertions among all groups of workers (both forced and free) and soldiers. Desertions among the enslaved are more difficult to gauge precisely. For all the monthly summaries of 1768 that give breakdowns of deserters, the total number of the enslaved who deserted was only 16 individuals.[33] Yet in the early years of the fort projects, desertions by the enslaved may have posed a greater problem. The summary of project expenses showed no outlays to stem desertions in the half year of 1763, but in 1764 and 1765, when 3,403 enslaved workers were purchased by the Crown, the cost of the desertion guard squad totaled 37,884 pesos. The state continued to fund the desertion squad at lesser levels through 1772.[34] Problems with desertion may also help to explain the concentration of prisoners in transport tasks such as carting that allowed workers considerable mobility, since the desertion of prisoners, while troublesome, would not have represented as much of a loss on Crown investment as the desertion of the enslaved workers of the king.

The numbers of the enslaved who died while working in the fortification projects is more difficult to determine. Cuban historian Francisco Pérez Guzmán estimates a death rate for the state's enslaved workers and convict laborers at about 15 percent to 20 percent. The actual numbers are obscured by the fact that there seems to have been an active trade in state enslaved workers by falsifying their deaths and selling them in the private sector.[35] Still, fragments of evidence suggest that deaths among the newly arrived enslaved Africans were a serious problem. Between the summer of 1763 and the end of 1764, the Crown purchased 2,762 enslaved Africans for the fort works. A report from the Hospital de Nuestra Señora del Pilar, which treated the enslaved and prisoners, listed the deaths of a total of 534 *bozales del Rey* between April and October of 1764, or 19.3 percent of the new, purchased enslaved Africans.[36] While death from disease and injury was difficult for colonial officials to stem, in October 1764 the Junta de Fortificación tried to control fraud and desertion by ordering that the king's enslaved workers be marked with the letters of the garrison brigade to which they were assigned.[37]

The work regimes endured by the state's enslaved workers and by prisoners also contributed to the high rates of disease, death, and desertion on the fort works. At the fort sites with over 1,000 workers, the contingents of the enslaved and convicts were generally mustered out separately in brigades of about 100 men. Each work brigade was assigned to and supervised by a specific brigade of soldiers from the Spanish garrison.[38] How workers would have been organized for tasks in settings with smaller, mixed groups of workers is less clear. At the limekilns, the ratio of prisoners to the enslaved was fairly even until the end of 1765, when prisoners began to predominate. In the extant records, there was only one soldier assigned to the kilns through 1765, and then two or three appear in records for 1767 and 1768 as the numbers of workers rose to over 90. In the warehouses as well, the workers were a mixed group, with only one or two soldiers assigned to them over the entire period from 1765 to 1768, even though the numbers of workers increased to over 200 by 1768.[39]

The workday at the fort sites began and ended with a roll call and an accounting of any tools issued. The workday in the summer months generally extended to 12 ½ hours, taking advantage of more hours of daylight. The winter months averaged a 9- to 10-hour day. Work discipline was maintained by armed guards assigned to each brigade. There was usually a brief break in the morning for breakfast, a longer break of some 3 to 4 hours with the main meal at midday, and dinner after the end of the workday in the evening. The chaplains were supposed to offer religious instruction during meal breaks and say mass on Sundays and holidays. The aim of this instruction was to ensure that "the spiritual well-being of those souls [of the enslaved], disposed by the grace of baptism, be reconciled with service to the king."[40] Religious instruction by the clergy only became the norm in 1764 with official regulation and payment of chaplains assigned to the fort works. Before 1764, these duties were carried out voluntarily by engineers, supervisors, and clergy at various work sites. Only after the state became responsible for some 2,000 newly arrived enslaved Africans did it directly commit itself to funding and regulating the conversion and instruction of its own enslaved workers.

Francisco Pérez Guzmán has studied the average diet of enslaved workers and prisoners on the fortification projects of the late eighteenth century. He concludes that it was generally adequate in protein and carbohydrates, including salted meats, rice, and root vegetables. The diet was rather shorter on other vegetables but did include legumes several days per week. He calculated a range of caloric intake between 3,400 and 4,400 calories per day as probably sufficient to sustain the workers, although it was not an especially varied diet.[41] Enslaved workers and convicts were also issued three rations of tobacco per day, and those working in particularly draining work were given *sambumbía*—a drink of sugarcane juice, water, and chilies—as refreshment.[42]

The clothing allowance seems to have been in line with the custom on the island. The king's enslaved workers were issued two suits of clothing per year, consisting of pants and shirts of ordinary linen and a blue or green overshirt for the cold season.[43] Shoes do not seem to have been a regular part of the clothing allotment.[44]

In terms of housing, the lot of those enslaved by the state was particularly hard. Because large numbers of the enslaved were acquired by the state quickly, their housing was somewhat makeshift and cramped even by plantation standards. The typical housing was a barracks constructed at about 137.5 feet in length but only 13.75 feet in width to house 200 to 220 enslaved workers or convicts. There was no division of the space inside the barracks to allow for any privacy, and the beds were generally made of wooden slats. There was little relief since fort regulations required all workers, enslaved and free, to remain on-site during the workweek. These cramped conditions were eased somewhat only as the number of workers confined to the hospital mounted into the hundreds.[45]

With labor expenses running at over 60 percent of total costs on the fort projects and losses by disease, death, and desertion mounting, by 1765 officials were increasingly concerned about the overwhelming expenses involved in so many large and complex projects. The king's enslaved laborers were the largest contingent of workers on the fortification projects in its most intense and urgent phase between 1763 and 1765. The highest yearly total of 1,967 enslaved people employed by the state had been reached in 1764.[46] In the following year, the king ordered the intendant to begin selling off the unskilled among the enslaved to raise money for the fort works.[47] After 1765, the proportion of workers enslaved by the king to convict laborers began to decline, and by 1769 prisoners outnumbered the enslaved.[48] The report on fort expenses of 1772 listed 423 enslaved workers still owned by the Crown after the state had recouped some 3,123,647 reales by selling many of its enslaved laborers. At prices for the purchase of enslaved laborers current in Cuba in the 1760s (250 to 300 pesos per individual), this would have involved the sale of between approximately 1,300 and 1,500 enslaved workers.

Another proposal to relieve the Crown of the expense of buying and maintaining its own enslaved workers on the construction sites was made by the intendant to the king in 1764. He proposed establishing a "colony" of king's enslaved workers in a suburb of Havana with "700 chosen male slaves and marry them to 700 female slaves of their choosing. . . . I would not give them land because being at the door of the city they will better earn their livelihood with carts working in the city and because it will be possible to keep them under my view and to intervene in their disorders which is the principal charge of this business, there are no inconveniences to conscience because here you may see by this means some residents that know how to conserve their goods more than the rest."[49]

This proposal does not seem to have been implemented, but it does offer some insights into the relationships the state could have with its own enslaved workers. Here the intendant was proposing establishing an urban colony of king's enslaved workers that bears some resemblance to the community of workers enslaved by the Crown in the copper mines of El Cobre in eastern Cuba. While those enslaved at El Cobre owed the state labor, they had been granted plots of land for their subsistence. This settled community relieved the Crown from the expense of their maintenance and provided a pool of people to defend the area as well. The enslaved miners of El Cobre and their families worked these plots for generations, establishing a permanent community that had a strong sense of privileged status by the grace of the king.[50] In the urban context of Havana, the intendant proposed allowing a colony of the enslaved to take advantage of the city's thriving economy through the opportunities to earn a living in carting and petty commerce. The skilled enslaved Crown workers employed outside the fort projects had more possibility of establishing families and working for wages than their counterparts in the forts. As discussed earlier, for instance, the enslaved employed in the artillery company seem to have enjoyed at least the comforts of family life that were denied the enslaved workers laboring on the fortifications.

Besides organizing the fortifications' workforce and the laborers' maintenance, Ricla was also charged with helping develop and implement a plan for commercial reform that would generate the revenue necessary for imperial defense on the island. He conducted private consultations beginning in the autumn of 1763 with members of the Havana elite to come to a mutually beneficial package of reforms.[51] When Ricla's tenure on the island ended in 1765, a final plan had been approved by the king.[52] News of the final regulations of the commercial reform plan became official in Cuba on March 1, 1766, with the arrival of the new captain-general, Antonio Bucarely. The new trade regulations represented some significant concessions to Cuban interests. There could now be "free" trade under which the Spanish ports of Alicante, Málaga, Cartagena, Barcelona, Santander, Gijón, La Coruña, Seville, and Cádiz were allowed to trade with Havana. This commerce could be carried in either Spanish or Cuban ships. Trade duties were also rationalized, converting older duties based on weight and volume to ad valorem duties in return for a hike in the excise tax (*alcabala*) from 2 to 4 percent to 6 percent. The new regulations were particularly advantageous to sugar interests. Cuban sugar now had greater access to the Spanish market, and, despite pressure from the French Bourbons, sugar from the French islands was refused privileged access to Spain. After 1765, the new *alcabala* generated between 40 and 50 percent of the island's revenues, and Cuba contributed a growing percentage of the revenue for its own defense. Yet the island still relied on subsidies for the bulk of its financial needs. Luckily for imperial finances, royal revenues experienced considerable growth in Mexico during this period, so the *situado* continued to be a fundamental part of Cuban financing.[53]

The new captain-general Bucarely retained some of the extraordinary powers granted to Ricla, and the principal goal of his administration continued to be the realization of the various defense projects.[54] Procuring the necessary funding and recruiting sufficient laborers remained a major problem in carrying out the fort works. The Mexican *situado* allocation for fortifications had been reduced from 500,000 to 300,000 pesos, a sum Bucarely deemed inadequate for the work necessary on La Cabaña alone. And even the reduced sum could not be counted upon, since the viceroy of New Spain rarely sent the full amount.

In May 1768, Bucarely called a meeting of the Junta de Fortificación to develop some initiatives to reduce costs while bringing the fort works to a speedy conclusion. After consultation and discussion, the Junta decided that the only place they could cut expenses was in the excavation of

Table 7.3. Free workers, prisoners, and King's enslaved workers at fort sites, May–September 1768

Month	Free	Forzados	Negros del Rey	Total
May	140	529	1,020	1,689
June	139	685	959	1,783
July	144	640	860	1,644
September	137	760	842	1,739
October	126	690	703	1,519

Source: AGI, SD, 2122, "Estado de Revista . . . de los Negros, esclavos del Rey y demas Individuos en las citadadas obras . . . ," May 15, 1768, June 19, 1768, July 24, 1768, and September 18, 1768. The heading "free workers" here includes *paysanos, mulatos,* and *negros libres.*

trenches on the forts. Some of this work had been contracted out since 1764. Bucarely tartly remarked that the contractors had left the most difficult parts of the excavation until the last and now would not complete the work without raising the price. In marked contrast to the strategy used at the start of the fort works in 1763, colonial officials were not looking to enslaved laborers to carry out this difficult work. Instead, the Junta decided that as prisoners arrived from New Spain, they would be assigned directly to the trenches, dismissing the day laborers presently working there in equal numbers as they were replaced with prisoners. To further offset costs, the Junta decided that the intendant should take charge of the sale of "some of the slaves less useful for such work, those most likely to lose their value."[55] The Junta saw no other way to cut expenses. This measure was taken to ensure that within the next three years the large works on La Cabaña would be finished and the resultant savings could be applied to beginning work on a smaller fort on the hill of Aróstegui to the west of the city.[56]

As this plan was put into action, the composition of the workforce at the fort sites began to change, as table 7.3 illustrates. In spite of the Junta's intention to reduce the contingent of day laborers in equal measure with the arrival of prisoners from New Spain, the number of free workers on the fort projects varied only by a handful over the five months. The dotation of king's enslaved workers, on the other hand, was reduced by 317 people, at least 160 of whom were sold to private owners, according to the monthly workforce summaries from June and July of 1768. Table 7.3 indicates that by the fall of 1768, the king's enslaved workers were rapidly declining as the main labor support of the fortification projects in Havana. With a steady supply of prisoners from New Spain, the state felt able to divest itself of some of its less-skilled enslaved workers to recoup their value and offset the tremendous expenses of the fort works. It seems that by 1768, in the changing circumstances of the empire's labor market, the skills acquired by the king's enslaved workers in the Havana fort projects rather than the projects' urgency for imperial defense determined the retention and deployment of enslaved labor at the forts.

Yet these changes in the organization and composition of the labor force were insufficient to put the fortifications' financing on a surer footing. Even after the Junta's meetings, Bucarely continued to press the issue of the desperate state of Havana's funding on the minister of the Indies. The insecurity of *situado* funds forced the captain-general to resort to considerable borrowing to keep the projects afloat, some 295,676 pesos in loans for the first four months of 1768.[57]

Bucarely and the Junta met again in the summer of 1768 to discuss the projects' funding. They had hoped that the sales of from 200 to 250 of the king's enslaved workers would cover fort works' expenses for two to three months. But the *situado* payment had been reduced almost by half in 1768, forcing Havana residents to absorb more of the costs and hold debts for the projects. The intendant expressed his sense that the government could no longer expect large amounts of help from local residents, neither in loans nor in donations.[58]

Bucarely's perseverance ultimately was rewarded, as a number of the fortification works around the plaza of Havana were completed during his tenure. When his successor, Felipe Fondesviela, the marqués de la Torre, arrived in 1771, only the small castle on the hill of Aróstegui and the major project of La Cabaña remained unfinished. The marqués de la Torre was also blessed with a period of relative peace in which to carry out the last of the major defense works in Havana. Peace with Britain relieved the captain-general of the desperate urgency suffered by his predecessors after the siege and occupation of Havana in 1763.

The available monthly summaries of those assigned to the fort works in the mid-1770s show a continuation of the trends in recruitment and deployment of state workers, both free and coerced, visible by the late 1760s. At the two remaining fort sites, La Cabaña and the Loma of Aróstegui (also known as the fort El Príncipe), prisoners had come to outnumber workers enslaved by the king by almost two to one. Free workers, both whites and free people of color, represented a growing percentage of the total workforce, rising from 11.1 percent in October 1774 to 16.5 percent in March 1775. In the summaries of 1765, free workers were

Table 7.4. Workers at La Cabaña and the Loma de Aróstegui, October 1774–March 1775

Year

Month	Paysanos	Prisoners	Free people of color	King's enslaved	Other enslaved	Total
1774						
October	61	366	16	168	4	615
November	61	387	19	168	4	639
1775						
January	80	291	26	161	8	566
February	83	288	24	159	7	561
March	78	287	28	160	7	560

Source: AGI, SD, 1211, "Estado que comprehende el numero de forzados existentes en la rebysta que pase en la Cavaña, y Loma de Arostegui, oy dia de la fecha, con exprecion de sus clases, y destinos en que se hallan travajando: A saver," summaries dated October 30, 1774, November 27, 1774, January 29, 1775, February 26, 1775, March 26, 1775.

only 1.9 percent of the total workforce. Table 7.4 shows the breakdown of the workforce on the fort sites by the mid-1770s.

La Cabaña, the major fortification project of the period, was finally finished in 1776. Hence, the number of workers employed at various tasks around the sites, in warehouses, carting, in woodcutting, at the limekilns, at skilled trades, and in the hospitals roughly equaled the number employed in actual fort work. Segregation of workers enslaved by the king and of prisoners by task was more pronounced in the workforce of the 1770s. Warehouse work was carried out almost exclusively by the king's enslaved workers by a ratio of 10:1. The transportation of supplies by both land and water was the exclusive domain of hundreds of prisoners and a mere handful of free workers.[59] As desertion was still a serious problem for fort works administrators throughout the period, the Crown sought to reduce losses of its own enslaved workers by continuing to employ them in more easily monitored areas.

The acquisition of a skill by the enslaved remained an important factor in their retention as enslaved workers of the Crown. The workers listed by specific skills in the summaries, such as coopers, armorers, masons, and smiths, were all king's enslaved workers. The numbers and breakdown of patients in the hospital continued to show the greater susceptibility to disease of new immigrants to the island, such as prisoners and soldiers. Among the king's enslaved workers assigned to the fort works, an average

Table 7.5. Yearly averages of King's enslaved workers and prisoners employed in Havana fort works, 1763–75

Year	King's enslaved	Prisoners	Total workers
1763	795	NA	NA
1764	1,967	NA	NA
1765	1,396	538	2,249
1766	NA	NA	NA
1767	1,158	964	2,309
1768	1,072	773	2,004
1774	321	980	1,517
1775	319	837	1,318

Source: Averages calculated from sources listed for Tables 7.1–7.4.

of 5.4 percent of their total number were in the hospital between the fall of 1774 and the early spring of 1775. For prisoners, the average was 12 percent. Soldiers assigned to the fort works suffered much higher rates of disease, as an average of 36.4 percent of them were confined to the hospital over the same period.[60]

Even though the total workforce employed on the fort projects had decreased by the mid-1770s, the state continued to employ over 1,000 workers at these sites a full decade after their inception. The most significant change in the state's deployment of labor on defense projects is visible in its divestiture of its dotation of workers enslaved by the king in favor of prisoners. Table 7.5 shows the available data.[61]

The state was able to recoup about 63 percent of its initial expenditure for enslaved Africans by selling them to private owners in Cuba as the urgency of the projects diminished and more prisoners became available. Between 1763 and 1765, 616,788 pesos were spent on the purchases of workers enslaved by the king. Sales of these enslaved workers between 1765 and 1772 netted 390,455 pesos for the Royal Treasury. The summary of 1772 also listed 423 enslaved workers still owned by the Crown at a value of 126,900 pesos, an average value of 300 pesos per enslaved worker, or close to double the original price paid by the Crown. The summary noted the increasing number of deaths and desertions among the king's enslaved workers as a reason for the loss of some 99,432 pesos. Yet the state's power to dictate the price at which it would buy enslaved workers from the contractors between 1763 and 1765 allowed it to offset some of the immense labor costs of the fortification projects.

By the time Spain entered the American War of Independence against the British in 1779, the major works of fortification in Havana had been completed. But the state still maintained a workforce of some 670 workers into the 1780s to keep the defense sites in good repair. The fort sites now employed only about 250 workers, 99 of whom were workers enslaved by the king. Even with the reduced number of workers in its charge, the state maintained considerable segregation by task, as it had over the past 20 years. Warehouse work and skilled occupations like iron working and carpentry were still dominated by the enslaved of the king. Prisoners were used exclusively on the ferries in the bay, at the slaughterhouse, and in cutting wood. The hospitals still employed a mixed group of workers, although here, too, prisoners predominated.[62]

By the 1780s, the seemingly endless supply of prisoners from New Spain must have been largely exhausted because colonial officials now devoted much of their attention to trying to recruit and control free day laborers.[63] Yet even with free workers, the state found it necessary to use coercion to carry out its public works, and this coercion may have fallen most heavily on free workers of color. The chief engineer Luis Huet proposed using an exemplary punishment of some of the missing black workers to reduce desertion. Huet claimed to know where a number of them were hiding and suggested that they be punished with the wearing of a shackle and chain. The captain-general agreed to the chaining of these deserters for several days "to serve as an example."[64] To little effect it seems, since by December 1782 Huet declared himself on the point of firing half the workers, so disgusted was he with the state of affairs.[65]

Even with the return of peace between Britain and Spain in 1783, the Spanish Crown continued to maintain a workforce of some 600 people on the fort sites. In marked contrast to the workforce 20 years earlier, prisoners now dominated, rather than workers enslaved by the king, as the major source of labor for state projects.

A full two decades after the most intense phase of fortification construction in Havana, in which the labor of the king's enslaved workers was crucial, their numbers employed on the fort sites had fallen below 100 people. But they continued to be employed in other jobs in which they had predominated from the 1760s, including warehousing, hospital work, and especially skilled jobs such as metalworking and carpentry. By the mid-1780s, the largest contingent of those enslaved by the king in Havana was not employed in the fortifications. Rather, the group of the Crown's enslaved workers attached to the Artillery Brigade still numbered 144 persons. Family groups seem to have been maintained, as the ratio of men to women was close to even. It is likely that this group of enslaved workers continued to be highly skilled and important to the Crown for almost 20

Table 7.6. Workers on fortifications, November 1784–January 1785

Year Month	Paysanos	Prisoners	Free people of color	King's enslaved	Other enslaved	Total
1784						
November	51	338	22	190	3	604
December	47	336	25	187	3	598
1785						
January	48	336	25	185	3	59

Source: AGI, Cuba, 1371, "Estado que comprehende el Numero de Forzados existentes en la Revista que pase en la Cavaña y Loma de Arostegui oy dia de la fha. Con exprecion de sus clases y destinos en que trabajan," summaries dated November 28, 1784, December 31, 1784, January 30, 1785.

years, allowing them to maintain their families and to be maintained by the state in their later years.[66] The thousands of enslaved Africans that had labored in the fortifications themselves most likely did not fare as well.

When free trade in enslaved workers was promulgated by the Spanish Crown in 1789, the bulk of the major defense works in Havana had been completed. The state was no longer a major purchaser of enslaved workers in the city's market, and sugar production was poised to take over the economy of the island. The evidence presented in this essay raises a number of questions regarding previous interpretations of the nature of enslavement in Cuba. In the historiography of Cuban enslavement, 1790 is the date after which most authors begin to talk of the "hardening" of the regime suffered by the enslaved, with large importations of enslaved workers, skewed gender ratios in favor of men, gang labor, high mortality, and diminished access to manumission. The evidence here suggests that many of these same conditions obtained in the urban context of state defense projects of the 1760s, before the advent of the sugar boom on the island. Many aspects of the work regimes attributed to plantation enslavement, especially those of sugar plantations, were not unique to plantations or even to rural areas. The much vaunted custom of *coartación*, the purchase of freedom by installments, seems to have been of slight use to the workers enslaved by the king working in fort construction.[67] In spite of legal precedents and custom favoring freedom, many of the king's enslaved workers in late-eighteenth-century Havana were newly arrived Africans, severely restricted in their access to the city itself and to the earning of cash. Those who gained their freedom were more likely to have achieved it as fugitives than as *coartados*. Whether the king's enslaved workers' chances to gain freedom improved over the 20-year period studied here, as the state sought to divest itself of its least-skilled enslaved workers, remains an open question. Any enslaved workers who acquired skills in the king's service and who were actually sold to private owners may have had improved opportunities ultimately to gain their freedom. But while they worked in service of the king, since the state seemed anxious to retain the Crown's enslaved workers with particular skills, freedom would have been elusive.

The state's access to the coerced labor of convicts ultimately allowed it to discontinue its large purchases of the enslaved after the initial rush to begin repairs and construction between 1763 and 1765. As expenses mounted after 1765, the state looked to these other coerced laborers to help recoup some funds for the defense projects by selling off some of its own enslaved workers. This practice slowed the progress of the defense works, but by 1790 most had been completed. In the historiography of enslavement in the Americas, this case of the king's enslaved workers of eighteenth-century Havana brings to the fore the factors of the geopolitics of imperial defense and the work regimes necessitated by massive public works projects in determinations of the nature of urban enslavement in Cuba. Diversity in the experience of enslavement was not only a result of differing colonial cultures. Within a single society and even within a single city, enslavement varied with respect to structural factors as well—the nature of the work to be performed and the level of coercion necessary to carry it out and the structure of the labor market in which decisions about labor deployment were made.

This essay also brings some new evidence to bear on discussions of Cuban economic development and its relation to enslavement. The enslavement of Africans for work in the Americas, especially in the Spanish colonies, was also significant in sectors outside the production of agricultural commodities, like sugar, for export. Considerable recent research has shown that there was overall, if modest, growth in the Cuban economy over the eighteenth century. In the years before 1760, state spending in shipbuilding and in outfitting the fleet was a particularly important form of investment and source of revenue, especially in Havana. Changes in colonial commercial policy discouraged private investment in tobacco production and favored a shift toward sugar. Yet while all this development encouraged greater importations of enslaved workers, it was the British siege and occupation of Havana that reoriented Spanish colonial policy in ways that favored a greater reliance on enslaved labor and greater investment in sugar. This is not to argue that exposure to British free trade during the occupation was the breath of fresh air that allowed Cuba to break out of the mercantilist stranglehold. Rather, the desperate urgency of shoring up Havana's defenses in the contested waters of the eighteenth-century Caribbean forced the Spanish state to think in new ways about how the empire would support and defend itself. While the Spanish state sought to centralize administration, further militarize the island, and increase revenue, it had to make concessions. The Crown was forced to allow the Cuban elite more commercial freedom in return for a greater Creole burden of taxation and of militia responsibilities. State initiatives also brought change to the distribution and use of the basic factors of production, like labor, in the island's economy.[68]

The state's demand for labor kept wages high, especially for skilled work. The urgent need for coercible labor on the fort projects was at least as great a stimulant to the trade in enslaved workers to the island as private demand and free trade had been under the British occupation. Income within the empire was redistributed as much of the higher quantities of silver extracted from Mexico were funneled into Havana. The local economy was enriched as the state contracted out many of the necessities of the fort projects—procurement of enslaved workers, transport, brick manufacture, and lime and charcoal production. The state purchased provisions and supplies for its troops, workers, and projects. It confiscated, purchased, and rented land and buildings in and around the city. The tremendous expenses associated with the fortification projects also made colonial subjects the state's creditors, as *situado* payments fell in arrears. As Allan J. Kuethe has noted, "this inflow of treasure established a level of financial liquidity that was unique in the empire."[69] Although it would be difficult to document, many scholars believe this capital was an important factor in the expansion of sugar production in Cuba after the Seven Years War (1756–63).[70]

The Spanish state's reaction to defeat and occupation at the hands of the British in Havana in 1762 ultimately brought profound economic and political change to Cuba. The colony emerged in the 1780s more heavily taxed but more prosperous, more tightly controlled by the metropolitan government but more open to the emerging Atlantic economy. As the state became less committed to the use of enslaved labor, the private sector became more so. Creole elites were more closely allied with peninsular bureaucrats and the military but were poised to take advantage of economic opportunities that the Spanish state would be unable to control. In the geopolitics of the Atlantic world, Spain was stronger than it had been for some years, and Havana was better defended than virtually any city in the Americas. This profound transformation of Cuban society took place before sugar production came to dominate the island's economy. In fact, state enslavement in the fort works of Havana between 1763 and 1790 was an integral part of that transformation. Spain's defense imperatives propelled it to resort to enslaved labor for its defense works. In the process of marshaling enslaved laborers and funding those projects, the state helped to create the conditions for the sugar boom of the nineteenth century.

Notes

1. The year 1790 is usually used in Cuban historiography to mark the accelerated expansion of sugar production on the island after the outbreak of revolution in Saint Domingue, although there is evidence of a shift toward sugar throughout the period from approximately 1750. See Franklin Knight, "Origins of Wealth and the Sugar Revolution in Cuba, 1750–1850," *Hispanic American Historical Review* 57, no. 2 (1977): 231–53. For a more detailed study of the growth of sugar production in Cuba, see Manuel Moreno Fraginals, *El ingenio: Complejo económico social cubano del azúcar,* tomos 1–3 (La Habana: Editorial de Ciencias Sociales, 1978); Pablo Tornero Tinajero, *Crecimiento económico y transformaciones sociales: Esclavos, hacendados y comerciantes en la Cuba colonial (1760–1840)* (Madrid: Ministerio de Trabajo y Seguridad Social, 1996).

2. There seems to be considerable scholarly consensus on the importance of the imperatives of imperial defense and services to the island's economic development. See, for instance, Moreno Fraginals, *El ingenio,* 1: 65; and Manuel Moreno Fraginals, "Peculiaridades de la esclavitud en Cuba," *Islas* 85 (1986): 3–12; Julio Le Riverend Brusone, *La Habana, espacio y vida,* (Madrid: MAPFRE, 1992), 67; Knight, "Origins of Wealth," 242–43; Allan J. Kuethe, "Havana in the Eighteenth Century," in *Atlantic Port Cities, Economy, Culture and Society in the Atlantic World, 1650–185,0* ed. Franklin W. Knight and Peggy K. Liss (Knoxville: University of Tennessee Press, 1992), 13–39, especially 17–19 and 24–25. Francisco Pérez Guzmán's book, *La Habana clave de un imperio* (La Habana: Editorial de Ciencias Sociales, 1997), 158–68, has the most information to date on state enslavement in Havana, particularly those employed in building fortifications. It also treats fort construction in other Cuban cities. On urban enslavement in Cuba more generally, see Pedro Deschamps Chapeaux, *El negro en la economía habanera del Siglo XIX* (La Habana: Unión de Escritores y Artistas de Cuba, 1971), which focuses on free people of color in nineteenth-century Havana but also contains some information on the enslaved. See also Pedro Deschamps Chapeaux, *Los cimarrones urbanos* (La Habana: Editorial de Ciencias Sociales, 1983), for the nineteenth century; Fernando Ortiz, *Los negros esclavos* (1916; reprint, La Habana: Editorial de Ciencias Sociales, 1996), 189–96; Robert Paquette, *Sugar Is Made with Blood: The Conspiracy of La Escalera and the Conflict Between Em-*

pires over Slavery in Cuba (Middletown, Conn.: Wesleyan University Press, 1988) especially 29–50.

3. Early travelers to Cuba often remarked on the ease with which the enslaved in Cuba attained their freedom. Most influential for later historiography on Cuba probably were the comments of Alexander von Humboldt on his trip to the island in the early decades of the nineteenth century: "In no part of the world, where slavery exists, is manumission so frequent as in the island of Cuba." Alexander von Humboldt, *The Island of Cuba,* trans. J. S. Thrasher (New York: Derby & Jackson, 1856), 212–13. Humboldt's translator Thrasher then further described the institution of *coartación,* or self-purchase by installments, in a footnote to the passage quoted here. The main elements of Humboldt's description of manumission in Cuba and of Thrasher's *coartación* resurface in virtually every subsequent discussion of the topic—its distinctly urban manifestation, its prevalence among domestic servants and skilled workers, the Iberian legal and religious tradition favoring freedom, an economy that supported hiring out and allowed slaves to retain a portion of their earnings and apply it in installments toward their freedom, and the resultant large free population of color. See Hubert H. S. Aimes, "Coartación: A Spanish Institution for the Advancement of Slaves into Freedmen," *Yale Review* 17 (1909): 412–31; Ortiz, *Los negros esclavos,* especially 189–95 and 204–41. The work of Humboldt and Ortiz formed an important part of the evidence grounding the thesis of Frank Tannenbaum in his influential book, *Slave and Citizen* (New York: Vintage Books, 1946). Tannenbaum saw manumission as "the crucial element in slavery; it implies the judgment of the moral status of the slave, and foreshadows his role in case of freedom" (69). By this criterion, Tannenbaum deemed enslavement in the Iberian colonies of the Americas to be more open and tolerant of freedom and mobility for people of African descent, basing much of his argument on the medieval Castilian legal code of the *Siete Partidas,* which proclaimed freedom as the most natural and reasonable of human states and made specific provisions to allow the state and enslavers to grant freedom and to allow the enslaved to pursue freedom through various means, including *coartación.*

4. See Stanley M. Elkins, *Slavery: A Problem in American Institutional and Intellectual Life* (New York: Grosset & Dunlap, 1959). Elkins's argument for the uniquely oppressive character of U.S. enslavement as compared to enslavement in Iberian colonized America was that in British-colonized North America, "a growing system of large-scale staple production for profit was free to develop in a society, where no prior traditional institutions with competing claims of their own, might interpose at any of a dozen points to [change the course of development]" (43). In other words, unbridled capitalism produced unmitigated enslavement. Building on both Tannenbaum and Elkins, Herbert Klein argued in his *Slavery in the Americas: A Comparative Study of Virginia and Cuba* (Chicago: University of Chicago Press, 1967) that it was the combination of the legal and religious codes

and practices and a diversified economy on the island that gave the enslaved in Cuba more possibilities to pursue freedom (124–64).

5. Diverging from the more sanguine view of the character of enslavement in Cuba put forth by Tannenbaum, Elkins, and Klein, Franklin Knight argued in his 1970 book, *Slave Society in Cuba during the Nineteenth Century* (Madison: University of Wisconsin Press, 1970), that generalizations about the nature of enslavement over long spans of time, based on legal codes or cultural traditions, "can be of only limited value in understanding or comparing the nature of slave plantation societies in tropical America" (193). Instead, he favored comparisons based on equivalent stages of economic and social growth since, in his analysis, plantation societies showed remarkable similarities wherever they appeared, regardless of the cultural heritage of the site (194). Knight does agree that the experience of the enslaved in urban areas was likely more moderate and open to the pursuit of freedom. He insists, however, that in the nineteenth century, it was the plantation model that characterized the institution in Cuba for the vast majority of the enslaved, not the urban model (60–62). The so-called Tannenbaum thesis has been revisited more favorably recently, see Moreno Fraginals, "Peculiaridades de la esclavitud en Cuba"; and Jane Landers, *Black Society in Spanish Florida* (Urbana and Chicago: University of Illinois Press, 1999), especially 1–3.

6. The number of the enslaved in Havana in the 1760s and of those people enslaved by the state is difficult to determine exactly. A recent attempt by J. R. McNeill to estimate the population of the entire island as well as in the city of Havana in the mid-eighteenth century gives the entire island's population as around 160,000 in 1757, with perhaps a quarter of those people being enslaved. Modifying figures projected by the bishop of Havana, Pedro Agustín Morell de Santa Cruz, in 1755, McNeill estimates the population of Havana at some 35,000 people. If the same proportion of people enslaved to those free lived in Havana, the enslaved population of the city would have been some 8,750 persons (although this is most likely a low estimate for the city's enslaved population since Havana had a higher proportion of the island's total enslaved population until the late 1700s). McNeill also estimates the number of enslaved Africans imported through Havana during the British occupation from 1762 to 1763 at approximately 4,000. While all of these enslaved people probably did not stay in Havana after being sold, the city's enslaved population may have grown before the Spanish state began purchasing enslaved workers in large numbers in the summer of 1763, although the exact number of Havana's enslaved population is not known. In any case, the 4,400 enslaved workers purchased by the state probably stayed in and around the city between 1763 and 1765 and could have represented, very approximately, 33.4 percent of the total population of the enslaved in Havana (adding the total of 8,750 to 4,400 = 13,150). The approximately 2,000 enslaved workers employed on the fort works would have been 15 percent of that total. For Bishop Morell's projections for Havana, see César García del Pino, ed., *La visita eclesiástica* (La

Habana: Editorial de Ciencias Sociales, 1985), 24–25. For estimates of the islandwide and city population and other demographic information, see John Rupert McNeill, *Atlantic Empires of France and Spain, Louisbourg and Havana, 1700–1763,* (Chapel Hill: University of North Carolina Press, 1985) 33–45.

7. See, for instance, Charles Verlinden, *L'esclavage dans l'Europe médiévale,* tome 1, *Péninsule ibérique-France* (Brugge: De Tempel, 1955), 286–88. See also Ruth Pike, *Penal Servitude in Early Modern Spain* (Madison: University of Wisconsin Press, 1983), 4–10. For enslavement in Spain more generally, see Antonio Domínguez Ortiz, "La esclavitud en Castilla durante la Edad Media," in *Estudios de Historia social en España* (Madrid: Consejo Superior de Investigaciones Científicas, 1952); Alfonso Franco Silva, *Los esclavos de Sevilla* (Sevilla: Diputación Provincial de Sevilla, 1980).

8. Paul Hoffman, *The Spanish Crown and the Defense of the Caribbean, 1535–1585, Precedent, Patrimonialism and Royal Parsimony* (Baton Rouge and London: Louisiana State University Press, 1980), 56–57.

9. On the Crown's use of the enslaved in the garrison forts, see Hoffman, *The Spanish Crown.* Cuban historian Francisco Pérez Guzmán cites numerous references in the archival records of the use of the enslaved and of convicts from the beginning of the sixteenth century. But he says that rising costs of hiring free workers toward the end of the seventeenth century increased the use of enslaved labor in state projects, especially the building of the city wall. Pérez Guzmán, *La Habana,* 59.

10. Archivo Histórico Nacional (hereafter AHN), Sección de Estado, legajo 3025, expediente 3. "Relacion del estado actual de las fortificaciones de la plaza de San Cristobal de la Habana y demas fuertes y castillos dependientes. Año de 1761 por el ingeniero don Francisco Ricaud de Tirgale." Eighteenth-century bureaucrats did not use a standardized format for spelling, accents, and capitalization. I have tried to preserve their orthography in the citations.

11. Jamie Delgado, "El Conde de Ricla, Capitán-General de Cuba," *Revista de Historia de America 55–56* (January–December 1963): 60.

12. Cuban historiography has been particularly harsh in its judgment of Portocarrero's leadership. His ineptitude, in large measure, is singled out as the cause of the English occupation. See, for instance, ibid.

13. As historian J. R. McNeill has noted, "The British lost an army at Havana—5,366 men died, 4,708 of them of disease. The British navy lost 1,300, of whom only 68 died in action; another 3,300 sailors fell ill." McNeill, *Atlantic Empires,* 104.

14. The urgency of Ricla's charge had prompted the king originally to grant Ricla "absolute faculty and jurisdiction." The document was subsequently altered to read "wide [*amplia*] faculty and jurisdiction." Archivo General de Indias (hereafter AGI), Santo Domingo (SD), leg. 1211, Buen Retiro March 29, 1763, in a bundle with the instructions to Ricla.

15. AGI, SD, 1212. Letters from Ricla to Arriaga, July 23 and 27, 1763. Also AGI, SD, 2119.

16. AGI, SD, 1211.

17. AGI, SD, 1647, bundle dated 1763–65, expediente sobre contratar. This bundle contains a number of contract proposals with different contractors with a range of prices, concessions, and numbers of the enslaved Africans to be delivered.

18. For the latest data compiled on the transatlantic trade in enslaved workers, see David Eltis, Stephen D. Behrendt, David Richardson, and Herbert Klein, *The Trans-Atlantic Slave Trade,* CD-Rom Database (Cambridge: Cambridge University Press, 1999). For the period under discussion here, see Gloria García, "El mercado de fuerza de trabajo en Cuba: El comercio esclavista (1760–1789)," in *La esclavitud en Cuba* (La Habana: Editorial Academia, 1986), 125–47.

19. AGI, SD, 1212, Carta de Ricla a Arriaga 27 Julio 1763. Ricla hoped to obtain 400 to 500 slaves donated by private owners and also was waiting *"con ansia"* for a group of Guachinango Indians to be sent from New Spain. In Delgado, "El Conde de Ricla," 90–97, the figure given for the laborers clearing La Cabaña is 700.

20. The figures for enslaved workers purchased by the state vary somewhat. A statement of fort works' expenses summarized in December 1772 gives 4,198 enslaved workers purchased between May 1763 and the end of 1765, with a credit to the Royal Account for the sale of 283 enslaved workers to the artillery company, yielding a total of 4481. AGI, SD, 2129, "Estado que manifiesta los gastos, y costos causados en las Reales Obras de Fortificacion proyectadas en la Plaza de la Habana desde 7 de Julio de 1763 que se dio prinicipio al Morro, y Cabaña, y en 25 de Mayo de 1764 al Fuerte de Atarés, hasta 31 de Diziembre de 1772." Pérez Guzmán, *La Habana,* 66, gives a figure of 4,400 total purchased for the state. Pablo Tornero cites 4,359 with the gender breakdown. See Tornero, *Crecimiento económico,* 36.

21. García, "El mercado de fuerza," 136; AGI, SD, 2129, "Estado que manifiesta los gastos, y costos causados en las Reales Obras de Fortificación," dated December 31, 1772.

22. AGI, SD, 1211. Indice de las cartas del Conde de Ricla, dated Havana September 31, 1764. See also AGI, SD, 2122.

23. See the sources listed for table 1.

24. The data for March 1765 do not differentiate fort sites from other tasks, as all workers are listed under the three major fort projects of El Morro, La Cabaña, and Atarés. The 60 prisoners employed in carting were subsumed under the fort sites' listings after 1765. Quarrying and fascine making, which employed some 450 to 475 of the workers enslaved by the king and approximately 105 prisoners, were listed under the fort works at Atarés after August 1765.

25. AGI, SD, 2136. Free skilled workers were to be given a salary of eight reales/day and were to be assigned king's enslaved workers, "not convicts" to be trained in their trade.

26. AGI, SD, 1647, "Extracto de revista . . . hecho por don Nicolas Joseph Rapun . . . [sobre] los individuos que se hallen empleados en el Hospital Real de San Ambrosio de la Habana para la asistencia de los enfermos de las Tropas de

ella," not dated but in a bundle with papers from February 1765. AGI, SD, 2122, contains listings of the hospital's employees for the following dates in 1767 and 1768, December 31, 1767; January 31, February 20, March 31, April 30, May 31, June 30, September 30, October 31, and November 3, 1768. "Relacion [or Revista] de empleados y sirvientes en el Hospital Real de San Ambrosio de la Havana."

27. *An Authentic Journal of the Siege of the Havana By an Officer,* printed for T. Jefferys (London, 1762), 25.

28. Jacobo de la Pezuela, *Diccionario geográfico, estadístico, histórico de la isla de Cuba,* tomo 2 (Madrid, 1863), 260. AGI, SD, 2122, "Estado de Revista pasada por mi a dn. Nicolas Joseph Rapun Caballero de la orden de Santiago Comisario ordenador de Marina y Ministros Interventor General de la Administracion y Real Factoria de Tabacos, obras de fortificacion y de la Artilleria, a los Negros esclavos del Rey destinados al servicio de ella, a las Negras de SM mugeres de aquellos, a sus hijos, y hijas que unos y otras se hallan aquartelados en el Quartel de San Isidro de esta diudad hoy dia en la fecha," for the dates December 13, 1767; January 17, February 21, March 20, April 17, May 12, June 12, July 10, September 11, October 23, and November 27, 1768. AGI, SD, 2122, contains a series of charts recording the enslaved workers housed in the Quartel de San Isidro for January–July and September–December 1768.

29. AGI, SD, 2129, "Estado que manifiesta los gastos, y costos," 31 diziembre 1772. The figures for the number of the enslaved purchased and their total value in reales are taken from this Estado. A footnote to the Estado states that the enslaved were purchased at prices of 130, 150, and 156 pesos, but since there is no way to determine how many were purchased at the different prices, an average was taken here. The Estado's final total in reales has been preserved in the table, though it differs slightly from the total obtained by using the average prices. One peso = 8 reales de vellón. For monetary equivalencies see McNeill, *Atlantic Empires,* 212, Appendix B.

30. Kuethe, "Havana in the Eighteenth Century," 18.

31. Ibid., 24.

32. Pérez Guzmán, *La Habana,* 254–55.

33. The table and all the data presented in this paragraph are derived from the "Estado[s] de Revista," in AGI, SD, 1647 and 2122.

34. AGI, SD, 2129, "Estado que manifiesta los gastos, y costos," December 31, 1772. Also AGI, SD, 1647, "Relacion de cargo y Data de esta Thesoreria general," Altarriba to Esquilache, November 5, 1765.

35. Pérez Guzmán, *La Habana,* 101–6.

36. Ibid., 55, reproduces this report dated October 23, 1764. The report listed 33 prisoners as having died in the same time period.

37. Francisco Pérez Guzmán, "Modo de vida de esclavos y forzados en las fortificaciones de Cuba: Siglo XVIII," *Anuario de estudios americanos* 47 (1990): 245.

38. AGI, SD, 1647. Letter from Altarriba to Esquilache included with papers of

extracts of reviews corresponding to February, letter dated (?) April 1765. Also Guzmán, "Modo de vida," 245.

39. AGI, SD, 1647 and 2122, "Estado[s] de Revista."

40. Pérez Guzmán, "Modo de vida," 255. Quote is from the regulation of religious instruction.

41. Ibid., 246–52. Pérez Guzmán also argues that although fraud and corruption probably took place in the provisioning of the slave and convict workers, it was not a serious problem. Since the slaves in particular would be sold after their stint in the fortification works, the state took considerable precautions (regular inspections, penalties for irregularities in the provisions, and so forth) to provide adequate food. See especially 251–52.

42. AGI. SD, 1647. Letter from Altarriba to Esquilache dated Havana, August 16, 1765.

43. AGI, SD, 1647. Letter from Arriaga, 22 diziembre 1763, notifying Crown of the customary clothing allowance. Letter dated 25 abril 1764 requesting manufacture of these garments in Spain and their remission to Cuba.

44. Pérez Guzmán, "Modo de vida," 252.

45. Ibid., 252–53.

46. AGI, SD, 2129, "Estado que manifiesta los gastos, y costos," December 31, 1772.

47. See, for instance, AGI, SD, 1647, "Relacion de cargo y Data de esta Thesoreria general," dated November 5, 1765, listing receipts for March 1–August 31, sale of blacks at 220,960 reales out of a total of 11,362,086 reales.

48. AGI, SD, 1647, for the summaries of 1765; AGI, SD, 2122, for 11 summaries from December 1767 to October 1768.

49. AGI, SD, 1647, bundle of letters of the intendant dated October 1765, letter from Arriaga, June 19, 1764.

50. See María Elena Díaz, "Constituting Identity: Sociocultural Changes in a Black Colonial Village (El Cobre, Cuba, 1670–1800)" (Ph. D. diss., University of Texas at Austin, 1992).

51. Allan J. Kuethe and G. Douglas Inglis, "Absolutism and Enlightened Reform: Charles II, the Establishment of the Alcabala, and the Commercial Reorganization in Cuba," *Past and Present* 109 (November 1985): 125–27.

52. Ibid., 140.

53. Ibid., 140–43.

54. For more on Bucarely's tenure, see Ramiro Guerra y Sánchez, *Manual de Historia de Cuba* (La Habana: Cultural, S. A. 1938), 173–76.

55. AGI, SD, 2122, bundle dated August 13, 1768, Letter from Bucarely to Arriaga, Havana, May 28, 1768.

56. Ibid.

57. Ibid.

58. AGI, SD, 2122, in bundle dated September 4, 1768, resolutions of the second Junta Extraordinaria that met on June 11, 1768.

59. See sources for table 5 for an occupational breakdown.

60. Ibid.

61. Ibid.

62. AGI, Cuba 1371, "Estado que comprehende el Numero de forzados Existentes en la Revista que pase en la Cavaña y Loma de Arostegui oy dia de la fha. Con Exprezion de sus clases y destinos en que trabajan," dated December 31, 1784, November 28, 1784, and January 30, 1785.

63. AGI, Cuba, 1311, Letter from Luis Huet to Captain-General Juan Manuel de Cagigal, Havana, July 29, 1782. Huet notes the scarcity of laborers and the lack of prisoners "that for years have not come from the kingdom of New Spain."

64. AGI, Cuba, 1311, Letter from Huet to Cagigal, Havana, November 8, 1782; Cagigal to Huet, Havana, November 10, 1782.

65. AGI, Cuba, 1311, Letter from Huet to Cagigal, Havana, December 6, 1782.

66. AGI, Cuba, 1371, "Estado que manifiesta el n° de Individuos que habitan en el Quartel de Negros esclavos de SM con distinccion de Clases, sus edades y el total de ellos oy dia de la fha," Havana, December 31, 1784.

67. See sources and discussion of manumission and *coartación* in note 3. For more recent work, see Laird Bergad, "Fe Iglesias García and María del Carmen Barcia," in *The Cuban Slave Market, 1790–1880* (New York: Cambridge University Press, 1995), but the evidence is mostly from the nineteenth century. See especially 122–42. Bergad, Iglesias, and Barcia have a useful discussion of the historiography of manumission and *coartación* in the Americas. They also argue for the uniqueness of the Cuban variant of *coartación* because the process was initiated by the enslaved themselves. But some recent studies have found evidence that it existed in other American societies with enslaved workers. See, for instance, Douglas Cole Libby and Clothilde Andrade Paiva, "Manumission Practices in Late Eighteenth Century Brazilian Slave Parish d'El Rey in 1795," *Slavery and Abolition* 21, no. 1 (April 2000): 96–127.

68. For changes in land use in and around Havana after the occupation and its benefits to the local economy, see Sherry Johnson, "'La Guerra Contra los Habitantes de los Arrabales': Changing Patterns of Land Use and Land Tenancy in and Around Havana, 1763–1800," *Hispanic American Historical Review* 77, no. 2 (1997): 181–209. She concludes that "military spending . . . brought economic benefits that began almost from the moment royal administrators disembarked in 1763. Equally important, royal policies benefited many levels of Havana's society" (208).

69. Kuethe, "Havana in the Eighteenth Century," 24.

70. See, for instance, Knight, "Origins of Wealth," 231–53, especially 242. See also Moreno, *El ingenio,* 1: 65. For a summary of this scholarship on revenues from defense spending in Cuba see Kuethe, "Havana in the Eighteenth Century," 14–25.

8

The Urban Context of the Life of the Enslaved

Views from Bridgetown, Barbados, in the Eighteenth
and Nineteenth Centuries

Pedro L. V. Welch

The island of Barbados that provides the physical and conceptual location for this essay is located southward of the Greater Antilles, to the east of the Caribbean chain. It has a total surface area of 166 square miles (or about 432 square kilometers). Despite the island's small size, in the early colonial period it was, perhaps, the premier colony in the British Caribbean. It was settled by the English in 1625, and by the 1680s, as a result of its pioneer status in the sugar revolution, it had achieved a status as the most important jewel in (his) majesty's crown.

The rural agricultural sector dominated the island's economic life, employing about 82 percent of the enslaved population on over 175 sugar plantations, some of them exceeding 450 acres. The planter class that emerged dominated social, political, and economic life. Despite the importance of the rural sector, however, the urban complex also played an important part in shaping the life of the colony. In 1680, the chief town and port at Bridgetown was home to about 3,500 enslaved people (about 4.5 percent of the island's total enslaved population). By 1715, however, the enslaved population in Bridgetown had risen to about 13,000 and by the end of the eighteenth century to about 17,000 (13 percent). In fact, throughout the period 1715 to 1834, the enslaved population of the town averaged about 13 percent of the total classified as enslaved by the island's tax assessor. When it is recognized that there were three other small towns—Oistins, on the southern coast; Holetown; and Speightstown, on the northern coast—the urban statistics for the enslaved population will become even more significant in any study of the slave population in that period.

The port at Bridgetown occupied a major place in the English transatlantic trading system. Indeed, trade statistics extracted from the Calendar of State Papers for the period 1697–1714 show that the comparative values for shipping, tonnage, and cargo placed Bridgetown ahead of other Caribbean and North American ports. Although the growth of these ports would displace Bridgetown from its position over time, the port continued to be a major conduit for trade to and from England and North America throughout the eighteenth and into the nineteenth centuries. In addition, a considerable intercolonial trade developed in which Bridgetown acted as the distributive hub. The maritime trade was an important economic factor impacting on the nature of the slave system in the town. An occupational profile developed there that was in direct contrast to the well-known profile for the rural enslaved. These considerations provide the impetus for the discussion that follows.

Identifying the Problem

There is little question that the nature of plantation enslavement was such that it touched every other aspect of colonial society in the Caribbean. Yet the rural dimension represents only one aspect of social reality. The urban context of the plantation system represents another aspect of the life of enslaved peoples in Caribbean slave systems that requires more specific treatment.[1]

When the urban scene is examined, it will be discovered that the conditions of enslaved people's lives and enslaver-enslaved social relations there do not fit easily into the rural descriptions. In commenting on this, Barry Gaspar observes that, within the urban perimeter, the enslaved faced conditions of life different from those on rural plantations. Moreover, these conditions nurtured a weakening of bonds of dependence of the enslaved upon enslavers, thereby undermining an important element in the social control of the enslaved.[2] Gaspar's comments underscore the need to identify the peculiar characteristics of the urban complex if a clearer reading of the complexities of slave systems in the Caribbean is to be achieved.

On the whole, the historiography of colonial life in the Caribbean slave systems conceptualizes developments in terms of a hegemonic rural enterprise. There is a tendency for many Caribbean historians to stay within the confines of plantation society models developed by European historians and some social anthropologists and a failure to follow through on the implications of their own urban evidence. An examination of some seminal contributions to the historiography of Caribbean societies based on slavery made by Elsa Goveia, Orlando Patterson, Karl Watson, Kamau Brathwaite, Jerome Handler, Richard Dunn, Richard Sheridan, and Gary Puckerin, for example, reveals this tendency to negate or minimize the role and function of the urban milieu in such societies.[3] A few comments on the work of Goveia in investigating the slave system in the Leeward Islands will provide some brief insights into the scope of the problem.

Goveia's investigation reveals that at least 50 percent of the white population lived and worked in the towns and urban parishes. In St. Kitts, for example, the total white population was 1,912 persons in 1788. Of this number, about 450 persons lived in the rural areas. In addition, if we use the ratios of enslaved to the white population that she provides, more than half of the enslaved population lived and operated in a nonplantation setting.[4]

While there is some attention to urban issues, however, the larger picture that Goveia pursues does not lend itself to an emphasis of her own urban evidence. An important analytical point is missed when, despite her observation that urban enslavers were more capable than rural owners in exercising a direct, personal discipline over their enslaved workers, it is reported that in the towns, "more than on plantations they [slaves] abound in information, in vice, in insolence and in discontent."[5] The implications of this for the development of the community that she seeks to identify are not fully realized.

If, as it appears, the urban environment represented a theater in which specific challenges/adjustments to the authority structure established by whites may be viewed, then an important window into the expectations and perceptions of the slave system held by the enslaved has not been developed. It is within the ambit of this brief discussion that this essay offers some insights into the urban social schema in which enslaved Africans in the Caribbean lived.

The focus here is on one area of importance in the socialization of the enslaved in this nonplantation environment, namely, the occupational environment within which they operated. In paying attention to this aspect of the life of the enslaved, it is useful to include some reference to free coloreds. Throughout the Caribbean, the free colored population was largely urban-based. More important, as members of the enslaved community interacted with their kin and with significant others in this population, they could hardly avoid taking notice of any successes that their freedmen and freedwomen counterparts had in challenging a system built on assumptions of white hegemony.[6]

Clearly, there are other aspects of the urban existence that differed in some ways from the rural profile, such as the family life of the enslaved, the residential aspects of their life, and the issue of white-black interaction at the social level, but these will not be covered here.[7] The data used in exploring the issues raised are extracted from material covering the period and will not necessarily follow a chronological form.

Occupation Culture in a Maritime Trade Environment

The port functions of the Caribbean colonial towns in the slavery period served to generate an occupational structure that differed markedly from that of the rural areas.[8] Indeed, the volume and variety of maritime trade in port towns such as Bridgetown engendered a demand for services that led to the appearance of specialized occupations there. Tables 8.1 and 8.2 will help to illustrate this point.

The large volume of shipping, associated as it was with the movement of considerable tonnage of cargo and the influx of thousands of sailors and other transients each year, gives some idea of the scale of activity that was driving occupational development in Bridgetown. Several ships anchored in the roadstead off the capital and chief port each year. Smaller ships, many involved in inter-island trade, anchored at the wharves that lay behind the storehouses that fronted on the main street. These provided work for enslaved skilled people and for freedmen artisans. It would appear that most of the small craft (droghers, flats, and lighters) used to ferry cargo from ships anchored offshore were staffed and supervised by black crews, most of whom were enslaved, although the possibility of freedmen crews is not ruled out. The discussion is widened as the data contained in table 8.2 are considered.

If we disaggregate the figures in the categories skilled tradesmen and transport workers and select the subcategories (shipwright, caulker, sailmaker, ship carpenter, coppersmith, goldsmith, tailor, cordwainer [shoemaker], seamstress/washer, sailor, mariner, boatman, seaman, and porter), greater differences, not revealed in the table, begin to appear between the Bridgetown profile and that of the rural parishes.[9] The differences appear even in comparing Bridgetown with rural areas of Saint Michael, which might be expected to share greater similarities with the town, as this was the parish where this port town was located. In many of the subcategories listed, there was simply no rural counterpart.

The maritime trade also provided opportunities for enslaved people on self-hire and jobbing and for freedmen and freedwomen to enter into protoproletarian activities that modified the typical enslaver-enslaved ra-

Table 8.1. Shipping outward from Barbados for selected years, 1788–1834

Year	No. of ships	Tonnage	No. of crew	Value of cargo (£)
1788	352	37,706	2,583[a]	506,507
1789	342	35,107	2,401	408,886
1790	378	39,826	2,728	437,183
1791	388	40,967	2,792	—
1822	331	40,922	2,849	648,131
1823	444	40,922	3,380	1,064,244
1824	456	50,907	3,501	845,924
1825	452	53,163	3,676	859,452
1826	534	59,752	3,900	1,307,889
1827	440	46,652	976[b]	557,423
1830	544	56,345	4,212	776,695
1832	659	74,189	4,842	408,363
1833	529	65,784	4,079	553,628
1834	632	74,497	5,195	736,006

Sources: Adapted from R. M. Martin, *History of the Colonies of the British Empire* (London: Dawsons of Pall Mall, 1967), 68, and CO 28/60/31.
a. Estimates for eighteenth century obtained by using a ton/men ratio derived from later period.
b. Appears to be an underestimate.

Table 8.2. Occupational profile of enslaved urban and rural workers in Barbados, 1817 (number of enslaved)

Occupation	Bridgetown	Saint Michael (rural)	Saint John (rural)
Field laborers	9	3,609	2,942
Drivers	—	105	99
Skilled trades	1,089	570	244
Domestics	4,660	1,728	551
Stock keepers	28	395	273
Transport workers	429	67	14
Watchmen	6	1	48
Fishermen	68	18	—
Vendors	51	24	—
Laborers	196	22	35
Hired out	35	6	1
Nurses	14	64	57

Source: Adapted from B. W. Higman *Slave Populations* (Baltimore: Johns Hopkins University Press, 1984), 552–58.

cial stereotypes associated with rural regimes. Two of the areas where this departure may be identified are in the business of hawking (sometimes referred to as huckstering) and tavern-keeping.

Frederick Bayley, who visited Barbados in the 1820s, noted that there was a large traffic of fishing boats and canoes "manned by natives of diverse kinds and colors who came out to the ships to offer various provisions and other island luxuries to dispose of to the crew."[10] He also observed that the lower class of stores in Bridgetown were kept by hucksters "for the most part black or mulatto."[11] Some idea of the impact of huckstering as a spin-off from a larger marine traffic may be derived from the concern of the authorities over the dominance of hucksters in the local distribution of foodstuffs and in the import trade for the same.

Legislation with regard to huckstering was passed in 1774 and renewed several times up to the 1830s. The preamble observed that "hucksters Negroes [which it specified as free mulattoes, free negroes, and slaves] went on board vessels arriving here and purchase from thence live stock to revend [sell]."[12] Furthermore, concern was expressed that the activities of these hucksters led to the result that "the prices of stocks and provisions are greatly advanced."[13] Whatever else may have been the concern underlying this piece of legislation, it is clear that the urban maritime trade played a major role in shaping the Caribbean economy based upon enslavement.

The act prescribed several penalties for this breach of the natural order; in addition, in a direct attack on the huckstering trade, it attempted to prohibit enslaved people and mulattoes from displaying their wares "upon any stall, bench, stand or table, or in any tub or tray in any of the . . . streets of the said Town[s]."[14] In spite of these attempts, huckstering continued to expand in the town, a clear indication of the demand for such services. The explanation for this expansion and survival rests, in part, on the reaction of the white hucksters, who found themselves hamstrung by legislation that, on the surface, was designed to limit black competition and by the survivalist strategies adopted by the black hucksters.

In 1811, white hucksters petitioned the House of Assembly for the repeal of the 1774 legislation. They argued that the law provided for penalties inflicted in a much smaller proportion on people of color in the same trade itself. Moreover, they asked: against whom does this law operate? "The retailers of this Island—a class of traders requisite in all countries, more peculiarly requisite in a country in which the bulk of the population is in slavery and born amid the habits of Barter and Exchange. . . . These retailers whom you are thus harsh against are Poor they are white men against whom the Act is most cruel and severe."[15]

This attempt to distance themselves from the black hucksters suggests that one survivalist strategy used by the latter was the "barter and exchange" mode of trade. It would appear that African Caribbean hucksters simply altered the terms of the debate on their future by withdrawing from the more visible cash exchange transactions in favor of barter transactions. Perhaps this offered the option of disposing of perishable items while providing for a material accumulation that could be liquidated when the situation improved. It would seem also that strong lobbying from the local white hucksters and their sympathizers in the Assembly forced the authorities to adopt less confrontational measures in dealing with the "problem."

The urban maritime trade also contributed to the growth of the so-called Tipling and Crimping Houses, which were largely owned by mulatto women. Here, too, white merchants found that urban departures from the strictures of the plantation social system exposed them to competition from their social inferiors. On November 10, 1801, a petition of Bridgetown merchants to the House of Assembly stated that "the number of Tipling and Crimping houses dispersed over the town is highly injurious to the mercantile Body of this Island."[16] The petitioners were concerned that these local taverns were pulling white seamen labor away from the wharves, leaving them to discharge cargoes "at a heavy expense by hired negroes." There is the strong suggestion, also, that the owners of these institutions were not averse to seizing the opportunity of garnishing extra income by contracting out the services of the very deserters they were accused of encouraging. The merchants complained: "[S]uch is the ascendancy which the owners of these houses acquire over [the seamen] that your Petitioners have no other means of getting furnished, but thro' the Crimps, their Landlords, and are forced to submit to the most unreasonable and extravagant demands rather than forego altogether the profits of the voyage."[17]

Another underlying factor in this complaint may well have been the competition that these Crimping Houses posed to the local white merchants, many of whom were importers/retailers of spirits. Indeed, a survey of returns for the month of March 1804, provided by local merchants to Governor Seaforth, reveals a stock of some 12,610 gallons of imported brandy and some 2,260 gallons of gin.[18] The Crimping Houses usually served the local rum "neat" or in rum punches. Thus they were in direct competition with the petitioners for the seamen's market. It is not surprising, therefore, that the complainers would "most humbly pray your Honourable House to . . . limit the number of the said Houses and adopt such other measures for their good conduct."[19]

Another aspect of the maritime trade is the employment of enslaved and freedmen in servicing and maintenance of vessels. While it is difficult to obtain statistics on the actual numbers involved, the returns for 1817 show that there were 14 shipwrights, 14 caulkers, 17 sailmakers, 84 sailors, 6 mariners (possibly indicating a skill above that of "able seamen"), 135 boatmen, 37 seamen, 160 porters, and 2 cabin boys, representing a total of 469 persons in an urban enslaved population of 9,297.[20] These were indispensable to the smooth functioning of the port, and their work might place them in situations that invited departures from the usual enslaver/black-white relationships.

William Senhouse, the surveyor general of Customs, with headquarters in Bridgetown, recorded the expenses of his voyages in a customs sloop during the 1760s and 1770s. His records show that the black seamen on the ship were paid the same sum as their white counterparts—about 15 pounds sterling for a four-month assignment.[21] This situation may well reflect a growing dependence on enslaved and freedmen sailors on ships in Caribbean waters. Moreover, it would seem that this dependence and an increasing specialization of services in the maritime economy was contributing to a monetarization of those services. Monetarization of services appears to be a major factor acting on relations between white bosses and enslaved labor in the maritime trade environment.

The changes taking place in the maritime labor market were noted by colonial officials. In 1786, Governor Parry of Barbados wrote a letter to the secretary of state for the colonies. Parry informed him that "the numbers of Negro slaves employed in navigating the Trading Vessels in these Seas [Caribbean] seem . . . to increase so much as to require the attention of the British Legislature, as it throws so many English Seamen out of Employment."[22] There is no indication of any reaction by colonial officials to this comment. Indeed, the employment of black seamen in the British navy had become commonplace by this period, and Parry's comment might not have caused any alarm.[23]

An indication of the way the requirements of the maritime economy might have an impact on racial mores in the urban context may be derived from an encounter recorded by Bayley. In 1826, Bayley was exposed to a scene that demonstrates the departure that has been identified and further illustrates the usefulness of an urban focus in accessing the totality of the experience of enslaved Africans in the Caribbean. When his ship entered Carlisle Bay, the captain made a signal for the pilot to come on board. The pilot who responded to this request was apparently an African who "took possession of the vessel, with as much importance as if he had been a fine, rough old English seaman bearing up Channel." What was even more remarkable was the way he addressed the man at the helm (clearly, a white seaman): "Vy you no teer [steer] [s]teady? Got tam [damn] you, Sir, Vy you no teer teady, I say."[24] After untangling the dialect recorded by Bayley, what emerges is an individual whose skills (and the demand for those skills in the port environment) gave him liberties that went against the image of the typical enslaved person. When Bayley enquired about the man's status, he was informed that he was a "jobbing slave" who contracted his services out on his own account, remitting a percentage to his enslaver.[25]

For many of the enslavers in the town, particularly females who possessed small numbers of enslaved captives, "hiring out" the time of those enslaved often provided the sole source of income. Under the system, enslaver and enslaved entered into an informal arrangement in which the latter were relatively free to seek their employment. In some cases, enslavers would advertise the services of those they enslaved in the local newspaper. Such services could range from that of the skilled artisan to the thinly veiled offer of prostitution services (often advertised by female enslavers), which so scandalized William Dickson during his stay in Barbados.[26] Dickson was an Englishman who visited the Caribbean in the late eighteenth century and wrote a book describing conditions in the various slave communities. His observations on the treatment of slaves were surprisingly objective by the standards of his time.

Under the "hiring out" arrangement, the enslaved often provided their own housing, food, and clothing. In return, a fixed payment was made to the owners. One comment on this system, made with respect to an urban community in North America, suggests that this type of arrangement "provided masters [and mistresses] with the profits of slave ownership without the accompanying managerial responsibilities."[27] Whatever the advantages it brought these enslavers, the attraction it held for the enslaved was clear. It is suggested that the enslaved actively sought such arrangements for a number of reasons. First, blurred lines of authority could lead to a hirer being unsure of the extent of his or her disciplinary control. Enslaved Africans could exploit this to their advantage. Second, hirers might have little interest in the hired man or woman's off-work activity, thus permitting a higher degree of independent action to the enslaved than would have been possible under the owner's supervision. Third, the flexibility created by the blurring of lines of authority often forced both owner and hirer to offer positive incentives to the enslaved to guarantee better compliance with their desires.[28] In the Barbadian context, the benefits of the system to owners of small numbers of enslaved people and to the enslaved underlie the fact that, in the period between 1817 and 1834, over 58 percent of the enslaved in Bridgetown could be classified as skilled.[29]

Enslaved skilled workers could merge with the free black population in the urban environment and use their service skills to ensure survival. The demand for some services was so acute that runaways might even solicit the aid of a white person in their efforts to escape detection. Such advertisements as those noted below give an indication of the problems that faced some white owners. On May 21, 1788, John Bryan advertised for the return of Fortune:

> Runaway from the Subscriber, a Short, Stout well-made Negro man named FORTUNE; he is round shouldered, parrot toed and speaks thick, plays well on the fiddle, and is frequently seen in the Old-Church Yard Bridge-town. Whoever will apprehend and deliver him . . . shall receive FIVE POUNDS reward, and if any person will given information of his being harbored by any white or free person [he] shall received FOUR MOIDORES reward.[30]

In another advertisement of January 17, 1809, Ely Lynch, a merchant of High Street, issued the following warning: "Caution: The Subscriber forbids any person hiring his Mulatto Man Richard, by trade a joiner, without first applying to him at his Store, the corner of High Street."[31]

The authorities were not oblivious to the threat that jobbing and "hired slaves" could pose to the slave system. As early as 1708 the Assembly passed an act (expanded and amended in 1733 and again in 1774) that sought to limit the competition which black vendors were posing to white merchants in the town. The 1708 act was entitled *An Act to prohibit the Inhabitants of the Island from Employing, their Negroes or other Slaves, in Selling or bartering.* Under the act, persons were prohibited from employing enslaved people in the sale of "enumerated" items such as "Wares, Merchandise, Stock, Poultry, Corn Fruit [and] Roots."[32] More specifically, however, the act went on to state:

> If any person or persons inhabiting this island, being owner or Possessor of any Negro or Negroes, or Slave or Slaves, shall permit such

Negro or Negroes or other slave or Slaves to go at large, and hire out to him, her, or themselves to any person or persons, to follow any trade, occupation or calling and receive the profits thereof to him, her, or themselves, or rendering to his or her said Master or Mistress or to any other person or persons whatsoever for their use, a daily, weekly, or monthly sum of money or any other income, or any manner of gratuity whatsoever, every such person . . . for every such offence shall forfeit the sum of ten pounds current money.[33]

The provisions of this legislation indicate a concern that goes beyond the mere prohibition of vending imported foodstuff and manufactured items.

Elizabeth Fenwick, who lived in Bridgetown between 1814 and 1820, found herself an unwilling participant in the hiring system. Her experience may well be based on the fact that she was a female operating in a system in which the "norms" of behavior of those enslaved were markedly different from those of the rural patriarchal system. She commented: "Our domestics are Negroes hired from their owners, and paid at what seems to me an extraordinary rate. . . . They are a sluggish, inert self-willed race of people, apparently inaccessible to gentle and kindly impulses. . . . Nothing but the threat of the whip seems capable of driving them to exertion."[34]

In a further comment on the hired under her charge, she noted that "nothing awes or governs them but the lash of the whip or the threat of being sent back into the fields of labour."[35] She was particularly incensed at the action of a female who "boasted to her owner's other slaves that she knew that I would not suffer her to be flogged and, therefore, she knew better than to work when she was not made to do it."[36]

One of the features of urban life is the gender specificity of some occupational categories. Within the households of urban residents, one of the more common occupations allocated exclusively to females was that of "washer." These workers catered to visitors and residents alike in fulfilling an essential function in the tropical environment. Another occupation that was predominantly allocated to women was that of "water carrier." The nature of these occupations was such that it permitted regular, unsupervised absences from the town residences. Dr. George Pinckard, Nathaniel Hawthorne, and Dr. George Bayley all record scenes that illustrate the relative freedom of association and movement that was associated with these categories of the enslaved.[37]

It is unlikely that the limited hours involved in water carrying or washing represented the sum total of these women's activities. As Barry Higman points out, the small scale of urban slaveholdings suggests that most of the enslaved were probably employed on minimal domestic staffs covering a wide range of duties. This contrasts with the rural plantation where in the great house there was a greater degree of occupational specialization and differentiation. However, those enslaved persons who staffed urban commercial establishments might also exhibit a high degree of specialization.[38] This would almost certainly be the case with staffs in establishments involved in providing services for the maritime traffic that used the port facilities.

Another issue that distinguished the urban from the rural context was the organization of labor resources. Labor was organized and extracted in quite different ways in each area. For example, in urban areas there was a relative absence of gang labor and a greater tendency toward individualized work than on a typical plantation. Gang labor was associated in urban areas with specific occupations, but even in these cases the degree of supervision appeared to have taken on a different complexion.

In Bridgetown, all urban slaveholders were required to provide an able-bodied man or woman to work on public works each year, and this represented one of the few spectacles of gang labor that a visitor to Bridgetown might see.[39] A few days after his arrival in Bridgetown, George Pinckard noticed a gang of enslaved laborers building a road to the governor's house. It "was the first large body of slaves" he had seen, and his description is in striking contrast to the picture of field labor associated with the rural context. He observed: "Nothing of diligence, nor industry appeared among them; and, verily, but a little of bodily labor was expended. . . . A mulatto overseer attended them, holding a whip at their backs; but he had every appearance of being a stranger to industry as the negroes; who proceeded very indolently, without seeming to be apprehensive of the driver or his whip."[40]

Other examples of gang labor were associated with the transportation sector and with the skilled trades in the wharf-side area. With such a large traffic of shipping as the town attracted through the years, the shipbuilding industry must have been vital to the urban economy. Businesses such as that owned by ship's carpenters John and Thomas Scott required laborers in adequate numbers to manage the difficult task of handling large timbers and spars, not to omit the large expanses of canvas that a merchantman might carry. In the early nineteenth century, their property consisted of a ship carpenter's yard of some 14,350 square feet and a blacksmith's shop. Their labor needs were supplied by five ship's carpenters, seven caulkers, and six blacksmiths.[41]

In such establishments, the skilled workers labored with a minimum of supervision, although they might work in gangs on specific tasks. Indeed, as Alexander Campbell stated in his evidence before a select committee of the British House of Commons in 1790, the enslaved who worked with skilled tradesmen "laid out the work," while the white tradesmen did the "light and nice jobs themselves." These white tradesmen seldom did the "heavy or fatiguing work." Campbell had several estates in the British Caribbean and was personally familiar with the various islands. Also, at the time of his testimony he had apparently recently liquidated his mercantile interests in Antigua. He was, therefore, qualified to comment on the nature of work organization among artisans.[42] His testimony reveals a situation in which the skills acquired by black artisans gave them some autonomy in the work environment.

There is some corroboration of this scenario in the research carried out by Higman on urban slavery in the Caribbean. He observes that in the towns, "slaves continued to perform many of the same tasks as whites. . . . While the owners reserved the most skilled tasks for themselves . . . the strictly supervisory role of most owners and white employees on large plantations was not repeated in the towns." Even where one might expect a high degree of supervision over unskilled labor as, for example, in the case of the boatmen who operated the sugar flats and passenger ferries, the picture is one of a diminished supervision. The generally relaxed and unsupervised ambience surrounding the life of the "negro" boatmen is one of the features or urban life that attracted the attention of visitors to the island.[43]

Conclusion

It is not suggested that the urban enslaved in general, and enslaved domestics in particular, lived an idyllic life. However, the evidence indicates a culture that could hardly avoid taking note of the special conditions of town life. The rhythm of urban occupational life was removed, in some respects, from the regimentation characteristic of the rural enslaved. From the enslaved skilled person to the enslaved domestic, those involved in self-hire and marketing/selling all found an ambience that offered "room-to-manoeuver" options.

Within the broad categories of urban occupations, the enslaved handled their enslavers' money and their own; they acquired skills that offered them some autonomy on the job; they worked in maritime occupations that offered them options not widely available in the rural environment. They were often in occupations that required unsupervised absences from their owners' residences. They lived and worked in environments where the entrepreneurial exploits of their free colored kin could not fail to expand their own expectations of freedom. These were all factors in an evolving urban identity—an identity that could not fail to impress itself on visitors to the town. Certainly, William Dickson, who visited Bridgetown in the 1780s, was struck by the contrasts between rural and urban life. He was convinced that the enslaved in the urban environment, particularly those who were skilled, lived a lifestyle not available to their rural counterparts.

Notes

1. An excellent survey that examines the demographics of enslaved populations in the Caribbean and finds time to examine the social lives of the enslaved in the two contexts, urban and rural, is found in Barry W. Higman, *Slave Populations of the British Caribbean 1807–1834* (Baltimore: Johns Hopkins University Press, 1984). A survey of the conditions of the urban slavery is also found in Pedro L. V. Welch, "The Urban Context of the Slave Plantation System: Bridgetown, Barbados, 1680–1834" (Ph.D. thesis, University of the West Indies, Cave Hill, Barbados, 1995).

2. David Barry Gaspar, *Bondmen and Rebels* (Baltimore: Johns Hopkins University Press, 1985), 107.

3. Elsa Goveia, *Slave Society in the British Leeward Islands at the End of the Eighteenth Century* (New Haven, Conn.: Yale University Press, 1965); Orlando Patterson, *The Sociology of Slavery* (London: Grenada, 1973); Karl Watson, *The Civilized Island—Barbados* (Barbados: Caribbean Graphics, 1979); [Edward] Kamau Brathwaite, *The Development of Creole Society in Jamaica 1770–1820* (Oxford: Clarendon Press, 1971; reprint, London: Oxford University Press, 1978); Jerome Handler, *Plantation Slavery in Barbados* (Cambridge: Harvard University Press, 1978); Gary Puckrein, *Little England: Plantation Slavery and Anglo-Barbadian Politics 1627–1700* (New York: New York University Press, 1984).

4. Goveia, *Slave Society,* 203, 240–41.

5. Ibid., 146, 242.

6. See Pedro L. V. Welch with Richard Goodridge, *"Red" and Black over White: Free Coloured Women in Pre-emancipation Barbados* (Bridgetown: Carib Research and Publications, 2000).

7. For a discussion of family life in the urban context of slave plantation society, see Pedro L. V. Welch. "The Slave Family in the Urban Context: Views from Bridgetown, Barbados 1780–1816," *Journal of Caribbean History* 29, no. 1 (1995): 11–24.

8. Pedro L. V. Welch, "Bridgetown as Port Town" (seminar paper, University of the West Indies, Cave Hill, Barbados, 1989), 19–25.

9. See table 8.2.

10. Frederick W. Bayley, *Four Years Residence in the West Indies* (London: William) 33, 32, 33.

11. Ibid., 33.

12. Act cited in Samuel Moore, *The Public Acts in Force* (London: Luke Hansard, 1801), 154–71.

13. Ibid., 166.

14. Ibid., 168.

15. Petition of Merchants to the Barbados House of Assembly, 5 May, 1811, *Minutes of the House of Assembly,* May 5, 1811, Barbados Department of Archives (hereafter BDA).

16. *Minutes of the House of Assembly,* November 10, 1801 (transcript) (BDA).

17. See ibid.

18. Seaforth Muniments, Returns of Merchants to Governor Seaforth of Barbados, microfilm GD46/17/(80) (BDA).

19. See *Minutes of the House of Assembly,* November 10, 1801 (transcript) (BDA).

20. See Higman, *Slave Populations,* 552–58.

21. Account and Letter Book of William Joseph Senhouse, 3 vols. (Microfilm JAC 21 of Johns Hopkins University.) Wages paid to their boatmen are recorded in several reports of their monthly expenses.

22. Ruth A. Fisher, "Manuscript Materials Bearing on the Negro in British Archives," *Journal of Negro History* 27, no. 1 (1942): 88.

23. For a discussion on the impressment of "negro" seamen into the British navy, see Edward Scobie, *Black Brittania* (Chicago: Thomas, 1972), 63.

24. Bayley, *Four Years,* 25.

25. Ibid., 26.

26. William Dickson, *Letters on Slavery* (Westport, Conn.: Negro Universities Press, 1970), 38–39.

27. Paul D. Lack, "An Urban Slave Community: Little Rock, 1831–1862," *Arkansas Historical Quarterly* (1982): 263.

28. Ibid., 263–64.

29. Higman, *Slave Populations,* 232–35.

30. *Barbados Mercury,* May 21, 1788.

31. *Barbados Mercury,* January 17, 1809.

32. Richard Hall, *Laws Passed in the Island of Barbados* (London, 1764), 185.

33. Ibid., 186.

34. A. F. Wedd, *The Fate of the Fenwicks* (London: Methuen, 1927), 163.

35. Ibid., 168.

36. Ibid., 175.

37. George Pinckard, *Notes on the West Indies,* 3 vols. (London: Longman, 1806), 1: 256, 257; Benjamin Browne, *The Yarn of a Yankee Privateer,* ed. Nathaniel Hawthorne (New York: Funk and Wagnalls, 1926), 113; Bayley, *Four Years,* 68.

38. Higman, *Slave Populations,* 230.

39. Pinckard, *Notes on the West Indies,* 1: 246–57.

40. Ibid., 256–57.

41. Inventory of John and Thomas Scott 1829 (BDA).

42. Minutes taken before the Selected Committee Appointed for the Examination of Witnesses on the Slave Trade, 12 Feb. 1790. Evidence of Alexander Campbell (mfm. A7.B7 held by Johns Hopkins University Library).

43. Higman, *Slave Populations,* 242.

9

Freedom without Liberty

Free Blacks in the Barbados Slave System

Hilary McD. Beckles

The need to explore and comprehend the life options available to free blacks in the Atlantic slave system, particularly in the period during and after the Haitian Revolution, has generated a lively, conceptually challenging historiography. Among the millions of blacks in slave societies, the few who gained freedom seemed to have been brought under a closer scrutiny by white enslaving elites. While it was understood that the enslaved majority constituted the principal threat to the survival of the slave system, there was considerable anxiety and fear among whites that antislavery revolution could be sparked by the politics of the free minority.[1]

Free blacks, then, were perceived as a possible catalyst and therefore enormously "dangerous." The general tendency among them, however, was to seek out and exploit niche opportunities for status mobility and wealth accumulation. The enslaved, too, sought to develop similar strategies, oftentimes to secure the basis for a possible flight from bondage. But the attainment of popular freedom required the enslaved to first imagine the idea of collective, violent political action. It also required free blacks to rise above and explode the personal paradoxical positions in which they found themselves. The evidence suggests that in general they found it impossible to escape the contradictory social forces that shaped and guided their lives within a formation based upon the ideology of white supremacy.[2]

Free blacks in Barbados, the oldest and most densely populated sugar-plantation colony in the Caribbean, were not sufficiently numerous, politically organized, or financially influential to determine in any meaningful way the character and directions of the slave society. Their presence and predicaments, however, served to highlight the practical limits of the social idealism of freedom projected by the enslaved and to illuminate the thinking that informed the choice of armed conflict. Importantly, the enslavement they had personally escaped and dreaded returning to could not be detached in any meaningful way from the texture and terms of everyday life. While in their heads and hearts they might have broken loose, their hands and feet remained firmly attached. All significant social arrangements or financial activity in which they engaged required their embrace of slavery as the enabling infrastructure.[3]

The kinds of social objectives pursued by free blacks in the colony, particularly before the 1816 rebellion of enslaved people in Barbados, required the adoption of strategic plans that included slaveholding. The colonial system was designed to ensure that ownership and possession of enslaved people constituted the primary engines of status mobility and wealth accumulation for all free people. Free blacks neither discovered nor devised any dependable alternative method but approached slave-owning relationships in ways more socially complex and liberating than their white counterparts. It is not entirely true to say therefore that free blacks had retreated from the idealist antislavery ethos of their race that facilitated personal flights from slavery and advanced in the direction of self-serving strategic economic reactions and political postures. Their slave-owning patterns and manumission rates indicate also the operation of moral economy forces that centered on a measure of commitment to antislavery.[4]

The politically empowered planter-merchant white community considered it important to social stability to police the working and living parameters within which free blacks operated. They took some comfort in the realization that free blacks had agreed that the ownership of enslaved people was the mechanism that could guarantee the maintenance and promotion of individual freedom, but these whites remained uncertain about the possible political effects of free blacks' seemingly ambiguous circumstance. Also, whites considered it a major victory in governance that the society based on black enslavement could carry within its bosom a minority of free blacks. Occasionally, however, they were torn by evidence that suggested that free blacks had also claimed success in their sociopolitical maneuverings.

Historians have had a great deal to say about all of this. Barry Higman is correct to draw attention to Jerome Handler's analysis of the so-called freedman category as a conflation of ideologically differentiated social groups. A distinction should be made, notes Higman, "between free colored and free black slave-owners," even if to demonstrate that the latter were "less conspicuously oriented to white culture." Critically, Higman has also shown the striking difference between free black, free colored, and white enslavers' attitudes toward the freeing of the enslaved. This is sufficient, he concludes, to reject Handler's general conclusion that all enslavers approached the matter of enslaving Africans with broadly similar intentions and results.[5]

Most free blacks functioned just above subsistence level in the urban socioeconomic system. This was not phenomenal. It reflected the ideological and institutional nature of the rural plantation sugar economy that could not embrace them in large numbers. Freedom in the rural society, more so than in towns, constituted the most important social asset an individual could possess, and the extent of its translation into multi-consumer benefits depended upon other criteria governing general institutional arrangements. Excluded on the basis of race and class from the system of sugar-plantation production (hence the dominant economy) and denied honorable access to the rural commercial services demanded by sugar planters, free blacks had no option but to huddle around the towns and participate in the design and development of a more elastic, pluralist urban culture. As petty enslavers, their exclusion from the mainline sugar economy placed a ceiling upon their financial and social status achievements and assured urban concentration as the common expectation.[6]

The emergence of free black communities throughout the Caribbean was therefore essentially an urban experience. In Barbados, the overwhelming majority of free blacks lived in Bridgetown and its neighboring communities in Saint Michael parish. Higman has suggested that, in general, manumission was more common in towns than in rural districts and that there was a definite bias toward towns in terms of manumitter residency. In the period 1817–20, when only 12 percent of the enslaved population lived in Bridgetown, 49 percent of all manumissions occurred there. There were broadly similar patterns in Saint Kitts, Dominica, and Jamaica. The explanation seems clear when it is realized that those who owned few enslaved persons, as was the case in towns, were twice as likely to grant freedom than rural owners of a large enslaved labor force. The strong negative correlations between mean slaveholding size and manumission rates that held across the English colonies, Higman concludes, had several implications for the kinds of blacks who were likely to be freed.[7]

There were free black individuals, however, of both sexes, few in number and socially conspicuous, who managed to escape the entrapment of market economy forces and secure considerable material advancement.

While their levels of wealth accumulation corresponded to those of many urban whites, they were never accorded comparable civil honors and social respectability on account of the determining power of white supremacy ideology. The principle of race first, on which the slave system was based and which was so clearly articulated by John Poyer, the leading local proslavery ideologue at the end of the eighteenth century, ensured the effectiveness of social rigidity even when economic barriers were breached.[8]

The free black community in Barbados developed in much the same way as that of most major slave systems with economies based on sugar plantations. Barbados, however, had a peculiar social feature that problematized free black presence at the outset: the relatively large white laboring class with which it competed in the eighteenth century for employment and a share of the small business sector. Feeling vulnerable and politically targeted, free blacks as a result tended to follow the trail made by the free coloreds who had more wealth, confidence, and social prestige. By the early nineteenth century, in response to the increasing pressure of English antislavery politics and the successes of the Haitian Revolution, they had evolved a more distinct separate political identity. Handler notes that during this time the expression "free black" was a common self-ascription. Furthermore, he states that the use of the term as distinct from "free-colored," which suggests mixed racial ancestry, "indicates that as the years progressed the proportion of black freed men became larger than it had been in earlier years."[9] By the end of slavery, the free black population was just under half of the total free non-white community (see table 9.1).[10]

The case of London Bourne is strikingly illustrative of the economic success and social exclusion of free blacks. Like his father, William, London began life enslaved. When he was born in 1793, his father had already established a reputation as a successful black businessman who had purchased a number of properties in the less prestigious commercial parts of Bridgetown. In 1818, William secured the freedom of his wife and four sons through a special negotiation with a Jewish London-based merchant, Moses Barrow Lousada. London Bourne, now free and literate, married a free black woman, Patience Grahme, who also owned in her own right a number of urban properties. Together they had seven children who were all born into freedom. By the late 1820s, London was being described as a successful sugar broker, merchant, and owner of several stores in Bridgetown. He was also categorized as one of the "wealthiest" entrepre-

Table 9.1. Free black and free colored population in Barbados, 1773–1829

Year	Number			Percentage	
	Colored	Black	Total	Colored	Black
1773	136	78	214	63.6	36.4
1825	2,066	1,760	3,829	54.0	46.0
1826	2,169	1,905	4,074	53.2	46.0
1827	2,201	1,947	4,148	53.1	46.9
1828	2,259	1,989	4,248	53.2	46.8
1829	2,313	2,027	4,340	53.3	46.7

Source: See note 10.

neurs in the town, with a commercial office in London that employed white clerks and agents.

Bourne was, however, a black man operating within an economic environment dominated by white men who considered it necessary and found it possible to exclude black men from all positions of honor, prestige, and power. As a result, he was not invited to the formal business meetings of white merchants in Bridgetown, even though he owned the very building that these merchants used for such gatherings. They rented the upper part of the building for the purposes of conducting a commercial exchange; London and his family inhabited the lower floor. He collected the rent but could not enter the meetings. It was not until 1840, following the abolition of African enslavement in the British-colonized Caribbean and as a result of the political agitation of the influential Samuel Prescod and the supportive intervention of Governor Evan John Murray McGregor, that the doors of the Barbados Chamber of Commerce were opened to the owners of the building—London Bourne and Son.[11]

Gender, Manumission, and Self-Purchase

Females constituted the majority within both the free black and free-colored populations. This was explained by social commentators in terms of the bias toward women in the enslavers' manumission decisions. Since the legal status of children at birth was derived from that of the mother, free black women were well placed to reproduce the free community. Enslavers, wishing to suppress this possibility, tended to manumit enslaved adult women after their childbearing period. The norm, then, was for free black women to experience freedom within the context of their children's en-

Table 9.2. Free Blacks in the Barbados population

Year	Free Blacks	Whites	Slaves	Free coloreds
1773	78	18,532	68,546	136
1825	1,760	14,630	78,096	2,066
1827	1,947	14,687	79,383	2,201
1829	2,027	14,959	81,902	2,313

Source: See note 12.

slavement. Also among the free black community in Bridgetown were persons who had escaped enslavement in neighboring islands and, during the period immediately after the abolition of the trade in enslaved African captives, Africans who were captured from slave ships and landed on the island. This latter category was gradually absorbed into the free black community that struggled to eke out a living in the intensely competitive economy of the nonsugar sector (see table 9.2).[12]

The path of the journey of blacks from enslavement to freedom by manumission was policed and politicized by enslavers at every stage; signposts along the way expressed in clearest terms the importance whites attached to controlling and limiting any flight from enslavement for blacks. Parliamentary debates and legislative provisions constitute the rich sources of data that illuminate the ideological positions and political arguments of the white elite. Emphasis upon careful social planning and guided institutional organizations emerges from these deliberations. Enslaved blacks understood all too well that the intensive guarding of manumission mechanisms was to ensure that even in freedom, liberty would be severely curtailed and easily compromised.

Whites who participated formally in the effective manumission of enslaved people, however, did not wish to see them destitute in freedom; neither did they desire a situation in which free blacks could rise above the white community in terms of wealth accumulation and social status. The vision of manumitters of enslaved peoples then, was circumscribed by considerations of white supremacy, particularly that aspect of it concerned with the enhancement of paternalist mastery. The consolidation and social effectiveness of enslavers' dominance required, at least occasionally, public symbolic displays of personal concern for the welfare of some of the enslaved. As a political ideology, paternalism served to sharpen the power instruments available to enslavers by virtue of its tendency to splinter and diffuse anger and opposition among the subordinated. By strategically liberating enslaved persons considered "loyal," enslavers signaled to the mass of enslaved peoples a willingness to hear and respond positively to their claim to humanity and freedom.[13]

The ideological concerns of free colored enslavers who freed their enslaved blacks were oftentimes quite different from those of whites, though some similarities can also be discerned. It was a common social occurrence for wealthy free colored persons to buy and then emancipate members of their enslaved family. This trend is particularly evident from the several cases of free colored women, for example, securing the freedom of their black mothers. In such instances, the emotional bonds that held together the mulatto and black children of a black woman were strong enough to remove the slave relations that divided them. The politics of this type of domesticity and kinship, more often than not, differentiated the free black experience along the lines of manumitter ethnicity.[14]

White enslavers, therefore, were not confronted with the kind of decisions that free black enslavers were forced to make with respect to the manumission of enslaved blacks. The decision that many free blacks made to purchase their friends and kin and keep them in legal slavery as an act of social and family reconstitution often entailed the outlay of a lifetime of accumulated money. The emotional intensity of choices was frequently matched by the complicated arrangements made to finance as cheaply as possible such manumissions. In 1818, for example, William Bourne resorted to the imperial option in seeking his sons' manumissions. He "sold" them (they were "his slaves") to Moses Lousada who resided in London for 200 pounds Barbados currency. Lousada, in turn, had a manumission deed drawn up for ten shillings by a London lawyer who secured the Lord Mayor's signature, thereby declaring them free.

The cost of a manumission in Barbados was made prohibitively high by legislative provision in 1739. The law provided that a payment of 50 pounds had to be made to the vestry by the manumitter, out of which an allowance in the form of 4 pounds annual pension to the freedman or freedwoman would be made. This law remained active until major revisions were made to it in 1801, by which the manumission fee was raised to an astonishing 300 pounds for females and 200 pounds for males; correspondingly, the allowance in the form of an annual pension was raised to 18 pounds for females and 12 pounds for males.[15]

Betty-Burk Poore's case of 1789 illustrates the typical predicament of less financially sound free black enslavers who wished to manumit a family member. Like many free black women, she had succeeded in securing by purchase the legal ownership of her three children—John, Thomas, and Sarah. Under the 1739 law, she needed to raise 150 pounds Barbados currency in order to free these children before she died so as to exclude them from any charge upon her estate. As her property and chattel, these children were attached to her estate and therefore alienable under law. Poore could find no easy way of freeing her children and chose before death to sell her two sons in order to raise cash to pay for her daughter's manumission. The compelling logic of her decision is that as a free black person, Sarah's children would be born free under law, while her sons, both artisans, had a reasonable chance of achieving freedom through self-purchase.[16]

Government officials complained consistently that far too many so-cially irresponsible and callous enslavers freed their unproductive en-slaved workers as a strategy to abandon financial responsibility for them, resulting in these workers' dependence upon the vestry for poor relief. This occurrence explains, in part, Parliament's concern about the rate and terms of private manumissions. For sure, freedom was expensive and costly to maintain. It was, nonetheless, greatly valued and aggressively pursued. Had this not been the case, there would be considerable evidence of freed blacks selling themselves back to slavery as a way of attaining subsistence. Also, many would have opted for an amelioration of enslaver-enslaved relations rather than an end to the institution itself. Fortunate, therefore, were those individuals who received a substantial asset from their manumitter upon which to build a viable future with freedom. Mary Ann, for example, a black woman owned by Sarah Kirton, received on her freedom in 1790 three acres of land. She may have done better in the long term than Margaret, also a black woman, who received from her manumitter in the same year 150 pounds in an interest-bearing account.[17]

Probably the most effective assets emancipated blacks could receive were gifts of enslaved Africans as chattel. In all cases, the transition from enslaved to enslaver was revolutionary in that it oftentimes laid the foun-dation for a quantum leap in psychological, social, and material well-being. While it is true that the black family and wider community were frequently divided and torn apart by such an extreme shift in social cir-cumstance, black slaveholding came to typify everyday social life. Further-more, it was legitimized as an acceptable strategy of enfranchisement by a substantial part of the black population. Enslaved people constituted an income-earning investment that also yielded publicly recognized social returns. black enslavers, then, whose "slaves" were not part of their kin-ship network, could seek to be as unrestrained in their use as whites and free coloreds. It was unlikely, however, that the social circumstances of everyday life in the black community life would have allowed for such a development.

White enslavers recognized and understood the significance of this predicament in emancipating enslaved individuals. Provisions for entry into freedom, therefore, were considered most supportive when productive, out-of-kin slaves were offered to be manumitted. In 1766, for example, Robert Harrison's will provided for the freedom of his enslaved black females, Betty and Grace. Betty received, in addition, a cash allowance of 150 pounds; more important, her former owner provided her with "two mulatto girl slaves, Phillis and Rachel." Grace's cash advance of 100 pounds was supplemented by the gift of an enslaved mulatto girl, Mary. Harrison also made arrangements for both women to receive a dwelling house. As owners of enslaved females, both women could reasonably expect over time to benefit financially from their enslaved women's production and, equally as important, their reproduction. No mention is made in the will of any kinship relation between Betty, Grace, and any of these mulatto girls. A fair assumption would be that these enslaved females were highly valued and specifically chosen as substantial compensation in Harrison's emancipation project.[18]

Like many other white enslavers, Harrison could have chosen the option of investing the manumitted blacks with possession and use of enslaved laborers rather than ownership, in which case his primary consideration would be the future comfort of the beneficiary rather than their independent accumulation of wealth. In 1772, for example, Francis Ford made provision in his will for the freedom of his enslaved blacks, Murria and her two children. In addition, Murria was to receive a stipend from his estate of 12 pounds half-year for life, possession of the house which she inhabited, and the "use and services" of an enslaved black girl. These allowances were made for the duration of Murria's life. While Ford did not sponsor Murria's ownership of these assets, he stipulated that her son, Thomas, was to be "put to school and decently clothed and bound to apprentice a trade." Altogether, the package was designed to improve the life chances of this family over time, though Ford, like Harrison, would have been keen to ensure the survival and consolidation of the slavery system on which his own accumulation depended.[19]

From the perspective of free blacks' capacity to own enslaved persons, accumulate wealth, and consolidate family status, importance should be attached to the process and character of blacks' self-purchase and their capacity for financial accumulation. In the free black community, considerable status was claimed by persons who secured by self-purchase their own freedom. In fact, such persons boasted possession of an independent character, which they held up by way of social distinction. If self-purchase was in any way proof of an affirmative, antislavery consciousness, then the subsequent ownership of enslaved persons by such free blacks would seem all the more paradoxical. This would be so, however, only within the context of antislavery ideology that dichotomized individual and collective strategies of liberation. Since in fact the vast majority of day-to-day acts against slavery were predicated upon individual searches for betterment, from marronage to negotiations for better jobs and nutrition, it should not be considered phenomenal that free blacks would include slave-owning as a necessary mechanism for personal advancement.

The Barbados evidence suggests that, while self-purchase was preferred by most of those enslaved and pursued by many, it was both discouraged and problematized by the white slave-owning elite. In 1803, a Barbadian noted that some enslaved blacks who were "prone to industry, desirous of becoming free, and careful of their profits" did occasionally "amass money with which they purchase themselves. . . . Purchasing themselves means the depositing in the hands of the master the sum which he values them at." Such funds were said to have been commonly accumulated by enslaved people who "work out," tradespeople in the towns, estate drivers who received money rewards for good performance, hucksters, prostitutes, mistresses, and persons with special skills such as medicine and midwifery.[20]

Freedom was always much easier to achieve in this way for less productive enslaved workers who were oftentimes encouraged to take this step by low market valuations. This was also the case for women engaged in intimate relations with politically empowered, wealthy white men. But equally, it was a common response for white enslavers to receive requests for self-purchase as an act of defiance, insubordination, and outright rebellion. Language and dialogue were always open to this interpretation since the object of the exercise was the effective termination of the enslaver's property rights and social power. When the enslaved was able to accumulate sufficient capital for self-purchase, a discourse of subservience and submission was still necessary in order to secure the enslaver's compliance and agreement. Self-purchase, then, would rarely begin within a spirit of radical self-determination.[21]

The majority of free blacks were female Creoles who worked as domestics while enslaved. Males tended to be artisans, Creole, and urban-based. Domestics, tradespeople, sellers, and hired enslaved laborers, notes Higman, were "three times more likely to be manumitted than any other occupational group." He shows that "in rural St Michael 23 enslaved people were manumitted between 1817–1820, fourteen of them domestics, three tradesmen, two seamstresses, and four listed no occupation." Furthermore, the Barbados evidence shows that free blacks and free colored enslavers were twice as likely as whites to manumit enslaved blacks. Higman concludes that, based on the period 1817–20, it seems necessary to reject Handler's conclusion that in Barbados "freedmen manumitted at a rate that was roughly comparable to, or even somewhat below, that of whites, and . . . were not disproportionately inclined to manumit their slaves."[22]

The slave registration data for Barbados show that free blacks were the most likely manumitters of enslaved blacks. In Bridgetown, free blacks freed their enslaved property at a greater rate than free coloreds or whites. For the period 1817–20, 10.4 percent of enslaved persons owned by free black men were freed, followed by those belonging to free mulatto men (3 percent), free black women (2.7 percent), free mulatto women (1.6 percent), white women (1.5 percent), and white men (0.6 percent). These figures suggest that free black men and white men resided at the extremes of the emancipation project and that the social process of patriarchal family reconstitution operated forcefully within the free black community. Free black men were more likely to own and free their families than free black women, which accounts for the substantial difference in manumission rates between the two groups.[23]

Free Blacks and Slaveholding in the Urban Context

The concentration in towns of free black enslavers also speaks to the specific conditions of the urban and rural economies and the nature of their interaction. The dominant sugar-plantation sector effectively marginalized and impoverished all persons without enslaved people or land. A feature of the urban economy was a substantial community of landless slaveholders, including mostly free blacks, free coloreds, and unmarried white women. Free blacks and the enslaved workers they owned, then, huddled together on the margins of the urban economy, seeking to accumulate capital against the forces of colonial racism. As property owners, however, their engagement in the slave-owning culture was marginal and minimum. Table 9.3 indicates that their share of enslaved people played a minor role in the economy.[24] In 1817, a total of 174 free blacks owned 563 enslaved people. At the same time, there were 476 "mulatto" enslavers

Table 9.3. Distribution of free black slaveholders, 1817

Parish	Black men		Black women	
	No. Owners	No. Enslaved	No. Owners	No. Enslaved
Saint Michael Bridgetown	42	144	196	296
Saint Michael rural	3	14	3	18
Saint Philip	6	14	4	20
Christ Church	2	9	1	4
Saint Thomas	2	5	2	4
Saint George	2	10	2	6
Saint James	—	—	—	—
Saint John	2	4	1	1
Saint Peter	1	1	5	13
Saint Andrew	—	—	—	—
Saint Lucy	—	—	—	—
Saint Joseph	—	—	—	—
Total	60	201	114	362

Source: See note 24.

who owned 1,990 enslaved people. The total number of enslaved people in the colony was an estimated 92,580. Free blacks then owned a mere 0.61 percent of all enslaved people, while free mulattoes owned 2.14 percent. The total number of enslavers in Bridgetown was 2,140, 6.44 percent of whom were free blacks who owned 8.15 percent of the 5,394 enslaved people in the town. Of these enslaved people, 50 percent were classified as domestics, 12 percent as skilled artisans, and the remaining 38 percent either had no specific occupation or were employed in selling, fishing, transport, or miscellaneous services. Among the enslaved there were 168 seamstresses, 124 tailors, and 140 shoemakers in Bridgetown, less than 25 percent of whom were owned by free blacks.[25]

Most free blacks, however, were not enslavers and made a living as workers alongside those enslaved mostly in the towns but also in the country. Inasmuch as those enslaved aspired to freedom, free blacks sought entry to slave-owning status for economic and social reasons. The worlds of both groups overlapped, since changing legal status could not in one generation lead to extensive reorganization of personal and kinship ties. Distinctions were often blurred, as the enslaved who "worked out" in the towns exercised as much social autonomy as free blacks and oftentimes possessed the support of influential owners to endorse their public conduct. Neither was it uncommon for free blacks without labor skills and driven to destitution by unemployment and propertylessness to depend upon the charity of those enslaved people who were more materially secure. Competition for scarce employment, then, did not always go in favor of unskilled free blacks, and their condition in some instances was not dissimilar to that of marginalized "poor whites" who were described as generally "sunk with despair and consequent indolence into a state of profligate and vagrant beggary."[26]

The condition of skilled free blacks was altogether more secure despite severe competition from skilled enslaved and white workers. An 1814 report on artisan services in Bridgetown tells us that "free Negroes carried on all the lighter mechanical trades, such as tailors, shoemakers, jewelers" and that the quality of their work was commendable. A description of the town at the end of slavery states that free blacks had cornered the market for skilled labor at the expense of enslaved artisan and white artisans because of "their superior industry."[27] A visitor to the island about this time remarked that "most of the respectable mechanics in Bridgetown are Negroes who own large establishments and employ only workmen of their own color." Here it is noted that free black businesses were committed to employing other free blacks in addition to hiring and buying enslaved people. Female free blacks approached their professions, whether as seamstresses, nurses, or hucksters, with a similar sense of social commitment to their group.[28]

Restrictive Legislation

The white community found it necessary and important to ensure that free black enterprises, whether they employed enslaved people or other free blacks, existed under a cloud of social suspicion with respect to the legality of their operations. The political tendency to criminalize free black businesses by linking them to transactions in illegal goods had the effect of stigmatizing their accumulation process. Throughout the eighteenth century, the legislature purposefully made this association, and laws designed to regulate illegal commercial activities focused on alleged criminal relations between larceny among enslaved persons and free black commerce. Free blacks were represented in the text of the legislative provisions, as well as in general proslavery literature, as the covert allies of the enslaved in the conspiracy to appropriate and dispose of properties owned by whites. In this regard, free black men were publicly represented by whites as participants in a criminal commercial subculture that paralleled the stereotype of free black women as living off immoral earnings.[29]

Joshua Steele, in the late eighteenth century an advocate of amelioration policies for enslaved people, made mention in 1788 of free blacks and
enslaved persons in Bridgetown constituting a marketing network in "all
sorts of stolen goods." Also involved in these arrangements were poor
whites who, according to Steele, found it convenient to hide behind free
blacks who in the event of prosecution could not give evidence in court in
which the accused was white.[30] The campaign against "Huckster Negroes," both enslaved and free, was carried out in the legislature against
the background of these charges, which gained intensity over time. The
objective of the white elite—to suppress, control, and where possible
eradicate the commercial culture of blacks—was intended to secure for the
white community hegemonic dominance at all levels of the economy.[31]

The resort to a licensing strategy by government was effected finally
through legislation in 1779. This law required all "Huckster Negroes" to
register annually with the colony's treasurer and receive a license on the
payment of ten pounds local currency and a service charge of 25 shillings.[32] An important effect of this financial imposition upon free blacks
was to undermine their capacity to purchase or hire enslaved workers to
expand their business operations. As a tax upon the black business sector,
the government's licensing policy was intended also to fracture the growing relations between urban white owners of rented enslaved laborers and
black employers. Small free black retail operators who normally hired
enslaved people to sell their products found the tax prohibitive. Many of
them opted to trade illegally, risking severe punishments, such as property
confiscation and imprisonment.

Free Black Slaveholders: Color and Gender Dynamics

Despite the oppressiveness of legislation within the radicalized social environment, some free blacks succeeded in establishing substantial businesses
that utilized large numbers of enslaved blacks. Without the large-scale
ownership or possession of enslaved workers, black entrepreneurs would
have been further handicapped with respect to the accumulation process.
In these businesses, the enslaved workers were oftentimes the main capital
investment and were used in the normal way as collateral on the money
market. A visitor from the United States in the colony in 1814 found it
significant that there was a concentration of free black enslavers in the
shopkeeping business. He suggested that in Bridgetown free blacks and
free coloreds managed and owned "the largest number of shops."[33] The
same was said of Speightstown, the second largest town. Critically, these

businesses operated in conjunction with highly organized trading links with enslaved plantation workers, who found outlets for their kitchen garden provisions and livestock.

The discriminatory policy of government significantly limited the scope of the economic relations between black shopkeepers and enslaved agricultural producers. Successful entrepreneurs such as Joseph Rachell, however, were able to emerge as testimony to the commercial acumen of free blacks. Described as "a Black merchant in Bridgetown, who had large and extensive concerns," Rachell's business success in the mid-eighteenth century was explained by white contemporaries in terms of his charismatic personality and humanitarian nature. They made reference to his slavery origins, manumission, rise through the dry goods business, and emergence as a leading moneylender and philanthropist. That he owned many enslaved blacks, employed white workers, and had good relations with prominent white merchants and planters were considered significant attributes of an entrepreneurial style. By 1750, success in his principal business, the inter-Caribbean trade, had set him apart within the mercantile community as a respected gentleman.[34] By the end of the century, Rachell's example had found expression in the achievements of other free blacks such as London Bourne.

Both men achieved a level of economic success to which free black women also aspired. While no black woman was able to attain the kind of economic status Rachell and Bourne achieved, several managed to establish businesses, purchase the freedom of their enslaved kin, and generally own enslaved workers as an expression of the personal freedom secured. One such woman was Phoebe Forde. Born enslaved, her determination to achieve freedom for herself and her family was intense and informed her strategic judgments as a young woman. "By her industry," the records tell us, "she earned and saved a sum of money with which she purchased her freedom from her owner." The negotiation over her manumission did not deplete her financial resources, and within a short time she was operating a retail store in Holetown and was known throughout the parish as a reputable businesswoman of strong character. An inventory of her assets at her death in 1823 establishes her as an owner of enslaved people, house owner, and mother of free children whom she had purchased and manumitted.[35]

Free blacks, then, were committed as a community to two immediate, paradoxical, and contradictory agendas. In most cases their personal experiences of slavery and understanding of the social order enabled them to develop aggressive antislavery attitudes with respect to family reconstitution. Records of their decision-making throughout the slavery period indicate commitment to the purchase and manumission of kith and kin as a principal social objective. To this end, however, free blacks found it in their financial interest, in most cases, to own or hire enslaved people. Freedom, therefore, for their free black families came as an end result of their entry into slave-owning. This process and relations, furthermore, were often blurred because the practical circumstances of economic activity necessitated the effective enslavement of family members as a precondition to attaining their freedom.

The tendency was, in addition, for free blacks to adopt attitudes toward work that corresponded with the dominant ideologies of the proslavery interest. Governor John Parry reported in 1788 that he had observed a mentality among them toward manual labor that was in no way dissimilar to that of whites. Distance from manual, degrading work was an important part of the meaning of freedom in Caribbean society, and free blacks, noted the governor, "are so proud and indolent that many of them will not labor for their own maintenance." The depth of this resistance, the governor suggested, was such an important feature of free black mentality that some chose to "become beggars" and be "supported by the parish" rather than labor in tasks normally performed by enslaved workers.[36] Steele tells us, however, that the few free blacks who found themselves in a destitute condition were outnumbered by whites who "pester" the colony and are seen begging "covered with only filthy rags."[37] In effect, Steele concludes, free blacks were not a significant element among the poorest of the poor, and the market economy had allocated their status to mostly unskilled white workers and "abandoned, infirm, and diseased" enslaved laborers.

There were no phenotypic black plantation owners during the eighteenth century, though several persons socially defined as "colored" entered the landed elite. Persons labeled as "mulattoes" were dominant within this small group, some of whom were described as sufficiently white "to go unmolested." Successful black merchants did appear. The white plantation elite seemed more accommodating to a minority of "coloreds" but resisted black entry with considerable tenacity. The ideological world of the sugar plantations constituted the effective force within the wider society. The unwillingness of whites to sell plantation properties to blacks was endemic and, as the evidence shows, survived slavery into the twentieth century.

The complex social circumstances that surrounded blacks' ownership of enslaved people, furthermore, could not facilitate their successful operations of large-scale sugar plantations. Clearly, the extreme cruelty surrounding slave relations in the plantation sector would have problematized black-on-black slavery in ways that the flexible, open conditions of urban slavery did not. It is possible, then, that blacks' confinement to the urban context was indicative of their realization that the social culture of towns represented the practical limits of their effective slave-owning. Essentially, their slave-owning demand was governed by the real need for domestic, artisanal, and casual labor rather than the desire for racial domination, sexual exploitation, and cultural superiority. As an expression of class relation, however, black slave-ownership operated its own distinct ideological agendas but would have contradicted the full range of ideological practices found within the sugar-plantation sector. While it is true, for example, that in the urban sex industry black male and female entrepreneurs were ruthless in the way they degraded and marketed the sexuality of enslaved black women, the vulgar culture of such a trade, it seemed, offered a measure of social liberty and opportunity for personal autonomy to some enslaved women not generally associated with sugar-plantation slavery.

Rachel Pringle, the famed colored woman who ran a hotel that offered enslaved women as prostitutes to guests, freed six of her enslaved women by terms of her will in 1791. When Dr. George Pinckard visited Barbados in the mid-1790s, he observed that enslaved females were commonly offered to guests as prostitutes in most Bridgetown taverns and inns. This activity, he concluded, offered enslaved women "the only hope they have of procuring a sum of money, wherewith to purchase their freedom." While many visitors to the colony noted the severe exploitation of enslaved black females in this way and saw it as evidence of the moral corruption of colonial society, the dominant observation was that prostitution was an important route used by enslaved black women to pursue and achieve freedom and financial independence.[38]

Alliance with Free Coloreds and Radicalized Slave Relations

By the end of the eighteenth century, free blacks had become accustomed to their slave-owning and employer status. In this context, they allied with free coloreds, wrote joint petitions and memoranda, and spoke with one public voice on issues of civil liberties. While their "colored" counterparts were financially more successful, having penetrated both the urban trade sector and rural plantation economy, they had no longer pedigree in the business of slave-owning. It is instructive to note, for example, that the Saint Michael vestry records as early as the 1670s and 1680s show two families of "free Negroes" as owners of several enslaved people.[39] This early start is reflected in Handler's conclusion that throughout the period of African enslavement there is no evidence that, as a group, free blacks "had any compunction against owning or employing slaves" and that they regarded slaves "as desirable forms of property." Furthermore, the "emphasis on slave-ownership was not restricted to those who had been born free, but also extended to former slaves who, after their manumission, often acquired their own human property."[40]

It is important, then, to discern two tendencies within the free black slave-owning experience, one that relates to strategies of liberating family reconstitution and another that was driven purely by the accumulation process. While some overlap occurred between the two, and the extent of this should be carefully assessed, they were effectively discrete social and economic actions. With regard to the latter, however, the dozens of free blacks who, along with over 200 free coloreds, signed the 1803 petition calling upon the Legislative Council not to approve legislation to limit their slave-owning and property accumulation rights may not have spoken for the majority within the group.

In the 1803 petition to the Council, free blacks made reference to their being "accustomed to the assistance of slaves" without which it would be required of them to "perform every menial office with [their] own hands." "Our children," the petitioners claimed, "who are now grown almost to the years of maturity have from their earliest infancy been accustomed to be attended by slaves." The "greatest blessing attending upon freedom," they concluded, "is the acquirement and enjoyment of property," and "surely death would be preferable to such a situation" of slavelessness.[41] While members of Parliament were swayed not to legislate limitations upon free blacks' capacity to own blacks and other forms of property, they remained generally disturbed by the trend that showed free blacks increasing activity on the property market.

Here again, two discernible trends in free black slave-owning culture are illuminated by the discourse on the relative "treatment" of the enslaved in which critics and defenders of slavery engaged. While the evidence shows that free black slaveholders manumitted enslaved people at a rate considerably above whites and were effectively the greatest emancipators of the enslaved, several observers of slavery noted that free blacks "treated" their slaves with less compassion than did whites. William Dickson, for example, who established a reputation in Barbados and England at the end of the eighteenth century as a knowledgeable critic of Barbadian slavery, paid particular attention to the social relations of free blacks. Dickson was not an emancipationist but an ameliorationist who believed that the terms and conditions of enslavement could be modified to meet the requirements of a liberal conscience. He promoted the civil rights of free blacks, encouraged whites to free enslaved skilled artisans in greater numbers, and spoke highly of the quality of the work of free black artisans. But he was at pains to point out that, with respect to the treatment of the enslaved, "free Blacks are generally more severe, because less enlightened owners than white people."[42]

Dickson provided no evidence to support this belief and may have been swayed by the view that, because of their ethnicity, free blacks should not participate in the promotion of radicalized slave relations and the inhumane excesses they imposed upon enslaved blacks. Such a perspective would carry as an assumption the existence of an ideologically monolithic mentality among blacks and an endorsement of the belief in the moral plurality of whites. Denying free blacks a diverse range of opinions, positions, and strategic responses on slavery would suggest that black antislavery politics were not rooted in a complex, sophisticated cosmology.

The enslaving practices of some blacks were undoubtedly consistent with Europeans' concept of Enlightenment modernity that articulated ideas about social freedom with the notion of human progress. Also, the commitment of free blacks to property accumulation and social mobility strategies that required engagement in enslaving other blacks was matched by their determination to preserve and protect freedom, as conceived by white intellectuals and enslavers. The belief that this ideological world, which defined the nature of the proslavery establishment, could be fractured by a race-based master politics of antislavery solidarity contradicts all that is known about gender, class, and race divisions within the colonial context. While contradictory subjective political circumstances oftentimes surrounded free and enslaved blacks, resolutions were sought in multiple ways, and the collective armed struggle for freedom was but one.

The United States commentator who resided in Bridgetown in 1814 appreciated the meaning of these wider issues and considerably problematized Dickson's thesis that black enslavers were the most severe of all. His method was to destabilize Dickson's claim with the observation that it was "a character given by Whites" rather than blacks and was open therefore to doubt and disbelief. Furthermore, the United States visitor showed that the negative opinion of free blacks was propagated by "Whites who seemed to entertain a hostile feeling against them."[43] The ability of proslavery advocates to tarnish the relations of free blacks with negative slave-owning images, then, was part of a wider campaign to limit the liberation projects of all blacks and to suggest to critics of slavery that race was not the critical issue in the slavery debate. Reformers and antislavery agents arrived at the same judgment with respect to black slave-owners because they wished to show the extent of the corrupting nature of the slave system. Their objective, then, was to show that even former enslaved persons were forced to participate aggressively in slavery in order to survive above subsistence.

Following the illegalization of the English trade in African captives in 1807, new levels of constraints upon the labor market forced all slave-owners to devise rationalization schemes to consolidate their investments in enslaved labor. By abolitioning the trade in Africans, the British government drove the majority of enslavers to resort to breeding as the main mechanism of labor reproduction. The scramble to secure an effective share of the internal supply of enslaved labor did not favor black enslavers, though sugar-plantation owners seemed satisfied that in general all was well within their sector. While the skilled labor of free blacks attracted better wages after 1807, their opportunities to purchase or hire enslaved blacks were diminished in the fierce competition with sugar producers.

The dominant political strategy free blacks developed during the period after 1807 was to campaign with free coloreds for an expansion of civil rights, particularly the ability to give evidence in courts against whites and to hold office in government. Their public politics at no stage involved support for the abolition of slavery. Indeed, they stayed clear of any open association with the locally reported and discussed activities of William Wilberforce in England, and the revolutionary antislavery movement was spearheaded by enslaved blacks. Neither did they promote any oppositional politics around specific issues of concern to those enslaved, such as the separation of families, desire for formal education, preventing the corporal punishment of women, and the wish for religious tolerance. In effect, the free black community showed its restricted opposition to slavery primarily in its manumission performance and in its own aggressive but fruitless search for civil rights equality with whites.

The failure of the civil rights movement in the decade after 1807 had effects throughout the entire political culture of the colony. Enslaved blacks knew by then that white society had no intention of either reforming or abolishing slavery. Free blacks' requests for judicial equality with whites were dismissed by the legislature, which threatened them with a reduction of civil rights if they persisted with their campaign. They were made to understand that the few rights they enjoyed were gifts to treasure and that they were impertinent to make further demands upon government. The veiled threat used by their counterparts in Jamaica, Grenada, and Saint Domingue, for example, of leading, supporting, or encouraging rebellion among those enslaved was not made in Barbados. Enslaved people in Barbados had not attempted a significant revolt on the island since 1692, and the entire eighteenth century was free of armed insurrection. Whites were confident in the public management of those they enslaved and thought they had good reasons to be complacent in their political achievement.

A major revolt of enslaved people finally came on April 14, 1816, two years after the Assembly had enacted the imperial Registry Bill that mandated a count and documentation of the entire enslaved population. The enslaved organized an islandwide conspiracy to overthrow the enslaving class and thereby obtain their freedom. The Haitian model of armed insurrection was their inspiration; this much was made clear later by the several confessions of black rebels. The leadership of the rebellion was located within the elite community of enslaved drivers, overseers, and artisans, that is, persons most likely to gain freedom by manumission from their owners. There were no enslaved field hands within the leadership group. It was a strike for freedom led by enslaved people who, according to whites, long enjoyed as many liberties as free blacks. No mention was made of a supportive role played by free blacks, though the official report of the Assembly on the rebellion shows that a small group of laboring free colored men with close kinship and social ties to enslaved laborers were coconspirators.[44]

A large number of free blacks, however, gave evidence before the Assembly's Investigative Committee. The published testimony of one of them, William Yard, indicates quite clearly his political disassociation from the revolt. In his deposition, Yard, a tailor by profession, stated that the enslaved were anxiously awaiting news of their freedom from England since the passage of the Registry Bill and that he was questioned by several of them regarding his knowledge of the same. He also stated that "one of his boys" was questioned at his shop outside of Bridgetown by "country slaves" "whether he know anything about their freedom." His "boy," Yard said, had "pretended to read to them from a newspaper that they were to be free," for which he "rebuked the boy for attempting to impose on the negroes."[45]

Within three days the revolt was crushed by a joint force of militia regiments and imperial soldiers who were stationed on the island as part of the operation to keep out the French. Some 1,000 enslaved persons, two soldiers, and one militiaman lost their lives. No free blacks but four free coloreds, according to the reports, were included among the fatalities. Three years later, another 123 slaves held in various prisons were deported to Honduras and then to Sierra Leone as political prisoners. Many whites, however, according to one report, died as a result of "fatigue" caused by the widespread devastation. Some 177 property holders across 7 of the 11 parishes submitted claims to the government for compensation.[46]

The political leadership of the colony highly commended both free blacks and free coloreds for their loyalty to whites and plantation society during the rebellion. This attachment to the cause of property holders, said John Beckles, Speaker of the House, was effective in quelling enslaved rebels and in his opinion deserved a reward. Addressing the Assembly in January 1817, Beckles noted that this "free" but "restricted" element of the society has always made their complaints "in respectful language, and in terms of moderation." Furthermore, he said, they "have manifested a determination to do their duty by the country, and a devotion to the interest of the whites."[47] Within the year the Assembly passed legislation to reward them with the long sought after right, to give evidence in court under all circumstances in order to protect their freedom and property. Finally, in 1831, they secured the final concession from the legislature: full civil rights equality with whites.

Conclusion

Black-on-black slavery reflected a range of peculiar and sometimes contradictory experiences specific to the aspirations of the black population. At the same time, it illuminated features of the deepest ends and most remote corners of the enslaving culture that underpinned the political economy of Caribbean and Atlantic colonialism. While enslaving as a brutal and alienating anti-black culture constituted the principal mechanism of wealth generation and status mobility, it also enabled some blacks to engage in a desperate attempt at family reconstitution, kinship protection, and social inclusion. Adjusted more to the urban context than the sugar-plantation sector, black-on-black slavery operated with a set of complex socioeconomic arrangements that promoted the quest for property accumulation, in itself a necessary activity for the long-term attainment and protection of freedom.

As a strategic response for status consolidation, free blacks generally formed political alliances with free coloreds, whose anti-black attitudes also reflected the depth of "Negrophobia" endemic to white society. Divided by the vein, free coloreds dealt with their social contradictions and projected a range of attitudes to slavery that were consistent with their multiethnic origins. The ultimate objective pursed by all blacks was flight from enslavement. The door of owning enslaved Africans was one that opened along the journey, and free blacks entered boldly but redefined important aspects of the room they entered and inhabited.

Notes

1. See N. A. T. Hall, "The 1816 Freedman Petition in the Danish West Indies: Its Background and Consequences," *Boletín de Estudios Latinoamericanos y del Caribe* 29 (1980): 55–73; Gad Heuman, "The Social Structure of Slave Societies in the Caribbean," in *General History of the Caribbean: The Slave Societies*, ed. Franklin W. Knight, (London: UNESCO, MacMillan, 1997), 3: 138–69; Michael Craton, "Forms of Resistance to Slavery," in Knight, *General History of the Caribbean*, 222–71; Arnold Sio, "Marginality and Free Colored Identity in Caribbean Slave Society," *Slavery and Abolition* 8 (1987): 166–68.

2. Hilary McD. Beckles, "The Literate Few: An Historical Sketch of the Slavery Origins of Black Elites in the English West Indies," *Caribbean Journal of Education* 11, no. 1 (1984): 19–35; Hilary McD. Beckles, "On the Backs of Blacks: The Barbados Free-Coloreds' Pursuit of Civil Rights and the 1816 Rebellion," *Immigrants and Minorities* 3, no. 2 (1984): 167–88.

3. See John Garrigus, "A Struggle for Respect: The Free Coloreds of Pre-Revolutionary Saint-Domingue, 1760–69" (Ph.D. diss., Johns Hopkins University, 1988); M. G. Smith, "Some Aspects of Social Structure in the British Caribbean about 1820," *Social and Economic Studies* 1 (1953): 55–79.

4. See Gwendolyn Midlo Hall, *Social Control in Slave Plantation Societies* (Baton Rouge: Louisiana State University Press, 1996), 113–32.

5. See Barry W. Higman, *Slave Populations of the British Caribbean, 1807–1834* (Baltimore: Johns Hopkins University Press, 1984; reprint, Kingston: The Press, University of the West Indies, 1995), 112; Jerome Handler, *The Unappropriated People: Freedmen in the Slave Society of Barbados* (Baltimore: Johns Hopkins University Press, 1974), 18–25, 150, 187.

6. See Carl Campbell, "The Rise of the Free Colored Plantocracy in Trinidad, 1783–1813," *Boletín de Estudios Latinoamericanos y del Caribe* 29 (1980): 33–54; Barry W. Higman, "Urban Slavery in the British Caribbean," in *Perspectives on Caribbean Regional Identity*, ed. E. Thomas-Hope (Liverpool: Centre for Latin American Studies, University of Liverpool, 1983), 39–56.

7. Higman, *Slave Populations*, 382.

8. [John Poyer], A letter addressed to (Lord Seaforth by a Barbadian" (Bridgetown, 1801). See also Ronald Hughes, "Jacob Hinds [?–1832], "White Father of a Colored Clan" (seminar paper 2, Department of History, University of the West Indies, Cave Hill, 1982–83).

9. Handler, *Unappropriated People*, 17.

10. Ibid., 21.

11. Celia Karch, "London Bourne of Barbados" (paper presented at the 15th Annual Conference of the Association of Caribbean Historians, University of the West Indies, Mona, Jamaica, 1983); Warren Alleyne, "London Bourne," *The Bajan and Caribbean Magazine*, April 1979; Handler, *Unappropriated People*, 132–33.

12. Handler, *Unappropriated People*, 20–21; see also Hilary McD. Beckles, *Natural Rebels: A Social History of Enslaved Black Women in Barbados* (New Brunswick, N.J.: Rutgers University Press, 1989), 15–17.

13. See Claudia Goldin, "The Economics of Emancipation," *Journal of Economic History* 33 (1973): 66–85; Gad Heuman, *Between Black and White: Race, Politics and the Free Coloreds in Jamaica, 1792–1865* (Westport, Conn.: Greenwood Press, 1981).

14. See Edward Cox, *Free Coloreds in the Slave Societies of St Kitts and Grenada, 1763–1865* (Knoxville: University of Tennessee Press, 1984); Handler, *Unappropriated People*, 29–82.

15. Karch, "London Bourne," 2–3; Karl Watson, *The Civilised Island: Barbados: A Social History, 1750–1816* (Bridgetown: self-published, 1979), 101.

16. Will of Betty-Burk, alias Betty-Burk Poore, free Negro, November 6, 1789. RB6/19, Barbados Archive.

17. These cases are set out in the wills of Sarah Kirton and Laurentia Lavine, 1790, RB6/19, Barbados Archives. See also Watson, *Civilized Island*, 102.

18. See B. M. Shilstone, "Harrison of Barbados," *Journal of the Barbados Museum and Historical Society* 8 (1941): 30–32.

19. The will of Francis Ford is cited in B. M. Cracknell, ed., *The Barbadian Diary of General Robert Haynes, 1787–1836* (Medstead, Hamspie, England: Azania P, 1934), 58–60.

20. Quotation from an anonymous author in *Letter from a Gentleman in Barbados to His Friends in London, on the Subject of Manumission from Slavery, Granted in the Cay of London and in the West Indian Colonies* (London, 1803), 21.

21. Higman, *Slave Populations*, 382.

22. Ibid., 384–85.

23. Ibid., 385–86.

24. Ibid., 233, 433–46.

25. Ibid., 436.

26. Cited in Samuel Moore, *The Public Acts in Force, Passed by the Legislature of Barbados from May 11, 1762–April 8, 1800 Inclusive* (London, 1801), 226–28.

27. Cited in Benjamin Browne, *The Yarn of a Yankee Privateer*, ed. Nathaniel Hawthorne (New York: Funk and Wagnalls, 1926), 112.

28. See Sylvester Hovey, *Letters from the West Indies* (New York, 1838), 205.

29. As early as October 1694, two bills were debated by the Assembly on the subject. The first was to prohibit "the sale of goods to Negroes" and the second to

prohibit "the employment of Negroes in selling." *Journal of the Assembly of Barbados*, October 17, 1694; *Calendar of State Papers, Colonial Series, 1693–1696*, fol. 381.

30. See Joshua Steele's reply to questions asked by Governor Parry on the subject in *Parliamentary Papers*, 1789, 26: 31.

31. See Hilary McD. Beckles, "An Economic Life of Their Own: Slaves as Commodity Producers and Distributors in Barbados," *Slavery and Abolition* 12, no. 1 (1991): 31–47.

32. Moore, *Public Acts in Force*, 154–70. See also Hilary McD. Beckles, *Black Rebellion in Barbados: The Struggles Against Slavery, 1627–1838* (Bridgetown: Antilles Press, 1983), 71–72.

33. Cited in Browne, *Yarn of a Yankee Privateer*, 103.

34. See Jerome Handler, "Joseph Rachell and Rachel Pringle-Polgreen: Petty Entrepreneurs," in *Struggle and Survival in Colonial America*, ed. D. Sweet and G. Nash (Berkeley: University of California Press, 1981), 376–91.

35. Phoebe Forde's case is outlined in *Petition of Samuel Gabriel, Catherine Duke and William Forde, Colored Persons, Inhabitants of this Island of Barbados, 8 March 1823*, CO28/92 Series, No. 16.

36. Cited in Handler, *Unappropriated People*, 138.

37. Steele's assessment is set out in a reply to Governor Parry, 1788, *Parliamentary Papers*, 1789, 26: 33. See also Daniel McKinnen, *A Tour Through the British West Indies in the Years 1802 and 1803* (London: 1804). McKinnen states that the filth and crowded slums of Bridgetown were the social effects of freed slaves concentrating their lives in the one place (15–16).

38. See Handler, *Unappropriated People*, 135–37.

39. Saint Michael Parish Register, Barbados, vol. 1A, R.L. 1/1, Barbados Archives.

40. Handler, *Unappropriated People*, 146.

41. The Humble Petition of the Free Colored People, Inhabitants of the Island, was submitted to the governor in Council on November 1, 1803. See Minutes of Council, November 1, 1803.

42. See William Dickson, *Letters on Slavery* (London, 1814), 55.

43. Cited in Browne, *Yarn of a Yankee Privateer*, 103.

44. See *Report from A Select Committee of the House of Assembly Appointed to Inquire into the Origins, Cause and Progress of the Late Insurrection*, April 1816 (Barbados, 1819).

45. Deposition of William Yard. Ibid.

46. Anon. An Account of the Late Negro Insurrection which took Place in the Island of Barbados on Easter Sunday, 14 April 1816. New York Public Library, Mss. Division; Beckles, *Black Rebellion*, 86–120.

47. Minutes of the Assembly, 7 January 1817; Beckles, *Black Rebellion*, 110; Hilary McD. Beckles, "On the Backs of Blacks: The Barbados Free-Coloreds Pursuit of Civil Rights and the 1816 Slave Rebellion," *Immigrants and Minorities* 3, no. 2 (1984): 1–12.

10

The Free Colored Population in Cuba during the Nineteenth Century

Franklin W. Knight

The free colored population represented a significant proportion of the overall inhabitants of the island of Cuba and an important dimension of its history during the nineteenth century. Both the demographic and historical experience greatly influenced the development of the non-European sectors of the Cuban population. The reverse was also true. The history of the free colored community in Cuba cannot therefore be separated from the indelible traditions and continuing impact of a Spanish Caribbean colony. More specifically, the social and moral influence of the evangelizing Spanish Catholic Church of the sixteenth century—greatly diluted by time and circumstances but nevertheless still effective—remained a recognizable aspect of society in the nineteenth century. As early as the first half of the sixteenth century, important officials such as Bartolomé de Las Casas, Juan Ginés de Sepúlveda, and Palacios Rubios and periodical papal pronouncements such as *Sublimis Deus,* the famous papal bull of 1537, fashioned a paternalistic and proactive colonial legal structure that influenced the nature of the entire Spanish American colonial experience.[1] While individual bureaucrats or churchmen frequently deviated in practice from the official principles, the importance of these legal and customary precedents was never entirely lost—especially by successive generations of free coloreds who sought every opportunity to escape the disabilities of the colonial slave system.[2] Indeed, late in the nineteenth century, a knowledgeable, articulate, and philanthropic opponent of slavery, Rafael María de Labra, declared conscientiously that Spanish slavery was "superior" to all others because of its humane laws.[3] He was not alone. Some twentieth-century scholars such as H. H. Johnson, Frank Tannenbaum, Gilberto Freyre, and Herbert Klein have followed that tradition.[4]

The timing of Cuba's economic development played an inordinately significant role in the ultimate nature of race relations in Cuba. As a Spanish colony, Cuba did not experience the early sugar revolutions or the profound social and economic metamorphosis that the plantation slave system produced in the Caribbean until the late eighteenth century and the beginning of the nineteenth century.[5] This delay had two important and indelible consequences. First, by 1800 Cuba had a large and diversified free black population—the largest of any Caribbean territory. Second, by 1800 the entire South Atlantic System based on the transatlantic trade in enslaved Africans was collapsing and under attack especially from the British, formerly the largest supplier of Africans to the Americas.[6] The massive Haitian revolution and the creation of an independent black republic also contributed to the collapse. Changes in international attitudes toward slavery as well as technological changes in the nineteenth century would seriously affect Cuban society and politics. The implementation of new technical processes in sugar production altered the labor systems of plantations, radically changing labor use after about 1840. At the same time, the rise of pseudoscientific racism complicated and eroded the previously amicable patterns of race relations in Cuba. The free colored population did not escape the impact of these changes.[7]

In the nineteenth century, Cuba developed a conventional society only slightly different from its earlier Caribbean counterparts like Jamaica or Barbados. While the demographic proportions varied from place to place, the pattern was familiar across the region. Caribbean society during slavery represented a segmented construct of mutually reinforcing social cleavages—a society of rigid racial castes complicated by a subdivision of social classes. At the top of this structure was the white population, or Spanish Creoles as they called themselves in Cuba.[8] Cuban whites were a heterogeneous group, comprising peninsular Spaniards, Cuban- and Latin American–born Creoles, Asian Indians, Chinese, and Mexican Indians. Until the abolition of slavery in 1886, free persons of color occupied an intermediate position, and occasionally small numbers merged into the group of whites by obtaining a legal document called a *limpieza de sangre* or *gracias al sacar*. The enslaved, who constituted the lowest order, were given the manual and menial occupations until the end of the nineteenth century. Together, these groups comprised what Spanish colonial convention called the *sociedad de castas*.

The free persons who could not be classified legally as white and yet were not enslaved spanned a wide spectrum both in color and in social position. This segment of the population enjoyed the clearest range of mobility as well. But it came at a great price. As Charles Boxer remarked, "One race cannot systematically enslave members of another for over three hundred years without acquiring a conscious or unconscious feeling of racial superiority."[9] Cuban free coloreds suffered enormously from the racism that permeated their society in the nineteenth century and after as whites sought to eliminate them in all sorts of ways.[10] But free blacks were too integral a part of the society to be easily eliminated by crude mass murder as after the La Escalera conspiracy in 1844 or by more subtle means of applied Social Darwinism.[11]

Demography of the Free Coloreds in the Nineteenth Century

The free colored community in Cuba, as elsewhere throughout the Americas, varied in its origin. Many were the descendants of a number of free or nearly free blacks who came to the Americas with the earliest Spanish colonists. Others were the illegitimate offspring of the profligate sexual encounters between white enslavers and enslaved blacks or with the free black and colored population. Although miscegenation transgressed the social mores of whites and was repeatedly banned by the Spanish colonial government, it nevertheless took place. Indeed, as early as 1580 some 65 percent of the population of the early Spanish towns of Cuba represented mixtures of some sort between the Spanish and the non-Spanish inhabitants, either Indians or Africans.[12] The free colored population usually found itself subdivided into *pardo,* or mulatto, and *moreno,* or black. "The mulattoes," wrote Jacobo de la Pezuela in 1863, "are the children of White men and Black women, or of White women and Black men. However, this latter case is so rare that it is considered a phenomenon throughout the country, although it is physiologically as feasible as the former."[13]

Prior to the abolition of slavery in 1886, the Cuban colored community increased itself in three ways: by natural reproduction, probably at the rate of about 3 percent per year; by voluntary manumission and self-purchase, or *coartación;* and by the freedom granted to a limited number of illegally landed Africans who were captured and declared free by the Courts of Mixed Commission in Havana between 1820 and 1886. This last category comprised the so-called *emancipados* who, rather than being liberated outright, were left in a semiservile condition not far removed from total slavery. Between 1824 and 1866 (the year that the trade in African captives to Cuba apparently ended), more than 26,000 Africans found aboard ships off the coast of Cuba became *emancipados.* These individuals were then contracted out to persons needing labor in an elabo-

Table 10.1. Growth of the free colored population in Cuba, 1792–1899

Year	Free coloreds	Total Cuban population (%)	Nonwhites (%)	Free people (%)
1792	54,154	19.0	45.6	
1827	106,494	15.1	27.1	
1841	154,546	15.1	25.9	
1860	225,843	16.2	37.4	
1877	272,478	20.0	55.7	
1887	528,798	32.5	100.0	32.5
1899	505,443	32.1	100.0	32.1

Sources: Kenneth F. Kiple, Blacks in Colonial Cuba, 1774–1899; U.S. Government, Informe sobre el Censo de Cuba, 1899.

rate, deceptive exercise from which few of those subjected emerged alive. Cristóbal Madán, a large planter, estimated that there were only 6,650 emancipados doing service in Cuba in 1864.[14]

As table 10.1 illustrates, the absolute growth of the free colored population was quite dramatic, although as a proportion of the total island population the performance was erratic. In 1792, the free coloreds numbered more than 106,000 and accounted for almost 20 percent of the total island population. The census of 1792 categorized as "mulattoes" nearly 34,000 of the more than 54,000 free persons of color, meaning that approximately three of every five free black and coloreds had some white ancestor. As the black and colored population increased with the introduction of new enslaved Africans, the proportion of free blacks and coloreds—as well as the proportion of mixed within that category of nonwhite free—would inevitably decline. By 1841, the free colored population had grown nearly three-fold, but the proportion of mulattoes had fallen to about two in five. The mulatto proportion stabilized at about 50 percent of the free colored population until the end of slavery. With the decline of the trade in African captives as well as slavery itself after 1841, the free colored population increased numerically as well as proportionally. After 1860, the Spanish authorities replaced the long-standing division of pardo and moreno with the undifferentiated classification of gente de color (colored person). It is possible that this change reflected a deterioration of both racial and class relations on the island. By 1899, the colored population numbered 520,400, slightly more than 32 percent of the Cuban population. The largest number then lived in Santiago de Cuba (146,605), followed by Havana city and province (112,214), Santa Clara

(111,768), Matanzas (84,527), Pinar del Río (47,439), and Puerto Príncipe (17,847).

One aspect of the demography of the free colored community that cannot be ascertained from the available data is the degree to which manumissions contributed to the overall growth of the free colored population during the nineteenth century. The evidence on manumissions from Cuban sources is not reliable enough to speculate on the frequency, but circumstantial evidence exists to suggest that manumissions decreased during the nineteenth century. The increasing demand for labor and the increasing sense of panic after the Haitian revolution made white enslavers less willing and less able to grant manumissions voluntarily.[15] At the same time, the legal route to *coartación* through which any enslaved person could negotiate the price of his or her self-purchase became increasingly more difficult, partly as a result of the sharper discrimination against blacks and coloreds. In any event, a traveler to Cuba in 1853 remarked that "emancipation of slaves very seldom occurs in Cuba, where they publicly shout that abolitionists are those who have no slaves."[16]

The Moret Law of gradual abolition would begin to drastically change the situation in the mid-1870s by guaranteeing the eventual freedom of all new-born children as well as superannuated enslaved persons.[17] Before that time, the greatest impetus to the population increase among the free coloreds came from its own natural increase. Between 1827 and 1841, for example, the free colored population increased by more than 46,000. Over the interval of 14 years the increase amounted to 43.5 percent, indicating a mean annual growth rate of about 3 percent. This is not an exceptionally high growth rate. Indeed, it only slightly surpasses the growth rate of the white population during the same period. The plausibility of natural increase is enhanced by the fact that some 45 percent of all free colored males and 48 percent of all free colored females were in the potentially fertile age group between 16 and 40 years of age as indicated in table 10.2.[18]

Free colored females exceeded free colored males everywhere across the island, with insignificant variation between rural and urban zones. The areas of greatest differences were found in the provinces of Puerto Príncipe, Santa Clara, Sancti-Spíritus, Trinidad, Cienfuegos, and San Juan de los Remedios, which now forms part of Santa Clara. In these provinces, the ratio of males to females was 49.2:50.8. This difference contrasts sharply with the white segment of the population as well as the enslaved population. White males outnumbered white females in all three major geographical divisions of the island. In the western region, including the

Table 10.2. Age and sex profile for the free colored population in 1841

Sex	Ages 1–15	% of total	Ages 16–40	% of total	Ages 41–60	% of total	Ages over 60	% of total
Male	27,988	37.0	34,268	45.2	10,939	14.5	2,507	3.3
Female	27,001	34.2	37,566	47.6	10,424	13.2	3,852	4.8
Total	54,989	35.6	71,835	46.5	21,363	13.8	6,359	4.1

Source: Resumen del censo de la población de la isla de Cuba en 1841 (Havana: Imprenta del Gobierno, 1842), 19.

city of Havana, males exceeded females by almost 11 percent. For the enslaved sector, the widest gender spread occurred in the plantation-developed Central Department where males proportionally exceeded females by more than 2:1. The pronounced sexual imbalance found among the enslaved population would be mitigated somewhat with the abolition of the slave system in the 1880s. The most important observations of the data provided in table 10.2 relate to the age-sex profile of the free colored population and their suggestiveness for other social considerations pertaining to that element of the overall population.

The most outstanding aspect of the population in 1841 was the relative youthfulness of the free colored sector.[19] Approximately 82 percent of all free colored males and 84 percent of all free colored females were less than 40 years of age. The potentially reproductive age group—those between 16 and 40 years of age—included 47 percent of all females in that category. Females exceeded males in that segment by 3,297 individuals. The relatively high proportion of the population below age 16[9]–37 percent of males and 35 percent of females—indicates a strong natural rate of increase. Nevertheless, in 1859 José García de Arboleya wrote that "the annual population increases of the island since 1774 when the first official census was made resulted more from immigration than from reproduction."[20] While applicable to the white and enslaved sectors of the population, García de Arboleya obviously overlooked the vital, natural growth of Cuba's free colored population.

The available evidence does not permit a close analysis of the statistics of births, marriages, and deaths since the free and nonfree data are combined. Of the 161,349 infants baptized in the period between 1842 and 1846, 74,302 (46 percent) were not white.[21] More than two-thirds of the registered births were by parents who were not legally married. Almost 25 percent of the marriages that took place between 1842 and 1846 were by nonwhites. Some of these marriages included the enslaved, but it is reasonable to assume that the majority involved free coloreds, reflecting an enthusiasm for marriage among the free coloreds. Of the 109,318 registered deaths, blacks and coloreds outnumbered whites by 57,762 to 51,456.

By 1860, the free colored population had increased to more than 200,000, of whom more than 120,000 lived in the Western Department, with the rest living in the large Eastern Department. In the plantation zones, as table 10.3 shows, the division between *pardo* and *moreno* tended to be nearly equal. In the Eastern Department, with only scattered pockets of plantations, *pardos* outnumbered *morenos* by more than 2:1. In a rapidly expanding and frequently mobile population such as that of Cuba during the nineteenth century, this pattern is not easily explained. The concentrated heavy introduction of enslaved Africans during the later eighteenth century and throughout the first half of the nineteenth century may have reversed the earlier preponderance of free coloreds over free blacks.

The location of the free colored population mirrored both the settlement pattern of the free population as a whole as well as the vicissitudes created by the conversion of the island into a plantation slave society. Free coloreds resided more in towns and cities than in the plantation zones and areas of dense sugar plantation concentration. Eastern Cuba, where the sugar and slavery system had been less developed, had a larger share of free blacks and coloreds, as did Havana. In five jurisdictions—Baracoa, Bayamo, Cuba, Manzanillo, and Tunas—the proportion of free coloreds exceeded 30 percent of the population. In Guantánamo and Guanabacoa, the percentage was close to 30.0 percent (see table 10.3).

In 1870, when the total free colored population amounted to 20 percent of the island's inhabitants, they comprised 30 percent of the inhabitants of the jurisdictions of the Eastern Department. The distribution of the free colored population, therefore, roughly corresponded to a pattern diagonally opposite to those of white and enslaved persons, as Ramiro Guerra y Sánchez notes in his study of the Ten Years War (1868–78).[22] In 1870, the 22 western jurisdictions had 600,840 white persons, 141,677 free persons of color, and 300,989 enslaved people. The seven easterly jurisdictions of Baracoa, Bayamo, Santiago de Cuba, Guantánamo, Holguín, Jiguaní, and Manzanillo totaled 113,702 whites, 83,189 free coloreds, and 47,410 enslaved.[23]

Table 10.3. Population distribution, 1861

Jurisdiction	Free nonwhites	%	Slaves	Whites	Total population
Bahia Honda	716	6.5	7,043	6,828	14,587
Baracoa	4,805	42.6	1,575	5,905	11,285
Bayamo	13,900	41.3	2,727	17,046	33,673
Bejucal	2,191	8.9	7,052	15,416	24,659
Cárdenas	3,214	5.5	24,418	28,355	57,987
Cienfuegos	7,812	14.3	16,985	29,714	54,511
Colon	3,703	5.9	33,699	26,476	62,878
Cuba	36,030	37.5	32,255	27,743	96,028
Guanabacoa	5,998	22.1	4,775	16,278	27,051
Guanajay	3,653	9.0	17,608	18,998	40,259
Guantánamo	5,627	28.7	8,561	5,331	19,619
Güines	4,473	7.2	24,817	32,630	61,920
Holguín	7,045	13.5	4,226	40,852	52,123
Jaruco	2,872	7.9	11,077	23,431	36,494
Jiguaní	Not Listed				
La Habana	37,765	18.4	29,013	138,445	205,223
Manzanillo	11,105	30.5	1,713	13,675	36,493
Matanzas	7,067	8.8	32,219	40,627	79,913
Nuevitas	533	8.4	1,622	4,189	6,376
Pinar del Río	10,408	15.1	14,996	43,522	68,926
Puerto Príncipe	10,786	17.2	13,185	38,556	62,527
Remedios	9,335	19.8	9,487	32,425	47,247
Sagua la Grande	2,416	4.7	19,150	30,420	51,986
San Antonio	2,022	6.5	10,737	21,127	30,896
San Cristóbal	3,289	11.3	7,771	17,917	28,977
Sanctí-Spíritus	7,134	15.6	8,949	29,624	45,707
Santa Clara	11,200	21.3	6,866	34,579	52,644
Santa María Del Rosario	828	10.2	2,173	5,045	8,046
Santiago De Cuba	2,041	12.0	4,507	9,302	15,850
Trinidad	9,034	24.0	10,539	17,936	37,509
Tunas	2,254	33.0	480	4,089	6,823
Total	227,356	16.5	370,220	776,481	1,374,057

Source: Jacobo de la Pezuela, *Diccionario geográfico, estadistico, histórico de la isla de Cuba,* 4 vols. (Madrid, 1863–66).

Economic Role and Property Holding

Before the expansion of the Cuban sugar industry, free coloreds seemed to have enjoyed a significant degree of economic and social mobility. They formed an important part of the Spanish colonial society and participated in the military defense of the colony. Black men participated in the military expeditions sent to fight the French in Florida in 1702 and to help defend Vera Cruz in 1720. Black regiments fought in the futile defense of Havana against the English in 1762. The tradition of mobilizing the militia in time of need continued into the later nineteenth century. In 1874, members of the colored militia fighting on the side of the Spanish in the Ten Years War numbered 7,216 men, forming, as one Loyalist put it, "part of the columns which kept alive the glory of our flag and the integrity of the fatherland in the face of the insurgents."[24]

While the sugar revolutions did expand economic opportunities for all sectors of the society, including the free coloreds, opportunities continued to remain circumscribed during the nineteenth century. Free coloreds still suffered from certain legal disabilities. Persons of color were legally barred from practicing the professions of priest, lawyer, doctor, pharmacist, businessperson, or public servant in the royal bureaucracy. In short, the highly public, remunerative, and prestigious positions were all closed off for blacks and coloreds. Some of these legal restrictions go back to early colonial days. Others were added later, and even during the nineteenth century more were being added.[25] Status and color, however, were extremely ambiguous in the nineteenth century. Distinctions between enslaved and other nonfree persons such as the indentured Asians were reasonably sharp, despite the existence of such transitional categories as the *coartados* (those who were in the process of buying their own freedom) and the *emancipados* (those manumitted for whatever reason). On the other hand, no such clear distinction existed between the "white" person and the free mulatto. The mutually reinforcing cleavage that operated between enslaved and free did not operate to the same extent across the free sectors. Because color distinctions were arbitrary and imprecise, it is possible that infringements of the laws did take place and that some free coloreds did practice prohibited professions. It is important that such persons passed as white and were never recognized in law or by their peers as persons of color, since these occupations remained exclusively white in the compilation of Jacobo de la Pezuela in 1861. In this case, therefore, the question of how many, if any, free persons of color were able to pass as whites assumes minor importance. As far as the society was concerned, the situation remained unchanged and the legal status quo was not challenged. Of course, blacks and coloreds also could be "elevated" to white status by the granting of a *limpieza de sangre,* a royal privilege that removed any disabilities and established social status. The sugar revolutions of the early nineteenth century affected the laws, and consequently, race relations. During the regime of Captain-General Géronimo Valdés (1841–43), a law stipulated that the overseer of every rural farm had to be a white man, "under penalty of one hundred pesos fine on any owner infringing this law, and against whom, moreover, the government will use every coercive measure to enforce its compliance."[26]

In addition to the legal exclusion of any free person of color from the professions, the Cuban system of landholding inhibited black and colored ownership. For whatever reason, free black and colored landholders constituted an insignificant proportion of real estate owners during the nineteenth century. As the sugar revolution rolled inexorably eastward from Havana and Pinar del Río, the nonurban free coloreds (as well as smallholding whites and the landless) faced two options: they could move farther east ahead of the engulfing capitalist tide of sugar plantations and slavery, or they could become absorbed into the residential labor force of the *ingenios.* The *ingenio,* as Manuel Moreno Fraginals notes in his excellent study, blurred racial differences in its insatiable demand for laborers:

> The *ingenios* absorbed all available free labor ... the displacement of the tobacco growers of the lands around San Julian de los Güines [southeast of Havana] was followed by, among other eventualities, the incorporation of the peasants in the *ingenio.* The account books of the period clearly reveal how [in] the falling and clearing of the forests, free laborers did the cutting of firewood, and even a good deal of the cutting and hauling of the sugar cane. Also, within the *ingenio,* in the manufacturing sector, white and black wage earners worked shoulder to shoulder with the slaves.[27]

Like so much else concerning the society and economy of Cuba, the patterns of the east differed from those in the western part of the island. Landholding patterns of the free colored, therefore, followed the earlier noted pattern of a propensity of free coloreds to concentrate in the nonsugar zones of the island. And in the east, Baracoa accounted for the densest concentration of free colored property holders. Of the nearly 14,000 proprietors listed throughout the island, blacks and coloreds accounted for slightly more than 1,000—a ratio of roughly 1:13. But in the seven eastern jurisdictions for which there is available data, black and coloreds owned 622 properties out of a total of 4,642, providing a ratio of approximately 1:6—roughly the same ratio as the division of free persons of both colors across the island. It is clear that where the opportunities presented themselves, free coloreds did engage in property owning, although the value of their properties tended to be less than their white counterparts. Nevertheless, as table 10.4 indicates, data for landholding are not available for Bahia Honda, Nuevitas (a moderately large although not densely populated eastern jurisdiction), Pinar del Río, San Cristóbal, Santa María del Rosario, and Santiago de Cuba. Further data would be required to assess the size and value of these properties. Rafael María de Labra observed in 1869 that only 230 free persons of color owned enslaved people.[28] About ten years earlier, the total number of enslavers in Cuba amounted to nearly 50,000, so the logical conclusion is that few free coloreds in Cuba could afford to own enslaved people or cared to do so.[29]

Legally prohibited from the professions and the bureaucracy and unable to establish themselves among the propertied classes, free coloreds turned to those occupations where a demand existed and where opportunities depended on individual merit rather than race. Indeed, free coloreds filled a substantial economic role, although their importance tended to be overlooked by the white sector of the population. Blinded by fear and racial prejudice, white people generally condemned the free colored sector as "lazy," "uncivilized," and "un-Christian."[30] The proslavery property owner Cristóbal Madán wrote in 1864: "The people of color scarcely contribute to the effective labor of the island in proportion to their population. They do not work on the farms, but congregate in the cities and towns, where they degenerate day by day into a lazy and vicious class. Their women are habitually depraved, and it can be said of the race that it is little or more of no use either to itself, or to the country in which it exists."[31]

José Antonio Saco wanted nothing more in the late 1840s than "most ardently . . . the extinction of the black race" that he believed jeopardized his island.[32] Writing from Paris in 1860, the count of Pozos Dulces, Francisco Frías Jacott, thought that blacks were "impotent and dangerous" and a "disturbing element" in the population.[33] An anonymous pamphleteer, writing from Madrid and ironically calling himself "a conscientious Negrophile," claimed that blacks were lazy, lacked ambition, and "would be the worst workers to replace the slaves."[34] A visitor from the United States joined the chorus of negativity by declaring that "the great majority of negroes are addicted [to] vice; few evince a virtuous disposition."[35]

Not all writers were as prejudiced against blacks as these just quoted.

Table 10.4. Property holdings, 1861

Jurisdiction	Nonwhite	White	Total	Nonwhite (%)
Bahia Honda	Not listed			n.a.
Baracoa	211	386	597	35.3
Bayamo	38	272	311	12.2
Bejucal	1	195	196	0.5
Cárdenas	2	465	467	0.4
Cienfuegos	48	784	832	5.7
Colon	8	448	456	1.8
Cuba	132	650	782	16.9
Guanabacoa	—	226	226	0.0
Guanajay	9	270	279	3.2
Guantánamo	116	175	291	39.9
Güines	5	676	681	0.7
Holguín	30	450	480	6.3
Jaruco	—	30	30	0.0
Jiguaní	Not available			n.a.
La Habana	107	1,487	1,594	6.7
Manzanillo	12	132	144	8.3
Matanzas	32	323	355	9.0
Nuevitas	Not listed			n.a.
Pinar del Río	Not listed			n.a.
Puerto Príncipe	44	1,711	1,755	2.5
Remedios	6	196	202	2.9
Sagua la Grande	—	150	150	0.0
San Antonio	13	1,708	1,721	0.7
San Cristóbal	Not listed			n.a.
Sancti-Spíritus	134	1,163	1,297	10.3
Santa Clara	59	787	846	6.9
Santa María del Rosario	Not listed			n.a.
Santiago de Cuba	Not listed			n.a.
Trinidad	Not listed			n.a.
Tunas	39	242	281	13.8
Total	1,046	12,928	13,974	7.5

Source: Jacobo de la Pezuela, *Diccionario geográfico, estadistico, histórico de la isla de Cuba,* 4 vols. (Madrid, 1863–66).

Around the middle of the nineteenth century, Antonio de las Barras y Prado wrote that "the people of color serve the whites in every domestic, agricultural, and industrial job."[36] According to the monumental statistical compilation of Jacobo de la Pezuela, blacks and coloreds showed amazing versatility and industry over a wide range of occupations.[37] The variation in occupational listings precludes an easy comparison across the island of the role of the free coloreds, but a general pattern can be clearly discerned.

Black and colored men featured prominently in the lower skilled and nonskilled occupations, such as bakers, barbers, bricklayers, carpenters, daily wage earners in industry and agriculture, hatters, house painters, masons, muleteers, musicians, potters, saddle makers, sawyers, shoemakers, silversmiths, tailors, water carriers, and watchmen. Free colored women predominated in dressmaking, washing, and other domestic services. Very few free colored ranked among merchants, skilled technicians in the sugar industry and the railroads, teachers, fishermen, *mayorales* (supervisors of enslaved, which was legal), or cattle dealers. Only one black *maestro de azúcar* was found on the entire island.[38] As mentioned, the priesthood, the regular military or police, and *mayordomo* (bookkeeper on an estate) were all duties prohibited by law to the free colored population.

Education

The nineteenth century was the age of mass exploitation, not mass education. Most people, regardless of color or condition, were illiterate. A formal education was not a prerequisite to practice most skills. Until the middle of the nineteenth century, even an important position such as an estate bookkeeper required no qualification other than a white skin color. The highly valued *maestro de azúcar* relied less on knowledge of chemistry than on luck and intuition. Since blacks and coloreds occupied the lowest rung of the social ladder, it is not surprising that their lack of education tended to be one of the mutually reinforcing circumstances of their position. Yet Cuban society was changing, especially after the beginning of the second sugar revolution after the later 1830s with the introduction of the railroads and major improvements in the technical production of sugar. The demand for a basic education increased, although opportunities for schooling did not keep pace with the changing needs of society. More and more, fundamental skills like reading and writing offered opportunities for social, economic, and physical mobility.

Educational data suggest that the free colored community lagged in its education, increasing neither in proportion to the numerical growth of the sector nor commensurate with the changing needs of the wider society. As the sugar industry became more mechanized after the 1830s, the demand for literate, skilled, or semiskilled persons increased. With good land at a premium and capital scarce, displaced free blacks, whites, and mulattoes needed some minimum education in order to succeed in the increasingly

Table 10.5. Teachers, 1861

Jurisdiction	Nonwhite	White	Total
Bahia Honda	Not listed		
Baracoa	0	26	26
Bayamo	3	79	82
Bejucal	2	38	40
Cárdenas	4	155	159
Cienfuegos	2	151	153
Colon	0	162	162
Cuba	18	333	351
Guanabacoa	4	130	134
Guanajay	40	59	99
Guantánamo	5	17	22
Güines	4	164	168
Holguín	Not listed		
Jaruco	0	13	13
Jiguaní	Not listed		
La Habana	86	2,596	2,682
Manzanillo	Not listed		
Matanzas	0	57	57
Nuevitas	0	5	5
Pinar del Río	Not listed		
Puerto Príncipe	6	34	40
Remedios	0	10	10
Sagua la Grande	0	8	8
San Antonio	0	8	8
San Cristóbal	Not listed		
Sancti-Spíritus	0	17	17
Santa Clara	0	7	7
Santa María Del Rosario	0	3	3
Trinidad	0	17	17
Tunas	Not listed		
Total	174 (4%)	4,089	4,263

Source: Jacobo de la Pezuela, *Diccionario geográfico, estadistico, histórico de la isla de Cuba,* 4 vols. (Madrid, 1863–66).

competitive labor marketplace of the towns and *bateys* (the main residential and manufacturing centers of the *ingenio*).

Figures for schooling show a dramatic neglect on the part of the free colored sector.[39] In 1817, Cuba had 192 schools with 6,651 white students and 316 black and colored students, or a ratio of white to blacks and coloreds of 21:1. By 1836, the number of black and colored students had increased to 340 while the number of white students rose to 8,442. The ratio of whites to blacks and coloreds fell to 13:1. The partial returns for 1860, however, reflect a sharp decline in the growth of the black and colored school population. In the interval, the number of schools had increased to 562, with the number of white schoolchildren growing to 21, 494—more than double the number in 1836—and the number of non-white students growing to 1,147. The ratio of whites to blacks and coloreds in the schools had dropped back to 20:1—almost the same as in 1817.

Most children attended schools that were de facto, although not de jure, segregated. Of the 562 public schools and private schools in Cuba in 1861, a mere 48 were racially integrated. As indicated in table 10.5 a mere 4 percent of the 4,263 teachers were blacks and coloreds. Only two juris-dictions—Las Tunas with 3 schools and Guantánamo with 5—had a com-pletely integrated school system. The Eastern Department, with 37 of 105 schools—and 77 percent of the racially mixed schools on the island—had far more integrated schools than the sugar-dominant Western Depart-ment.

Yet it would be egregious to conclude that non-whites eschewed formal education. Rather, it is obvious that slavery and the plantation system in Cuba militated against the education of black and colored persons. Eight of the principal sugar-producing jurisdictions—Bejucal, Cárdenas, Colon, Güines, Remedios, Sagua la Grande, Santa Clara, and Trinidad—con-tained a combined total of 642 of the 1,365 working sugar estates on the island in 1861 but not one of the 3,607 students in the 106 schools was black or colored. Cienfuegos, Santiago de Cuba, Guanajay, Matanzas, and Puerto Príncipe together had 455 *ingenios* and 137 schools (of which 31 were racially integrated) yet a mere 458 of the 5,814 students were blacks and coloreds. The superficially cosmopolitan city of Havana had no sugar estates within its metropolitan boundaries but was the home of many of the leading sugar producers in Cuba. Only 357 black and colored students were among Havana's 7,829 schoolchildren in 1861.[40] In Cuba, it seemed that sugar production and the plantation did not coincide with schools and education.

In the disrupted social and economic conditions of the postwar period in 1899, it is not surprising that the unemployed would constitute a sub-stantial proportion of the population. As indicated in table 10.6, the cen-sus of 1899 shows that 68 percent of local whites and 57 percent of blacks and coloreds were unemployed. Since a large proportion of these unem-ployed would be women and children, the situation of blacks and coloreds was not as dire as it first appears. In postslavery Cuban society, non-

Table 10.6. Occupational profile in 1899

	Total	Agriculture, fishing, and mining	Commerce and transport	Manufacturing and mechanics	Domestic service	Unemployed
Cuba	1,572,797	299,197	79,427	93,034	141,936	950,467
Nonwhites	520,400	100,967	7,625	38,647	71,478	301,129
Whites	910,299	166,960	29,434	39,684	47,221	621,050

Source: Departamento de la Guerra, *Informe sobre el censo de Cuba, 1899*. Tradacido del inglés por F. L. Joannini (Washington, D.C.: Government Printing Office, 1900).

Europeans were performing creditably against the mounting resistance of whites and an atmosphere that became increasingly more racially charged. With about 32 percent of the total population, blacks and Coloreds represented 33.7 percent of those engaged in agriculture, fishing, and mining; 50.3 percent of those in domestic service; 41.5 percent of those in manufacturing and the mechanical trades; and 31 percent of those unemployed. They were conspicuously underrepresented in two categories. blacks and coloreds were only 9.6 percent of those employed in commerce and transport services and 6.3 percent of professionals.

The Social Condition of Free Coloreds

After the outbreak of the Haitian revolution in 1791, things would never be the same for slave systems in the Americas. Whites everywhere began to demonstrate a hostile "terrified consciousness" that manifested itself in increasingly stringent police-control measures against free coloreds as well as enslaved persons. In Cuba, one of the first casualties of the changing attitudes to non-Europeans was the Afro-Cuban *cabildo,* an important socioreligious organization that served both free and enslaved blacks. Founded in frontier Iberia, the *cabildo* underwent some transformation in Cuba. Based on Africanized Catholicism, the associations served the salutary purpose of bringing urbanized blacks and coloreds together for recreation, mutual assistance, sick and poor relief, and even the collective purchase and manumission of the enslaved. These organizations regulated the free black community to a certain extent and afforded a measure of communication between the white elite and the enslaved.[41] As early as 1792, a series of orders forced the *cabildos* to meet outside the walls of the city of Havana and restricted their meetings to Sundays and watch nights. At the same time, the members suddenly needed special permission to hold meetings. The increased control of the *cabildo* represented only one indication of the increasing legal and extralegal discrimination against Cuba's black and colored communities.

In 1837, a royal decree—published 12 years later in Havana—prohibited the landing on the island of any person of color, enslaved or free.[42] Arriving black and colored seamen were immediately incarcerated in Cuban ports for the duration of the visit of their ships. The *Bando de gobernación y policía* of Captain-General Gerónimo Valdés, first issued in 1842, not only reactivated some of the old discriminatory laws but added some new ones. Occupations such as farm overseers and bookkeepers were legally designated to be exclusively for white persons. Blacks and coloreds had to be licensed to enter farms to seek work. Article 143 declared that "no colored person may carry arms permitted to white persons."[43] Federico de Roncali, the count of Alcoy, added further restrictions on free persons of color. They could not travel after 11 o'clock at night except in emergencies, when they could travel with a lit lantern and after reporting to the *sereno*, or watchman. Free persons of color could also not drive cattle in the streets unless accompanied by a white person, and attempts were made to restrict intercourse between free coloreds and enslaved. As Article 24 of the *Reglamento de esclavos* put it: "The greatest care should be taken to eliminate excess drink or intercourse with free colored Persons."

On September 30, 1844, in a confidential dispatch to the Colonial Department of the Royal Council, Captain-General Leopoldo O'Donnell confessed that the racial situation was critical on the island.[44] The white sector was becoming alarmed at the numerical majority of blacks and coloreds. Plans to augment the white population through immigration proliferated, as did suggestions to segregate and expatriate the free coloreds. In an address to the Cuban Bureau for the Encouragement of white Immigration, Attorney General Vicente Vásquez Queipo attacked mixed marriages, probably hoping to stem the growth of the free mixed population: "We do not think that the Real Junta has forgotten, concerning this point, the severe lesson of the neighboring island of Santo Domingo, whose loss depended to a great deal on the close intimacy in which white inhabitants of the French part lived with their slaves, and the numerous colored population resulting from this foreboding association."[45] José Antonio Saco joined the ranks of racists popularizing the cry "Remember Haiti" in order to boost his scheme for ending the trade in African captives, decreasing the black population, and restoring the "moral and numerical preponderance" of the white sector.[46]

The climate of suspicion and fear reached a climax in the so-called La Escalera affair of 1844. On the basis of rumors of a massive slave revolt in Matanzas in which it was alleged that the free colored were fomenting rebellion, the white planters called for blood. Captain-General Leopoldo O'Donnell, the corrupt friend of planters and slavocrats, responded with delight. Despite the fact that both whites and free coloreds were associated with every organized slave revolt, nothing was said of white complicity on this occasion. O'Donnell exacted harsh penalties from the entire free colored community across the island, notwithstanding the localized nature of the presumed conspiracy. In a savage campaign in which a number of persons lost their lives, the army indiscriminately arrested all leaders of the free colored community, some of whom they brought back from abroad. Twenty-three mulattoes—including the poet Gabriel de la Concepción Valdés, otherwise known as Plácido; the doctor and linguist Andrés José Dodge; and the remarkable poet Juan Francisco Manzano—as well as 11 free blacks faced execution or exile, as did thousands of other blacks and coloreds.[47] The event constituted a sort of catharsis for the white population of Cuba. Ten years later, Captain-General José de la Concha, decrying the travesty of justice, remarked: "The findings of the military commission produced the execution, confiscation of property, and expulsion from the island of a great many persons of color, but it did not find arms, munitions, documents, or any other incriminating object which proved that there was such a conspiracy, much less on such a vast scale."[48]

The catharsis accomplished, a sort of normalcy returned in which the whites could again concentrate on sugar production relieved from the major preoccupation of an enslaved and free colored revolt. The superordinacy of the whites had been established. Antonio Barras y Prado remembered: "The free Negroes enjoy the same liberty as the rest of the other citizens, they may own property and even slaves, and many live from this profit; but always, the Negro, whether slave or free, is obliged to respect the white, for the law gives to the latter a superiority which has as its object, the preservation of moral dominance in order to subject the black race."[49] By the late 1850s, the black militias were reestablished and the mutual aid societies of the free coloreds began to flourish.[50] Indeed, the mutual aid societies of the blacks and coloreds often accepted white participation over the objection of the authorities.

Conclusion

Whites in general might have opposed black presence in Cuban society, but free coloreds and the enslaved were indispensable to the viability of Cuba in the nineteenth century. White plantation owners wanted labor, irrespective of provenience or color, provided that it was cheap. Lower-class whites might have feared the wage competition from the free coloreds and abhorred the stigma attached to much manual labor, especially on the sugar estates. But by the late 1860s, the labor force had become so racially integrated that it was fallacious to argue that only black people could do manual and menial work. With the transatlantic trade in African captives to Cuba effectively curtailed, demand for labor outstripped supply, and wage labor was inexorably replacing the regime of enslaved labor. Moreover, whites realized that blacks were creating important opportunities for education and labor organization through their associations, and some wanted to be a part of it. Black associations were both nationalist and integrationist, as Joan Casanovas points out in her study of the Cuban working class in the later part of the nineteenth century.[51]

The free colored people preferred to stick to the towns where they could enjoy more employment options. They were especially prominent in those urban services that were neglected or undersupplied by white workers—such as cab driving, cooking, washing, street vending, music making, and leather crafts.

The Ten Years War between 1868 and 1878 was a difficult time for all Cubans. Many writers, encouraged by the Spanish government propaganda, saw the war as essentially a "race war" rather than a nationalist campaign against Spanish colonial rule. While it is true that, although some were not native Cubans, the most outstanding military leaders of the insurrection came from the free colored community—men like Antonio Maceo, Máximo Gómez, and Modesto Díaz—there is little support for José de la Concha's assertion that the "vast majority of the rebels are Negroes, mulattoes, Chinese and deserters from our [that is, the Spanish] army."[52]

The last decades of the nineteenth century saw a proliferation of mutual aid associations among the free colored community. In the urban areas, some of these associations developed into fully fledged labor unions, but labor organization in the countryside lagged owing to the aftermath of the slave system and the prevalence of banditry.[53] In both urban and rural areas, colored people formed alliances with whites to improve their economic condition as well as foment a political consciousness that constituted a sort of protonationalism.[54] One feature of these new associations was the prominent role played by blacks and coloreds. As Casanovas notes:

A remarkable feature of Afro-Cuban societies, compared to the white led associations, is the prominent role played by women. For instance, at the beginning of 1879 in Cienfuegos, black women formed the *Sociedad de Socorros Mútuos La Caridad del Cobre;* in Trinidad, Santa Clara Province, they founded the *Sociedad Las Hijas del Progreso. . . .* By contrast, there is no record that working-class white women ever founded an association or occupied official positions in mutual aid or cultural associations. A major reason for this difference is that, with the gradual elimination of slavery, many freedwomen migrated to the cities, while many freedmen continued to work in the fields. Furthermore, black and mulatto women had a stronger tradition of participation in Cuban public life than their white counterparts, and the African *cabildos* institutionalized the participation of women, who sometimes composed the majority of members. . . . [In] nineteenth century Cuba, it was considered improper for white women to walk alone in public spaces.[55]

Attempts at constructing a racially integrated society floundered against the strong political passions generated by the continuing Cuban War of Independence in the 1890s. As Aline Helg demonstrates, race, class, and nationalism became inextricably intertwined.[56] Spain tried to paint the Cuban insurgency as a race war, continuing the old propaganda from the 1860s that, if lost by Spain, the island would inevitably become another Haiti. Nevertheless, blacks fought on both sides of the war. More colored people supported a free Cuba than the continuation of Spanish rule. Many were indifferent to the political outcome, and a number chose to leave Cuba permanently. Some black Cubans—including a number of freed blacks—also returned to Africa.[57]

Notes

1. For Spanish American colonial experience in general, see Charles Gibson, *Spain in America* (New York: Harper, 1966); Lewis Hanke. *The Spanish Struggle for Justice in the Conquest of America* (Philadelphia: American Historical Association, 1949); Eric Wolfe, *Sons of the Shaking Earth* (Chicago: University of Chicago Press, 1966); J. H. Parry, *The Spanish Theory of Empire in the Sixteenth*

Century (Cambridge: Cambridge University Press, 1940); John L. Phelan, *The Millennial Kingdom of the Kingdom of the Franciscans in the New World: A Study of the Writings of Géronimo de Mendieta* (Berkeley: University of California Press, 1956); David Brading, *The First America. The Spanish Monarchy, Creole Patriots and the Liberal State, 1492–1867* (Cambridge: Cambridge University Press, 1991); and Colin M. MacLachlan, *Spain's Empire in the New World: The Role of Ideas in Institutional and Social Change* (Berkeley: University of California Press, 1988).

2. For an acute awareness of Spanish laws and the ability of black and coloreds to exploit them, see Olga Portuondo Zúñiga, *La virgen de la caridad del Cobre: Símbolo de Cubanía* (Santiago de Cuba: Editorial Oriente, 1995); and Maria Elena Díaz, *The Virgin, the King and the Royal Slaves of El Cobre: Negotiating Freedom in Colonial Cuba, 1670–1780* (Stanford, Calif.: Stanford University Press, 2000).

3. Rafael María de Labra y Cadrana, *La abolición de la esclavitud en las Antilles Españolas* (Madrid, 1869), 25–63. Labra was born in Havana in 1841, where his father was serving with the Spanish regiment from Galicia, and returned to Spain when he was ten years old. He was a prolific writer and died in 1918. His ardently pro-Spanish views gained wide currency both in Spain and in Cuba.

4. Frank Tannenbaum, *Slave and Citizen* (New York: Random House, 1946); Gilberto Freyre, *The Mansions and the Shanties* (New York: Random House, 1946); Herbert Klein, *Slavery in the Americas: A Comparative Study of Virginia and Cuba* (Chicago: University of Chicago Press, 1967); H. H. Johnson, *Views and Reviews from the Outlook of an Anthropologist* (London: Williams and Norgate, 1912).

5. See Franklin W. Knight, *Slave Society in Cuba during the Nineteenth Century* (Madison: University of Wisconsin Press, 1970); Manuel Moreno Fraginals, *El ingenio: Complejo socio-económico del azúcar en Cuba* (1964; reprint, Havana: Ciencias Sociales, 1978); and Philip D. Curtin, *The Rise and Fall of the Plantation Complex: Essays in Atlantic History* (New York: Cambridge University Press, 1990). The phrase "South Atlantic System" belongs to Philip Curtin and first occurs in his book, *Two Jamaicans: The Role of Ideas in a Tropical Colony, 1830–1865* (Cambridge: Harvard University Press, 1955), 4–6.

6. Philip D. Curtin, *The Atlantic Slave Trade: A Census* (Madison: University of Wisconsin Press, 1969); Paul Lovejoy, "The Volume of the Atlantic Slave Trade: A Synthesis," *Journal of African History* 23, no. 4 (1982): 473–501; Herbert Klein, *African Slavery in Latin America and the Caribbean* (New York: Oxford University Press, 1986); David Eltis, *The Rise of African Slavery in the Americas* (Cambridge: Cambridge University Press, 2000); Hugh Thomas, *The Slave Trade: The Story of the Atlantic Slave Trade, 1440–1870* (New York: Touchstone Books, 1997); Robin Blackburn, *The Overthrow of Colonial Slavery, 1776–1848* (London: Verso, 1988).

7. For the political and social changes, see Rebecca J. Scott, *Slave Emancipation*

in Cuba: The Transition to Free Labor, 1860–1899 (Princeton, N.J.: Princeton University Press, 1985); Rosalie Schwartz, *Lawless Liberators: Political Banditry and Cuban Independence* (Durham, N.C.: Duke University Press, 1989); Christopher Schmidt-Novara, *Empire and Anti-Slavery: Spain, Cuba and Puerto Rico, 1833–1874* (Pittsburgh: University of Pittsburgh Press, 1999); Joan Casanovas, *Bread or Bullets! Urban Labor and Spanish Colonialism in Cuba, 1850–1898* (Pittsburgh: University of Pittsburgh Press, 1998); and Ada Ferrer, *Insurgent Cuba: Race, Nation, and Revolution, 1868–1898* (Chapel Hill: University of North Carolina Press, 1999).

8. The term "Creole" described all persons born in the Americas, regardless of ancestry. It has had a varied application, however, and developed local peculiarities from place to place. There has been no systematic study of the way the expression has been used across the Americas, but one extremely interesting case is Edmund T. Morgan, *Disparate Diasporas: Identity and Politics in an African-Nicaraguan Community* (Austin: University of Texas Press, 1998).

9. Charles Boxer, *Race Relations in the Portuguese Colonial Empire, 1415–1825* (Oxford: Clarendon Press, 1963), 58.

10. Verena Martinez Alier, *Marriage, Class and Colour in Cuba in the Nineteenth Century: A Study of Racial Attitudes and Sexual Values in a Slave Society,* 2nd ed. (Ann Arbor: University of Michigan Press, 1989); Robert Paquette, *Sugar Is Made with Blood* (Middletown, Conn.: Wesleyan University Press, 1988); Aline Helg, *Our Rightful Share: The Afro-Cuban Struggle for Equality, 1886–1912* (Chapel Hill: University of North Carolina Press, 1995); Ferrer, *Insurgent Cuba;* Alejandro de la Fuente, *"With All and For All": Race, Inequality, and Politics in Cuba, 1898–1995* (Chapel Hill: University of North Carolina Press, 2001); Vera Kutzinski, *Sugar's Secrets: Race and the Erotics of Cuban Nationalism* (Charlottesville: University Press of Virginia, 1993).

11. See Helg, *Our Rightful Share,* esp. 15–42.

12. Levi Marrero, *Cuba: Economia y sociedad,* 14 vols. (Madrid: Playor, 1974–89), 2: 329–70.

13. Jacobo de la Pezuela, *Diccionario geográfico, estadistico, histórico de la isla de Cuba,* 4 vols. (Madrid, 1863–66), 1: 153.

14. Cristóbal Madán, *El trabajo libre y el libre cambio en Cuba* (Paris, 1864).

15. Knight, *Slave Society in Cuba,* 130–33; Moreno Fraginals, *El ingenio.*

16. Demoticus Philalethes [pseud.], *Yankee Travels Through the Island of Cuba* (New York, 1856), 393.

17. Arthur F. Corwin, *Spain and the Abolition of Slavery in Cuba, 1817–1886* (Austin: University of Texas Press, 1967), 239–54.

18. *Resumen del censo de la poblacion de la isla de Cuba . . . 1841* (Havana: Imprenta del Gobierno, 1842), 19.

19. Kenneth Kiple argues persuasively that the 1841 Cuban census was probably inaccurate: "For a variety of reasons, then, the veracity of the 1841 count should be highly suspect while, by contrast, the 1846 enumeration 'squares' re-

markably well with contemporary estimates of natality, mortality, and migration."
See Kenneth F. Kiple, *Blacks in Colonial Cuba, 1774–1899* (Gainesville: University Press of Florida, 1976), 58.

20. José García de Arboleya, *Manual de la isla de Cuba* (Havana: Imprenta del Tiempo, 1859), 118.

21. Figures derived from Pezuela, *Diccionario,* 1: 153.

22. Ramiro Guerra y Sánchez, *Guerra de los Diez Años, 1868–1878* (Havana: Cultural, S.A., 1950), 4–15.

23. *Cuba desde 1850 á 1873: Colección de informes memorias, etc. . . . que ha reunido Don Carlos de Sedano y Cruzat* (Madrid: Imprenta Nacional, 1973), 152–53.

24. Miguel Blanco Herrero, *La política de España en Ultramar* (Madrid, 1886), 431.

25. See, for example, José M. Zamora y Coronado, comp., *Biblioteca de legislación ultramarina,* 7 vols. (Madrid, 1844–49), especially 4: 461–68; and *Boletín official de la capitanía general de la isla de Cuba* (Havana: Imprenta de la capitanía general, 1869–98).

26. *Bando de gobernación y policía de la isla de Cuba expedido por el Excmo Sr. D. Gerónimo Valdés, presidente, governador, y capitán general* (Havana, 1842), article 77.

27. Moreno Fraginals, *El ingenio,* 141. See also Knight, *Slave Society in Cuba,* 25–46.

28. Labra y Cadrana, *La abolición,* 63.

29. *Archico Histórico Nacional* (Madrid) Sección de Ultramar, Subsección de Esclavitud, leg. 3553 (hereafter *AHN*); see also Knight, *Slave Society in Cuba,* 135.

30. See, for example, Francisco de Armas y Céspedes, *Regimen político de las Antillas Españolas,* 2nd ed. (Palma, 1883), 89; Demoticus Philalethes [pseud.], *Thoughts upon the incorporation of Cuba into the American Confederation . . .* (Havana, 1849), 8.

31. Cristóbal Madán, *El trabajo libre y el libre cambio en Cuba* (Paris, 1864), 3.

32. José Antonio Saco, *Replica a la contestación . . .* (Madrid, 1847), 18.

33. Francisco Frías y Jacott (count of Pozos Dulces), *La isla de Cuba: Colección de escritos sobre la agricultura, industria, ciencias y otros ramos de interés* (Paris, 1860), 23, 371.

34. *Cuba Y Puerto Rico medios de conservar estas dos Antillas en su estado de esplendor, a "short treatise" by "a conscientious Negrophile"* (Madrid, 1866), 92–93. This "short treatise" runs for 157 pages.

35. Philalethes, *Yankee Travels,* 33.

36. Antonio Barras y Prado, *Memorias: La Habana a mediados del siglo XIX* (Madrid: Ciudad Lineal, 1925), 107. The memoir was written sometime between 1850 and 1862, when the author left Havana for the last time.

37. Pezuela, *Diccionario,* passim.

38. The *maestro de azúcar*, chief of the boiler house, had principal responsibility for the quality of the sugar produced by his control of the entire operations, indicating when changes were to be made in the various stages of production. The *maestro de azúcar* relied more on experience, intuition, and guesswork than knowledge of sugar chemistry. This skill was passed from father to son. In the seventeenth century, a white person held the position in Brazil. During the eighteenth century, the job was done by a slave throughout most of the British West Indies. It reverted to whites in Cuba during the nineteenth century.

39. The school figures are taken from Rafael Soto Paz, *La falsa cubanidad de saco, luz y del monte* (Havana: Editorial "Alfa," 1941), 8.

40. The figures on schools and students are compiled from Pezuela, *Diccionario*, 1: 38–39; Carlos Rebel, *Estados relativos a la producción azucarera de la isla de Cuba* (Havana, 1860); Raul Cepero Bonilla, *Obras Históricas* (Havana: Instituto de Historia, 1963), 31; Francisco Pérez de la Riva, *El café historia de su cultivo y explotación en Cuba* (Havana: Montero, 1944), 68–75; H. E. Friedlaender, *Historia económica de Cuba* (Havana: Montero, 1944), 544–48; José García de Arboleya, *Manual de la isla de Cuba* (Havana, 1859), 238.

41. Fernando Ortiz, "Los cabildos afro-Cubanos," *Revista Bimestre Cubana* 16, no. 1 (1921): 5–39.

42. *Instrucción reglamentaria . . . de la formalidad para llegada, circulación y salida de gentes en esta isla* (Havana, 1849).

43. *Bando de gobernación*, articles 23, 143.

44. *AHN Ultramar*, Esclavitud 3552, legajo 1, indice 3, no. 3.

45. Vicente Vásquez Queipo, *Informe fiscal sobre fomento de la población blanca en la isla de Cuba . . .* (Madrid, 1845), 33.

46. Fernando Ortiz, *José Antonio Saco y sus ideas cubanas* (Havana: El Universo, 1929), 73–74.

47. For the official records, see *AHN*, Estado, Esclavitud. Legajo 8057, esp. no 1. For a review of the literature see, Paquette, *Sugar Is Made with Blood.*

48. José Gutierrez de la Concha y de Irigoyen, *Memoria sobre la Guerra de la isla de Cuba y su estado político y económico desde 1871 hasta 1874* (Madrid: Labajas, 1875), 15.

49. Barras y Prado, *Memorias,* 111–12.

50. Joan Casanovas, *Urban Labor and Spanish Colonialism in Cuba, 1850–1898* (Pittsburgh: University of Pittsburgh Press, 1998), 132–34.

51. Casanovas, *Urban Labor.*

52. José Gutierrez de la Concha y de Irigoyen, *Memoria sobre la Guerra,* 100.

53. Schwartz, *Lawless Liberators,* 120–21.

54. Schmidt-Novara, *Empire and Antislavery,* 101.

55. Casanovas, *Urban Labor,* 134.

56. Helg, *Our Rightful Share.*

57. Rodolfo Saracino, *Los que volvieron a Africa* (Havana: Editorial Ciencias Sociales, 1988).

11

"¿Quién Trabajará?"

Domestics, Urban Enslaved Workers, and the Abolition of Slavery in Puerto Rico

Félix V. Matos Rodríguez

This essay analyzes the role that domestic work and urban enslavement played in the process of the abolition of slavery in Puerto Rico. Puerto Rico's historiography has shown that economic, demographic, and social changes among enslaved rural workers played a significant role in the abolition of African enslavement. In this essay, on the other hand, I will discuss the importance that colonial authorities and the local urban elites gave to their perceived domestic labor shortage "problem" in San Juan and other cities. The evidence from continuous specific work regulations, the proabolition literature and propaganda, the struggles and frictions with colonial authorities, and the connections with the development of beneficence institutions indicate that the concern regarding domestic work—although virtually forgotten in Puerto Rican historiography—was far from marginal in the island's economic, political, and social processes during the second half of the nineteenth century.

Puerto Rico's historians have written extensively on the events leading to the abolition of slavery in 1873.[1] Recently, there has been growing interest in exploring not only the transition from enslaved labor into so-called free labor but also the processes through which different agents defined complementary and contradictory notions of the concept of "freedom."[2] The exploration of these themes is not an isolated phenomenon in Puerto Rico's historiography but part of a larger dialogue regarding the forces that led to the eradication of the system of African enslavement in the Americas and the behavior and expectations of the different groups involved in the process, including enslavers, enslaved, merchants, and politicians.[3]

My interest in domestic work comes from the need to add new elements to the debates about enslavement and its eventual abolition in Puerto Rico. Furthermore, domestic work has begun to be studied more carefully given the developments in the fields of women's and gender studies.[4] Historically, domestic work in Latin America has been done by women, and nineteenth-century Puerto Rico was no exception to this rule. Recent research has stressed the importance of domestic work to the general economy, particularly in relation to the development of capitalism and urbanization in different regions.[5] In urban enclaves, domestic services—paid or not—such as washing, cooking, ironing, cleaning, supervising children, and caring for ill people and the elderly have been key to the growth and development of other sectors of the economy. Although the chores we traditionally associate with domestic work apparently have not changed much over the years—with the exception, perhaps, of technological innovations that have supposedly simplified the work—it is important to recognize that, as with many other sectors of the economy, domestic work has a history. The development and historical evolution of domestic work must be problematised in order to appreciate its contribution to the socioeconomic transformations in Caribbean and Latin American history. This essay is a contribution to reevaluating the importance of domestic work in Puerto Rico's history.

There was a direct connection between domestic work and urban enslavement in nineteenth-century Puerto Rico. If it is true that not all enslaved urban women were domestics, it is also true that a majority of enslaved urban women performed domestic chores, such as being servants, cooks, laundresses, nannies, and maids.[6] Given the comparative lack of interest in domestic work in Puerto Rican and wider Caribbean historiography, it should not be surprising that urban slavery is also understudied in the region.[7] In most Caribbean slavery studies, the emphasis has been on plantation work and sugar processing. In this essay, I will regard domestic work and urban slavery as virtually synonymous, even when aware that not all urban enslaved laborers worked as domestics and that in rural plantations the distinctions between enslaved domestic and field hands were often murky.

The selection of San Juan as the focus for this essay is based on several important criteria. During the first two-thirds of the nineteenth century, San Juan was the island's most important political, intellectual, and economic urban center.[8] During the first half of the nineteenth century, the importation of enslaved persons increased in San Juan and throughout Puerto Rico. Halfway through the century, the processes that led to the abolition of slavery started. At the time of abolition, San Juan was the city with the highest number of enslaved domestics.[9] This is particularly significant considering that other cities such as Mayaguez and Ponce had far higher total numbers of enslaved people, both rural and urban. San Juan is, therefore, an appropriate place to analyze the role played by enslaved domestics and urban workers in the abolition process during the second half of the nineteenth century in Puerto Rico.

Domestic Work in the Capital

We can obtain a description of the characteristics of the women who performed domestic chores in mid-nineteenth-century San Juan through the use of census data and notarial records. Unfortunately, information regarding the lives of domestics is not abundant.[10] Census data, however, allow us to determine the geographic, racial, and marital status distribution of domestics. The only surviving midcentury manuscript census in San Juan is the one taken in 1846.[11] In that census, there is information about three of the four barrios (quarters) that composed the walled city: Santa Bárbara, Santo Domingo, and San Francisco. There is also a slave registry for 1872, which has been studied by Negrón Portillo and Mayo Santana.[12] This registry, however, does not have information regarding free women of color.

Who were San Juan's mid-nineteenth-century domestics, and what kinds of jobs did they perform? Table 11.1 shows the number of domestics in the three San Juan quarters included in the 1846 census data.[13] Almost all the individuals listed as domestics in the 1846 census were women. Servants or maids were the most common type of domestics, followed by laundresses. The number of domestics, 1,101, is significant, particularly if we consider that San Juan's total population at that time was around 13,000 inhabitants.[14] Domestics, then, comprised at a minimum 8 percent of San Juan's population in 1846. These numbers, however, must be taken with caution because they could be affected by several factors. One can assume, for example, that many men and women classified as enslaved in the census perhaps performed domestic chores in their owners' homes, even if they were not classified with any occupation. Thus the number of domestics in 1846 was probably higher than the census figures indicate.

Tables 11.1 and 11.2 show the racial composition and the *condición* (free or enslaved status), respectively, of San Juan's domestics. There was a marked difference among domestics in the city: the majority of the laundresses were free women (73 percent), while the majority of the servants

Table 11.1. Domestic workers by race in San Juan, 1846 (Santa Bárbara, Santo Domingo, and San Francisco Barrios)

	White	Black	Parda	Mulatto	Total
Laundresses	19	158	81	101	359
Cooks	2	78	12	8	100
Servants	10	460	115	57	642
Total	31	696	208	166	1,101

Source: AGPR, Censos San Juan, Barrios Santa Bárbara, Santo Domingo y San Francisco, 1846.

or maids (90 percent) and the cooks (77 percent) were enslaved women. In 1846, enslaved people comprised about 20 percent of San Juan's total population.[15] Given these data, it should not be unexpected to find that a high percentage of the cooks (78 percent) and the maids (72 percent) in San Juan were black. Among domestics, only laundresses had a less polarized racial breakdown: 49 percent of them were black, 23 percent were *pardas*, and 28 percent were mulattoes.[16] Irrespective of the racial differences found among the laundresses and other domestics, it is clear that a majority of San Juan's domestics were black or colored (97 percent) and that a high percentage of them were enslaved people (68 percent).

The 1846 census also allows us to explore other characteristics of San Juan's domestics. The census data show that most domestics were between 10 and 44 years of age.[17] Servants or maids tended to be younger than cooks and laundresses. Table 11.3 shows the marital status of San Juan's domestics. The great majority of the city's domestics were single (93 percent). Almost all the servants were single (99 percent). These servants usually lived in the residence of their owner or employer. Most of the cooks were also single (91 percent). Finally, among the laundresses, four

Table 11.2. Domestic workers by "status" in San Juan, 1846 (Santa Bárbara, Santo Domingo, and San Francisco Barrios)

	Free	Enslaved	Total
Laundresses	265	94	359
Cooks	23	77	100
Servants	67	575	642
Total	355	746	1,101

Source: AGPR, Censos San Juan, Barrios Santa Bárbara, Santo Domingo y San Francisco, 1846.

Table 11.3. Domestic workers by marital status in San Juan, 1846 (Santa Bárbara, Santo Domingo, and San Francisco Barrios)

	Married	Single	Widows	Total
Laundresses	30	291	39	360
Cooks	5	94	4	103
Servants	4	657	1	662
Ironer	—	1	—	1
Total	39	1,043	44	1,126

Source: AGPR, Censos San Juan, Barrios Santa Bárbara, Santo Domingo y San Francisco, 1846.

out five were single. In the case of laundresses, even though most were single, there was a high percentage of heads of households.[18] Thirty-eight percent of the laundresses and 13 percent of the cooks were heads of households. These figures contrast with those of the servants, given that not one servant was a head of a household in 1846. The percentage of heads of households among laundresses points to a high number of single mothers among them.

The 1872 data from San Juan's slave registry confirm some of the trends identified in the 1846 data, even when the 1872 data do not include free domestics. In 1872, a majority of the enslaved domestics in San Juan were women between 10 and 40 years of age.[19] Although by 1872 the total number of enslaved people in the city had decreased compared to the midcentury numbers, it seems that the characteristics of enslaved domestics had not changed much.

The work done by domestics was quite arduous. Laundry work, for example, required much physical strength. Laundresses could be employees or enslaved people working full-time in a single residence, military barracks, or monastery, or they could sell their services to multiple clients. In the latter case, laundresses probably collected clothes from their clients and took them to wash in their own homes or to one of the city's public water fountains. Among these itinerant laundresses one could find enslaved people who, although mostly responsible for washing and folding their owners' family clothes, also rented their services—or were rented out by their owners—to other families.[20] This system of rental was fairly frequent in the city, to the extent that it drew heavy criticism, censure, and requests for its eradication from the both the *cabildo* (city council) and the central government.[21]

Washing clothes was not a simple task in a city lacking easy access to fresh water. In other Puerto Rican towns or cities, women took their wash to the nearest river, usually located at the outskirts of the town or city. San Juan had no such nearby rivers. San Juan's residents depended on three water fountains and several wells to supply them with water. The fountain with the highest volume and best quality of water was located in the Condado area—near the San Antonio bridge—a considerable walk from the city's walls.[22] Another well was located in the Puntilla area, but the water quality there was poor, and the city's residents stopped using it during the mid-nineteenth century. The Miraflores islet, located even farther away than the Condado fountain, had water of excellent quality. The city also had three intramural wells located in the plazas facing the Carmelite and Franciscan convents and the San Justo gate. These wells were opened at the onset of the nineteenth century, but their water supply and volume were unreliable. The intramural wells were closed in the 1860s after repeated complaints from religious leaders regarding the noise, public scandals, and general unruly behavior of the people who used the wells.[23]

Many laundresses took their wash to the Condado fountain or the wells located within the city walls. Other laundresses took water to their homes or used water collected in cisterns. Some had access to the cisterns at the military garrisons or the city's hospital. In all cases, the laundresses' work required carrying a heavy load of clothes or water for a considerable distance. Laundry work ended with the task of drying the washed clothes so they could be ironed and returned to their owners. In many cases, the laundresses' children helped with collecting the soiled clothes and with the drying and ironing processes. The Condado fountain and the other intramural wells were public gathering places for the laundresses and their children.

Very little is known about the work performed by other domestics. Most cooks and servants in San Juan were enslaved and lived in their enslavers' residence. These domestics were in proximity to their enslavers' families, a situation that invited greater intimacy and, at the same time, greater friction with the family. The intimacy that allowed some of the enslaved to receive their manumission given "good and admirable services" made other enslaved domestics the victims of suspicious accusations by their enslavers, including, for example, poisoning of food.[24] Although domestic chores required many hours of work, San Juan's urban setting and the errands owners often required of their domestics allowed these enslaved people to spend a considerable amount of time on their own and outside their enslavers' residences. Some enslaved domestics even rented their services to others outside their owners' families.

Enslavement remained an active practice in San Juan and the rest of the island until abolition. During the decade prior to abolition, enslaved people were still being bought and sold in San Juan.[25] Many of these were later sold to the haciendas in San Juan's periphery, as the demand for agricultural workers remained high and hacienda owners paid higher prices to obtain them. Although the sale of enslaved people continued in Puerto Rico, statistics show that the enslaved population decreased in the decade prior to abolition. In San Juan's case, the number of enslaved people decreased from 1,334 in 1869 to 890 in 1872.[26] The decreasing number of enslaved people in San Juan was certainly a factor affecting the demand for domestic work in the city.

Domestic Work and Urban Slavery in the Abolitionist Debate

The debates regarding the potential abolition of slavery in Puerto Rico, debates that gathered momentum and intensity in the second half of the nineteenth century, made few references to the situation of enslaved domestics. From the perspective of hacendados, merchants, politicians, and intellectuals, the key concerns of the abolition debate were: Would the sugar industry survive? Would there be a cheap and abundant workforce? Would the repercussions of abolition be in the social and political realms? Would masters get compensated for their slaves? What would the diplomatic and international fallout be? How would such a process be handled? The enslaved, for their part, also articulated their own visions of what a postslavery Puerto Rico would be like.

Although the future of enslaved domestics and urban workers was not a central theme in the abolitionist debates, it is important to acknowledge that enslaved domestics did figure in the rhetorical strategies of the warring sides of the debate. In the first place, proabolition groups used the figures of the total number of domestic slaves to argue that Puerto Rico's agriculture would not be affected by the elimination of slavery. *El Abolicionista*, the propaganda newspaper of the proabolition forces, gave the following rationale in Madrid's press: "Of the 30,000 slaves that exist in the tiny Antille, 25,000 are dedicated to domestic service and their manumission will not affect agricultural production at all. Agriculture right now is done with free laborers, except for the 8,000 slaves that complete the total number of slaves for the entire Puerto Rico."[27]

The manipulation of numbers (not always exact or reliable) and the arbitrary designation of enslaved people as either agricultural or domestic were some of the ways in which the supporters of abolition presented their argument to minimize fears of a financial and agricultural disaster in Puerto Rico resulting from abolition. Other proabolitionist leaders used the numbers of domestics and the nature of domestic work not to mitigate fears of a potential economic crisis following abolition but to mitigate fears of a social revolt. Many whites opposed abolition because of social order concerns, not because of financial considerations. The racial hierarchy that slavery provided Puerto Rico could be altered or inverted with the end of slavery, something that worried members of the white elite. Others feared the potentially damaging effects on society of the supposed intellectual and moral inferiority of the enslaved. To appease these fears, proabolitionists used enslaved domestics as an example of the docility and obedience that the ruling elite wanted to see perpetuated in a postabolition Puerto Rico. To this end, the famous Puerto Rican abolitionists Segundo Ruiz Belvis, José Julián Acosta, and Francisco Mariano Quiñones wrote in 1867: "Of the 41,000 total slaves, the 28,000 employed in mechanical tasks and in domestic service have always seen public authority over the master's authority, respecting both. If this situation keeps the slaves today away from any idea of disturbance, with more reason will it keep it away the day they obtain their freedom."[28]

With explanations such as this, abolitionist leaders tried to dissipate fears of a freed peoples' revolt or of any other kind of racial protest. The abolitionists manipulated the images associated with enslaved domestics—their supposed docility and loyalty toward their enslavers—to minimize the threats suggested by the antiabolitionist forces.

One last argument used by the promoters of abolition was to accentuate the lack of employment and work options the domestics would face once slavery disappeared. Abolitionists again used domestic slavery to counter the arguments of their antagonists. The proslavery forces argued that abolition would create a major havoc in the labor market given that freed people would seek only well-paid jobs or that they would filter to the countryside to engage in subsistence agriculture.[29] Although abolitionists like Acosta and Ruiz Belvis acknowledged that some alteration in the labor supply was likely once slavery ended, these leaders emphasized the volume of domestics that would probably end up working in the same kind of jobs they had as enslaved workers. Acosta and Ruiz Belvis presented their views in Proyecto para la abolición de la esclavitud (1867): "Because it has occurred to no one that domestic slaves, most of them women, and those dedicated to mechanical tasks in the towns, will abandon their ordinary tasks when they become free, given that their actual situation is far more benign than that of slaves living in the countryside. The transition from slavery to freedom will be, therefore, less violent."[30]

The abolitionist leaders promoted the image of an orderly and pacific transition after abolition. In the quotation above, abolitionists used the strategy of feminizing domestic slavery by accentuating that the majority of the enslaved domestics were women. This feminization attempted to conjure images of docility and submission destined to appease those fearful of the effects of abolition. Proabolition leaders utilized the nature of domestic slavery itself, the apparent lack of employment options for the new freedmen and freedwomen, and the myth of the enslaved domestic as a loyal and docile subject in order to promote the eradication of slavery in Puerto Rico.

The Labor "Crisis" and the Struggle to Control the Supply of Domestics in San Juan

Aside from the manipulation in the propaganda in favor of and against the abolition of slavery in Puerto Rico, the colonial authorities and the commercial and agricultural elite had faced what they described as a *"crisis de brazos"* (labor crisis) since mid-nineteenth century. Governor Miguel López de Baños instituted a registry for wage-laborers (*jornaleros*) in 1838, forcing every landless person age 16 through 60 to register with the municipal Vagrancy Juntas and list his or her occupation.[31] The so-called labor crisis occurred not because there were not enough workers in Puerto Rico but because the government and the elite wanted to dictate working conditions and wages on the island.[32] Social and labor control regulations of those without land continued throughout the nineteenth century as profits in the sugar sector dwindled and the possibilities of reproducing an enslaved labor force decreased. Perhaps the best known of these regulations was the *jornalero* legislation issued by Governor Juan de la Pezuela in 1849. Pezuela's regulations combined all labor control laws approved by previous governors and added a new requirement that forced *jornaleros* to carry a notebook or passbook in which information regarding their labor history was kept. Although labor control mechanisms were applied all across the island, in San Juan's case repressive and preventive regulations were issued around the reproduction, access, and control of domestic workers.

The apparent shortage of workers affected San Juan in the second half of the nineteenth century. Not only did the debate over the abolition of slavery cause concerns and renegotiations, but also the city's elite faced the problem of recruiting domestics in order to keep their privileged lifestyle. There were enough women ready to work as domestics, but given demographic and economic changes in San Juan, there were fewer women willing to accept the elite's terms of remuneration and working conditions. Among the factors that affected the supply of domestic workers in San Juan were demographic changes (fewer women and fewer people of color), the effects of the cholera epidemic in 1855, the rise in the price of enslaved people given the end of the trade in African captives, and the fears rising out of the impending abolition of slavery on the island.[33]

On the economic side, urban enslavement in San Juan—as well as on the rest of the island—entered a crisis beginning in the second half of the nineteenth century. Rising inflation, ever-increasing prices of basic goods, the shortage of enslaved domestics, and the difficulty in providing for those enslaved persons directly affected the viability of the system of urban enslavement in San Juan. This crisis, similar to the ones that affected several other Caribbean and Latin American urban centers, combined with the changing demographic patterns in San Juan, marked the limits of the attempts at regulating domestic work and also regulating the terms of the supply of and demand for domestic work in the capital.[34]

Faced with the difficulty of obtaining domestics, Spanish authorities initiated a campaign of identifying and controlling workers. In 1858, for example, the central government prepared a list of domestics, agricultural workers, and unemployed people in each town.[35] Lists such as these indicate the importance the insular government placed on domestic work—it was, after all, one of the categories on the list—although most official communiqués and contemporary accounts privileged the work of agricultural workers. In 1864, San Juan's *cabildo* started another listing of women and men over 14 years of age who "rent themselves for permanent domestic work in someone else's home, cooking, washing, cleaning and taking care of a home or family or analogous occupations."[36] This municipal listing, created from an islandwide one, included information regarding all the work contracts issued to domestics. The 1864 regulations required "obedience, fidelity and respect" from the domestics to their employers, a requirement that was not expected to be reciprocated by employers. Violations of the regulations—which included losing work passbooks or not having updated information in the passbooks—were stipulated only for domestic workers. The penalties were: "If you were male you faced six days of correction working in public works in the region at half-pay, and if female a fine of four *reales* or a day in jail."[37] The only punishment to the employers in the 1864 regulations was that they were to go to court if they were behind in their payments to the domestic worker. The 1864 regulations were part of ongoing islandwide efforts throughout the 1860s to reinstate and reinforce some of the coercive labor measures designed in the 1830s and 1840s given the perceived failure to increase the supply of workers.[38] In 1871, the government enacted another set of regulations pertaining to domestic work. Official authorities themselves recognized that these 1871 regulations were not enforced, "perhaps because at that time domestic work was still performed for the most part by slaves."[39]

The impact of the abolition of slavery on the supply of workers in Puerto Rico after 1873, particularly in urban centers, needs to be studied with more care. Nevertheless, it is clear that Spanish authorities and the local elite both were convinced that there was a shortage of domestics in San Juan. The Spanish governor, for example, commented on the negative effects of it a few years after abolition was enacted: "After the abolition of slavery, there was the need to mitigate one of its effects, in the Capital particularly, which was the shortage of domestics, even for the most necessary chores. There were not then, as now, any available replacements."[40] The governor's commentary referred to a petition to transfer 25 inmates from the local jail to perform domestic chores in San Juan due to the difficulty experienced by the elite in finding workers willing to do domestic chores.

In 1876—three years after the abolition of slavery in Puerto Rico—the city regulated domestic work by forcing domestics to carry a passbook and to register at the town hall.[41] City authorities justified the new regulations not just because of the so-called shortage of domestics but also to defend the rights of both workers and employers during contracting. The registry had information regarding the conduct, physical traits, place of birth, marital status, and the name of the parents of each domestic.[42] Besides the standard regulations of movement, scheduling, and residency, the 1876 law also attempted to limit the pool of domestics to city residents and thus avoid encouraging immigration into San Juan from other parts of the island. Domestics not complying with the passbook and the registry were fined three pesos for the first infraction. In the case of a second infraction, the fine increased to six pesos, and the domestic was exiled to her or his city of origin.[43]

It is ironic that city officials complained about a shortage of domestic employees at the same time that they were legislating to ship potential workers out of San Juan. This points to the real purpose behind all the domestic work regulations: to control and manipulate the supply of domestics and dictate the terms of the working conditions of those domestics in the city. Also, the 1876 regulations coincided with the last year of the mandatory contracting the enslaved "liberated" in 1873. Although there are no clear data about the effects of the actual abolition of slavery in 1876 in San Juan, studies from towns such as Guayama showed a significant number of enslaved persons, particularly women, migrating to cities seeking employment as domestics.[44] The 1876 regulations in San Juan were perhaps destined to dictate the terms of employment in the city as well as to prevent a massive migration of *libertos* who might become a safety and economic hazard to the colonial officials and the urban elite.

The different domestic service regulations issued by the colonial government, starting in the 1850s and continuing in various years after slavery was abolished, show similar patterns. First, all regulations were drafted to ameliorate the so-called labor crisis among domestics in San Juan and other parts of Puerto Rico. Second, the regulations copied the mechanisms—registries, passbooks, spatial and geographical restrictions, punitive measures ranging from fines to forced hard labor—employed by insular authorities in the legislation regulating *jornaleros* and other landless people on the island. Third, the passbooks subordinated workers to the bureaucratic whims and fancies of colonial officials and employers. Given that any improper conduct, from the employers' perspective, had to be recorded in the passbook, domestics were vulnerable to their employers' caprices, in addition to the control the employers had in the areas of contracting and determining wages. Finally, the continuous passing of regulations indicated that, even if Puerto Rico's historiography has neglected the importance of domestic work, that was not the case with Spanish authorities and the dominant classes in nineteenth-century Puerto Rico.

Beneficence and Social and Labor Control

Another response by colonial Spanish officials and Puerto Rico's elite to the problem of securing an abundant, cheap, and docile supply of domestics was the proliferation of public and semiprivate beneficence institutions in the nineteenth century. The liberal conception of beneficence superseded old notions of charity, which had shaped the way the state, church, and dominant classes had responded to the needs of the poor on the island.[45] Beneficence institutions became the locale where liberal and modernizing discourses in Puerto Rican society merged with social engineering projects destined to make economic and medically marginal individuals into productive members of society. In the *casas de amparo*, the asylums and hospitals, the elite and the government experimented with their recipes for rehabilitation, vocational instruction, discipline, and job placements in order to, among other objectives, guarantee the reproduction of domestic workers and artisans who could be lost as a result of the abolition of slavery.

The Casa de Beneficencia in San Juan was inaugurated in 1844. From the specific original intent to serve as a *"casa de recogidas, amparo o reclusión"* (shelter and almshouse), the Casa was turned into a multipurpose establishment by the time of its opening.[46] In the Casa, mental patients were committed, enslaved persons and women awaiting trial were "deposited," prostitutes and indigent people were cloistered, and vocational instruction was provided to poor children to turn them into artisans and domestics. On several occasions, the Casa also housed and distributed so-called *emancipados*—slaves illegally shipped into Puerto Rico after the slave trade was abolished—to hacienda owners in need of agricultural or domestic workers.[47] In order to generate its operating revenue, the Casa relied on the profits made by interns who did laundry for the nearby hospitals and military garrisons. This type of arrangement—in which the institution generated its own revenue, women learned domestic service skills that would make them "useful" and productive in the future, and the Spanish bureaucracy's domestic service needs were supplied—was considered ideal by the colonial authorities. It is not surprising, then, in the period between 1844 and 1873 to discover multiple petitions by the city's elite requesting to house a domestic from the Casa in their residences. Doña Ana María Crosas de Vidal, for example, asked the *cabildo* for an orphan girl from the Casa to be employed as a domestic. Crosas de Vidal promised "to take care of and provide for her as if she were one of our own family," and the *cabildo* accepted her petition.[48]

The Casa de Beneficencia was not the only institution created in San Juan that combined the rhetoric of beneficence with the training, placement, and control of domestic workers during the decades of the so-called labor shortage prior to abolition. In 1859, for instance, a group of women in San Juan requested permission to create a beneficence asylum to provide elementary and vocational education to poor children. In 1861, after an intense struggle between San Juan's bishop and the island's governor regarding who would have jurisdiction over the institution, the Asilo de San Ildefonso opened its doors.[49] The Asilo, administered by a board of elite women and staffed by nuns and volunteers, provided elementary and religious education to poor girls. As in other beneficence institutions established in Puerto Rico at the time—in Ponce, for example, the Asilo de Damas was opened in 1866 and the Asilo Tricoche in 1868—elite women organized institutions that guaranteed a reliable, accessible, and trained supply of domestic workers.[50]

Beneficence in San Juan, like in the rest of Puerto Rico, emerged partly as a response from the colonial authorities and the elite to the labor shortage problems they thought affected the island starting at midcentury. In San Juan, beneficence establishments were oriented toward recruiting, training, and placing domestic workers. The city's elite women played an important role in creating and administering these institutions, which helped to guarantee their privileged lifestyle and kept them in charge in the public sphere of the domestic staff they supervised in the private sphere of the home. Although much remains to be researched and studied regarding the emergence of beneficence institutions during the second half of the nineteenth century, it is clear that their emergence concurs with the attempts by the dominant class to mitigate the repercussions of the so-called labor crisis on the island and to prepare themselves for the eventual labor market changes caused by the impending abolition of slavery.

Domestic Workers and Their Conflicts with City Officials

The perception of a lack of domestic workers and their even greater shortage once slavery was abolished was not the only reason why colonial authorities and the elite attempted several labor and social control strategies. Although it is not easy to recover the responses and the activities of nineteenth-century domestics, there is evidence that they fought to improve their working conditions and the remuneration they received for their services. The colonial bureaucracy and the municipal policing authorities had constant clashes with domestics from the mid-nineteenth century on. These clashes were another reason why new mechanisms of labor and social control were tried in San Juan during the second half of the nineteenth century.

Of all the domestic workers in San Juan, it was the laundresses with whom city officials had the most problems and frictions. The reasons for these frictions were many. First, laundresses, for the most part, were black, mulatto, or *parda*. This, added to their access to visible public spaces (such as water fountains and plazas) and to private spaces (the homes and the bedrooms of their employers or clients), made laundresses highly suspicious in the eyes of city officials. It must be kept in mind that, until the

1850s, San Juan was a demographically black and colored city and that the Creole and Spanish elites were always fearful of a revolt by enslaved black and colored people.[51] For public safety officials—all of them male—it must also have been uncomfortable and difficult to operate in predominantly female public spaces, such as a water fountain crowded with laundresses and their children.

The fears regarding the behavior of laundresses in San Juan were not merely abstract. At several junctures, city laundresses challenged colonial and police officials. The laundresses at the Hospital de la Caridad, for example, organized work stoppages on several occasions to protest the lack of access to water and the poor working conditions at the hospital.[52] In one of their disputes, the laundresses requested from the *cabildo* in 1842 permission to use the water cisterns at the military barracks in Ballajá. A Laundresses' Guild existed in 1876, although there is not much information regarding its activities or membership.[53]

Another incident that shows the repeated frictions between city officials and laundresses occurred in 1857 at Condado's water fountain. The *alcalde* (municipal judge) of Cangrejos—a small suburb outside San Juan—chastised several laundresses at the Condado fountain not only for the noise and bustle they were causing but also for encroaching on private property as they washed and dried their clothes. The *alcalde* argued that his job was

> to prevent, as it is expected by the government, all causes of scandal and disorder in the section of the territory to the right of the road leading to San Juan and in the fountain's surroundings, which were being committed by the mentioned laundresses who behaved without any respect to my authority or to the property. Since the laundresses were invading all the land, I asked them to leave the premises given that it was not political nor convenient that they stayed there, particularly when their presence there had led others, not interested in earning a precarious subsistence washing clothes but in creating a scandal and demoralizing the general public and those who traveled near the fountain with their improper and unruly behavior disregarding the provisos of the island's government.[54]

After a heated exchange, the laundresses replied that they did not recognize the *alcalde*'s jurisdiction because the water fountain was located in San Juan and not in Cangrejos. The dispute between the laundresses and the *alcalde* ended up on the governor's desk.

If the clashes with colonial officials did not enhance the laundresses' poor reputations, their status as women who earned a living working in the city's streets did not help them either. Their public persona excluded laundresses from the considerations and respect of men. Laundresses were not protected like other women who did not venture into the streets without an escort and otherwise stayed behind closed doors. The laundresses who worked outside their homes were frequent victims of physical, verbal, and sexual abuse. Not only were they targets of these kinds of abuse, but their condition as public women limited their attempts at vindicating themselves after the abuse was committed. The documentation from the civil courts provides ample evidence of the "presumption of guilt" in cases against women whose work forced them out to the streets escorted only, perhaps, by their children or by other domestics, or against women whose work forced them in and out of their clients' homes. Juana de Dios González's status as a laundress, for instance, was enough for the court to dismiss her lawsuit against Pasqual García. González was suing García, a soldier, for "seduction and rape" under the pretension and promise of marriage.[55] González claimed that García visited her house, promised to marry her, and had given her a child; therefore, he had to marry her. In these kinds of cases it was usually enough to know that a man had visited a women's house for the court to rule in favor of the woman, forcing the man either to marry her or to provide her with an adequate dowry. García defended himself by arguing that it was well known that González and her mother were laundresses and that it was logical to assume that his going in and out of their house had nothing to do with romance but with his laundry. The public nature of González's work had cost her her day in court.

Another laundress, Ysabel Avilés, faced a similar fate. She was sued by the soldier don Julián Gutiérrez for having insulted him publicly. Gutiérrez argued that Avilés, who normally took care of his laundry, had entered his house and told him that "it was enough for him to be a soldier to be indecent, a scoundrel and a thief."[56] Avilés, in her defense, accepted having insulted Gutiérrez but only after explaining that since he owed her money, she went to his house to collect her payment, only to be publicly insulted by Gutiérrez and violently thrown out of his house into the street. The judge accepted Gutiérrez's version of the story and asked Avilés for a public apology. Avilés did not accept the judge's decision.

Colonial and ecclesiastical authorities both complained about the lack of decorum and order present in San Juan's public plazas. As the nineteenth century advanced, uneasiness grew among the elite regarding the possible abolition of slavery and the potential challenges to the social and economic hierarchy it could unleash. Furthermore, by midcentury San

Juan was beginning to feel the first European influences regarding urban beautification, decoration, and hygiene in open public spaces.[57] This combination of factors led city officials to approve in the late 1860s the construction of a public washing area to move all the laundresses into Puerta de Tierra, an extramural barrio.[58] In Puerta de Tierra, the laundresses would be sufficiently near the city to be able to provide adequate laundry services and sufficiently far away not to be a public safety, hygiene, and beauty problem. Under the mask of beautification, decoration, and hygiene, Spanish officials and the city's elite hid their fears and insecurities regarding the dislocations and changes that the postabolition world would bring to San Juan.

Conclusion

The access to and control of domestic work in San Juan played an important role during the 1840–73 period, as shown by the multiple regulatory attempts and by the recurring conflicts between domestics and city officials. Although it did not play a leading role, domestic work did figure in the comments and strategies of the two sides in the debate over the abolition of slavery in Puerto Rico. Even when the island's historiography has marginalized the study of domestic work on the island, it is clear that these workers worried many in Puerto Rico during the second half of the nineteenth century.

I have identified three responses to the socioeconomic transformations occurring just prior to the abolition of slavery, particularly as it related to the supply of domestics. The first was the attempt at increasing the social and spatial control over domestics using lists, registries, and punitive legislation in response to what the government and the elite saw as a labor shortage. This was not a new pattern in the history of the Spanish colonial government's ongoing struggle to guarantee a cheap, docile, and abundant labor force in Puerto Rico. These attempts trace their ideological roots to the insular laws of the 1840s and the parallel campaigns to eradicate vagrancy and common-law marriage on the island.[59] Instead of visionary public policy solutions targeted at improving and modernizing the island's economy, Spanish officials and their allies opted for a tough policing stand to face their perceived labor shortage problems.

The second response was a struggle to control the city's public and private spaces. This struggle had been going on in San Juan, if in a less intense manner, since the beginning of the nineteenth century. The city's elites' policies effectively pushed significant numbers of people of color (the majority of them women) out of the city and into the surrounding extramural barrios.[60] The idea of the public washing area in Puerta de Tierra, although it was never constructed, shows the way in which San Juan's upper classes wished to reconfigure the city's social, economic, and racial space. In terms of private spaces, more research is still needed regarding the struggles for control and distance in these spaces. The renegotiations between domestics and their owners or employers that occurred as abolition approached and the uncertainty regarding the rules that would apply in the postslavery world await the careful scrutiny of future Puerto Rican historians.

The third response was provided through the creation of beneficence institutions. The advocates of beneficence pointed to the intellectual and public policy currents in Europe to rally support for the establishment of beneficence institutions. The ironic twist of this influence is that the elite still needed domestic work to carry out its modernizing agenda. Domestics guaranteed the free time that the elite and the new professional classes needed to dedicate to their modernizing social, economic, and cultural projects. Public and semiprivate beneficence was a mechanism used to experiment with new forms of social control, vigilance, job placement, rehabilitation, and vocational and religious training.

A significant part of this essay has focused on analyzing some of the reactions of San Juan's elite to the changes in the mid-nineteenth-century labor market. Unfortunately, I have not been able to document with equal precision the domestics' reactions to such transformations. Logically, the mere existence of all the registries and regulations indicates that there was some resistance to doing domestic work under the conditions dictated by the upper classes. Perhaps other sources—diaries, letters, or court testimonies—will allow the exploration of domestic workers' quotidian engagement or distancing from this process. If the experiences of the laundresses are indications, one can argue that the Spanish authorities and the elite faced groups of women intent on defining, to the best of their abilities and resources, the terms of their working conditions.

Another element that could shed some light on the development of domestic work in Puerto Rico during the second half of the nineteenth century would be the experience of other Caribbean and Latin American urban centers. In Barbados, for example, Pedro Welch has shown how the experiences with enslaved urban workers in Bridgetown prepared the governmental and commercial elite to consolidate control mechanisms for the period after abolition. Among the mechanisms they instituted were the control and regulation of emigration and the creation of a city police corps to monitor and punish the new freedmen and freedwomen.[61] The attempts to regulate postslavery domestic work in San Juan with mechanisms from the pre-1873 world indicate that in Puerto Rico the colonial authorities also learned from their experiences with the mobility and resistance of urban slaves and *libertos*. It is likely that the authorities in Puerto Rico were acquainted with the various mechanisms of social and labor control employed in the British and French Caribbean possessions after slavery was abolished there in 1833 and 1848, respectively. The experiences in other urban areas of Puerto Rico, such as Ponce, Mayaguez, and Arecibo, could help to corroborate this hypothesis.

San Juan's domestics, many of them urban enslaved females, were part of the cast of characters that worried colonial officials, elite members, and those debating the wisdom of abolition. This essay has attempted to highlight the importance of domestic service to the urban economy of San Juan at a time of transition from enslaved labor to so-called free labor. I have also analyzed how domestic service was linked to other developments in San Juan, such as the institutionalization of public and semiprivate beneficence establishments. Many questions emerge from the evidence presented here regarding San Juan that merit further study. What can be learned from the evidence of other urban centers in Puerto Rico? How do they compare with San Juan's experiences? Why have domestic labor and urban slavery attracted so little attention in Puerto Rican historiography? How can the history of abolition and slavery in Puerto Rico begin to be rewritten considering the experiences of urban centers? I hope that this essay stimulates further historical research regarding domestic work and its connections with the significant socioeconomic transformations of Puerto Rico, such as the abolition of slavery.

Notes

This essay was originally published as "¿Quién trabajará? Trabajo doméstico, esclavitud urbana y abolición en San Juan en el siglo XIX" in *Revista de Ciencias Sociales* 4 (January 1998): 219–45 and is reproduced (with editorial changes) with permission. The author wishes to thanks Emilio Kourí, Luis Figueroa, Eileen Findlay, Jorge Duany, Pedro San Miguel, and Joan Krizack for their helpful comments and suggestions.

Abbreviations

AGPR	Archivo General de Puerto Rico
AHD	Archivo Histórico Diocesano
AHN	Archivo Histórico Nacional
C	Caja
CP	Fondo Colecciones Particulares
E	Expediente
f	folio
FAT	Fondo Audiencia Territorial
FGEPR	Fondo Gobernadores Españoles
FMSJ	Fondo Municipal San Juan
FOP	Fondo Obras Públicas
FPN	Fondo Protocolos Notariales
L	Legajo
P	Pieza/Parte
S	Serie
Se	Sección
v	vuelto

1. See, among others, Centro de Investigaciones Históricas, *El proceso abolicionista en Puerto Rico: Documentos para su estudio,* 2 vols. (San Juan: Instituto de Cultura Puertorriqueña, 1974–78); José Curet, "About Slavery and the Order of Things: Puerto Rico, 1845–1873," in *Between Slavery and Free Labor: The Spanish Speaking Caribbean in the Nineteenth Century,* ed. Manuel Moreno Fraginals, Frank Moya Pons, and Stanley L. Engerman (Baltimore: Johns Hopkins University Press, 1985), 117–40; Luis M. Díaz Soler, *Historia de la esclavitud en Puerto Rico,* 3rd ed. (Río Piedras: Editorial Universitaria, 1981); Arturo Morales Carrión, *Auge y decadencia de la trata negrera en Puerto Rico (1820–1860)* (San Juan: Centro de Estudios Avanzados de Puerto Rico y el Caribe & Instituto de Cultura Puertorriqueña, 1978); Benjamín Nistal-Moret, "Problems in the Social Structure of Slavery in Puerto Rico during the Process of Abolition, 1872," in Moreno Fraginals, Moya Pons, and Engerman, *Between Slavery and Free Labor,* 141–57; and Andrés Ramos Mattei, *La hacienda azucarera: Su crecimiento y crisis en Puerto Rico (siglo xix)* (San Juan: Centro de Estudios de la Realidad Puertorriqueña [CEREP], 1981).

2. See Curet, "About Slavery"; Andrés Ramos Mattei, ed., *Azucar y esclavitud* (Río Piedras: Editorial Universitaria, 1982); Luis Figueroa, "Facing Freedom: The Transition from Slavery to Free Labor in Guayama, Puerto Rico, 1860–1898" (Ph.D. diss., University of Wisconsin–Madison, 1991).

3. This literature is quite extensive. See, among others, Robin Blackburn, *The Overthrow of Colonial Slavery, 1776–1848* (London: Verso Books, 1988); Arthur F. Corwin, *Spain and the Abolition of Slavery in Cuba, 1817–1886* (Austin: University of Texas Press, 1967); David Brion Davis, *The Problem of Slavery in the*

Age of Revolution, 1770–1823 (Ithaca, N.Y.: Cornell University Press, 1975); Seymour Drescher, *Capitalism and Slavery: British Mobilization in Comparative Perspective* (New York: Oxford University Press, 1986); William A. Green, *British Slave Emancipation: The Sugar Colonies and the Great Experiment, 1830–1865* (Oxford: Oxford University Press, 1976); Thomas C. Holt, *The Problem of Freedom: Race, Labour and Politics in Jamaica and Britain, 1832–1938* (Baltimore: Johns Hopkins University Press, 1992); Moreno Fraginals, Moya Pons, and Engerman, *Between Slavery and Free Labor;* Rebecca Scott, *Slave Emancipation in Cuba: The Transition to Free Labor, 1860–1899* (Princeton, N.J.: Princeton University Press, 1985); Rebecca Scott, "Comparing Emancipations: A Review Essay," *Journal of Social History* 20, no. 3 (1987): 565–83; Rebecca Scott, "Exploring the Meaning of Freedom: Postemancipation Societies in Comparative Perspective," *Hispanic American Historical Review* 68, no. 3 (1988): 407–28; Dale W. Tomich, *Slavery in the Circuit of Sugar: Martinique and the World Economy* (Baltimore: Johns Hopkins University Press, 1990); and Pedro L. V. Welch, "Notes from the Bridgetown Underground: Control and Protest in Post-Emancipation Barbados" (paper presented at the 28th Annual Meeting of the Society of Caribbean Historians, Bridgetown, Barbados, April 17, 1996).

4. See, for example, Elsa Chaney and May G. Castro, eds., *Muchachas No More: Household Workers in Latin America and the Caribbean* (Philadelphia: Temple University Press, 1989); Sandra L. Graham, *House and Street: The Domestic World of Servants and Masters in Nineteenth-Century Rio de Janeiro* (Cambridge: Cambridge University Press, 1988); Mary Romero, *Maid in the USA* (New York: Routledge, 1992); and Heidi Tisman, "The Indispensable Services of Sisters: Considering Domestic Service in Latin America and the Caribbean," *Journal of Women's History* 4, no. 1 (1992): 37–59.

5. Tera Hunter, "Household Workers in the Making: Afro-American Women in Atlanta and the New South, 1861 to 1921" (Ph.D. diss., Yale University, 1990); Elizabeth Kuznesof, "A History of Domestic Service in Spanish America, 1492–1980," in Chaney and Castro, *Muchachas No More,* 17–36; Tisman, "Indispensable Services."

6. Mariano Negrón Portillo and Raúl Mayo Santana, *La esclavitud urbana en San Juan: Estudio del Registro de Jornaleros de Esclavos de 1872* (Río Piedras: Ediciones Huracán, 1992), 80–81.

7. Rubén Carbonell Fernández, "Las compra-ventas de esclavos en San Juan, 1817–1873" (master's thesis, University of Puerto Rico–Río Piedras, 1976); Félix V. Matos Rodríguez, "Street Vendors, Shop-Owners and Domestics: Some Aspects of Women's Economic Roles in 19th Century San Juan, Puerto Rico," in *Engendering History: Caribbean Women in Historical Perspective,* ed. Verene Shepherd, Bridget Brereton, and Barbara Bailey (Kingston: Ian Randle, 1995), 176–96; Negrón Portillo and Mayo Santana, *La esclavitud urbana;* Pedro L. V. Welch, "The Urban Context of the Slave Plantation System: Bridgetown, Barbados,

1680–1834" (Ph.D. diss., University of the West Indies, Cave Hill, Barbados, 1994).

8. Luis Aponte-Parés, "Casas y Bohios: Territorial Development and Urban Growth in XIXth Century Puerto Rico" (Ph.D. diss., Columbia University, 1990), 291–99; Aníbal Sepúlveda Rivera, *San Juan: Historia ilustrada de su desarollo urbano, 1508–1898* (San Juan: Carimar, 1989), 222–24.

9. Centro de Investigaciones Históricas, *El proceso*, 2: 181–82.

10. Aixa Merino Falú, "El Gremio de Lavanderas de Puerta de Tierra," in *Historias vivas: Historiografía puertorriqueña contemporánea*, ed. Antonio Gaztambide Géigel and Silvia Alvarez Curbelo (San Juan: Asociación Puertorriqueña de Historiadores & Editorial Postdata), 74–79.

11. Félix V. Matos Rodríguez, "Economy, Society and Urban Life: Women in Nineteenth Century San Juan, Puerto Rico (1820–1870)" (Ph.D. diss., Columbia University, 1994), 32, 96–97.

12. Negrón Portillo and Mayo Santana, *La esclavitud urbana*, 9–14.

13. The 1846 census is the first one providing the occupation or employment of women in San Juan. The 1846 data come from three out of the four quarters that made up the city of San Juan then. AGPR, FMSJ, Censos San Juan (Santa Bárbara, Santo Domingo, and San Francisco barrios), 1846.

14. Adolfo De Hostos, *Historia de San Juan, cuidad murada* (San Juan: Instituto de Cultura Puertorriqueña, 1983), 21.

15. Matos Rodríguez, "Economy, Society," 105.

16. *Pardo/a* usually refers to light-skinned mulattoes.

17. AGPR, FMSJ, Censos San Juan, 1846.

18. I have included as "heads of households" those individuals listed in the 1846 censuses as *jefes* (head) or *inquilino* (tenant). The data come from AGPR, FMSJ, Censos San Juan, 1846.

19. Negrón Portilla and Mayo Santana, *La esclavitud urbana*, 114–17.

20. Ibid., 81–89.

21. Díaz Soler, *Historia,* 158–61.

22. De Hostos, *Historia de San Juan,* 477–79.

23. Sepúlveda Rivera, *San Juan,* 288–90.

24. An example of this type of accusation can be found in the testament of don Patricio Fogarty. Fogarty accused his mulatto cook of poisoning his food. AGPR, FPN, San Juan, José María León de Urbina, February 21, 1827, C-442, 84f-85v.

25. Carbonell Fernández, "Las compra-ventas," 29–32.

26. Negrón Portillo and Mayo Santana, *La esclavitud urbana,* 97.

27. Centro de Investigaciones Históricas, *El proceso,* 2: 437. This and all subsequent direct block citations have been translated by the author. The discrepancy in the numbers appears in the original document.

28. Segundo Ruiz Belvis, José J. Acosta, and Francisco M. Quiñones, *Proyecto para la abolición de la esclavitud,* 2nd ed. (Rio Piedras: Editorial Edil, 1978), 70.

29. Díaz Soler, *Historia,* 278–79.

30. Ruiz Belvis, *Proyecto,* 70–71.

31. Fernando Picó, *Historia general de Puerto Rico,* 2nd ed. (Río Piedras: Ediciones Huracán, 1986), 170.

32. Francisco Scarano, "Labor and Society in the Nineteenth Century," in *The Modern Caribbean,* ed. Franklin Knight and Colin Palmer (Chapel Hill: University of North Carolina Press, 1989), 51–84.

33. Matos Rodríguez, "Economy, Society," 88–129.

34. Maria Odila Silva Dias, *Power and Everyday Life: The Lives of Working Women in 19th Century Brazil* (New Brunswick, N.J.: Rutgers University Press, 1995).

35. AGPR, FGEPR, Censo y Riqueza, 1858, C-16.

36. AGPR, FMSJ, Actas del Cabildo, C-24, 19 de mayo de 1864, 93f-v.

37. "Reglamento que ha de observarse en la locación del trabajo personal para el servicio doméstico," Chapter 5, Article 6. AGPR, FGEPR, S-Municipios, C-480, June 8, 1964.

38. Gómez Acevedo, *Organización y reglamentación,* 117–23.

39. AGPR, FMSJ, L-24G, E-941, April 3, 1876.

40. AHN, Se-Ultramar, Serie-Gobierno de Puerto Rico, L-5113, E-60, September 5, 1879.

41. De Hostos, *Historia de San Juan,* 81.

42. Article 4, AGPR, FMSJ, L-24G, E-941, April 3, 1876.

43. Article 1, AGPR, FMSJ, L-24G, E-941, April 3, 1876.

44. Figueroa, "Facing Freedom," 359–64.

45. Teresita Martínez Vergne, "The Liberal Concept of Charity: Beneficencia Applied to Puerto Rico, 1821–1868," in *The Middle Period in Latin America: Values and Attitudes in the 17th–19th Centuries,* ed. Mark D. Szuchman (Boulder, Colo.: Lynne Rienner, 1989), 167–84.

46. Matos Rodríguez, "Economy, Society," 272–73.

47. Teresita Martínez Vergne, "The Allocation of Liberated African Labour through the Casa de Beneficencia—San Juan, Puerto Rico, 1859–1864," *Slavery and Abolition* 12, no. 3 (1991): 200–216.

48. AGPR, FMSJ, Actas del Cabildo, C-24, December 23, 1864, 216v.

49. Matos Rodríguez, "Economy, Society," 295–97.

50. Ramón Marín, *Las fiestas populares de Ponce* (1875; reprint, Río Piedras: Editorial de la Universidad de Puerto Rico, 1994), 227–28.

51. Matos Rodríguez, "Economy, Society," 102–7.

52. See, for example, AGPR, FMSJ, Actas del Cabildo, May 4, 1842, 88v. & June 30, 1842, 122f.

53. Merino Falú, "El Gremio de Lavanderas," 74.

54. The *alcalde*'s version is found in AGPR, FOP, Obras Municipales, L-62LL, E-13, C-236, July 14, 1857. Unfortunately, the record does not contain the governor's decision regarding the controversy. The chief naval officer of the island

testified in favor of the laundresses, arguing that the property in question was within his jurisdiction.

55. AGPR, FMSJ, L-73E, (P.I.), E-3, December 22, 1822.

56. AGPR, FMSJ, L-73E, (P.I.), E-12, October 10, 1841.

57. Angel G. Quintero Rivera, *Patricios y plebeyos. Burgueses, hacendados, artesanos y obreros (Las relaciones de clase en el Puerto Rico de cambio de siglo)* (Río Piedras: Ediciones Huracán, 1988), 23–98; Sepúlveda Rivera, *San Juan,* 158–91.

58. The public facility was never constructed, although discussion regarding its possible construction lasted into the 1880s. See AGPR, FOP, Obras Municipales, L-62LL, E-15, C-326.

59. Picó, *Historia,* 173–74. See also Antonia Rivera Rivera, "El problema de la vagancia en el Puerto Rico del siglo XIX," *Exegesis* 5, no. 14 (1992): 12–19.

60. Matos Rodríguez, "Economy, Society," 130–32.

61. Welch, "Notes from the Underground," 20–21.

Contributors

Hilary McD. Beckles is professor of history and principal of the Cave Hill campus of the University of the West Indies. He has authored numerous scholarly articles and books, including *Centering Woman: Gender Discourses in Caribbean Slave Society* (1999); *A History of Barbados: From Amerindian Settlement to Nation-State* (1990); *Natural Rebels: A Social History of Enslaved Women in Barbados* (1989); and *White Servitude and Black Slavery in Barbados* (1989).

O. Nigel Bolland is professor of sociology at Colgate University in New York, where he also teaches Caribbean studies. He has published several books about colonialism and decolonization in Belize. Among his publications are *The Politics of Labour in the British Caribbean* (2001); *On the March: Labour Rebellions in the British Caribbean, 1934–39* (1995); and *Colonialism and Resistance in Belize* (1988).

David Geggus is professor of history at the University of Florida. He is the author of *Slavery, War and Revolution: The British Occupation of St. Domingue* (1982), author of more than 60 scholarly articles, and coeditor (with Barry Gaspar) of *A Turbulent Time: The French Revolution and the Greater Caribbean* (1997).

B. W. Higman is professor of history and director of the history program in the Research School for Social Sciences at the Australian National University in Canberra. He is the author of numerous publications, including *Writing West Indian Histories* (1999); *Montpelier, Jamaica: A Plantation Community in Slavery and Freedom* (1998); *Jamaica Surveyed: Plantation Maps and Plans of the Eighteenth and Nineteenth Centuries* (1988); *Slave Populations of the British Caribbean, 1807–1834* (1984); and *Slave Population and Economy in Jamaica, 1807–1834* (1976). He also edited Volume 6 of the UNESCO *General History of the Caribbean* titled *Methodology and Historiography of the Caribbean* (1999).

Franklin W. Knight is Leonard and Helen R. Stulman Professor of History at Johns Hopkins University, Baltimore, and president of the Latin American Studies Association. His numerous publications include *Slave Society in Cuba during the Nineteenth Century* (1970); *The African Dimension of Latin American Societies* (1974); *The Caribbean* (1978, 1990); and *The Modern Caribbean* (1989, coedited with Colin A. Palmer). He edited volume 3 of the UNESCO *General History of the Caribbean* titled *The Slave Societies of the Caribbean* (1997).

Félix V. Matos Rodríguez, a graduate of Columbia University and a former faculty member at Northeastern University, is the director of the Center for Puerto Rican Studies at Hunter College (CUNY). He is the author of *Women and Urban Change in San Juan, Puerto Rico* (1999); coauthor, with Pedro Juan Hernandez, of *"Pioneros": Puerto Ricans in New York City, 1896–1948* (2001); and coeditor, with Linda Delgado, of *Puerto Rican Women's History: New Perspectives* (1998). He has published numerous articles in scholarly journals on women's studies and Puerto Rican, Caribbean, and Latino history.

Kathleen E. A. Monteith is a lecturer in the department of history, University of the West Indies, Mona, Jamaica. She has published in the areas of the social, economic, and financial history of Jamaica and the Caribbean. She is coeditor (with Glen Richards) of *Jamaica in Slavery and Freedom* (2002).

Evelyn Powell Jennings is a predoctoral fellow of the Frederick Douglass Institute for African and African-American Studies and a doctoral candidate in modern European and Atlantic history at the University of Rochester in Rochester, New York. She holds a master's degree in Latin American history from the State University of New York at Stony Brook and a bachelor's degree in Spanish language and literature from the State University of New York at Oswego.

Gail Saunders, past president of the Association of Caribbean Historians, is director of archives, Nassau, Bahamas. She is the author of several publications, including *Slavery in the Bahamas, 1638–1838* (1985), and is coauthor, with Michael Craton, of *Islanders in the Stream: A History of the Bahamian People*, vols. 1 and 2 (1992–98).

Verene A. Shepherd is professor of history at the University of the West Indies, Mona, Jamaica, and 2000–2001 network professor with the York University/UNESCO Nigerian Hinterland Project. She is the author of *Transients to Settlers: The Experiences of Indians in Jamaica* (1994); editor of *Working Slavery, Pricing Freedom: Perspectives from the Caribbean, Africa, and the African Diaspora* (2002); editor/compiler of *Women in Caribbean History* (1999); coeditor, with Glen Richards, of *Questioning Creole: Creolization Discourses in Caribbean Culture* (2002); coeditor, with Hilary McD. Beckles, of *Caribbean Slavery in the Atlantic World* (2000) and *Caribbean Freedom* (1993); and coeditor, with Bridget Brereton and Barbara Bailey, of *Engendering History: Caribbean Women in Historical Perspective* (1995).

S. D. Smith is lecturer in economic history at the University of York. He is currently researching British coffee consumption from the seventeenth century to the present. Among his publications are "Accounting for Taste: British Coffee Consumption in Historical Perspective," *Journal of Interdisciplinary History* 27 (1996); "Sugar's Poor Relation: Coffee Planting in the BWI, 1721–1833," *Slavery and Abolition* (1998); and a forthcoming book, "*An Exact and Industrious Tradesman*": *The Letter Book of Joseph Symson of Kendal.*

Pedro L. V. Welch is assistant registrar at the University of the West Indies, Cave Hill Campus. He is coauthor, with Richard Goodridge, of *"Red" and Black over White: Free Coloured Women in Pre-emancipation Barbados* (2000) and author of "The Slave Family in the Urban Context: Views from Bridgetown, Barbados, 1780–1816," *Journal of Caribbean History* 29, no. 1 (1995); "In Search of a Barbadian Identity: Historical Factors in the Development of a Barbadian Literary Tradition," *Journal of the Barbadian Museum and Historical Society* 40 (1992); and "Educational Selection, Inequality and Development in Barbados: Which Way Now?" *Bulletin of Eastern Caribbean Affairs* 14, nos. 1, 2 (1988).

Index